The Idiot's Frightful Laughter

Sheridan Peterson

1st Edition Dec. 15, 2007
2nd Edition Nov. 2018

Copyright © 2001 by Sheridan Peterson TXu000996928 / 2001-05-04

All rights reserved. This book or any portion thereof may not be reproduced or used in any manner whatsoever without the express written permission of the author except for the use of brief quotations in a book review or scholarly journal.

First Printing: 2018

ISBN 978-0-359-20731-2

Editor's Notes

Welcome to Sheridan's literary documentary/protest novel. Be forewarned that some readers will be disturbed by some passages.

This 2nd edition began with the 1st edition, dated 12/15/2007. The 1st edition had 682 pages in the distributed pdf. It was only available in digital form, and cost $25. However, there were multiple cover pages and duplicated pages. Sheridan himself noted his chagrin on Lulu.com where the publication was available for a short time in 2008.

It appears that, over time, Sheridan lost the ability to publish his cherished work. This 2nd edition aims to restore Sheridan's work in modern forms that are more reader-friendly.

There were 339 text pages in the 1st edition. This 2nd edition now has 470 text pages in a Palatino Linotype font. The original copyright by Sheridan on 5/4/01 claimed 680 pages. In various internet posts, Sheridan has claimed 826 pages.

I made the decision to reformat the book into US 6x9 Trade size, to allow wider distribution. At the same time, I decided it would make a smoother read to do some light editing:

- Consistent indented paragraph style, with no (few) blank lines.
- Spelling, hyphenation, and punctuation were updated where it seemed appropriate. Commas were both added and removed. In some situations, I left the use of upper case, in case it was being used for emphasis. I left "piaster" as singular everywhere, since I think it evokes common verbal use then.
- There is a sparsity of date references. I added none, although the novel's events cover the span of time from 1926 to 1970, with 1962 mentioned.
- I shortened the back-cover text.
- The front cover art was important to Sheridan. A friend apparently made it for him. I kept the cover art but switched the title/author font to a typewriter font. The prior font

didn't match the tone of the book, and the new font is a nod to Sheridan's history as a journalist.
- No words were added or removed. The reader can rest assured that if any surprising words or phrases are used, they are from Sheridan, not the editor.
- I took the editorial liberty of adding a copy of Rimbaud's poem as a foreword. Sheridan did not do this, but I think it adds a richness to the understanding of the book's title phrase if the reader is not familiar with Rimbaud.
- The author's picture is the same picture that was used in the 1st edition. My understanding is that it was from a passport or visa situation in Saudi Arabia, sometime between 1975 and 1977. Since the original photo had crinkled and was damaged over the years, I took the liberty of retouching it for use as in the 1st edition.
- I did not update the Vietnamese place names to correct accents/diacritics.
- The 1st edition was subtitled "Part 1: The Refugee Advisor" but I have dropped that subtitle. It implied there was additional text, but to my knowledge, there is not.

There is an issue with some Vietnamese words and place names. Vietnamese has nine accents/diacritics: four to create additional sounds, five to indicate tone. There are some place names that have two diacritics on the same vowel.

I did not edit Sheridan's writing to make the Vietnamese "correct". Mostly because I did not want to deal with the complexity of double diacritics, but also because it may reflect the American speaking Vietnamese, better. Sheridan did have some command of Vietnamese.

My goal was to help Sheridan achieve his desire for wider publication of his work. I hope readers will enjoy the result. In the past, Sheridan noted:

I was stunned to find out that people were reading my book.

Hopefully, the same result occurs here, but in a good way.

Contents

The Village That Vanished 1
The Outsider 6
The Callow Youth 20
Max Gutschinritter 33
The Prison Professor 37
A Fifth of Scotch 44
The Province Chief 53
A Way of Life 57
Hank Barban 65
The Hatchet Man 68
The Foreign Service Officer 74
The Spy Chief 78
Vince Grecco 91
Generating Refugee 95
Whitewash Corrigan 123
Friday Night Poker Game 129
Fire in the Hole 137
Scrounging 151
The Chieu Hoi Advisor 154
Her French Gentleman 164
A Jungle Ambush 180
Suburbia, U.S.A. 185
The Proletariat Dictatorship 193
Smokejumpers 199
The Saigon Sport Parachute Club 207
Vietnam's Voltaire 235
The Photos They Took 252

The Precocious Young Lawyer	256
Working for the Yankee Dollar	265
His Kind of People	271
To End a Feud	277
Lieutenant Hank Hesse's Best Shot	282
The Sea of Reeds	290
A Volunteer	299
Sneaky Little Fuckers	316
The Swiss Bank Account	319
Vincent Grecco, II	322
A Hearts and Minds Sort of Guy	331
Them People Lack Will	352
Banana Cat	363
That Perfect Place	366
A Final Appeal	375
The Hamlet of Thoi Binh	382
A Real Can of Worms	405
Alden Wordsworth-Adams, Esq.	409
The Late Night Massacre	424
Like a Child with a Toy	433
That Déjà Vu Feeling	439
Killer Cong	446
The Colonel's Hasty Exit	457
They're Out to Win	461
He's the Worst	466

A Season in Hell, Arthur Rimbaud

Once, if I remember well, my life was a feast where all hearts opened and all wines flowed.

One evening I seated Beauty on my knees. And I found her bitter. And I cursed her.

I armed myself against justice.

I fled. O Witches, O Misery, O Hate, to you has my treasure been entrusted!

I contrived to purge my mind of all human hope. On all joy, to strangle it, I pounced with the stealth of a wild beast.

I called to the executioners that I might gnaw their rifle-butts while dying. I called to the plagues to smother me in blood, in sand. Misfortune was my God. I laid myself down in the mud. I dried myself in the air of crime. I played sly tricks on madness.

And spring brought me the idiot's frightful laughter.

Now, only recently, being on the point of giving my last squawk, I thought of looking for the key to the ancient feast where I might find my appetite again.

Charity is that Key.--This inspiration proves that I have dreamed!

"You will always be a hyena. . ." etc., protest the devil who crowned me with such pleasant poppies. "Attain death with all your appetites, your selfishness and all the capital sins!"

Ah! I'm fed up:--But, dear Satan, a less fiery eye I beg you! And while awaiting a few small infamies in arrears, you who love the absence of the instructive or descriptive faculty in a writer, for you let me tear out these few, hideous pages from my notebook of one of the damned

The Village That Vanished

It was the season of the monsoon, and every day it rained. It came like a great tidal wave of the South China Sea lashing across the Mekong Delta's table-top surface. The earth would turn to tar, thick and black, holding firmly to one's foot, so that he would have to strain with each step, pressing one foot ankle-deep in it, and then pushing with all his strength with the other, to pry it loose. Then within an hour or so, the rain would move on, and the sun would again shine heating the moist air until one felt as though he was in a steam bath, his clothing drenched in sweat. When it was like this, one would look for a cool place to rest, for it was not good to work while it was so hot and humid.

Before the rain was welcome, for it meant plowing the rich alluvium soil. Wading waist deep in the rice paddies that looked like a checkerboard of swimming pools spreading as far as one could see. Slipping the point of the wooden plow into the thick oozy mud, the peasant would steer his giant, lumbering water buffalo lurching up and down often sinking so deep into the goo that all one saw were the tips of the beast's large crescent horns and flared nostrils.

Then the rice was planted, placing the seedlings one at a time beneath the muddy water so that the slender leaves poked above the surface. It was pleasing to watch them grow into thick glossy green mats, then turn yellow and finally golden. Each stock was crowned with a cluster of grain. By then the soil was dry so that the peasants could cut the plants close to the earth with sickles. Gathering handfuls of the stocks in their hands, they would strike them hard against a wooden frame knocking the kernels loose, so they fell into wicker baskets.

After the landlord had driven out from his villa in the city to collect his share of the yield which was large, much too large, there was usually just enough to last until next year's harvest if one was careful, supplementing his diet with fish caught from canals and rivers, rats trapped in the marshes and paddies, and aromatic leaves picked from plants that grew from human waste spread about among the thatched huts.

Now throughout most of the delta, the rain was no longer welcome, for many of the peasants had been driven from the land, and vast areas lay abandon. The people were herded into camps surrounded by barbwire crowned with razor-edged concertina and guarded by soldiers peering down at them from lookout towers. The delta was a great battlefield where tanks and armored personnel carriers rumbled over the land knocking down the dikes of the rice paddies. Planes and artillery bombarded the earth leaving it pockmarked with deep craters. Whenever a peasant dare slip out under cover of darkness to plant a plot or two of rice, planes would swoop down and spray it with herbicides. Dioxins that poisoned the earth for decades to come.

Once there was a village named My Anh, but now it was gone. My Anh was like so many other villages throughout the Mekong Delta that had disappeared. Villages that had been there for hundreds of years, and then within a matter of minutes had vanished. Blown into oblivion.

For centuries My Anh had remained the same. The people had wanted it that way. They had liked their way of life and had not wanted to change it. But there were things that they had not liked. They had not liked the wealthy landlord who insisted on anywhere from forty to sixty percent of their harvest. This had always angered them. It had seemed wrong for someone to drive out to the village once a year and demand the rice that they had worked so hard to raise. His bully boys came with him to beat those who could not meet their quotas.

Furthermore, the people of My Anh had not liked the district chief telling the village elders how to run their affairs and always insisting on higher and higher taxes. Money that was dearly needed to pay the school teacher, or buy medicine for the dispensary, or pay for repairs of the public market or community damn. This too had made them angry, for what had the district chief done for them? They had heard that their money had been used to build him a large concrete villa with a glazed tile roof. Once insurgents had fired a rocket at the house blowing a hole large enough for a carabao to pass through. This had pleased the peasants, but then they'd had to pay more taxes in order to repair the damage.

However, what had done more to anger the people of My Anh than anything else were the foreigner troops who suddenly seemed to be everywhere. Tanks and armored personnel carriers raced over the farmland trampling the rice and smashing the dikes. Helicopters swooped low over the village; their great rotor blades ripping loose the thatched roofs of their nepa huts sending the palm frond sailing in all directions. Jet propelled assault boats raced back and forth on their canals and rivers sinking the tiny sampans and smashing the larger junks and barges against the shore. Often foreign soldiers would come to My Anh poking about in the huts checking the people's identity cards. They were tall and fat like giant demons. Some had pink skin and eerie blue eyes. Others were as black as charcoal. The Vietnamese soldiers, who came with them, were always demanding money. "Give us money, or we'll tell the foreigners that you are Communists. Then they will burn your homes and kill your elders," they'd say.

In spite of all this, the people loved their village and their way of life and did not want to change it no matter how difficult things became. They were like a family. Of course, like anywhere there were those who were troublesome and sometimes vicious. But they understood these individuals and knew how to handle them. The village elders were more like fathers than officials. They took a personal interest in each and every one and settled conflicts by offering solutions that were agreeable to both sides. Neither was wrong, but one was usually less right than the other. And he who was less right had somehow to resolve the difference.

The people liked the slow easy pace of village life. There was always plenty of work for everyone. There was no time for idleness. But then no one was made to work harder. When one was not wading behind his slow lumbering buffalo waist deep in the rich delta mud, he might be floating along the shore of a canal in his sampan placing fish traps resembling wicker baskets in among the reeds or gathering palm frond from the mangroves to repair his home. There were any number of things one could do if he felt like it.

One day an official came from the province capital and informed the people of My Anh that they must leave their village. It was explained that the village was in the midst of a free-fire zone. Anyone found in the area would be shot without warning. Everything was to be destroyed – homes, school, market, ancestral tombs, trees, bushes. Anything that the enemy might hide behind would be razed. Nothing would remain. But the people refused to leave. They did not care. They would stay. They would sooner die in their village; then be herded like cattle to a resettlement camp. The spirits of their ancestors were there. They could not abandon their forbearers, for what would become of them when they had died? Who would look after their remains? Who would comfort their spirit?

One morning helicopters landed at the village of My Anh, and hundreds of foreign soldiers herded the peasants aboard the aircraft. Those who tried to escape were shot. Vietnamese soldiers, who accompanied the foreign demons, took whatever the people could not carry with them. Their homes were burned, and bulldozers came and scraped and dug at the earth until there was nothing but a flat bare field.

However, the destruction was not always like this. Sometimes it came suddenly without warning. Bombs and napalm rained down unexpectedly from the sky. Fighter planes and helicopters would swoop low over the charred smoldering ruins spraying it with bullets until everything was quite still. This often happened when an aircraft was shot at or enemy were in the village or it was suspected that the villagers were enemy sympathizers. However, none of this had occurred at My Anh. It was because My Anh was near an enemy supply route. And so to stop the infiltrators, it was decided that everything in the area must be razed. Not one tree or a single bush was left for one to hide behind. Thus My Anh like thousands of other villages throughout the country vanished.

Thousands of years of existence obliterated in an instant.

The Outsider

"Oh my God! It's Thong! Old Mr. Nguyen Van Thong, the village elder, running! Hobbling on his staff. Yes, everyone, running," Vince Grecco blurted. He could see the whole village from the hood of his jeep. Hundreds running for their lives. And then vanished. Engulfed in flame. Blankets of orange, yellow-red flames billowing hundreds of feet into the sky. He scanned the area with his binoculars. Nothing was left. The village of Cu Cat gone. Every scrap of vegetation incinerated. "Bastards!" Vince screamed waving his fist at the planes as they roared overhead. "Dirty fucking bastards." And then Grecco was awake, wound up in his mosquito net. "The same goddamn nightmare," he said as he untangled himself from the gossamer. "Every morning the same fucking thing." He lay back on the bunk and tried to calm down. His heart was pounding, and his breath came in gasps. Shit, I'll have a stroke if I'm not careful, he thought. What am I doing here working for these Nazi bastards? What good had he done? None. None at all.

Then he heard it. A far-off drone. He checked his watch. "Six forty-five," he muttered. "Right on time." Squadrons of B-52 bombers were passing overhead at thirty thousand feet. This happened every morning since Grecco first arrived at Phu Vinh deep in the Mekong Delta three weeks ago. It was his early morning wake up call. In a few moments, the 500-pound bombs would explode like a string of firecrackers shaking the house.

Vince thought of how Elbert Winiford, the USIS rep, would be sending a lot of crap to the Little Pentagon in Saigon about an NVA command post being wiped out. And then that evening there would be all sorts of bullshit being slung about at the colonel's briefing about the body count. He could see it in his mind's eye. The S-2, a small squat warrant officer with square rimless glasses,

The Idiot's Frightful Laughter

standing ramrod stiff before Colonel Winters saying; "Sir, base camp of NVA Second Battalion, 217st Division sustained 37 KIA and 52 WIA." His pointer taping at a shaded area on the wall map.

It was a charade, Grecco thought as he slipped off the cot. No one was fooled. They all knew that it was a crock of shit. The victims weren't even Viet Cong. He was sure of that. They never were. He was at the province hospital after yesterday's blitzkrieg. The victims were all women and children and old people. One must have been in his nineties. Some were blown all to hell. There was the little girl. No more than five or six with both legs blown off at the knees. And the old man with no eyeballs. Blood oozing from empty sockets. Well, it didn't make a shit what they called them. They could call them any damn thing they wanted, but they weren't kidding him. Not for a frigging second, they weren't. But he wasn't going to let it bother him. What good would it do? He couldn't change these warmongers if he had to.

Picking up an aerosol can from beneath the bunk, Vince examined the net. There were six blood-bloated mosquitoes trapped in a corner of the webbing. "Never learn," he muttered giving them a couple short bursts of spray. "You may get my blood, but I'll be damned if you'll get away with it." He picked the insects up gingerly one at a time and dropped them on the floor careful not to smear the blood on the sheets.

What cowards we are, Grecco thought. Why can't we fight man for man? The Viet Cong have nothing. They don't even have shoes. Make their sandals from our old worn out tires and strap them on with strips of inner tube. What are a rifle and a few mortar shells compared to a jet plane armed with cannons, guided missiles, machine guns, five-hundred-pound bombs, and canisters of napalm all operated by computer programmed radar. Have we no pride? No courage? What do the ordinary GI's have? Basically they are supplied with steel centered, nylon covered flak jacket; a radio transmitter; an M-60 machine gun; an M-79 grenade launcher; M-16 rifles; Claymore antipersonnel mines; fragmentation grenades; tear gas; white phosphorus grenades; a mine detector; starlight scopes; and blocks of pentrite high explosives usually transported by helicopter, and what do they do when they make contact with the enemy? Drops back and calls in artillery and aircraft support. Let them obliterate the enemy. What sort of war is that? Is there no honor?

Glancing at the cot across the room, Grecco saw that Max Gutschinritter had made it back. He was lying on his side curled up in the fetal position. He never used a net. Claimed the mosquitoes didn't like him. Too much alcohol in his blood. However, Gutschinritter wasn't a drinker. Said he hated the stuff. Vince had never seen him touch it around the quarters. However, whenever he visited the Vietnamese province officials, which was nearly every night, he felt obliged to drink as much and frequently more than his host. He'd come back long after curfew loaded on a brew that smelled like formaldehyde. He believed that drinking was part of the Vietnamese culture and that if one wished to make a good impression, he must get drunk with them. It was a matter of trust. Grecco didn't see it that way. The only time he saw drunk Vietnamese was when they were entertaining Americans. He assumed that they drank because they felt very ill at lease around Westerners. He could hardly blame them. Most of the province's American advisors acted so goddamn phony with their counterparts addressing them as "sir" and "mister" and passing out a lot of shit about what a great job they were doing and not meaning a word of it. However, Gutschinritter wasn't like that at all, Vince thought. Max really like the Vietnamese and would never dream of patronizing them. He worked hard at earning their confidence and was always rationalizing their shortcomings. As far as Gutschinritter was concerned, the Vietnamese, just as long as they weren't Communist, never did anything wrong. The way Max saw it, it was always the Viet Cong's fault. What's more, he spoke the language so fluently that he would fool Vietnamese speaking to him on the phone. They had no idea that he was American.

He's one hell of a good man, Grecco thought. If I was Colonel Winters, I'd appoint him as my deputy senior advisor and can all the rest of the bums. Well, I might keep a couple, he mused. There was Elmo Bledsoe and Major William Jack. Bledsoe knew his job

The Idiot's Frightful Laughter

and was a damn efficient administrator, and Major Jack had a brain on his shoulders and got along well with the Vietnamese. However, they disgusted Vince. They were a couple of real Uncle Toms. That was their problem. Always kissing that peckerwood Hank Barban's ass.

Downstairs Grecco could hear Ong Son rattling the pots and pans in the kitchen getting ready to cook breakfast. The smell of freshly brewed coffee filled the room. Vince shivered slightly. As always, Gutschinritter had turned the air conditioner on high. He opened the window and then pried loose a couple of tacks that fixed a sheet of plastic to the window frame. A gust of hot humid air invaded the room. Grecco hated air conditioning. It was unhealthy, he thought. How was one to become accustomed to the climate?

Vince glanced back at Gutschinritter who now had both arms and legs wound about his pillow. Dreaming of his wife, Grecco thought. He makes me want to puke whenever he talks about her. What she says just before she cums. How she behaves when she's horny. Nothing's sacred with that guy, he figured. And if it isn't the intimacies with his wife, it's his hang-ups with communism. Christ! Does he ever hate the Viet Cong. Hate! Hate! Hate! Kill! Kill! Kill! He's a real psychotic when it comes to the commies. Vince couldn't figure it out. He had all this undying love for the Vietnamese, but just let one of them go soft on the Viet Cong, and he's ready to tear the guy limb from limb. Grecco thought of all the people he himself hated. Shit! There were lots of them. He'd gladly have them all shot if he could. But they were people he knew. Those who had gone out of their way to give him a hard time. Just what had the commies ever done to Max? Gang raped his wife? Cut his balls out? Robbed him of his life's savings? Not hardly. Vince thought back of all the cheap crap that he and a lot of the other guys on the team had heaped on Gutschinritter. He never seemed to mind. He was the only one who didn't hate Hank Barban's guts. Grecco couldn't remember ever hearing him say a disparaging word about the cheap prick. As a matter of fact, on a number of occasions, he had stuck up for the bastard, and Barban was always piling shit on him.

On the other hand, Grecco once remembered making Gutschinritter so angry that his face turned scarlet. He was so incensed he couldn't speak. Just sat there sort of sputtering at Vince. It happened one evening in the rec room. Grecco and two Aussie Seabees were getting smashed on gin tonics when Max came in. He was quite upset. A village chief whom he had known quite well had been executed by the Viet Cong. Gutschinritter started off on a long tirade about the evils of communism. After putting up with this for a while, Vince said: "Look, Max, just what did the Viet Cong ever do to you?"

Gutschinritter stared open mouth at Grecco for several moments, his eyes red with rage. He had then walked abruptly outside slamming the door. Two MP's escorted him home at two the next morning. They had found him wandering about town muttering to himself. After that Vince was careful what he said around Max about the commies. One never knew, he thought. A fanatic like that could really crucify a guy. He might even go so far as to send a report to the CIA. Have some assassin ambush him some dark night and blame it on the Victor Charlie, he thought. So, after that, whenever Gutschinritter started off on one of his Red hating diatribes, Grecco would try to change the subject.

Grecco braced himself. There was a booming sound like a string of firecrackers exploding; then the house shook convulsively. "Bombs away," He muttered to himself. A fragmentation grenade toppled over and rolled off the nightstand striking the floor with a loud thud. Gutschinritter had brought it in the previous week after S-2 warned that a VC sapper squad was planning to infiltrate the town.

"Hot Dogs," Max said springing out of bed. "Some VC just got their asses blown off."

"Don't count on it," Grecco said picking up the grenade and setting it back on the table. He crimped the ends of the pin to make sure they were good and tight.

"What do you mean, don't count on it?"

"Just don't count on it. That's all," Vince said picking up his toilet articles and slinging a towel over his shoulder.

The Idiot's Frightful Laughter

"Hey," Gutschinritter call as Grecco started down the stair, "Still moaning about your commie pals that got barbecued?"

"They're not my 'commie pals'," Vince said stepping back into the room. He was furious. "They're poor simple peasants who have never heard of communism. All they wanted was to be left alone."

"Yea sure," Max sneered. "Wouldn't hurt a flea. Ha, ha."

"Suck on this," Grecco said jabbing his index finger at him. Starting back down the stairs, he muttered to himself: "There you go. When are you going to learn?"

In the bathroom, Vince gazed at himself in the mirror studying his features carefully as though he had never seen them before. This always came as sort of a surprise, for he thought of himself as being quite young. In his mind's eye, he looked as he had in his high school yearbook more than twenty years ago. The guy in the mirror was some sort of imposture. He didn't like his lean haggard look. The left eye with the tilted brow gazing back at him with a quizzical haughtiness. The cynical twist of the lip. The lined sunken cheeks. He didn't like it one bit. Where was the charm? The mirth? The casual air? The gay indifference? That's how he imagined himself to look. However, what he saw was a sort of weary outrage.

Grecco turned the shower's hot tap on full force spraying the sides and floorboards of the stall in order to wash away the black mold that had accumulated during the night. He then lifted the wooden mat with a stick to make sure that a snake or salamander wasn't hiding there. It seemed to be a favorite hangout for reptiles. Then reaching behind the shower module, he pulled out a pair of plastic sandals. One couldn't be too careful, he thought. He'd had his share of jungle rot. It would start between the toes, and within a week, the feet were covered with white watery blisters. And the smell! It made him retch just to think about it. The Vietnamese used an aromatic resin called Tiger Balm. Most of them wore sandals and were constantly rubbing the medication between their toes. It had a strong pungent odor, but Grecco didn't mind. It was far better than the sweet nauseous stench of tropic fungus.

However, the Americans had little faith in the oriental balm. They preferred gentian violet. It was useless, Vince figured, but then that was their business. He used an acerbic acid that a Chinese doctor in Cholon had recommended. It burned like hell, but it did the job, at least to some extent. It slowed it down. Kept it in check but left the skin sore and tender.

It was the color. Grecco hated purple gentian's deep crimson luster, but it was more than that. The feet weren't simply purple. They had a phosphorescent gleam to them. He'd stopped going to the lounge of an evening, for someone would invariably slump down on the sofa across from him and prop his feet up on the coffee table between them. Vince was disgusted. What could be more repulsive than a pair of ugly crimson feet thrust in one's face? He had an overwhelming impulse to stomp on them as though they were slimy slugs.

The troops called it the "purple plague," and Doc Dudley, the medic at the dispensary, was known as "Purple Paws" because his fingers were stained a deep lustrous violet. It was assumed that the stain would gradually creep up his arms and eventually transform him into a purple person. Doc was fanatic about the ointment. He used it everywhere. If one had a fever blister on the mouth, he'd paint his lips and gums with it and splash some on the teeth transforming the hapless patient into a Halloween goblin.

Grecco turned the hot tap on full force; then turned up the cold until the heat was just bearable. Good and hot, he thought. That's the way I like it. Nothing like a good hot shower. When he had been told that he was being transferred to Yen Chau, a tiny province capital deep in the Mekong Delta in the midst of a North Vietnamese Army, he had not thought that he would have it so good. He was living better now than he had in The States. Hot shower, a housekeeper, and a first-class Chinese cook. He gradually turned down the cold tap until the water was scalding. He did this twice a day more as a sort of therapy than for cleanliness. His tensions would ebb away leaving him limp and tranquil.

Grecco thought of MACV, an acronym for Military Assistance Command for Vietnam. There was a team of them in Yen Bay, whom he worked with, and whom he depended on for protection. The civilians and the soldiers were all on the same team, Advisory team 57. However, it was no wonder that the grunts hated the civilian members, Vince thought. They were billeted on the second floor of an old mandarin's mansion, their bunks stacked one on top of the other. There was barely enough room to squeeze between the cots. What's more, there were no air conditioners, no hot showers, and no topnotch Chinese cook.

Back upstairs, Grecco put on a white dress shirt, black slacks and a pair of oxfords. He was a civilian and he didn't want any mistake about it. If others wanted to wear army fatigues, go on patrol with the troops, and ambush Viet Cong, that was their business. He wanted no part of the military. Sure. Colonel Edward Winters, The Province Senior Advisor, was his boss. He was a West Point Graduate, and in command of the advisory team; however, the only contact Grecco had with the colonel was at his Saturday evening briefings when Vince gave his weekly progress report.

Some of the civilians were more militant than the grunts. Hank Barban, The Deputy Senior Advisor, was a real martinet. He was always driving about the province in his jeep with an automatic rifle across his lap. Everyone said that his days were numbered, but Grecco knew that pricks like him never died.

As he started back downstairs, Vince could hear Gutschinritter's whiny voice. As usual, he was talking about his wife. Grecco paused for a moment. Perhaps he should wait until Max had finished; however, he was already late for breakfast, and there'd be nothing left if he waited too long.

Gutschinritter was attempting to pick up a glass bead with a slender pair of lacquered chopsticks. "It's like trying to screw with a piss hard-on," he said looking up from his plate and smiling coyly. He looked like a child who had just done something quite mischievous and was gloating over it. "I remember waking up with a piss hard-on one morning", he said. "My wife reached over and took hold of my cock. 'Oh Darling', she said, 'it's so big and hard. Wait'll I go to the can', I told her. When I came back, she said, 'Oh Honey! It's so little and soft. What happened?'" No one but Coffee Koffman laughed, and it sounded forced and mirthless. The others concentrated on their food appearing not to have heard anything.

Grecco looked forward to Ong Son's breakfasts. He couldn't remember ever having had better. They were excellent. This morning there was a platter heaped high with golden squares of French toast, a huge bowl of hot cereal with a mound of brown sugar melting on top and plates of omelets mixed with chunks of cheese surrounded by thick slices of crisp bacon.

As always, Koffman complained about the food. "Where's the goddamn hash browns? Every morning it's the same old shit." he raved pointing his finger at the bowl of cereal. "It ain't fit fer pigs."

Grecco resented having his breakfast ruined every day. At first, he had wanted to punch Coffee's fat stupid face, but no one else seemed to mind his continual haranguing, and Ong Son seemed quite indifferent to it all, so Vince tried his best to ignore the jerk. Koffman was an air force sergeant on loan to the team as a logistics advisor. He wore civilian clothes and took their side whenever there was a confrontation with the grunts. No one could remember when he wasn't complaining about something. He behaved as though it was an inalienable right of his and seemed gravely offended whenever Vince objected.

There were usually two or three vehicles at the quarters to ride to work in, but Grecco preferred to walk. In spite of the fierce fighting that had ensued recently throughout the province capital, Yen Chau was still a picturesque country town. It was one of the few towns in the delta that still retained that old French colonial charm. The ugly U.S. Army prefabs that dominated so much of the landscape elsewhere were of little evidence here. It was still pretty much the way it had been when the French left some twenty years ago.

Grecco still had plenty of time to get to the office, so he sat in a wicker chair on the front porch. It was a bright clear day. It was always that way during the dry season. Even during the monsoon, there was sunshine. Suddenly without warning, the rain would pour down, and then in an hour or so, it was gone, and the sky was bright and clear again. Grecco liked the hot humid climate. It was so much better than Seattle where it nearly always drizzled. There the sky would be thick with mist for weeks. The sun might peek through for an hour or so every couple of days. Weather deeply affected Vince. He had never felt so depressed as he had in Western Washington. However, in Vietnam, there were those few days just prior to the monsoon when the weather was incredibly hot. Grecco's clothes would become drenched with sweat. At times like that, he longed for the cool misty Puget Sounds. But those occasions were few and far between. The month of May marked the end of the dry season, and although the roads were ankle deep with dust, the air was sultry. Even the Vietnamese found it oppressive and would extend their two-hour noon siestas to three and often up to four. Coming out of an air-conditioned office was like stepping into a blast furnace. But soon the monsoon would come, and the countryside would become green, and the dusty roads turn into rivers of thick sticky mud.

The front yard was small. There were no coils of concertina barbwire nor sandbags surrounding the house as was usually the case at the compounds elsewhere in the countryside. However, there was a concrete bomb shelter just to the side of the porch. It was beneath the ground, and even during the dry season, it was half-full of stagnant scummy water. It was an excellent place to spawn mosquitoes. It was also a habitat for snakes and salamanders. What a dilemma, Grecco thought. Either get hit by a mortar shell or bit by a poisonous snake. A lychee nut laden with clusters of golden-brown fruit was at either end of the yard. Someone had begun to mow the weeds with a sickle and quit after cutting less than half of it.

Across the street was Vietnamese Army compound. Coils of razor-sharp concertina were heaped one on top of another about the camp's concrete wall. Spaced at regular intervals behind the barbwire were sandbag bunkers. Directly across from Grecco was a lookout tower. The sentry was asleep. All he could see of the soldier were the soles of his sandals propped V-like beside a 50-caliber machine gun. Vince didn't like the idea of living across from an ARVN compound. It not only drew mortar fire but in case of an attack, his quarters were in the sentry's line of fire. He wouldn't hesitate to riddle the house with bullets, Grecco thought. The building would look like a slice of Swiss cheese. Arvin despised Americans. They were all too aware of the U.S. advisors bias. Their cheerful good-natured behavior didn't fool them. Vietnamese were a very perceptive people, Vince thought. They were hard to fool.

It took Grecco about ten minutes to walk to his office at the province headquarters. He could take a shortcut and get there in half the time, but he preferred the long route. The streets were lined with tall lean tamarinds. Along either side were faded ochre villas once the homes of French civil servants. They were now occupied by Vietnamese officials. Some of the homes were surrounded by high adobe walls crowned with jagged pieces of broken bottles and window pane. Other had strands of barbwire. A few of the occupants had made a half-hearted effort to restore their gardens, but most were overgrown with weeds and littered with rubbish.

Grecco passed groups of Chinese youth on their way to a high school east of town. They wore school uniforms. The name of the institute was embroidered in red characters on the left just above the heart. The girls wore white blouses and blue skirts that came just beneath the knee. The boys had white short-sleeve shirts and blue shorts. The youths wore either rubber sandals or canvas sneakers and took big aggressive steps swinging their arms as they walked. The girls' hair was cut short, just even with the earlobe.

However, the Vietnamese students walked west in Grecco's direction. The girls were dressed in the traditional white ao dia and black pantaloons. They were very slender. The long loose strips of cloth hanging from the waist at the front and back floated about them in the morning breeze giving the appearance of butterflies fluttering near the ground. They wore high heel wooden sandals and took short, very precise steps. The foot was brought almost straight up and then placed down in nearly the same spot. Their hair fell to just above the waist and looked very smooth and silken. They wore straw cone-shaped hats covered with clear plastic and held in place with a ribbon tied in a bow beneath the chin. Some would gaze coyly up at Vince as he passed by, their eyes sparkling mischievously.

The comparison interested Grecco. It told him how very different the two people were, and how stubbornly the Chinese had clung to their identity even in such isolated areas as Phu Vinh. It also gave him a better understanding of the Vietnamese, and why China had not been able to absorb them into their culture. After thousands of years of occupation, the Chinese had failed to change them. The Vietnamese had taken what they wanted from China – literature, architecture, philosophy, medicine, music – but this had not lessened their national fervor. Later the French and the Japanese and now the Americans tried to mold them into their image, but Vince could see that they would never change, and this pleased him. It was good that they were proud of whom they were. He had seen what America had done to The Philippines. The Filipino wanted so much to be American. He both worshipped and hated the Americans. Worshipped them because he'd been taught that the American way was the only way. The best of all possible worlds. Hated them because he knew that it could never be. The Filipino would always be mired in poverty.

Turning north at an intersection, Grecco passed a group of Arvin wearing U.S. uniforms. They were seated at roadside tables sheltered from the dust by reed mats hung over a bamboo lattice. The soldiers were drinking beer. They looked so lethargic. Forty years of war had sapped the will, he thought. First the French, then the Japanese, then again the French, and now the Americans. Would it ever end? They had ceased to care. It was not their fight. It was the Russians and Chinese against the Americans. They were nothing more than pawns. That's how they saw it. And the more they disassociated themselves from the war, the more the American troops despised them. They were over here fighting for a people who wouldn't fight for themselves. That's how the GI's saw it. Why couldn't the Arvin be like the Viet Cong? They were the same people. But a different cause, Vince would point out when asked.

Next door was a whorehouse. A long rectangular shed made from scraps of wood and flattened tin cans. Inside were several rickety tables and stools. Beer was served in large glasses with big chunks of ice. That was where negotiations were made. The cribs were at the back facing a narrow courtyard. A bamboo fence separated the barroom from the cages. It was there to thwart the MP's. These whores were for the Americans. They were too costly for the Vietnamese and besides their cunts were no longer suitable for the smaller Arvin cock. They had their own hookers on the top floor of a dilapidated Chinese hotel near the public market. The Arvin resented their second-class status. Revenge was meted out in various sly ways. However, sometimes it was both bold and brutal.

As he neared the province headquarters, Grecco glanced about at the destruction that had occurred last February during the Viet Cong's Têt Offensive. During the early morning hours of the Lunar New Year, a detachment of VC had slipped into the unguarded compound. They had set up machine guns on the headquarters' rooftop and barricaded its doors and windows. Jet fighters had pounded the structure with rockets blowing away the top floor. It was now enmeshed in bamboo scaffolding and supports. The education building had also been badly damaged and was under repair. A mason stood on a platform at the top of the scaffold turning a crank pulling buckets of concrete up by means of a rope pulley. The menial work was done by women. They carried the heavy loads, dug the ditches, shoveled the sand and gravel mixing it with cement. The skilled jobs were reserved for men. They were the carpenters, masons, electricians, and plumbers. The men might be physically stronger, but their work was much less strenuous. Grecco wondered how such an irrational system ever got started. But then there were many nonsensical customs throughout the world, he surmised. Many more absurd than this. At the center of the compound was the pale-yellow administration building where Vince worked. It was like most government buildings everywhere throughout South Vietnam. A reminder of over a hundred years of French colonialism and three hundred years of European intrigue. However, this structure was unique, for it was polka dotted with white circles of varying circumferences and shapes. Masons had recently plugged the bullet and rocket holes that has riddled the walls with white shiny plaster.

The Idiot's Frightful Laughter

For five days a detachment of Viet Cong guerrillas had barricaded themselves inside the building beating back one assault after another. Two blocks away the GI's set up machine guns on the rooftop of their garrison and pounded away at the structure until Colonel Winters had ordered them to stop. What was the point? Why destroy the only office building in the province capital? The VC would have to leave sooner or later. They only had so much ammunition and food.

The enemy slipped away in the dead of night and hid in a Cambodian pagoda on the outskirts of town. A bonze made the fatal mistake of telling the province chief, an Arvin colonel, where the Viet Cong were. The chief, a Catholic, who had fled North Vietnam with the French, had no use for either the Cambodians nor the Buddhists. He'd called for an air strike on the ancient sanctuary killing the VC along with many of the monks and razing the pagoda. Grecco was vexed. He supposed that it had been one of the most picturesque pieces of architecture in the province. Was it the American military's intent to reduce Indochina's culture to a pile of rubble? Send them back to the Stone Age? he pondered. What was their rationale?

Stepping inside the section reserved for Americans and their clerical staff, Grecco saw that Gutschinritter was already hard at work. He was seated at his desk cluttered with stacks of papers awaiting translation into English. Some were highly confidential documents taken from the enemy. At the moment Max was speaking in Vietnamese to a hamlet chief about resurfacing their soccer field. Another village elder sat beside his desk waiting to talk with him about a new resettlement camp. It had been finished several months ago. All it needed was the Province Chief's official recognition. He wanted Gutschinritter to speak with the chief's deputy. Max had a better rapport with the colonel than any of the village officials. Two more were standing by with similar requests. He was the only American the Vietnamese ever came to see unless it was Major William Jack, the civil action officer; a black man from rural South Carolina. They just didn't trust the others. The feeling was mutual.

The Callow Youth

Long ago, a French architect had designed the interior of Yen Chau's province headquarters to protect top management from assault. The director's office was a thick windless cubical in the center of the building. The corridor surrounding the room was where the clerks and administrators had their desks. Hank Barban, the Deputy Senior Advisor, along with assistants, Major William Jack and Elmo Bledsoe occupied the inner sanctum. Barban also had a Vietnamese secretary, Lu Di. She was ravishingly beautiful. Her main job was to make sure that no one intruded on the Deputy Senior Advisor's privacy unless he authorized it. During the noon siesta, he would fuck her on Major Jack's desk. It was one of the condition's she agreed to, in order to get the job. A half-dozen other candidates had refused. The major would stand guard outside the door as an added precaution. It wouldn't do for her husband, An Arvin officer, to get wind of the affair. The fucking wouldn't have mattered to Lu Di. It was the cold mechanical way that Barban had gone about it that she hated. It was as though he were buying fish at the market. He was so inhuman, so goddamn haughty. He never showed any feeling, any tenderness. He treated her as though she were a slab of meat. Lu Di hated that, and because of it, she plotted her revenge; a revenge that would turn the tide of war in Vinh Binh Province.

Grecco knew about the assignation, for his desk was in the corridor facing Barban's door. He once got a glimpse of Lu Di lying spread leg across Major Jack's desk, her pantaloons pulled free of one leg, and her ao dia thrown across her face. Barban was standing braced against the edge of the desk pressed against her thighs, a leg of hers on either shoulder. What alarmed Vince most was the expression on Hank's face. It was one of cool disdain. He's raping her, Vince thought. Raping the enemy just as he probably had done to the black girls on his father's peanut plantation in Mississippi. Grecco knew instinctively how Lu Di must feel. It was the price she had to pay for her job.

Vince was jammed so closely to the doorway, that he had to constantly shift his heavy metal desk about so that people could pass by. This constant disruption evidently pleased Barban, for he would not allow Grecco to move even so much as an inch. He insisted that the desks be a precise distance apart. He had the space between each desk measured, and had lines painted on the floor to mark their exact location.

The work environment didn't matter much to Vince. Why should it? His job was quite routine and required no thought whatsoever. However, although it was dull and pointless, he was never able to meet the deadline. This puzzled him a bit, for he was a journalist and had spent many years in big city newsrooms racing against the clock, so to speak. However, that was interesting challenging work.

His desk was always cluttered with piles of memos, reports, and communiqués that he rarely looked at. Many were documents from the head office in Saigon. Usually, he'd simply initial and pass them on Gutschinritter, for most were so full of bureaucratic jargon that they were quite incomprehensible. At first, he'd made an earnest effort to decipher them, but after a week or so, he'd concluded that it wasn't worth the trouble.

The ones who read them were the nitwits who were more numerous than he had first imagined. And then there were the career men who had to pretend that the directives were of great importance if they hoped to survive. To admit to themselves that they weren't would make their own existence seem so senseless.

Grecco thought of the hundreds, possibly thousands of nameless people in small cubicles in Saigon writing this stuff, and the tens of thousands more in Washington and countless more in offices throughout America writing gobbledygook that no one ever read. That could not be read. It was job security, he reasoned. As long as they cranked it out, their jobs were secure. Just how many billions of dollars did this cause the taxpayer every year? he wondered. The waste must be astronomical.

Stacked at one corner of Vince's desk was a pile of computer printouts. Spread out in a straight line, they'd measure about fifteen feet. They were loaded with highly inflated statistics concerning welfare recipients throughout the province. Every month Grecco had to bring the figures up to date. And it suddenly occurred to him that the deadline was 1600 that very day.

"Shit," he muttered. "Shit almighty," He would have to meet with his counterpart, Nguyen Chu, the Social Welfare Chief.

For the first couple months, Vince had visited the resettlement centers throughout Vinh Binh Province. If he was lucky, he could hitch a ride on a helicopter, but frequently he went alone by jeep right though Viet Cong controlled territory. He took great pains getting accurate data. However, Nguyen Chu always had a very different set of figures. Where did he get them? He never left Yen Chau. Grecco was the only one to visit the resettlement camps. He was sure of that. It was the Social Welfare Chief's discrepancy that threatened Vince's credibility. The US State Department's Chief of the Refugee Division was angry. "Grecco was being stubborn. He was not cooperating with Mr. Chu, his counterpart. Why didn't the figures match? That was the whole point of him being there. 'Vietnamization'! Didn't he understand what the word "advisor" meant? He was a social welfare advisor. His job was to inspire the Social Welfare Chief to take the initiative. That's what was meant by 'Vietnamization'. Get the Vietnamese to take control and do things efficiently.

Bill Bailey had laughed at Grecco. "Take it easy, Vince," he'd cautioned. "You're taking your job too seriously. Your predecessor and Mr. Chu were great buddies. They used to play chess all the time."

"I know," Grecco said. "But Barban wasn't too pleased about that."
"Fuck that prissy ass prick," Bailey retorted. "Nothing 'ill please that asshole."

It was the bribery that Grecco found most distasteful. However, Bailey assured him that they all had to do it. Even Barban did it. He was the worst of all.

In order to get a copy of Chu's bogus refugee figures, Grecco had to buy him a fifth of Scotch at the Post Exchange. What bothered Vince most was not the bribery per se, but the charade he had to go through. He couldn't simply hand him a bottle of whiskey. First, an appointment had to be made. Then at the prescribed time, he would enter the Social Welfare Chief's office with the bottle of Scotch concealed in a paper bag. Chu would be seated at his desk with the pages of the bogus figures before him. Grecco would sit down and place the bag beside the desk. The chief would then reach down and slide it around beneath his chair. Then with great decorum, he'd stand and hand the report to Vince. Chu's secretary had carefully explained the formality to him repeating the procedure until she was certain that he had it right. "Protocol is so important to Mr. Chu," she'd said.

Bailey was so reassuring. "You're getting off light, Vince. A bottle of whiskey is nothing. That's just the preliminaries. He's softening you up for the big kill," Bailey said. "Sheet, the other day Colonel Winters had to get the Province Chief a fridge. A little grease makes things move more smoothly," he added nudging Grecco in the ribs with his elbow. "Oh, by the way, none of that cheap stuff. Chu likes Johnny Walker Black Label." Bailey was an ag advisor and spent much of his time testing soil samples and figuring out ways to reclaim mash land.

The radio operator's desk was only a couple meters from Grecco's desk. Tony Sanchez, a Filipino, sat all day dispatching coded messages to the regional office in Can Tho. "Papa Alpha, this is Bravo Whiskey. Come in Papa Alpha," he would shout over and over again into his microphone. Grecco was surprised at how oblivious everyone was to the noise or at least they seemed to be. Vince could hardly restrain himself. At times it was all he could do to keep from smashing the radio to bits. What were all those

Sheridan Peterson

messages? Just how confidential were they? Were they all that urgent? He was sure they weren't.

At a right angle to Grecco between Sanchez and Gutschinritter's desks was another Filipino, Eduardo Perez. He was the self-help advisor and had been there for years. The American civilians seldom stayed more than eighteen months and the GIs less than a year. However, Perez had been around since 1962. Over six years. He had come with the first advisor team and stayed ever since. Perez's desk drawers were jammed with trays of cards on which he kept a great assortment of facts and figures. He was always shuffling them about and copying data from them to send to the self-help director in Saigon. He seldom left his desk during the day and never went outside the province capital. At first, Grecco had asked Perez a great many questions about the province and its people supposing that he must be somewhat of an authority of the area. But Vince had soon stopped, realizing that the self-help advisor's information was false. What's more, he didn't seem to know a word of Vietnamese and saw no reason to learn it. What's more, Grecco had trouble understanding his English. The Vietnamese never had anything to do with the Filipino, and he never made any effort to meet with them. As for self-help projects, as far as anyone knew, he had never bothered to start one.

On the other side of Gutschinritter sat Buu Hoang, an ethnic Chinese whose ancestors had lived in the province for over three hundred years. They were here when the Vietnamese invaded the delta two hundred years ago defeating the Chams and Cambodians. His title was interpreter-translator. Before the Viet Cong had taken control of most of the rice land in the province, he was a prosperous landlord. He loathed the Vietnamese and spoke very disdainfully of them. "They're all lazy and dirty," he had once told Grecco. "You can't trust any of them." He had not let Vietnamese work his land. All his tenant farmers were ethnic Cambodian. He didn't like them either. He considered them even dirtier than the Vietnamese. However, they were hard workers and honest. Well, more so than Vietnamese, he'd declared.

The Idiot's Frightful Laughter

Behind Buu Hoang opposite the entranceway was Ms. Nguyen Thi Van's desk. She never spoke to Hoang, and he never spoke to her. When he spoke about the Vietnamese, she appeared not to hear. She was an excellent secretary by anyone's standards, and she knew it. Barban was continually trying to lay her, but he had no success. She'd been hired before he came and had friends in the regional office, so Barban was hesitant to push things too far. Besides he was afraid of what her husband, a Marine Colonel in I Corps, might do if he found out. Nevertheless, Hank had tried to bribe her by giving her a truckload of sheet metal roofing and another of cement which had been earmarked for a resettlement camp. Ms. Van had taken it and built a house, but Barban had got nothing, not so much as a smile.

Ms. Van's beauty was quite different from Lu Di's. She was exotic whereas Lu Di had an ordinary sort of beauty. Some might regard it as sexy. On the other hand, Ms. Van was not the least bit sexy. Her beauty was that of a classic princess. Grecco envisioned her at the Emperor's Court in Hue before the French intruded and changed all that. She had long tapering fingers. Her face was slender and her features very delicate. He eyes were large and soft like those of a doe. She had slender lips and a straight aquiline nose seen only among the gentry of Central Vietnam. It was believed that this trait came from the Chams whose Hindu Kingdom ruled central Vietnam around the second century A.D.

There was something regal about her poise, and the way she walked with such grace and preciseness. Grecco remembered so well the Sunday afternoon when she paid the team a visit. She was wearing a violet ao dia and white pantaloons. Her black glossy hair hung in ripplets down to her down to her waist. A light blue parasol shone like a halo about her head. Grecco had taken her picture standing beneath the litchi nut tree. He had sent it to Glamour Magazine. Perhaps someone had stolen it, for he had never heard from them.

What was she doing in Yen Chau with this sordid gang of foreign misfits? Grecco was puzzled. A pearl among swine. That's how Vince saw it. What a fool her husband must be. Didn't he realize what a precious jewel he had?

Grecco looked about at the calendar on the wall behind him. Today was Friday. "Not Friday!" he gasped to no one in particular. "Not the last Friday of the month!" He had marked the square with a red felt pen "MRD", monthly report due. Barban would be looking for his input for the monthly report. "Holy shit!" he murmured. "The monthly report is due today."

Theoretically, Grecco was responsible for three refugee centers and one temporary camp. A day or so before the report was due, he made a point of visiting two of the centers to see if anything was amiss. The third was inaccessible. The Viet Cong had liberated it during the Tết offensive, and it was still under their control. Even the military with all its air power and heavy artillery had not yet bothered retaken it. Vince had spoken with Colonel Winters about providing him with some protection, but the Province Senior Advisor had advised him that it was impossible. It was now a VC base camp, and that it would take a fully mechanized battalion to root them out.

However, the other day, Vince had learned that there was no longer any camp left. It had been bombed by a squadron of B-52 Stratofortresses, blowing it into oblivion. Sergeant Clint Braileanu, the team's forward observer, had reported directly to MACV Headquarters at Tan Son Nhut that the camp was a VC stronghold. However, neither Colonel Winters nor Barban wanted it known that some eight hundred Vietnamese, mainly women and children who were under their care, were blown to smithereens. Thus, Grecco was ordered to report to the head office for refugees in Saigon that the camp was temporarily inaccessible. Vince was incensed. He was under orders from the team commander to commit perjury, to cover up for a heinous crime. The Nuremberg War Crimes Trial had made it a capital offense to obey an order condoning genocide. Nazis, that what they were, Grecco thought. I'm working for a gang of Nazis. He had half a mind to tell his pal, who was *Time Magazine's* Bureau Chief in Saigon. That would be an honorable thing to do. However, the CIA would surely kill him if he did. He'd just be another statistic. Missing in action. Who would care?

There was a temporary camp just a couple clicks south of town. It was built more than a year ago. The team had planned to move some four hundred people there from a Viet Cong controlled village in the southwest corner of the province and then declare the area a free-fire zone. It had been Vince's predecessor's responsibility to look after these instantaneous refugees. However, he had refused to have any part of it. Crispin Tucker was a Harvard Law lecturer who had applied for the job through the U. S. Agency for International Development. He wanted to see for himself just what America was doing in Vietnam and insisted on being sent to the field as a refugee advisor. He spent a lot of time wandering about speaking with Vietnamese. Gutschinritter had accused him of being a Communist, and Blaine Bruce, the CIA's province director, had called him a fucking gook lover. That was after he had alerted his colleagues at Harvard of the enforced internment of villagers. As a consequence, a group of U. S. Congressmen and reporters came to Phu Vinh on a fact-finding junket. Barban made sure that Tucker was out of town. He prepared an elaborate banquet for them, and Nguyen Du Bo, the province chief, speaking in flawless French, told the guests what a marvelous job both Barban and Colonel Winters were doing. He would occasionally pause to correct his translator's English. "Please, Mr. Suu, the verb tense is future perfect. You should have said: 'They will have completed'." He would then shrug his shoulders and roll his eyes in mock despair. His address was followed by Buu Hoang who explained in great detail about all the wonderful things that the Americans were accomplishing.

It was Coffee Koffman who put things in the proper perspective. "They're a couple bullshit artists," he said.

"Yea," said Elmo Bledsoe after looking about to make sure that Barban was out of earshot, "They sure can pile the shit on. They're the greatest."

Tucker and Barban had had a fight over the matter. It wasn't much of a fight. If it had been, Tucker would have pounded Barban to death. He was built like a bull and had played rugby at Harvard. It seemed strange to be playing rugby in America, but then at Harvard most anything was possible. Anyhow that's how Grecco saw it. Barban had called Tucker a "smartass", and he had taken a swing at him smacking him just beneath the right eye. The blow had sent him flying across the rec room and onto a ping pong table which snapped in two.

Cowering behind Major Jack, Barban had given Tucker twenty-four hours to leave the province; otherwise, he'd have him locked up for striking a superior officer. Actually, Crispin had a higher GS rating than Hank, and besides, they were both civilians and thus not subject to military discipline. Barban wrote up a poor efficiency report, accusing Tucker of being both uncooperative and antagonistic. A month later he was fired and sent back to The States. Tucker wrote an article for the *Wall Street Journal* about the proposed razing of a village and the deportation of some four hundred people to a concentration camp; however, Barban and Colonel Winters' names had been omitted.

Barban ordered Gutschinritter to set up the camp. The Viet Cong's big Tết offensive of '68 occurred soon after the quarters were built, and so the project was destroyed.

Now Barban was trying to renew interest in the project. He had been after Grecco to get things in order. Vince could well empathize with Tucker, but why fight the system? The individual invariably lost. Why waste one's time and energy? Take his old' buddy, Grant Olson? He was always off on some crusade. And now here he was in Vietnam heading a training center for some corrupt construction conglomerate. What a place for an idealist? "Eat your heart out, Grant," he muttered to himself. "You simple shit. Won't you ever learn?"

Grecco rummaged through his drawers until he found a copy of the previous month's report. He went through it changing dates; then he took it into Barban's office. No one was there but Lu Di. Bledsoe and Major Jack were with Barban at the colonel's morning briefing. They wouldn't be back for another hour. Lu Di was reading an English grammar text. Barban had made it clear to

The Idiot's Frightful Laughter

everyone that she was his private secretary and not to bother her. She was only to type for him; however, he rarely had anything for her to do. On the other hand, Nguyen Thi Van had too much to do. She was always busy typing translations of long awkwardly written Vietnamese government documents. Lu Di would type for Grecco if she was in an agreeable mood, and she was so inclined about fifty percent of the time. The other half of the time, she took her hate for Barban out on the other Americans in the office. When she felt irritable, she'd shake her head and smile very apologetically pretending that she could not understand what was being asked of her. This had infuriated others, but Grecco understood the very humiliating circumstances that she had been forced into, and so had never pushed her. Consequently, she was unusually friendly to him whenever Barban was gone.

"*Ong minh yo come*? How are you, sir?" she said very softly and very sweetly.

"*am on. Come on co*. I'm fine. Thank you, Miss," he replied. "You look very lovely today, Lu Di," he said shifting back to English.

"Today? Only today?" she asked looking at him with mock despair. "I only look lovely today? How did I look yesterday? Did I look dreadful?" she said smiling coquettishly.

"No! No! Lu Di!" he said raising his hands in protest. "You are always lovely."

"More lovely than Co Van?" she murmured with a mischievous glint in her eye, for everyone knew how much Vince adored Nguyen Thi Van.

Grecco felt his face grow warm. Lu Di burst out laughing. "I see! I see!" she shrieked pointing an accusing finger at his flushed face. "She is more lovely? Yes? Yes? Yes?" Lu Di shook her head and shoulders up and down with glee.

Why deny it, Grecco thought. Co Van was a goddess. There was no comparison. How could he compare a mere mortal with a goddess from heaven? He gave Lu Di a wide-eyed smile ruffling his eyebrows.

"See! See!" she screeched shaking with glee. "True! True!"

Grecco always felt like a loser when it came to women. They always had the last laugh. And yet Lu Di couldn't be pleased with such a hollow victory. She must surely feel let down. "Lu Di," he said suddenly looking quite earnest. "When's your next day off?" And without giving her time to answer, he added, "How about this weekend? How about meeting me at the Bong Mai Café in Can Tho?"

"I sorry Vin…cent," she said slurring his name. "I can't. I have husband. He *ca ka dou* me," she said pretending to strike herself on the head. She looked genuinely sorry to have had to say it.

"What you got?" she asked. "Same old report as last month?"

"Yep," Grecco said trying to sound very casual. "Mind typing it up for me?" "Okay," she said suddenly looking quite serious. Then curling the corners of her lips down slightly and motioning towards Barban's desk, she added: "But shit-for-brains beaucoup mad if he know." Grecco wondered where she picked up the term. Probably from Barban.

"Don't worry, Lu Di. I'm not about to tell and don't you tell either," he said winking as though they were plotting some unsavory conspiracy.

A half hour later, as Lu Di had just finished typing the report and was handing it to Grecco, Hank Barban walked in. He was followed by Elmo Bledsoe and Major Jack.

The first time Vince saw Barban, he had instantly hated him. He envisioned a callow youth blatantly in love with himself. A real narcissus. It brought to mind a quote from Shakespeare's *Merchant of Venice*. "I am Sir Oliver. When I speak let no dog bark."

"Vince, ya finish your report?" Hank demanded. He had stepped behind his desk, pressed both fists down on it and leaned forward. Grecco had to admit that he looked rather imposing. He was wearing an African safari outfit and an Aussie bush hat. The jacket had large pleated pockets and a wide lapel. It was referred to derisively as a "Jungle Jim" suit. The name came from the costumes Johnnie Weissmuller wore as the fabled Jungle Jim in his big game hunter movies. Barban had had an Indian tailor on Saigon's notorious Tu Do Street make a half dozen for him. He had a tiger

The Idiot's Frightful Laughter

stripe, two black, a gray, an olive drab and a khaki with bush hats to match. He wore his hat at a rakish tilt and a pistol slung low on his hip. As he walked, the holster with a 45-caliber automatic slapped at his side. In one hand he carried a bullet-tip swagger stick and slung over the shoulder, chrome-plated Swedish K automatic rifle. How did he get away with such buffoonery? Vince wondered.

"Yea," Grecco muttered shrugging his shoulders.

"Yea what?" Barban said rearing back slightly and raising his eyebrows.

"Yea, I finished the report," he replied trying to sound as casual as possible.

That wasn't the reply Barban wanted. If he'd directed the question to either Bledsoe or Major Jack, they'd have snapped to attention and replied: "Yes Sir, the report is finished, Sir." Barban had passed out a directive ordering all civilian personnel to address their superiors as "Mister" and "Sir". He had also insisted that everyone stand at attention whenever he entered the office and salute him. His rationale was that the team was headed by an army colonel; making the civilians paramilitary and thus subject to military discipline.

Grecco made a deliberate effort to ignore the directive. He'd served his time in the Marine Corps fighting the Japanese. What had Barban ever done? Get a deferment because of a weak back. That was a pretty feeble excuse, Vince thought especially considering that he was a weightlifter.

Grecco's pretense was obvious to everyone, and Barban let it be known that he didn't like it one damn bit, but there was no way to enforce such a command without looking ridiculous. However, he used subtle threats reminding Vince of how important an efficiency report was if he was thinking of making a career of the Foreign Service or finding another government job. What's more, he told everyone of the poor rating he'd had to give Tucker, and how sorry he was, but then he believed in being honest. It wasn't fair to gloss over a man's deficiencies, now was it? He'd ask smiling sardonically.

Grecco disguised his disgust. As long as everyone else was going to eat shit, why should he be the martyr? He'd played the role before, and what had it gained him? Stoic indifference, that was how he planned to play it.

"And stop bothering Lu Di," Barban added. "She's got work to do."

Lu Di looked expectantly at Vince. Her eyes were bulging, and her lips pressed tightly together as though she was about to burst out laughing. Grecco had to bite down hard on his lip. Her looks said more than words could possibly express. "Okay," Vince said trying to affect an innocent smile. Waving casually, he turned and sauntered from the room closing the door slowly behind him.

"There's no place for men like that on this team," Barban said pointing his swagger stick at the door. "He's got a bad attitude. No team spirit." Major Jack's expression indicated that he was in full agreement, but he said nothing. It was Bledsoe as usual who took Barban's side.

"That's right, Sir. Everyone has to work for the good of the team." Lu Di turned her head so that she couldn't be seen and stuck out her tongue.

Max Gutschinritter

The team's New Life Development Advisor had been a Marine up along the DMZ for several years, but there was none of the Leather Neck bravado in his demeanor. He was so casual and shy that at first glance, one might assume that he was effeminate. But nothing could be further from the truth. He was tough and quite fearless, but not foolhardy like Blaine Bruce, the province's CIA Chief. Yet what estranged him from even the most ardent hawks was an insane hatred of Communism. It was a monomania. No punishment was too severe for the Viet Cong.

Some thought that his mania had occurred when his best friend was killed in a mortar attack near Da Nang. However, a Public Safety Advisor who had known him in high school said that he was just as fanatic then. His whole family were far-right extremists. They adored Senator Joe McCarthy. Max did not see the Viet Cong as people who sought a different way of life for the horribly oppressed peasant. To him, they were monsters who could perform the most dastardly crime without remorse.

Gutschinritter only read books that confirmed his deeply rooted conviction and reinforced his hate. He wouldn't dream of reading Karl Marx or Frederick Engle. He considered their views lies to dupe the fuzzy-minded intellect. Others had to lock up books by liberals or even mild-minded conservatives in their trunks, or they would disappear never to be seen again. It was suspected that Max burned them.

Gutschinritter was so disturbed by Grecco's left-wing outbursts that he wrote a report to the FBI stating that he suspected Vince of being a Communist and demanded a more thorough investigation of his security clearance. Soon other members of the team began receiving inquiries about Grecco. The CIA kept watch of his daily activities.

However, there was an ambiguity. Gutschinritter was a paradox in capital letters. Grecco both admired and despised Max; however, if he had known Max's parents, he might have felt more conciliatory. Actually, Gutschinritter knew little of them. He only knew what they chose to tell him. He knew that they were members of the Third Reich and had served under Hitler. They had come to America in 1945 immediately after the war. But that was it. They kept their Nazi past hidden from him, and he sensed that it would not be prudent of him to ask too many questions. There were things that he best not know.

Max father, Fritz Gutschinritter, served as a Gestapo Agent in the Ukraine. He was in command of a company of SS troops. Among other things, he made cut-throats of his men. He could transform ordinary youth who had never harmed a living thing into cold-blooded killers. His men followed behind the combat troops. They would go from town to town in search of communist commissars. The heads of the city and provincial governments. Teachers were also apprehended. Anyone who had any sort of influence over the populous was a prime target. Once they had a sizable number of prisoners, they would load them on trucks and drive to a field or wooded area. The condemned were ordered to dig their own mass grave. Fritz was very exact about the size of the pit. He made certain that it was three meters deep by six meters square. Once this fete had been completed, the prisoners were lined up and made to stand at the edge of the trench exactly ten centimeters apart. An SS trooper would position himself behind each prisoner; his pistol held at the base of the victim's skull. Then Captain Gutschinritter would raise his hand in the Nazi salute. "Heil Hitler," he'd shout as he dropped his arm. At that instant, the soldiers would fire simultaneously, and the prisoner's bodies would topple into the pit. Lime was spread over the corpse, and the trench was filled in. The remaining soil was shoveled onto the trucks and dumped in a stream or river. Grass seed was then sown over the grave site. The remains would vanish without a trace.

Max father met his mother at a special rest camp for Nazi officers of Nordic descent in the Bavarian. When Sarah von Burger

The Idiot's Frightful Laughter

was seventeen and had just graduated from secondary school, she was sent to the camp. Sarah like tens of thousands of other girls just like her from throughout Germany and Austria were informed that they were to have the great honor of serving the Fatherland. Sarah had been singled out because of her Nordic heritage. She was larger than most girls her age and had long flaxen hair and clear blue eyes.

There was nothing romantic or courtly about Captain Fritz Gutschinritter and Sarah von Burgen's courtship. It was an arranged marriage. They were introduced by a high-ranking official of the Third Reich. He informed them quite matter-of-factly that it was their duty to produce children for the Fatherland. It was a great honor. The wish of their beloved Fuhrer. They had been specially selected to participate in the creation of a race of Nordic Supermen and women who would rule the earth. And so, ironically it was Max who had become the answer to a Fuhrer's dream.

Fritz had been careful what he said to his son about America. He realized that a negative attitude would hamper the boy's success, and Fritz most certainly did not want that. But it was not easy, for he and his wife had little use for the country. When they were alone, they would speak with each other of how stupid Americans were. They were so naïve, like children babbling about the most nonsensical drivel. "They are so easy to be duped by the English and French and so soft on Communism," Fritz would say, and Sarah would nod. How long could such a mongrelized society survive? They wondered. Fritz knew what he would do if he were the leader. This is a white man's country, he would declare. The blacks and Asians and Latin Americans would have to go before it was too late.

From as early as he could recall, Max remembered his father telling him about the evils of Communism. It was a fight to the death, he told his son. We must get them before they get us. It was always those damn Communists, or those damn Reds, or those damn Bolsheviks. That was all Max ever heard. The rest his father kept to himself.

Soon after the war, former OSS agents slipped Captain Gutschinritter into the U.S. He along with hundreds of other Nazi officers were of use to the newly formed Central Intelligence Agency. It was preparing for an eventual clash with the Soviet Union. The German officers were assigned to train Special Forces such things as espionage, terrorism, counter-insurgency, and interrogation. He had access to a large warehouse full of SS Gestapo training film that the CIA had confiscated. Many were documentaries taken at the scenes of actual interrogations, tortures, and mass executions. Captain Gutschinritter was once attacked by a Jewish officer who had recognized him in command of an execution in a film. Soon after that, he resigned afraid that Israel's Mossad would find him and try him as a war criminal.

Grecco suspected that Max had been brainwashed. Someone had worked on his psyche when he was just an infant pressing the hate into the moist emulsion of his subconscious, leaving an indelible imprint on his mind. Vince knew all about being brainwashed. Priests had embedded the fear of hell and the devil into his tender mind. Not just of hell and the devil, but of a vengeful, wrathful God. Even now that he knew that it was all bullshit. The notions still haunted him.

To Gutschinritter, the Communists were devils who delighted in the slaughter of babies and the rape of virgins. He saw it as a blight creeping across the earth contaminating everything in its wake. However, Grecco figured that the Commies were fed the same sort of bullshit. They had their fair share of Gutschinritters brainwashed since infancy, psychically blinded seeing the Americans as vile monsters intent on ravish and plunder. Now with the advent of television, prejudice would spread much more rapidly, he thought. Is there no way to stop this bigotry? Why couldn't people just leave their children alone? Let them be free to form their own opinions?

The Prison Professor

At the age of twelve, Chanh was a real man. Short, dark and stocky, he looked more Cambodian than Vietnamese. He grew up on the bank of the Cong Hoa Canal in the very midst of the great Sea of Reeds. During the monsoon which lasts from June until September, everything as far as one can see is beneath water except for the mounds of dirt spread out along the south bank of the canal. The rest is a plain of reeds that covered more than seventy square kilometers of marshland. Chanh's home and eleven other thatched huts were perched on the mounds of earth piled there by an army of laborers who dug the canal some fifty years ago. Thousands of men and women were forced to dig the channel forty-five kilometers south to the great Mekong River. These prisoners hacked at the thick gummy clay with short-handled hoes and carried the muck in wicker baskets up the steep sides to pile along its bank. Dozens of smaller canals crisscrossed it making the delta look like a great if not a somewhat disproportioned checkerboard.

Chanh's father, a tenant farmer, was held to a bare subsistence by his wealthy landlord. Once the water receded somewhat, he'd work all day waist deep in the muddy alkali soil raising rice. However, if it hadn't been for the fish he caught in wicker traps beneath the reeds along the bank of the canal, Chanh's family would have starved during the lean years when crops failed.

Chanh would never forget the day two strangers came to his home and beat his father. Someone had informed the landlord that he'd been hiding part of the rice harvest, for he'd received just forty percent of the yield rather than the customary sixty. The two strangers had used clubs striking his father until he was unconscious. Afterward, he was not the same. He no longer cared to work in the fields but sat all day and often late into the night in front of their hut staring off across the kilometers of swaying bulrushes. Chanh's mother wove reed mats, and he sold them at the market in Tram Chim. But there was little demand for them, for most peasants made their own. Forced off the land, the family moved to Hong Ngu, a port town on one of the Mekong River's vast maze of tributaries called Tien Giang. The village was just three kilometers from the Cambodian border.

Chanh's mother went to work as a day laborer loading and unloading barges and junks. The work was hard. She had to pack hundred-pound sacks of rice, bamboo baskets of brick, and large earthen jugs of pungent fish sauce up narrow planks that bent beneath her weight. She worked from dawn to dusk. The pay was never more than thirty piaster a day. Less than thirty cents. In the meantime, his father grew more and more despondent, rarely speaking to anyone. He lost interest in food and began to resemble a skeleton.

It was here that Chanh began working for the Binh Xuyen Gang. Among other things, it controlled the rivers and canals throughout the delta. Chanh first worked as a spotter on the Tien Giang River. His job was to report any vessel trying to slip across the border into Cambodia without paying the customary tribute. Most of the boatmen made monthly payments at the gang's police headquarters in Saigon and were issued a safe conduct pass that the skipper presented to the mob's chief at either Hong Ngu or Chau Duc. Those caught trying to sneak across the border without a pass had to pay double and suffer the loss of their cargo. Repeat offenders had their vessels seized and sold to those willing to abide by the rules.

The following year, Chanh was assigned to an assault squad. Their task was to halt vessels trying to evade payment. They would fire several shots across the prow of the boat, then board it and were then supposed to tow it to port. However, the gang found it more lucrative deal directly with the skipper. He was always more willing to pay them double or even triple to save his cargo. However, as soon as he was on his way again, they would notify the next patrol further upstream, and the skipper would be fleeced a second time. This might occur a half dozen times before he

The Idiot's Frightful Laughter

reached Phnom Penh. One thing was certain. He learned his lesson. He never tried to slip through again without first securing a safe conduct pass.

It was on one of these raids that Chanh and his cohorts were captured. They were arrested by the police who only a month before were on the Binh Xuyen's payroll. When the U.S. put Ngo Ding Diem at the head of the newly created South Vietnam, the premier set out to consolidate his power by declaring war on any group legal or illegal that challenged his command. The Binh Xuyen gang was one of Diem's prime targets. His first act in office was to take charge of the police force. The commissioner was publicly guillotined. Diem then closed down the gang's gambling casinos in Cholon. The big showdown came a month later when the Binh Xuyen massed all its forces, some six battalions of fully armed troops, in the Rung Sat's mangrove jungles. It fortified itself along the Nha Be River, Saigon's trade route to the South China Sea. However, within less than three weeks, Diem's forces equipped with gunboats and landing craft crushed the pirate army.

Chanh along with hundreds of his cohorts was sent to prison at Con Son Island, a sun-baked speck of coral rock some fifty miles off the eastern tip of Vietnam. It was there that Chanh made his first encounter with the Communists. Soon after being confined to a small brick compound crammed with other Binh Xuyen culprits, he met Luu-Y. Captain Luu-Y was the former commander of Headquarters Company, Second Battalion of the Viet Ming's famed 316th Division which was instrumental in defeating the French Foreign Legion at Dinh Binh Phu. The captain never mentioned the Communist's aims or ideals to Chanh. That would have been too difficult for him to grasp. He only spoke of the country's ills. Things that the lad was all too well aware of. He talked about the rich indolent landlords, the corrupt officials and the Americans, especially the Americans. They were worse than the French. They were there to take what the French had left. They had chopped Vietnam in half. The people must drive them out and reunite the country. Luu-Y spoke of how the foreigner, the white man, had robbed the people for hundreds of years. It was time to put an end

Sheridan Peterson

to it. He said that one owed it to his family, his village, and his nation's future generations to drive the white devils into the sea. He assured Chanh that he would own his own land. His children could go to school. There would be no more corruption. No wealthy landlords nor crooked officials to bother with. Luu-Y was an idealist and believed this with all his heart. Chanh could see it in his eyes, in his tone of voice, by the way he pounded his fists on the table to empathize a point. One could not doubt his sincerity. It was a dream too marvelous to imagine.

Chanh thought frequently of the two strangers who had come to his village years ago and beaten his father. He could remember it so clearly. How they had first gone to a tiny thatched shop and drunk rice wine, their staffs left outside leaning against the wall. They had sat there for a long time before they had looked for his father. A little boy had taken them to where he was plowing waist deep in the mud. They had motioned for him to come to the dike where they were standing. One took a piece of paper and read aloud from it. Chanh saw his father's bone lean body grow taut. He looked so expectant. The other man took his pole and struck the back of his father's head. Striking with the cold deliberate motion of one swinging at a ball. He stood motionless for several seconds and then pitched forward striking the dike and slipping face down into the mud. The two strangers took hold of either shoulder and lifted him up onto the dike careful not to soil their clothing. They wiped their hands on his shirt and then turned him over on his back with their poles. Squatting at either side, they struck at his face with short wooden clubs they carried beneath their belts. They smashed his nose. Knocked out his teeth. Then they took turns striking at his face with wrist-snapping motions until it was a soft pulpy mass of blood. They did it without any display of emotion. That was what bothered Chanh the most. If they had been angry, full of passion and outrage, it would not have distressed him nearly so much. It was their cool, business-like behavior that made it so horrible, so cold-blooded. He yearned for revenge. He often thought of what he might do if he ever found those two thugs. How he would make them beg and whimper for mercy before he chopped them up into tiny pieces and fed them to the dogs.

Until now the hate had not gone beyond the two strangers and the landlord who'd sent them. He had not thought of the brutal beating as a class war. The consequence of a system made up of the oppressed and the oppressors. He had not realized that the two thugs were simply the tools of a tyranny that ruled their lives. The two strangers were just as much victims as his father was. It was the system that was evil, Luu-Y explained. A system that must be destroyed. That was how Chanh must avenge his father's brutal beating. Killing the two hooligans would solve nothing. There were plenty who would promptly take their place. Men who needed money to feed their families. Even the wealthy landlord didn't count. He had little power. It was the leaders, the province chiefs, and the generals and the politicians that kept the proverbial rope bound about the peasant's neck. They were the ones who were in essence responsible for the beating, the captain explained. And of course, there were the foreign devils, the Americans, who were promoting this oppression. They were the real tyrants. The others were just lackeys.

Chanh thought of how alike the two strangers looked. They had the round swollen faces of people from Saigon. Too much rich food and alcohol. Their pale brown eyes were like panes of smoked glass. When he first saw them walk into the hamlet wearing the same white shirts, black slacks, and pith helmets, he had thought how lifeless they appeared. Now he understood that they were without souls. Men who had lost interest in life, in other people, in themselves. Perhaps they had never cared. Like cows, simply doing what they were told. They were just like so many of the guards at the prison. It was the leaders who were to blame for his father and countless others' misery. They were the ones whom he must get. That was how to settle the score. And, of course, especially those foreign devils.

"But first we must get you out of here," Luu-Y told Chanh one day. You're not doing anyone any good rotting on this rock."

"How about you?" Chanh had asked.

"With me it is different," he replied. "I came here by choice."

"By choice?" Chanh was alarmed. He knew that Luu-Y was serious, for he never joked.

"Yes, by choice," he said. "How would you and all these others have known about the National Liberation Front if I hadn't been here to tell you? Several dozen of us have been sent here by the party as teachers to guide men like yourself in the right direction. We are here to enlighten those who have been made victims of corruption and oppression. To help them find justice," he said.

The day Chanh was released from Con Son Prison, Luu-Y gave him a phone number of a comrade. "The password is: 'feed the tiger's greed'," he said. "He will put you in contact with a unit of the NFL. Enemies will be watching you, so be careful," he cautioned.

Things had worked out just as Luu-Y had said. Chanh was one of several dozen Binh Xuyen gangsters assigned to a Viet Cong guerrilla unit in the jungles a kilometer or so inside Cambodia. They spent most of their time digging underground fortifications. In the beginning, Chanh was terrified. Without warning, dozens of five-hundred-pound bombs would drop quite unexpectedly out of the sky. Beneath a three-layer canopy of jungle, the muffled drone of the flying fortresses some thirty thousand feet above could not be heard. And so there was no time to escape. Tons of earth, trees, stone, buildings, and bodies would cascade into space blown to oblivion. Miles of twenty-meter-deep craters were left in the wake. Then there were the planes that sprayed the forest with herbicides, soaking the vegetation with deadly dioxins. The jungle would gradually wither and die. Water was poisoned, and crops destroyed. Soldiers grew sick dying slow painful deaths. Some of the guerrillas fled. But where could they go? Enemy aircraft were everywhere shooting at anything that moved.

At sixteen Chanh was a hardened warrior. However, he never overcame the fear of the bombardments. That wasn't humanly possible. But he was able to bring the fright under control. He used it to fuel his rage for the enemy. Those foreign devils who were blowing his country apart, intent on annihilating him and his comrades. He fantasized of overrunning an American outpost, his assault rifle blazing at his hip, killing the Yankee devils by the hundreds. He was so obsessed. His craving for revenge was insatiable.

He did not have to wait long. All one day, artillery shells pounded what was left of the jungle. The next morning, Chanh heard the clatter of hundreds of helicopters' rotor blades whirling above. He mounted his 7.62mm Chicom machine gun on its swivel and fired 150 rounds a minute at the choppers hovering a few hundred meters overhead. The door gunners fired back spraying the woods about them. Never had Chanh felt such exhilaration. He was quite oblivious to his own safety. Helicopter after helicopter crashed about him bursting into balls of flame and black clouds of smoke. Then out of the clouds fighter jets dived for him passing overhead with a deafening roar. Canisters of napalm tumbled from beneath their wings, striking the earth in bursts of billowing flame. The thick burning gel swept over Chanh. Ablaze, he ran screaming for several meters before crumpling into a mound of carbon.

"Smells like roast pig, don't it?" a GI said kicking at Chanh's burnt carcass. "It's a hell of a way ta go, ain't it, even if he is a gook?"

"He ain't no gook," another soldier said. "Shit asshole, he's more of a man than you'll ever be."

"Ah thought you hated Vietnamese?"

"Ah hates Arvin, those yellow-bellied mothafuckers," he said. "But ah has the highest respect for the Viet Cong. They put us to shame." He stood at attention and saluted Chanh's burnt remains.

A Fifth of Scotch

Grecco stopped by his desk just long enough to roll up his computer printout and cram it into his briefcase before paying the Social Welfare Chief a visit. It then occurred to him that he had forgotten the fifth of whiskey. He'd left it in a box beneath his cot.

As he crossed the living room and started up the stairs, he could hear Ong Son talking with his teenage daughter, Co Chi. She was only fifteen. She'd had an affair with a cop from St. Cloud, Minnesota a year and a half ago when she was just thirteen. He was now in I Corps on the DMZ training death squads. They wrote each other regularly. Once she showed Grecco a family snapshot of him with his wife and two teenage sons. He looked to be fifty; a good thirty-year age difference, Vince figured. What makes it worse, she's in love with the slimy bastard.

Sitting on the edge of his bunk, Grecco reached beneath it and pulled out the box. A paper bag with a fifth of Johnny Walker Red Label was at one corner. The rest was filled with mementos that he had picked up while traveling about the country as a newspaper correspondent. There were a pair of sandals carved from a truck tire which he had removed from a dead Viet Cong, a faded National Liberation Forces flag, a small Buddha figurine he'd found in the rubble of a pagoda bombarded during the Têt Offensive, some Chieu Hoi safe conduct passes, a small lacquer vase inlaid with mother of pearl from an abalone shell, a conical hat made of palm leaves, a Montagnard bracelet, a pair of bamboo chopsticks, and a small carved stone from Emperor Khai Dinh's Mausoleum in Hue.

As Grecco sorted through the souvenirs, Co Chi came very quietly into the room. She walked past him as though she didn't see him, set a feather duster, a broom, and a wicker basket on the floor and then stepped backward dropping into his lap. Her head leaned

The Idiot's Frightful Laughter

back lying on his shoulder. She turned her face to his as though wanting to be kissed.

Grecco stared at the child's parted lips only inches from his own for what seemed like a very long time. He could hear Ong Son moving about down in the kitchen humming a tune, and people playing tennis next door. Rubber soles slapped the concrete court. The ball thump thumped against the rackets. He felt his cock swell. It seemed as though it would burst. Flesh is weak, he thought. It had been a long time since he'd had a piece of ass. He wanted so badly to fuck her.

"No Co Chi. No, no" he whispered taking her by the shoulders and raising her to her feet. "Ong Son has very big ears. He caca dau me," he added making a cutting motion across his throat with the edge of his hand. She smiled which seemed both innocent and coquettish. Then she turned still smiling back at him and went out the door. Listening to her footsteps moving very slowly down the stairs, he thought, what the hell. The damage has been done. What difference would it make now? And then how many others were slipping over here during the day just for that? He figured that they all were, most of them anyway.

Nguyen Chinh, The Social Welfare Chief, rose and came around from behind his desk to greet Grecco when he stepped into the room. He took the American's hand in both of his and shook it for what might pass for warmth. "Ah, my friend," he said grimacing broadly. "Long time don't see. Where you go?" he asked.

"Out checking on refugees," Grecco replied.

"Ah yes, yes," Chinh said scurrying back behind his desk and dropping his eyes to the floor. "Yes, good, good."

It was anything but good, Grecco thought. The refugees had none of the things they'd been promised. They didn't even have potable water. At one site, it was brackish. At another, the wells hadn't been dug. Consequently, many were returning to their razed villages in the free fire zone. They would sooner die than live like that.

"Sit down. Sit down," Chinh said grimacing even more broadly than before. Unlike the other public officials in Vinh Binh, he was quite thin, so thin that he resembled a skeleton with skin stretched tightly over it. His arms were the thickness of mop handles, and his head had no flesh. Just a skull. The skin pressed taunt against it. Grecco thought of a specter in one of Edgar Allen Poe's horror tales. The sunken-eyed sockets, the flat nose with large nostrils, the lipless mouth and the bared teeth. Death incarnate. Perhaps he has tapeworms? Vince thought, for he had accompanied him to the Province Chief's Tết banquet and was so amazed at what an enormous appetite the tiny man had. He ate more than anyone else.

Grecco glanced about the office. A thick coat of dust lay over everything. The floor was littered with cigarette butts and scraps of paper. Large, loose-leaf binders bulging with yellowed papers lay stacked along the wall behind Chinh and on top of cabinets. They, in turn, were crammed with old moldy ledgers and bundles of papers tied together with strips of cloth. Additional binders, papers, and ledgers lay haphazardly about on Chinh's and his clerks' desks. One man was busy sealing a pile of legal-looking documents with red wax, pressing the department's logo firmly into the warm emulsion. A secretary wearing a colorful ao dia had one foot propped up on an open drawer pairing her toenails. Overhead an antique propeller fan turned lazily making a creaky-door sound. Its blades were black with grime. Shit, thought Grecco, pigs live better than this. It wouldn't hurt them to clean the place out once in a while. He supposed that many of the stacks of paper were left there by the French decades ago.

Trying to be as discreet as possible, Grecco set the bag with the bottle of whiskey at the side of the desk next to the wall. Chinh instantly grabbed it and slipped it into a bottom drawer grimacing at Vince the whole time as though to say" "Aren't we clever chaps though."

Why so much caution? Grecco wondered. Who's going to complain? They all do it. The booze will probably be passed up the line from one official to the next until someone at the head office in Saigon eventually consumes it.

The Idiot's Frightful Laughter

Chinh opened the top drawer of his desk and took out the report. Bowing slightly, he handed it to Grecco extending both hands in a gesture of great formality. He behaved as though he were doing Vince a great favor. Vince was mesmerized by the nostrils boring back into the skull like the snout of a pig.

"Thanks," Grecco muttered. He was certainly not going to address his counterpart as "Mister" or "Sir" like the other advisors on the team did. That was carrying things a bit too far. After all, he thought. I've got to live with myself, haven't I?

"Lots of new refugees this month," Chinh said. "The 123rd have a big operation at Cam Dinh."

"Oh yea?" Grecco said smiling sardonically. He wasn't going to be any phonier than he absolutely had to. And he most definitely wasn't going to discuss the figures with Chinh as though they were genuine. If the chief needed to save face, he'd have to find someone else to bullshit. The whiskey was enough, he thought getting up and shaking hands. "Sorry, but I've got to hurry," he said. Then waving the report at Chinh, he added, "Must send this to Saigon. Today's the deadline." Wait'll he sees that it's Red Label, not Black, he mused. Next time he'll check more carefully.

As he left, he noticed that the secretary had finished with her toenails and was daintily picking her nose with a three-inch fingernail. She had the chief's sinister grimace. Perhaps his daughter, Vince thought.

This is what the American taxpayer pays me for, Grecco thought as he headed back to his office. Boy oh boy, if they only knew where their hard-earned cash was going. A bribe for a phony set of figures.

The protocol was different this time, Grecco thought as he trudged back across town. Why the grimace full of mock disdain? And why did he grab the bottle of Scotch and jam it inside his bottom drawer? Before Chinh had been different. He had been quite matter-of-fact about it. He'd simply said: "No whiskey; no report." And then quite abruptly motioned for Vince to leave. Obviously, something was going on. What was it? He hadn't the vaguest notion. Was it simply a ploy to keep him off balance?

In search of a diversion, Grecco glanced about at the outdoor market. Anything to wash away the sour taste, especially the memory of that deathhead grimace. He wondered if the ceremonial offering was an omen of ill tidings. What had caused such an erratic change of behavior? He was noticeably anxious about something. In a civil war such as this, anything was possible. Families were divided. Father against son. Brother against brother. One often had no choice but to betray the thing he held most sacred. Grecco could well imagine how perplexed these people's lives were. If his brother or father had been taken prisoner and was being tortured by the people he was in close association with, what would he do? What could he do? Had Chinh been asked to denounce a member of his family? That was certainly a strong possibility. No matter how despicable the chief might appear to the casual observer, his life might be one of immense turmoil. Far worse than anything an American could possibly imagine.

Grecco felt a tug at his pant leg. A wizen old crone was squatting on the ground smiling up at him. It had been a while since he'd seen such an unsightly person. Her teeth were coated with shiny black lacquer. She was chewing betel nut and spitting the reddish liquid at Vince's feet. Her mouth looked as though it were full of blood like that of a carnivorous beast feasting on a freshly killed prey. The spectacle of red saliva dripping from shiny black teeth was nauseous. For a moment, he was not able to hide his disgust. However, she appeared not to notice.

"Ong xihuan?" "You like?" she said pointing to a huge wicker basket full of slimy squirming eels. They were nearly a yard long and very slender glistening silver in the bright sunlight. They had small beady eyes and mouths like dragons with plier-like clamps at the very tip of their jaws. A hush fell over the noisy bickering fishmongers. Grecco noted their anxious stares. They were watching him intently.

"Dau co." "Oh no," he said softly. "Cam on ba." "Thank you, madam." This was followed by an outburst of laughter. They were all smiling at him good-humoredly. It was important to show an

The Idiot's Frightful Laughter

elderly person respect, Vince assumed. She too was pleased, smiling and nodding her head cheerfully.

Nearby a woman with a checkered cloth bound about her head was chopping fish and putting the pieces into a pan of murky water. Another fishmonger was bargaining with a genteel matron in a blue silk ao dia. Her hair was coiled into a grand coiffure. The two women were haggling over a shark that was much too large for the tiny basket it protruded from. However, the thing that held Grecco's attention was a huge leopard-spotted manta ray. It was at least four feet in diameter. Two men carrying it impaled on a quarter-inch water pipe. It had been thrust through its pectoral fins that protruded like great horns at either side of its bulbous eyes. Its whip-like stinger had been chopped off leaving a four-inch stump. What annoyed Vince most was the large glob of betel nut juice someone had spit on its glossy opalescent skin. Such a degrading end for such a magnificent creature, he thought.

Life goes on, Grecco thought as he gazed about the busy marketplace. Are these people the least bit aware of how corrupt and incompetent their leaders are? The Americans like to pass it off as a way of life. It was a generalization that they applied to all Asians. However, most Vietnamese were honest hardworking peasants. Vietnam was the victim of a system that began with the French colonialists several hundred years ago. Corruption had started as a way of evening the score with their colonial masters. Now it was too deeply ingrained into the bureaucratic system to change easily. The peasants were struggling for survival while their leaders spent their time figuring out how best to exploit them. It was no wonder that there was a revolution. Why is it, Grecco wondered, that we Americans always end up supporting the crooks? It's the same old story wherever one looks. There was Batiste in Cuba, a front man for the Mafia, Marcus in The Philippines, The Shah of Iran, Somoza in Nicaragua and Generalissimo Chiang Kai-shek. He and his in-laws plundered China before fleeing to Taiwan and the U.S. willingly helped them. The list of greedy despots we've supported is endless. And now its Nguyen Cao Ky and Nguyen Van Thieu. Who would lay down their life for such swindlers? The answer is appalling. We are doing it by the thousands. Tens of thousands of young American boys are being slaughtered so that these criminals can get rich and hightail it to the French Riviera. It was no wonder that morale was so low among the Arvin enlisted men. Grecco thought of how he'd once had to give the Public Works Chief five rolls of color film in order to borrow a U.S. truck so that he could deliver a load of bulgur wheat and cooking oil to some war victims. They would have starved otherwise. But this was of no concern to the chief. He had a new camera that his American counterpart had bought for him at the post exchange in Saigon, and he wanted to take some pictures at the Province Chief's party that evening.

Grecco tried to shrug it off. So what if that's the way they feel? Why should he care? It was none of his business. Yet he found that their callous disregard for their own people was forcing him to become more and more involved. This contemptuous indifference for the refugees had caused him to grow increasingly concerned. It was the very thing that he had set out to avoid. He had rationalized his purpose for taking the job. He was a newsman. Here was a chance to see the Vietnam War at the grassroots. See how Vietnamese bureaucracy works from within. He'd have a firsthand knowledge of its day to day routine. And then there was the money. Sixteen thousand dollars plus four thousand bucks hardship pay. Twenty thousand dollars a year, and for doing what? Turning a couple phony reports in each month. He was determined not to let the situation bother him. Not for one instant. Well, he was wrong. It was troubling him. He couldn't help it. The greed. The incompetence. The ignorance. The cruelty. They were all gnawing at his guts. Never, even in his maddest dreams, had he ever imagined such a thorough lack of scruples. Oh, sure, there was plenty of corruption in The States. He wasn't about to deny that. There was always someone out to screw you. However, it was not so matter of fact. Here dishonesty was so systematic. So carefully orchestrated. Vietnamese officials behaved as though it was an inalienable privilege that went with the job.

The Idiot's Frightful Laughter

When Grecco was a police reporter for the Tribune in Chicago, he'd heard cops boast about the price they'd paid for their beat, and how much they figured on netting in payoffs. The one on Division Street where the bookies and drug pushers hung out was said to be worth forty thousand a year, and so a cop had to pay the chief for such a lucrative beat. Well hell, Vince thought, that was the way it was with everything in Vietnam. Even down to the lowly washwoman at a U.S. Army outpost. She had to pay off the Vietnamese police in order to get a security pass. That's as far as it went. She was never investigated. Every Vietnamese that worked for the Yankee dollar had to pay someone off. Sometimes it was the personnel clerk or the one with the most clout in the office where an applicant was seeking employment.

Grecco had tried to figure it out. One might put the blame on the French, he thought. Colonialism had alienated these officials from the people. They were no longer Vietnamese. They had been raised to imagine themselves as French. They were a mark above the masses. Each generation had been trained to assist the French colonialist in exploiting their people and keeping whatever they could for themselves. It was a conspiracy. However, first, they had to be made to feel that they were different. A superior species. Once that was achieved, their French masters knew that the rest would be easy. It had taken hundreds of years for the French to produce this hybrid. Their culture. Their religious faith. Their mannerisms. Their prejudices. Even the furnishings of their homes and the clothes they wore were French. And then when these misnomers had all the wealth that they could squeeze from their people, they would leave. Flee to the Riviera or the French Alps and live the lives of noblemen. How could such an indelible imprint on one's soul be erased? Never, Grecco assumed. Ship them off to France. That was his solution.

These Vietnamese Officials had not defeated the French Foreign Legion. They had not liberated Vietnam from colonial oppression. They had fought with them against the Viet Minh. Hundreds of thousands had given their lives fighting for the French empire. Huge crowds had lined the streets of Saigon and wept openly as the French troops marched past and boarded ships for home. They could not be blamed. They had been carefully conditioned since infancy, Grecco thought. Their ancestors were the ones who made the choice. It was their decision that made the difference. Out of sheer greed and power, they had chosen to turn their backs on their ancient heritage and do the colonialists' dirty work.

The Province Chief

Colonel Nguyen Duc Bo, the Province Chief of Yen Bay Province, disliked a lot of things about the Americans; however, the thing he disliked the most was the way they'd knifed the French in the back. He, like all the other province chiefs and most of the Arvin staff officers, had fought with the French as a platoon sergeant. Colonel Bo had not wanted the French to leave. He knew what would happen, and he knew what he'd have to do to survive the impending disaster. The country would be ravished. And when there was nothing left, those who could, would leave. Flee to France. He for one would grab all that he could before it was too late.

It angered Colonel Bo at how America had stood by and watched the Viet Minh annihilate the French forces at Dinh Binh Phu. He had been wounded in the hip there. Many of his comrades, Vietnamese trained at French academies, had been killed. Men whom America could have saved. But it had chosen to wait, and then when the French had surrendered and withdrawn, the Yanks had moved in and imposed their rules. Rules that shift and change from one month to the next; until he is tired, fed up with all their nonsense and will no longer pay any attention to any of it.

For a while, he had pretended to be interested. But now he can no longer bear even to hear about some new policy that contradicts all he's been taught at the French academy. Whenever his counterpart, Colonel Winters, starts in on some plan of theirs, Colonel Bo abruptly changes the subject. Winters was so typical, he thought. Each year he had a new American counterpart. They were all the same. Colonel Winters was a graduate of West Point, the cream of the army's officer corps, and yet what did he know? He knew nothing of Vietnam. Nothing. Not even the simplest words. Colonel Bo had visited a village recently with the colonel. What fun that had been. He had told the village "Aren't you pleased with these gentlemen?" he had asked pointing to the village elders. "Yes, yes," Colonel Winters had said smiling and nodding his head. "See," he said turning back to the villagers. "He agrees that he is a fool." Everyone laughed including Winters and his interpreter. What a charade it all was, the Province Chief thought. He must not forget to tell his French friends at the Circle Sportif about this. It will amuse them immensely.

The Yankees are always complaining about the red tape imposed on Vietnam by the French, but it is nothing, absolutely nothing compared to the great rolls of shit that belches forth from their computers. Reams and reams of statistics. Senseless, useless, pointless columns and columns of erroneous figures.

Another thing that Colonel Bo disliked about Americans was their naïveté. He had hoped that they would maintain some order. That they would keep the Chinese merchants in check, but they've done quite the opposite. They've encouraged corruption. Tempting even the most scrupulous by turning billions of dollars over to the government of South Vietnam. Simply giving it away. Never bothering to check on how it is spent. And then later, they have the audacity to accuse the very leaders that they have handpicked of being thieves. This had outraged The Province Chief. What had they expected?

Have they never heard of greed? Have they thought the Vietnamese so different? Are the Yankees so perfect? Given the chance, won't they do the same thing? He knew quite well that they would. That they have.

The Province Chief's hate of Americans had begun when he was commander of an Arvin infantry company some five years ago. He had resented the American advisors' impatience, their condescension, the way they pushed the Vietnamese troops about. He recalled with glee the time he'd gotten rid of his counterpart, Captain Ike Becker, a fat arrogant bigot. For three weeks the Yank had been pestering him to make a sweep of a thickly forested mangrove swamp. Reconnaissance planes had spotted activity in the area. The Colonel, who was then a captain, had sent out recon

The Idiot's Frightful Laughter

patrols to probe the guerrillas' position, so he had a fairly good idea of how well entrenched the Viet Cong were. He had not shared this information with Captain Becker. However, he had sent a report to his battalion commander complaining that Becker was an unsuitable advisor. He had described the VC encampment and called his American counterpart a laggard. "I need an advisor who inspires more aggression," Colonel Bo had said. The report went all the way up to the U.S. Army Chief of Staff. Within less than a week, Captain Becker was transferred to a desk at Saigon's Little Pentagon. A month later he resigned his commission. Colonel Bo was amazed at how easy it was to destroy an American commission officer's career. He had never felt quite so powerful before.

Colonel Bo had studied philosophy at the Sorbonne in Paris. He wrote his dissertation on the *Critique of Pure Reason* by Emanuel Kant. "I have nothing in common with these Americans," he told his French friends at dinner one evening at the Circle Sportif, Saigon's elite social center. "Since the French have left, Vietnam has become a cultural wasteland. These Yanks are barbarians," he added. "They care nothing for art, music, literature, not even their own great Emerson. They are a nation of mechanics, or should I say grease monkeys."

"The French. Ah, a French officer," Colonel Bo said raising his glass of wine in salute. "The French officer is so proud, a true scholar. He is a man of good taste and refinement. He does not trouble himself with gadgets. He is too intellectual for such trifles. With him, one can talk of art and music and philosophy – Kant, Fichte, Hegel. That is what makes one an officer and a gentleman. The way one stands. That expression of subtle disdain. His voice." Colonel Bo said pressing his fingers to his lips and then throwing a kiss to the wind. "How he speaks to the enlisted men, to fellow officers, to his superiors. Ah yes, all this is what commands respect. The troops know that their officers are superior. Worthy of respect and unquestionable obedience. Ah, but these Americans." Colonel Bo's face grew somber. "If it were not for the insignia, one could not tell the difference between a colonel and a private. They are like children playing games with expensive toys – tanks, planes, helicopters and oh such deadly weapons. I must talk with them as though I were talking to an unruly adolescent spoiled by all their privilege. What do they read?" The Province Chief raised his hands in mock despair. "Cowboy and Indian thrillers. Detective mysteries. Comic books. And their music? Noise for drunken savages. And art? What would they know about that? Pictures of naked sluts torn from cheap erotic magazines. Ah but then there's the food!" He shook his head in disgust. "What has become of their tongues that they cannot taste? Their food is not fit for an ignorant peasant. Tasteless, bland slop that they soak with ketchup and other condiments to give it some semblance of food. It is only the French who know what truly fine food is. Where else could one find such exquisite dishes? Nowhere! Nowhere in all the world!" Colonel Bo waited only for the day when he could flee to France. Once he had squeezed enough money from these children, he would go. He'd have a villa on the Riviera and a chalet in the Alps. Ah, then he would live. So many of his good friends were already there. It was so amusing to note that those who had been his bitter rivals here were now such good friends. If only the Americans knew what a charade it all was. What fools we are making of them. They are so naïve. Too innocent to even see what's right there before their eyes. Too busy playing with their gadgets to take interest. "Ha! Ha! Give us your dollars, Yankee. You may keep your toys," the Province Chief said downing a glass of wine in one gulp. France's finest.

A Way of Life

Grecco stopped his jeep at a narrow bridge. A Vietnamese wearing army fatigues sat on the railing holding a pole with a disk at one end. The side facing Vince was red with a black line across it, the international traffic signal for "stop". As he waited watching the loose planks rock up and down beneath the wheels of the oncoming traffic, he grew impatient. H felt suddenly anxious to get back to the office. But for what? What was so important that he could not wait a moment or so? Why was he in such a hurry? Was he worried about losing his job? Was he afraid of Barban? Had he fooled himself into believing that he had something of great urgency to do? No, he knew that it wasn't because of any of those things. It was simply the way he was. He too was the product of generations of conditioning. Patience was something he had little of. He had tried at times to cultivate it. He had even tried meditation and yoga; however, they took more discipline than he could muster. Nevertheless, he yearned for it. For him, it represented many things. It meant strength, peace of mind, success, insight, tolerance, friendship, and love. He believed that all these things and more were possible with patience.

Coming to Vietnam had momentarily rekindled this aspiration. Grecco had looked to the East through the eyes of such pop mystics as D. T. Suzuki and Alan Watts, present-day stress healers whose maxims had been exploited worldwide by cults, such as the Hare Krishna and the Moonies. Vince embraced their platitudes as though they had sprung from the Godhead. They were a salvation. He had decided that he would live among the Orientals. Exposure to their stoic resignation would free him from his gut twisting anxieties. He would become like them.

However, the Orient was not at all as he had imagined. If it was in their best interest, Vietnamese could assume a façade of patience and politeness. But that was a charade. Beneath their cool exterior lurked a furor far more intense than the Westerner's impetuosity. There were occasions that called for a special sort of politeness. However, these were ceremonial and had nothing to do with daily life. They reminded Grecco of how he'd been taught as a child to genuflect before the altar at holy mass. He had done it simply because that was what was expected of him. However, it was quite out of keeping with daily life and bored him immensely.

Grecco was quite unprepared for the Asian's herd instinct. Wherever he went, he was pushed about by surging mindless mobs. The onslaught orchestrated by a bedlam of blaring horns, ear-piercing shrieks, and raucous laughter. In self-defense, he soon learned to elbow his way through the throngs. In order to exit a bus, he'd crouch low as though he were a football linesman and ram his way through those intent on pressing him back inside. The charge was frequently led by little old women with looks of fierce intent. The simple task of crossing a street was a harrowing experience. Often, he saw the body of a hapless victim left by the roadside. Stopping or even slowing down for a pedestrian was quite unheard of. Such an unexpected action would have infuriated the other motorists and quite like have caused a traffic disaster. There was no escaping these onslaughts.

What's more no one ever stood in line. Cueing up was unheard of. Such a routine would have been thought absurd. They fought their way to the ticket counter at a train station or to buy stamps at the post office, pushing those ahead aside. No one was exempt. The feeble, the aged, the crippled were all treated alike. What would Buddha have thought of all this? Grecco wondered. But then the Orient had probably always been like this. Nearly a hundred years ago, Rudyard Kipling had depicted a frenzied urgency much the same as now, even worse if that was possible, Vince thought.

On the other hand, whenever Grecco sought the help of a Vietnamese bureaucrat, time was of no consequence. He may be in quest of a work permit, the renewal of his visa or a custom's clearance. It didn't matter. The clerk would sit sipping his tea looking listlessly through Vince at the wall behind as if he was

The Idiot's Frightful Laughter

invisible. He spoke with infinite patience and icy condescension making Grecco feel as though he was being a dreadful imposition. The bureaucrat would frequently advise him to come back in a week or two or even a month or so. In the meantime, he would see what could be done. And when Vince returned, his records were apt to be lost, and he would be sent on a round-robin going from one department to another until he was finally back where he'd started, for it had really been there all the time. There had been mistakes. There were always mistakes. They must study the regulations in more detail. His case was more complex. Come back in a couple weeks, they would say waiting patiently until Grecco became wise to their tactics and slipped a five hundred piaster note or more, much more depending what the requirement was. And then and only then would he get help. It was a studied sort of patience couched in deceit and cunning. The sort of thing that Westerners have difficulty coping with. It drove some mad, stark raving mad. And after they had exhausted all their fury and were weak and quite defenseless, The Vietnamese bureaucrat was still calmly sipping his tea and gazing through them speaking softly to the wall behind. "Come back in a couple of weeks," he'd say grinning sinisterly to no one in particular. "We may have it for you then."

In the beginning, Grecco had lost his temper, but that had only boosted the price higher and made the time longer. And so, Vince learned to be patient or at least pretend to be. He had not felt patient. His stomach would twist into tight knots, and afterward it took a couple shots of bourbon to ease the tension. But he soon learned the necessity of appearing patient, forcing all expression from his face. Retreating behind a glazed-eyed placid mask. The hypocrisy troubled him. Perhaps, he thought, if one were to act as though he condoned bribery long enough, he might surely become the person he pretended to be. But was it possible for him to actually become such a loathsome creature? The thought was too revolting to imagine. After such dealings, he was plagued with guilt. Oh, how he abhorred it.

"Don't sweat it, Vince," Bill Bailey would say. "This is Vietnam. It's a way of life," Grecco both envied and despised Bailey. He like so many expats had no character. He believed in nothing and was true to no one. He was like the bamboo bending in the direction of least resistance. If one was to ask him what he believed in, he'd have no answer, for the very act of believing in something would force him to make a stand and that he'd never do. "Survival. That's what it's all about, Vince," he'd say. "Look out for number one. No one else will." Bailey was simply articulating what most of the others were doing. Barban, Bledsoe, Major Jack. They were all alike, Grecco thought.

Crossing the rickety bridge, Grecco turned left along the canal. The water looked like dirty oil. The kind that had been in an engine much too long. Several dozen barges were tied up along the bank. A couple were being unloaded. Women wearing straw conical hats and black silky pajamas labored up swaying planks hauling large sacks on their backs. "Cement!" Grecco exclaimed. "Cement for war victims!" However, he knew that little or none would reach them. As always it would be stored in the province warehouse, and little by little would disappear. Sold to some wealthy Chinese merchant for his home or business, or then it might find its way back to Saigon where it would be bought by some U.S. Army procurement officer to build a state-of-the-art clubhouse and sports facility for staff officer. The money would end up in the Province Chief's numbered account at some Swiss Bank.

Even though everyone knew what was happening, the cement kept coming, tons and tons of it by plane, truck, and boat. Even if the war victims were to get cement, what could they do with it? Grecco thought. There was no sand or rock in the Mekong Delta. Nothing but mud, black rich gooey mud. Vince and others had pointed this out. They had written their bosses in Saigon. And what had happened? Ambassador "Blowtorch" Komer, Vietnam's Chief of Pacification, had notified each and every Deputy Senior Advisors throughout the delta. The message was short and blunt. "The cement will be sent, and it will be used."

The Idiot's Frightful Laughter

Grecco was perplexed. Komer was behaving as though he had been defied; that Vince and the other advisors were somehow responsible for the lack of sand and rock in the delta. It was evident that Saigon did not want to know about such unpleasant realities. They did not want to admit to themselves that they were behaving incompetently. They would only acknowledge success. Those in the field must shoulder failures stoically. It sickened Grecco to think that his real function was helping a gang of thieves get rich.

That afternoon as Grecco entered the office complex at province headquarters, Truong sprung in front of him and cockily drove a fist into his stomach. "Mr. Barban wants to see you," he said smiling sinisterly up at Vince. The runt was only four-nine, and although he was twenty-seven, looked fifteen.

"What about?" he asked.

"Going to chew your ass out about something, I guess," Truong said shrugging his shoulders.

Grecco raised his eyebrows and smirked at his tiny antagonist. "No shit," he said. Vince hated Truong almost as much as he did Barban. Officially Truong was Hank's personal interpreter; however unofficially he was much more. Among other things, he was his spy and informer. It was also rumored that he was on the Province Chief's payroll. Truong not only mimicked Barban's mannerisms by swinging his shoulders and clicking his heels as he walked, but he also dressed like Hank. They wore matching Jungle Jim suites and Aussie bush hats; however, instead of a forty-five slung at his hip, he carried a thirty-eight in a shoulder holster tucked beneath the left arm.

No one ever said anything about Barban when Truong was nearby. Even Calloway, the Public Safety Advisor, kept quiet. "If I got anything to say about that prick, I'll say it to his face," the police officer said.

Once Grecco had struck a picture of Barban with his fist. The photo was on the front page of *Helping Hand,* the IV Corps' weekly news sheet which had been left on his desk. Barban was marching at the head of a Home Defense Unit with all the pomp and swagger of General George Patton. Later Barban had called Vince into his office. He wanted to know why he'd struck his photo. It dawned on Grecco that Truong had so obviously set him up. He'd planted it on his desk. Later when Vince passed Truong in the hall, he'd called him a sneaky sonofabitch.

When Grecco entered his office, Barban was leaning back in his swivel chair, his feet propped up on the desk. Vince met the deputy's gaze with what he hoped would pass for bored indifference. It was all a game with Barban, a very serious game. But still a game. However, Grecco wasn't going to play. Not by Hank's rules anyhow.

Prior to coming to Vietnam, Barban had acted in TV commercials. He always played the same part – smug and quite conceited which was easy for him, for that's the way he was all the time anyway. Now he was trying to cast himself as the dashing, hardboiled commander.

Grecco knew the routine. He had seen others go through it with Barban countless times. They would march briskly up to the desk, click their heels, salute and say: "You wish to see me, Sir? However, Vince chose to amble slowly across the room, his hands shoved in his pockets, and in a very off-handed way, say: "Hi. What's up, Hank?"

"Yea," Barban said rearing up in his chair and dropping his boots on the floor with a thud. "Why didn't you send that report of the Têt war victims in?"

"It's the same as last week," Grecco said. "I sent Simoni a note saying that we hadn't made any payment this week."

"I don't give a goddamn. I want that report sent every week regardless. Is that clear?" Barban said jabbing a finger at Vince.

"Okay," Grecco said wheeling about and stomping out of the room. "Fuck you," he muttered flourishing a middle finger at the closed door. He was seething with rage. From the corner of his eye, he saw Truong standing by the radio operator smiling at him. "Fuck you too, Truong," he muttered. "Fuck you all."

Têt war victims, Grecco thought as he pulled a form from his file cabinet marked "classified". What a joke. They should have got this money six months ago when they really needed it. Waiting half

The Idiot's Frightful Laughter

a year to help these people who lost everything is outrageous, he reflected

He laid the form next to the one he'd filled out the previous week and began to copy it. "War victims paid: 311. Not paid: 2,205. Homes under 50% destroyed: 809. Homes 50% or more destroyed: 362. Killed: 191. Wounded: 301. Then there was the breakdown for those under eighteen and those eighteen and older. Well, they'd eventually get something, Grecco thought. That was more than the refugees who were forced to abandon their villages ever got. But then just how long they could keep it was still another matter. The district chief and the other local officials would have their hands out for a cut. The aid was little enough as it was. Fifty bucks for a house and twenty for the death of an adult and ten for a child. What sort of compensation was that, especially here in Vietnam where prices were so inflated? They were as high as anywhere else in the world and higher than most places thanks to the big spending Americans. Twenty dollars? A Tu Do Street Hooker could make that much in thirty minutes.

Barban was gone when Grecco laid the form in his "in" basket. He had already forgotten about it, Vince Assumed. It'll probably lie there for a week before he gets around to looking at it. That's how urgent it is. He glanced about the deputy's desk. At one corner was a large photo of a flashy blonde with an Ipana toothpaste smile. His wife, Vince assumed. Poor kid. Married to such a jerk. At the other corner were two Vietnamese medals mounted in nicely crafted picture frames. I'd hide those if I was he, Grecco thought. Better yet, I'd bury the fuckers. Who's he trying to fool? Everyone knows what it takes to get one of those dime store trinkets. All one has to do is help the Province Chief screw Uncle Sam for a couple of grand and the medal's yours. Colonel Bo will even throw in a presentation ceremony with all the trimmings to boot. It's as easy as that.

Beneath the glass top were a couple dozen snapshots. Several were of Barban standing over the tiny emaciated body of a Vietnamese, his rifle aimed at the victim's head. Another showed him slicing an ear from a severed head. One more had him firing a fifty-caliber machine gun that hung from a belt slung across his shoulder. He's just an overgrown kid running about playing cowboys and Indians and sore because I won't play, he mused. Grecco slipped the picture of the ear cutting from beneath the glass and tucked it in his wallet. One never knows, he thought. One just never knows.

Hank Barban

You couldn't say that he was handsome, for that implies a sort of manly ruggedness, and there was no trace of that in Hank. It would be more correct to say that he was pretty. Prettier than most women. With long hair and some makeup, he would pass for a very beautiful woman. His dark eyes were large and limpid like those of a gazelle, and the lashes unnaturally long and curled. His lips were full and sensual. And he wore an expression of sullen arrogance that is so characteristic of very attractive women.

Hank's father, Jeb Barban, had never quite figured him out. "Wall, Sir, now, Hank weren't like the othas. He had a pretty high opinion of hisself. That, ah course, was his ma's doins. Liz was all the time ah puttin' ideas in the boy's head that he was better than everyone else. That he had no business working on the plantation like the other chilins."

Jeb often thought of his wife. She'd broken his heart when she ran off to Hollywood with a fast-talking Yankee. Gave her a big line about becoming a movie star. "Weren't no truth in it at all. No Siree, not one bit. She was a beautiful woman. She'd turn men's heads when she walked down the street. Made me real proud ta be alongside ah her. Ah felt as though I'd been sorta blessed. But then she had her bad side. Real bad. One time when she was real mad at me for sumpin, she said that Hank weren't my flesh and blood. Said that when she went up ta visit her folks in Richmond, she'd had a fling with some Dago gigolo, and that Hank was the splittin' image ah this gigolo fella. After that ah neva felt quite the same about Hank. Sorta ignored him. Tried ta erase 'em from mah mind."

Jeb Barban had a four-hundred-acre peanut plantation about ten miles south of Guntersville, Alabama. Since way before the Civil War, the Barbans had raised cotton. But then back about twenty years ago, Jeb had asked Fred Smithers, the farm agent, what he should do, because he was getting less cotton each year. Fred advised him to rotate the crop. Plant peanuts. They'll enrich the soil. Do that for three or four years, the agent said. Jeb never regretted switching to peanuts. It made things so much simpler. Harvesting peanuts was easy. Machines did everything. The first thing he did was to get rid of his Negro laborers and tear down their shanties. Out of fifty-five, he only kept seven to maintain and operate the machinery.

However, when his pa, Thaddeus Barban, died, he came close to losing most of the plantation. "Wall, Sir, Pa went plumb loco over this here nigger gal, Billy Sue, down by Cat Tail Swamp, Jeb said. "Built 'er a right fine house and give 'er all sorts ah nice things. He even bought 'er a car. One ah them where the roof folds down so's everyone can git a good look at ya. Well, they had these two half breed boys, Jackson and Lee. Jackson was so white ya had ta look at 'em real close ta see if he were a nigger. Well, jist before Pa died, he went and tore up his old will and made out a new one leavin' a third ah the plantation to each ah them half breeds. Well, ya know, we all figured Pa was a little soft in the head before he died. Otherwise he'd neva have done such a bird brain thing as that. Well, now I'm a God fearin' man. I ain't all the time gittin' drunk and chasen around lookin' fer trouble like them KKK's all the time a doin'. But then I weren't gonna let no half breeds take this here plantation right out from unda my nose. So's ah let the word git out that ah might consider makin' a little donation to the Klan's cause if they were ta put the fear of God Almighty inta them niggers. Well, now ah'll say one thing. The Klan neva does nothin' halfway. They burnt down that house that Pa built for Billy Sue, and the three of 'em got out by the skin of their teeth. Well, ya know it was a little more than I'd bargained fer, but anyhow ah donated a thousand dollas to the cause which was a heap ah money back in them days. But ah reckon ah'd ah lost a whole lot more if them half breeds had taken two thirds ah the plantation, so's ah figured it was a worthwhile investment."

"But then ya were askin' about Hank. Wall Sir, he was different. He weren't a bit like the otha boys. No Sireee. Hank neva wanted ta do nothin' but chase around after them little pickaninnies at the plantation. Ahm not sayin' that the othas didn't do the same. But Hank was afta them nigger gals all the time. Couldn't neva git pussy off his mind. At school he was all the time gittin' some gal in trouble. Ah reckon he got it from that gigolo fella. It were in his blood. That's the dadburn truth. It sure as shootin' was. When I owned up and told 'em so, he neva said nothin'. Jus packed up and left fer Hollywood. His ma wrote an said he was doin' real good. Makin' lots a money doing commercials on TV. Ah saw one of 'em. It weren't too bad. Can't figure out why he threw it all up ta go ta Vietnam. Musta had the idea that he was gonna be a big hero ova there. He was all the time a watchin' them John Wayne kinda movies. His favorite were High Noon. The one where Gary Cooper walks down the middle ah town and shoots it out with a real bad hombre. He musta watched that film a dozen times. I'd see 'em out behind the barn with Pa's ol' Colt six shooter pretendin' he was one ah them gun slingers. His brotha, Jake was all the time pokin' fun at 'em. 'How many Injuns ya kill taday, Hank?' he'd tease."

Hank Barban never spoke of his father nor the one who the people in Guntersville believed to be his father. He had all the traits of a farm boy from the South, but he never once admitted to it. "Why I was born and raised right here in LA," he'd insist. That was all he ever said about his childhood. As far as he was concerned, it was dead and buried.

The Hatchet Man

Whenever Grecco thought of the previous year he'd spent at the Refugee Division's main office at Saigon, it was like trying to remember a dream, a very bad dream. His mind would float back through a fog looking for something to lock onto – a face, the office, its furnishings, a document stamped "Confidential". But it all eluded his grasp swirling about like smoke in a whirlwind. He had turned to Kafka's *Castle* to make some sense of the bureaucracy. When he'd first read the surrealistic novel at the university, it had made no impression on him. It seemed highly implausible. Now he saw that Kafka was right on target.

Before coming to Phu Vinh, Grecco was a reports officer. At any rate that was the title, he'd been given. He'd been hired to write reports for the Refugee Division, a branch of a monolithic military-civilian complex whose innumerable bureaus overlapped and duplicated one another's tasks.

Harry Botts, however, was no bureaucrat. He'd hired Grecco because he was a journalist. Someone who could write with clarity, completeness, and simplicity. Botts was tired of wading through tons of gobbledygook. "Write with an appreciation for the reader's point of view," Botts had told Vince. "That's all I ask."

When Grecco was introduced at a staff meeting, Botts said that he had hired him because he knew how to write so that one could understand what he was saying. Waving a stack of papers in the air, he added that he had wasted all the time he was going to with this bureaucratic jargon. From now on everyone would model their reports after Vince.

Grecco glanced about at the sullen faces. Several were glaring angrily at him. Botts was a good man, he thought, but he didn't understand bureaucratic sensitivities. They do not take criticisms lightly. Surely Botts must realize the damage he's caused. If he

The Idiot's Frightful Laughter

figures that he can erase such deeply entrenched prejudices with a newspaper guy's simple terse style, he's in for a big surprise. There's was a coup de grace couched in a velvet glove. Vince became the invisible man. No one seemed aware of his existence. They would pass him in the hall without so much as a nod. At parties, it was worse. Whenever he'd approach a group, they'd move away or form a tight circle turning their backs on him. If he tried to speak to someone, the person would look blandly at him widening his eyes and lifting his brows. He would then shrug slightly and walk away.

Less than a month after he'd hired Grecco, Botts quit. He turned in his resignation, and two days later he was aboard a plane for The States. Rumors had it that he'd been offered a better post with the Rockefeller Foundation. However, the truth was that he had all the wrong ingredients for a successful Foreign Service director. He was intelligent, straightforward, industrious, and worst of all had a penchant for the truth. He insisted on knowing precisely what was being done for the refugees. Ignoring the advice of others, Botts sent the data he'd collected first hand to Washington D.C. Even more distressing, he handed over copies of his reports to the press corps. The Refugee Department came under fire from all sides, and the more that the power elite asked him to tone things down, the more outspoken he became. It was when the head of the mission ordered that all Botts' reports be cleared through him that he turned in his resignation.

Two hours before his plane was due to depart, Botts had to suffer through a farewell party with the usual Kool-Aid and cupcakes. Winfred Haynes, a Foreign Service officer, gave the farewell speech. It was loaded with the usual platitudes and glittering generalities for just such an occasion. No doubt he had given it at countless farewell departures about the world.

When Haynes had finished, no one clapped. There was an ominous silence. Botts swung about in his swivel chair and smiled amiably at a handful of Vietnamese secretaries, clerks, interpreters, and translators huddled in a corner of the room. He told them that it had been a pleasure to have known them and that he would always remember them as his friends. Then without so much as a nod to his staff, he picked up his briefcase and was gone. It all happened so fast that before Haynes could get downstairs, Botts had left. Two weeks later, Grecco received a letter from him apologizing for neglecting to bid him farewell. He hoped that Vince would understand why he had chosen to leave in such a manner. Grecco never showed the letter to anyone. What was the point?

Botts' position was filled several weeks later by Gilbert Jones, a very timid black man who spoke in a whisper. He had survived public service for thirty-two years by maintaining a low profile. He was not pleased with the lax, open manner that the operation was being run and was aghast at the bold frankness of Grecco's reports. Their short terse sentences leaped out at him like the crescendo of machinegun fire. He felt threatened by their straightforward appraisals and demands for action. Always in the past, reports had provided him with a shield. A way to hold his critics at bay. They caused others to suppose that Jones knew a lot more than he cared to reveal. They were not sure just where things stood. However, Grecco's reports tore away the façade and left him nowhere to hide. He was stripped naked, standing in the raw where his opponents could chop away at him. It was suicidal, Jones thought.

The first thing that Gilbert Jones did was find a new job for Grecco. He was placed in charge of statistics; reams and reams of it that came in large manila envelopes from all parts of South Vietnam. The work had been handled by a Vietnamese woman who recently married an American from another department and left for The States. The job offered Vince little challenge. He hated the monotonous routine and thus had asked his backstop at personnel for a transfer.

It was like working on an assembly line. Eight hours a day he would run the figures through a calculator and then enter the totals on numerous forms that made little sense to him. He had no idea at the time that the figures were highly inflated. They were used to justify America's involvement in what was essentially a civil war. Truth was the enemy.

The Idiot's Frightful Laughter

Each Friday morning, Grecco would stack the boxes of forms in the back seat of a limousine and take them across town to the Little Pentagon, headquarters for Vietnam's U.S. Military Advisory Corps at Tan Son Nhut Air Base. The chauffeur-driven limousine took him careening through a dense maze of traffic. The agency's drivers were all alike, swerving recklessly from one side of the street to the other through thick clusters of trucks, buses, motorcycles, cyclos, oxen-drawn wagons and vendors' pushcarts. They were an impatient, discourteous bunch who figured that they had special privileges, Vince thought. They were continually honking their horns and screeching to within inches of some hapless pedestrian. The more Vince screamed at the driver to slow down and drive carefully, the more erratic his driving became. "Toi khong hieu," the driver would say shaking his head as though he could not understand what Grecco was saying.

At the entrance to MACV's immense compound, military police checked Grecco's credentials and searched the vehicle for explosives. One MP would walk about the car holding a mirror fixed to a long pole beneath the limousine to see if a bomb was attached to the frame. It was simply a ritual, for Vince noticed that the guard seldom glanced at the mirror.

Pentagon East was larger than anything Grecco had seen in Asia, and he had been just about everywhere. From the outside, it looked like a gigantic warehouse. A chainlinked fence reinforced with barbwire surrounded the complex. Concrete bunkers covered with sandbags lined the inside of the barricade. Within the building was an endless maze of corridors all looking alike. Nothing distinguished one passageway or office door from another. The first time Vince had wandered about for nearly an hour looking for the Ambassador of Pacification's office. However, by now the route was etched into his mind. He went straight to room 1102; then turned left and went as far as 1344, and then right to 1966. Here he handed the box to a colonel, Pacification Ambassador "Blowtorch" Komer's special aide, who always seemed absurdly delighted, acting as though they were some precious gift that he had been anxiously waiting for a long time.

Once Gil Jones had got the report writing task into safe hands, he searched among his staff for a hatchet man. Someone who was tough, outspoken, aggressive and not too bright. One who would block interference for him and yet allow him to score the points. The flack catcher was Boris Eisenschiml, a retired army major who was full of raw ambition and narrow-minded conceit. He was a short stout man with close-cropped hair and fierce suspicious eyes. The type one would expect to see running a maximum-security ward at a military stockade. His sudden rise from a logistics dispatcher to the deputy director of the Refugee Division momentarily stunned the staff, but fear of survival quickly subdued any urge to object; for they knew that he would try to get rid of anyone who appeared to oppose him. Grecco saw the danger signs, but pride would not permit him to grovel at Eisenschiml's feet. Vince was no kissass. And so, it was Grecco who was the first to leave. When the henchman suggested it to Jones, the director had difficulty hiding his delight. "Yes, your observation is well founded. He doesn't quite fit in here, does he?" he replied. "He doesn't seem all that amiable, and I don't believe he cares much for his work," he added. "He's told others that it's monotonous. However, he isn't apt to find the work at the province level so dull, and perhaps the people there are more his type," he said chuckling softly to himself. "Tell him that Chuck Simoni, IV Corps Refugee Chief, just phoned us from Can Tho. He's in urgent need of a Refugee Advisor, and that we feel that Grecco's the best man for the job."

It was, of course, true that Grecco was not pleased with his new assignment and furthermore had as little as possible to do with the others at the office. As a matter of fact, he'd been earnestly thinking of putting in for a transfer but being railroaded by the likes of Eisenschiml did not sit well with him.

As Grecco had suspected, speaking to Jones was a waste of time. He told the director that he had no objections of being transferred to the province. That it would be an interesting experience. However, he had been hired as a reports officer. He was a journalist. All his education and experience dealt with writing. He knew nothing about caring for refugees. Wasn't it a bit presumptuous to suppose that he could advise a social welfare chief about an expertise he'd very likely been working at all his adult life?

Jones insisted that Vince was much too modest. His six months in the main office had given him a very suitable background for the job. He was much better prepared for it than the other advisors. Why, he exclaimed, they'd had only a two-week orientation course in The States prior to being shipped directly to the province. Most of them were nothing but kids fresh from college.

Well, it was either that or resign, so Grecco decided to take a crack at it. At any rate, the experience may prove useful when he returned to newspaper work again. Perhaps he could file some reports on the sly. Unethical perhaps, but what wasn't?

The last time Grecco had heard about former Deputy Director Wilfred Haynes, he was being shipped off to Quang Tri up next to the Demilitarization Zone that separated North and South Vietnam. A little bureaucratic arm-twisting on the part of Eisenschiml had convinced the Foreign Officer that it would be the best thing possible for a well-rounded career in the Foreign Service. Something one could point to with pride. Yes, with glory, no less.

Jones drew further back into the inner sanctums of his private office placing Deputy Director Boris Eisenschiml at a large metal desk in the vestibule where a receptionist had been. His orders were not to let anyone pass unless so instructed. The major was the idea hatchet man.

The Foreign Service Officer

Getting Wilfred Haynes as assistant had been the final blow. Haynes was even in the eyes of the most staid bureaucrat an utter ass. A lesser man might have transferred him to the field and given him a post as a regional director. But that wasn't Harry Botts' way of doing things. He was quite above such tactics. However, having Haynes in the adjoining office interrupting him all day with trivial nonsense called for a special kind of heroism that Botts didn't have.

On his arrival at Tanh Son Nhut Airport, Haynes came straight to Botts' office to present his credentials, so to speak. Such formality was not necessary, but he was a foreign service officer, had been one for twenty-three years. He had a foreign service rating of one, and that was nothing to sneeze at. According to the book, it carried all the prestige and benefits of a four-star general. However, in Haynes' case, one was inclined to overlook the book.

The meeting with Botts had gone badly. It was short and brusque. Haynes complained that the chief had none of the social graces that should go with a rank such as his. In Haynes estimation, Botts was a very ordinary person. But then Harry Botts was not a career officer and never pretended to be. This was his first government job and quite likely his last. He was an outsider. Not a member of the "good old boys' club", so to speak.

Haynes was informed that he would be in the number three slot and would channel everything through the Deputy Director. Well, that would be the day. He wasn't an FS-1 for nothing. Who was the Deputy? A mere FSR-3. Since when were three's placed above ones? It was unheard of. And the Director, who was he? He wasn't even Foreign Service. A reserve. That's what he was. An FSR filling a gap until a regular could be found to take his place.

Well, Wilfred Haynes was not one to sit around and sulk. After his meeting with Harry Botts, he got the housing section at personnel to get him a villa. He would most certainly not be stuck in one of those apartments surrounded by clerks and secretaries and other such riffraff. And the villa was to have a swimming pool and a tennis court, and both must be well lighted, of course. What did they expect of a top-grade foreign service officer, anyhow?

Haynes then went personally to the agency's warehouse at the outskirts of town to see about his "hospitality kit". He had learned from past experience that if one did not attend to these matters oneself, they would give him the ordinary kit that everyone else got. Well, he deserved something a little better than an FSR-7, now didn't he? After all, where was the incentive if everyone was given the same? That was pure and simple communism. He'd have no part of that. They'd have to break open three or four ordinary kits and make up a special one for him.

Before the day had ended, Haynes had selected a cook, three housekeepers, and two gardeners. They were all placed on three months' probation with the option of firing them without warning at any time during that period.

On the second day, Haynes went shopping. He visited the U.S. commissary in Cholon and then made the rounds of all four post exchanges in the Saigon area. The trunk and back seat of his limousine were filled with groceries, liquors, and toilet articles. He also bought a state-of-the-art television set, a stereo, a movie projector, a camera, a microwave, and a VCR. He had all these things in The States but saw no point in lugging them about with him, and besides these were all tax and duty-free. They could be sold for a hefty little profit in his hometown compliments of the American taxpayer.

The next day, Haynes was sitting in Willie Fisher, the Director of Confidential Records, office when he walked in ten minutes late. Haynes wore a gray flannel suit and black tie. The first things one noticed about him was his narrow sloping shoulders and egg-shaped pouch that pressed out over his belt. "Do you make a point of coming to work at this time?" was the first thing that he said to the records director as he held up his wrist and gazed at his watch with wide-eyed wonder as though something repugnant had dropped there.

Fisher was always very amiable; however, he was not obsequious. He had never worked for the government before. Previously he'd been a business manager for an NGO in charge of schools, hospitals, and refugee centers throughout most of Asia. Status had very little importance at such institutions, so Fisher's response was not what Haynes felt suitable for one of his stature. Fisher had simply said: "No, I'm usually here on time, but the shuttle bus was late. The traffic is bad in Saigon."

"Yes, yes, well, well, tsk, tsk, all right, all right," he said snapping open his attaché case and pulling out a large notebook. For the rest of the day, Haynes asked Fisher questions, such as: how many homes were damaged less than fifty percent during the last Communist offensive? How many tons of IR-8 rice were distributed during the past six months? How many refugee children were enrolled in school? Fisher had a handout prepared for just such occasions. A thick booklet of statistics of refugees at every province in South Vietnam. But Haynes wanted none of that. That was for newspaper reporters and clerks. Didn't this man realize to whom he was speaking? Well, he would surely tell him. He would be brief and to the point just as anyone in his position was expected to be. There would be no shirking of one's responsibility. One must respect their superiors. And why wasn't there a special room with maps and charts and lounge chairs and a podium? Well, there soon would be. He'd see to that.

Haynes wrote down everything Fisher said in his notebook continually questioning the source. Verifying every figure but not really caring. It was simply his way of imposing his authority on his subordinates. He wanted to show Fisher and everyone else in the department that he was someone to be reckoned with, that he was not to be taken lightly. To be spoken with on a casual basis. Most assuredly not.

He'd seen a few snap-to when he passed their desks. They knew a man of consequence when they saw one. Must remember them. See that they get the key slots when the shuffle came. Can't have ingrates running things. That would never do. Pearls to swine; that's what it was. No appreciation. No discipline. Hollow men. That's what T. S. Eliot called them. Well, he would have none of their mediocrity.

The Spy Chief

At first, Hank Barban had gone out of his way to befriend Grecco. He'd heard that Vince was a journalist and had hoped that he might write glowing articles about him.

One evening soon after Grecco had arrived at the province, he was invited to Barban and Colonel Edward Winters' French villa for drinks. The first thing that Vince noted was a bamboo bar at one corner of a large living room. It was stocked with the best brands of stateside liquor. Crystal glassware hung in rows above the bar sparked in the well-lighted room. A large bay window opened out onto a sun porch. The furniture was polished mahogany. The floors glazed turquoise tile. There was a stereo with speakers hung from the ceiling. Ella Fitzgerald was singing with the Philharmonic Jazz Orchestra.

Vince had come with Elmo Bledsoe. As soon as they arrived, Colonel Winters laid out the chessboard, and he and Bledsoe became deeply engrossed in the game.

Grecco hadn't been there ten minutes before Barban handed him a dozen typewritten pages. It was Hank's firsthand account of the Viet Cong attack on Yen Bay Province's headquarters during the Tết Offensive. The town had awoken on the morning of the Lunar New Year to discover that a squad of VC had barricaded themselves in the province compound.

The villa was directly across the street from the compound's main entrance. Barban peered out a bay window to see the barrel of a 12.7mm machine gun pointing at him from behind a makeshift barricade. The Viet Cong had fortified the government complex by stacking metal desks, chairs, filing cabinets and such against the doors and windows. Barban had slipped out the door of the villa and crawled through the garden to a wrought iron fence that bordered the street. While making a sketch of how the guerrillas appeared to be deployed in and about the building, he claimed that his cheek was nicked by a sliver of shrapnel. The scar was so faint that Grecco had to stand very close in order to see it. It looked more like an old razor nick.

Vince wondered what the Senior Province Advisor was doing all this time. Who was leading the troops? How about the Province Chief? Where was the MAT Team? Where was the ARVN Battalion? What about the home defense forces? How in the blazes could a squad of insurgents just walk into the province capital and hold it at ransom, so to speak? He was flabbergasted. However, what he said was: "Looks like you had a ringside seat, Colonel."

Colonel Winters smiled sheepishly. "Well, I guess Hank sort of embellished things a little," he said. It was all so bizarre, Vince thought. What was to keep a sapper from throwing a satchel charge of explosives on to the veranda some quiet night and blowing the villa to smithereens? Who would stop him?

As he and Bledsoe were leaving, Grecco looked about the garden. There was no sign of a shell landing near the villa. There wasn't a scrap of evidence.

"Did you read the paper Barban wrote?" Grecco asked Bledsoe as they walked across town pulling aside coils of concertina barbwire every so often. Any Viet Cong could do the same, he thought.

"Ah sure did," Elmo said shaking his head vigorously. "Ah sore did read it."

"What did you make of it?" Vince asked.

Bledsoe looked at Grecco for a moment blinking his eyes nervously. "That Mr. Barban's got guts. Ya sure got to give him credit for that." One had to be careful, he thought. These honkies are a wily bunch. They couldn't be trusted.

I should have expected that sort of reply from Bledsoe, he thought. It would have been better not to have asked. Grecco had found it hard to fall asleep that night. Barban's paper had disturbed him. His motive was all too obvious. Well, Vince had his limits, and this was one of them. He was not going to write any war hero shit about that narcissus. You could bet your rosy red ass on that.

However, a few weeks later, Barban got his publicity. A three-page feature in *Time Magazine* with a photo of him showing an Arvin soldier how to fire a Browning Automatic Rifle. There was another of him parading down the main street of Yen Chau at the head of a home defense unit.

Barban had heard that there was a news correspondent in Can Tho. He'd found him quite drunk in a pick-up bar and had persuaded him to come to Yen Chau as his special guest. He'd assured him that there was an unlimited supply of good whiskey and plenty of beautiful women.

Co My wasn't happy about being passed on to the journalist. However, she agreed after Barban intimated that in this way she would be buying her freedom from him. A promise he never intended to keep.

"And what am I to do for all this fine hospitality?" the reporter asked soon after arriving.

"Why, I thought you'd like to see the province," Barban smiled quite innocently.

"Ought to make a good story. Good for the troops. Need some morale boosting."

"How about Hank Barban? Wouldn't he make an even better story?"

Barban's smile faded. The newsman couldn't have come near the mark. It was so obviously true. He was being laughed at. The thing he could least endure.

"No offense, Hank," the reporter said shaking Barban by the shoulder. "Guess you haven't been around many journalists? We've got a pretty rough brand of humor." Barban tried to look jovial, but it appeared more as though he were smirking than smiling. The newsman spent four days in town. During that time, he and Barban were always together.

It was Blaine Bruce, the province's CIA chief, not Barban, who was the real hero. Or was it the death wish? Most everyone thought so.

About the time that Hank was supposed to be making his surveillance of the Viet Cong entrenchment, Bruce turned up at the

The Idiot's Frightful Laughter

back door of the villa. He was carrying two Swedish K automatic rifles. The CIA agent's status symbol that set him off from the army's grunts.

Bruce tossed one of the rifles to Barban. "Lets you and me take them, Hank?"

"Oh yea, sure," Barban said placing the weapon carefully on the table and slowly backing away from it. "You and me are gonna charge that machine gun?" he said looking at Blaine with wide-eyed disbelief.

"No sweat, Hank," Bruce said. "Had you figured wrong. Thought you were gung-ho." The spy chief stepped out the back door. Rounding the corner of the villa, he ran straight for the machine gun emplacement firing his rifle from the hip. He swivel-hipped across the street and into the compound twisting from side to side as though he were running for a touchdown.

A stream of machine gun fire hit Bruce from the left side ripping open his stomach. He collapsed in a pool of blood just beyond the gate.

Within seconds, a jeep armed with a fifty-caliber machine gun mounted on a steel post headed straight for the gate. Sergeant Pete Riviera stood at the gun mount firing into the makeshift bunker. Two GI's crouching at the back of the jeep grabbed Bruce and tossed him into the back of the vehicle. The driver shifted into reverse and backed off swerving from side to side until he had swung about behind the villa.

It was a miracle. Dr. Harry Sloans, a civilian physician from Scottsbluff, Nebraska, sewed Bruce up at the province hospital just a block from where he'd been shot. Within a week, the CIA chief was up and walking about.

Blaine Bruce was not the gung-ho warrior he appeared to be. He simply wanted to die. At any rate, that was how Grecco saw it. And as usual, it was because of a woman. Vince could relate to that. Hadn't he been on the brink once himself?

Foxy was the woman; a platinum blonde nurse whose quarters were directly behind Grecco's. Bruce spent his nights there leaving around 6:30 a.m. Frequently Vince was awakened by angry shouts.

It was Bruce yelling at Foxy. He could not tell what the spy chief was saying but had a very good idea.

Soon after Bruce drove off to work each morning, Grecco would see Colonel Nguyen Duc Bo, The Province Chief, and his three bodyguards emerged from his villa and walked slowly across the parade grounds to Foxy's quarters. Vince had never seen anything quite so theatrical. One of the guards walked several yards to the front of the colonel. The other two were a yard or two to either side of him. Each had his right hand in his jacket pocket. Grecco assumed that they were clutching revolvers, probably 45 Colts. The Province chief was smoking a Sherlock Holmes' pipe. He looked both casual and cautious. When the point man reached Foxy's quarters, he'd step inside. After several minutes, he'd reappear, and the others would then enter.

Vince wondered what the bodyguards did while Colonel Bo was busy fucking the nurse. Perhaps it was a gangbang. They'd take turns once the chief had finished. However, Foxy shared her quarters with another nurse. Perhaps they fucked her too. Grecco would have like to peer in a window, but he assumed that that might be somewhat risky.

Vince imagined seeing the death-defying spy chief attack the nurse's quarters with his Swedish K, but that never occurred. It would have been a piece of cake compared to his single-handed assault on the machine gun emplacement, Grecco thought. But that wasn't his style. Later Bruce and Foxy married and transferred to another province . . . and another province chief. That poor sonofabitch, Grecco thought, shaking his head. What some guys won't do for a steady piece of pussy. But then maybe it was retribution, for it was common knowledge that Bruce had been laying Co Chi on a regular basis for some time. Perhaps this was Foxy's way of getting even.

Hank Barban rolled over in bed. It was growing light, and he could barely see Co Lin seated before the mirror brushing her long sleek hair. She doesn't have much of a shape, he thought. No breasts. No meat on the hips. But you can't knock her face. She was damn good looking and neat too. She was cleaner than any

The Idiot's Frightful Laughter

American broad he'd ever had, and that went for his wife. Nancy could be downright raunchy. What's more, Co Lin's satin ao dia and spike-heeled sandals really turned him on.

Co Lin was preparing to leave. She always slipped off before sun up, so she wouldn't be seen. Barban had had to lay it on the line to her. If she wanted to work for him, she'd have to put out. That was all there was to it. She hadn't liked the idea. He'd given her two weeks to make up her mind. During that time, she'd made the rounds of the other offices asking for work. However, Barban had passed the word along that she was his property and to keep hands off. So, on the final day, she'd agreed.

She wasn't much of a screw, Hank thought. She'd just lie there like a corpse, but it was better than nothing, he figured. There wasn't a guy in the unit who wouldn't give his left nut to get into her pants. She seemed to have the hots for Gutschinritter. Every time he came into the office, she'd flash him a big smile. Well, he'd better wise up. One false move and he'd find himself at some district outpost up to his ass in mud.

Barban glanced about the room. He could just see the outlines of his furnishings. He really had a good set up, he figured. To the left of his king size bed stood a large stereo. To the right was a hi-fi set and at the foot of the bed was a large TV set. At the corner of the room was a fridge loaded with cans of coke and beer. There were two air conditioners set in the wall near the ceiling. The furniture – bed, dresser, table, and chairs – was all made of Thai teak. He'd made a deal with IV Corps' logistics director. It had cost Barban three Chicom AK-47 assault rifles and two Viet Cong flags. The furnishings were intended for the VIP guest house at Can Tho but had been reported lost, and a requisition was sent to Saigon for a replacement. The Province Chief had offered Hank five hundred dollars for it when he left. Shit, it was worth a hell of a lot more than that, he figured. Throughout the twelve rooms of the villa, there was a total of forty-two pieces of furniture. Some very artistically designed. But then there was no use rubbing Colonel Bo the wrong way. Who knows? Barban thought. He might need a reference from the chief someday, and besides the five hundred dollars was all clear profit. He hadn't paid a cent for the stuff.

In the next room, Barban could hear Colonel Winters and Co Thè whispering. He had given her to the colonel when he first arrived ten months ago. Hank was anxious to make a good impression on his new boss, for he needed a good performance evaluation if he hoped to get promoted to senior advisor. His previous boss, Colonel "Hardball" Hardy, had hated Barban and had nothing good to say about his deputy. "He's nothing but a fucking peacock," he told Major Jack. "Strutting about like a big game hunter. Needs his ass kicked good and hard. Don't be taking no shit of him, Major, ya hear?"

Winters was different. He was an organizational man intent on keeping harmony among the troops. He'd spent time in Japan and was impressed with their concept of teamwork. Anyhow, Barban thought, the Colonel was due to rotate back to The States in two months, so he'd be getting Co Thè back. He wasn't worried about Winter's replacement. He'd be more careful this time.

Hank hadn't liked the way Co Thè had taken to the Colonel. She really put her heart into screwing. It was hard to figure Vietnamese chicks out. Just what did they want anyhow? Winters was old enough to be her grandfather. His face had deep furrows that ran from his eyes to his chin and his hair was thin and gray. Yep, they were sure tough to figure out. Why didn't he turn her on? He was young and handsome and ready to go. Wasn't that what women wanted?

As always Co Linh had slipped out of the house without saying a word. It was several minutes before Barban realized that she had gone. She never left anything, not even so much as a hairpin. It was as though she was not coming back. Evidently, that was what she liked to think even though she knew she was simply fooling herself.

Barban rolled out of bed and stood naked before a full-length mirror. He smiled amiably at his reflection turning his head from side to side. Then he picked up a comb from the dresser and began to part his hair with great care checking it from the back and sides with a hand mirror. It was the first thing that he did each morning

The Idiot's Frightful Laughter

when he got up. He was paying homage to a revered idol. He then took an athletic supporter that he'd dyed maroon and slipped it on. Picking up a set of barbells in either hand, he watched his biceps bulge, as he slowly raised and lowered the weights. He did this for exactly fifteen minutes. Then he spent another quarter hour flexing his muscles. He subscribed to several bodybuilding magazines and had pinned a number of photos of physical culturalists assuming various poises on the wall at either side of the mirror. He would start with the top photo to his right mimicking each poise in turn. He'd accompany each position with a wink or nod of approval. He was so marvelous, he thought. Like the Greek God Apollo.

Before coming to Vietnam, Barban used to grease his body and use photographic lighting to enhance the effect. He once had a professional photographer take two dozen eight by tens enlargements of him. He mailed them to seven physical culture magazines. They were all returned within several weeks. A rejection slip accompanied each set of photographs. "Dear Contestant, Due to the large volume of submissions, we are unable to use your photos at the present time," they stated or something to the effect.

Occasionally Colonel Winters watched Barban go through his egocentric rituals. At first, the colonel had felt loathing. Such conceit. Such unabashed egotism, he thought. But then things never bothered the Province Senior Advisor for very long. Give him a little time, and he could adjust to just about anything. His wife had been largely responsible for this. If he could live with the old bitch, he could live with just about anyone. She was a chronic nagger. The moment he got home of an evening, he'd be bombarded with a long list of complaints that she had been saving up for him all day. Friends had sometimes asked him why he stood for it, and he always made the same reply. "Patience, my good man. Patience. From her, I have learned patience."

"Hank's just a kid," the colonel would tell himself. "That's the way kids are. Give him time, and he'll grow out of it." However, Colonel Winters knew that he was fooling himself because it was to his advantage to do so. It was due to Barban's wiles that he had such a splendid setup. He felt guilty every time he saw how the troops were squeezed into that old two-story adobe building. But then how many of them would willingly change places with him if they'd had half the chance? Every damn one of them would. He'd bet on that.

Winters never tired of wandering about the twelve-room villa with its ornate tile floors and hand-carved teak wood furnishings. It was more luxurious than anywhere he'd ever lived. During colonial days, it was the French provincial governor's home.

As for Co Thè, there was one precious gem. The colonel had never known such affection, such devotion from a woman before. The parting would be grim. He thought of it constantly with great melancholy. He would gladly marry her if he only could. But it was not possible, and he knew it. He could, of course, extend for another six months or a year; however, he'd very likely be transferred to an outpost up along the DMZ. Where would Co Thè stay? What assurance would he have that he could see her for more than a night or two a month? He would quite likely be assigned to a combat unit; thus exposing her to possible danger. It was all so impossible. "Sayonara Co Thè", he murmured. "Sayonara."

In spite of all the insurmountable obstacles that he'd had to confront on a daily basis, the year at Phu Vinh was the most pleasant experience of his life, and he had only Barban to thank for it. Sure, Hank had his reasons. He'd seen the lad's last performance rating. It was damn poor. Winter's predecessor, Colonel Hardy, obviously despised him. He had nothing good to say about the callow kid. What's more, Barban had trouble with his Vietnamese employees. They'd written objecting to his high handedness and sent it to the Minister of Labor in Saigon. Everyone but Truong had signed it. Since then Hank had avoided any association with them. His orders were channeled through Truong. His career with the Foreign Service hinged on the sort of evaluation Colonel Winters wrote. Frankly, the colonel wasn't all that pleased with the way Barban handled his job. For one thing, his relationship with the Vietnamese staff had grown even worse since they'd submitted the petition. What's more, he and Truong were always racing about in

The Idiot's Frightful Laughter

his jeep checking on district outposts. Taunting the CO's with poor performance ratings. It was Hank's way of evening the score. This troubled Winters, for it was undermining authority and weakening morale.

But, of course, where was the inspiration? Who gave a damn? What were the Vietnamese officials doing for their people? Robbing the poor peasants blind. Driving them into the welcoming arms of the enemy. Colonel Winters wondered if men like Gutschinritter with all their good intentions and hard work were accomplishing anything? If it wasn't all a waste of time? Perhaps Barban with all his conceit and self-interest did have the right idea. For Hank, it was all a game, and he was getting the most out of it while it lasted.

Colonel Winters pondered over all his own frustrations. What had he been able to accomplish? Colonel Nguyen Duc Bo, The Province Chief, was his counterpart. His primary duty was to advise Colonel Bo, but he had never wanted any of Winter's advice. He only came to him when he needed either money or supplies for some nebulous enterprises that never seemed to materialize. Winter's would follow the pompous little potentate about feeling useless and frequently ridiculous. Only twice had he wanted any advice. They had to do with accounting problems. An expertise that Winters knew nothing about. The first time the Province Chief had smiled rather sinisterly. On the second occasion, he had said: "Oh, but it is a pity. You have come all the way from America to advise me, and now you cannot help me." He had chuckled and said something in Vietnamese to his deputy. They had both looked at Colonel Winters and laughed loudly. Later he had asked his interpreter what the Province Chief had said. "Why did he laugh at me?" he asked. The interpreter said that he did not know. He had not been listening. Why then had he smiled so derisively, Winters wondered.

After his workout with the weights, Hank Barban took a hot shower and then lay on his bed. A Chinese youth wearing a white starched jacket and black trousers came in carrying a silver pot of coffee and a cup of fine porcelain on a tray. He set it on a nightstand beside the bed. "Your coffee, Sir," he said. His face was void of any expression. Barban resented it as much as if the servant had smirked at him.

"Where's the goddamn cream?" he snarled as the youth was about to close the door behind him.

"Very sorry," he said without turning about. In a few minutes, he was back with a small silver pitcher. He poured some cream into the cup and stirred it.

Barban looked coldly at the youth. Curling his lips into a faint sneer, he snarled. "Let's get on the ball Tu. Another fuck up, and I'll see you get drafted. A word to Colonel Bo is all it takes."

"Very sorry, Sir," he replied. His face still a mask of indifference. Tu hated Barban. He had not like most of the Americans he'd served, but Barban was the first one he'd permitted himself to hate. Tu had worked for the French. They had been harsh, demanding, occasionally cruel, but they never humiliated him. They had never tampered with his pride. It wasn't that they didn't speak coarsely of Vietnamese. He had heard them speak contemptuously of them countless times. But the criticisms had never been directed at him. And besides, he was Chinese. He had no use for the Vietnamese either. With the Americans, things were different. Most of them delighted in telling him over and over again how corrupt everyone was as though he was to blame. Barban went one step further. He made Tu responsible for the vice in the country. "You people," Hank would say. "You'd steal your grandmother's gold teeth."

Tu had never stolen anything from Barban, nor from anyone for that matter. And there were plenty of things that he could have stolen. Once Barban had misplaced his camera, a three-hundred-dollar Pentax. He'd left it in a pocket of his raincoat and accused Tu of stealing it. When the youth found it for him, Barban had said that Tu was only making an excuse. Tu knew that Hank trusted him; otherwise, he wouldn't leave his wallet lying about the bedroom. It would have been locked up in his trunk. Such treachery only intensified Tu's hate. It seemed as though Barban was deliberately trying to force him into doing something irrational. That he was setting him up. Forcing him into a showdown. Barban was a

The Idiot's Frightful Laughter

dilemma. Whatever Tu did was never right. He had begun to harbor thought of revenge. It was so easy to hire a hit man. One could only take so much, and Tu had about reached his limit.

When Barban came in for breakfast, Colonel Winters had already finished eating and was reading *The Stars and Stripes.*

"Good morning, Colonel. How'd it go last night?" Barban asked with a smile that he supposed was both sardonic and full of good fellowship; however, to the colonel, it appeared smug and arrogant. Barban had practiced it for hours before the mirror after seeing a Robert Mitchem movie some years ago. He imagined that it made him appear quite dashing.

"Good morning, Hank," the colonel said looking up from his paper. "Oh, can't complain. How about yourself?"

"Same as always," Barban said. "She just lies there as though she was dead. Might as well be screwing a corpse." His expression had changed to one of dejection.

Wants to let me know what a great sacrifice he's making. Remind me of how generous he's been, Winters thought smiling to himself. He must think I'm pretty naïve. It's he who's the callow one. "How are things in your department?" he asked in an effort to change the subject.

"Fair," Barban replied. "But I've got to get rid of Grecco. He can't cut the mustard. Gets everything all balled up. Got to have Major Jack go over all his reports."

"Oh yea?" Colonel Winters said raising his eyebrows as though surprised and nodding his head in a slow decisive manner. "Sounds bad." He knew that Barban was lying. Grecco was a damn good man. Probably the best of the civilians with the exception of Gutschinritter and Bledsoe. It was Vince's rank that troubled Barban. He outranked him by two steps. Hank was afraid he might take his job. That's what it added up to. At first, Barban had thought it was some sort of conspiracy, and that the colonel was in on it. The day he found out about Grecco's rank, he'd asked Winters quite pointedly why an FSR-4 had been assigned to an FSR-7 slot?

"A Reports Officer from the Refugee Division's main office sent here as a Refugee Advisor. It smells sort of fishy," Barban had said looking accusingly at the colonel. That was two months ago, and Hank still thought that it was a plot of some sort; however, he no longer suspected Winters.

"If he can't do the job, get rid of him and get someone who can," the colonel said keeping his eyes fixed on the newsprint. Getting rid of a good man was standard procedure in the military. It was a cut-throat business. There was no room for sentiment, the colonel mused. It was every man for himself. He hadn't liked it at the beginning, but people are very adaptable. One can adjust to anything. That's how Colonel Winter's saw it. Loyalty was for suckers. Those who couldn't take it, resigned. He'd known lots of that type. Well, he'd adapted and survived. Do or die, that was his motto.

I'll fire off a cable to Simoni right after morning briefing and let him know, Barban said.

Tu brought Barban's breakfast on a large platter. There were four thick slices of ham, six eggs sunny-side up and eight hotcakes.

"Where's the fucking juice?" Hank snapped.

Tu hurried from the room and returned with a large pitcher of pineapple juice. "Remember what I said about getting on the ball, Tu?" Barban growled. Tu nodded slightly looking into Barban's eyes with that same bland expression.

"We've got to find another houseboy," Barban told Winters.

"Yea," the colonel muttered continuing to read his paper. He figured he'd done enough appeasing for one morning.

Vince Grecco

As a child, Vince Grecco lived in two separate worlds. There was his home. That was one world. Then there was school. That was the other. The two were totally different.

Vince's parents were Italian immigrants. Peasants from the heel of the Italian boot near the village of Casarano. They arrived in America with nothing. Now they were prosperous. In just ten years, they'd been able to buy a hundred and fifty acres of Northern California's finest farmland.

The first thing that the Grecco's did was to plant grapes. They pulled up rows and rows of prune, apricot and apple trees. Their Anglo-Saxon neighbors were aghast. The trees had just reached their prime and were beginning to bear bumper crops. There was a good market for California fruit. It was the best. However, the neighbors soon realized that the Grecco's were right. Grapes were a far better investment, and vines required a lot less work than trees. The rich soil and temperate climate of the Sonoma Valley were ideal for grapes. In the fall, they took great truckloads to the winery to be crushed into juice. Aged in casks in dark, cool cellars, it produced wine to rival France's finest.

Grecco didn't know what to make of his parents. The spoke only their local dialect at home. Too poor to attend school in Italy, they could neither read nor write. When Vince first heard his father speak English, he was alarmed. He was only six, but he was painfully aware of the effect that his father had on others. They were noticeably amused. It embarrassed the child. He felt both pity and disillusion. He was ashamed that his parents were not like others. He saw mockery in his playmates' eyes, and frequently open unabashed smirks. Some parodied his father's speech. Why couldn't he be like his neighbor, Captain Olson? A war hero with a chest full of medals. When the captain spoke, people listened. They were serious and respectful. And Mrs. Olson, who was Vince's teacher at Hill School, looked so smart. She was slim and tall and wore nice clothing. Their son, Grant, was so lucky. Vince envied him. He could not understand why Grant hated his parents. Why was he afraid of them especially his father? Captain Olson was such a fine gentleman. Vince figured that Mrs. Olson was right. Grant was a little strange. Not like normal kids. It was that kick in his head by his Shetland pony. That's why, Vince thought.

Vince loved school. It was the real world where people spoke English and learned to be real honest-to-goodness Americans. He enjoyed Pledging Allegiance to the Flag and singing *God Bless America* and *The Star Spangled Banner.* It filled his heart with pride. He wanted so much to be like everyone else; to compensate for all those things his parents lacked. He memorized the national anthem and sang it aloud as he walked the narrow country road to and from school.

Grant's mother, Tessie, forbid him to go to Vince's home, for he came home smelling of wine. She had asked Vince not to let him drink. Alcohol was not good for children. "Yes, Mam," he'd say politely; however he knew how futile that would be. His father would not hear of such nonsense. It was insulting. Drinking wine was so basic to their culture. It was the staff of life. It made a child strong and full of life. Look at him. Look how strong he was. He had drunk wine every day of his life. It was the embodiment of Our Lord. Didn't Father John turn wine into the blood of Our Savior, Jesus Christ, at Holy Mass every Sunday? It was a grievous sin to deny anyone the right to drink wine. That was the essence of what he'd told his son in his provincial dialect.

Vince mother, Avalina, adored Grant. She loved his blond hair and blue eyes. He was so beautiful, like a Roman God. Avalina was huge. She was the fattest person Grant had ever seen, but he loved her more than anyone else on earth. Whenever he went to see the Greccos, she'd grab him in her enormous arms and hug him against her great breasts until he could barely breathe. "Where you been?" she would scold. "Why you no come to see your mama? Maybe you no like her no more?"

"Come here, kiddo," Pietro, the father, would say handing Grant a glass of Chianti. "Drink da vino." He would roar with deep belly-shaking laughter. "It putta hair on ya chest. Make a bigga man ah ya."

Grant thought of how very different Pietro was from his father. He was so jolly. Always waving his arms about and laughing that deep rich laugh. How lucky Vince was. Oh sure, he got angry with Vince, but he never struck him. That was the mother's job. She had a big wooden spoon that she'd swat Vince on the butt with if his grades ever dropped below A's. "Your father and I work hard so you'll get a good education. We weren't lucky like you. In our village, only the upper-class children were permitted to attend school. We were damn peasants. You must study hard and become a great man, so that we can be proud of you. If I see a B on your report card again, I'll beat your rump so hard you won't be able to sit down for a month." This was the gist of what she told Vince in her Italian vernacular, and she meant every word of it. Education was a very precious commodity. To waste it was the gravest of all sins.

Vince was Tessie Olson's favorite. She could not imagine how such a bright little boy could have such crude ignorant parents. Although Mrs. Olson was prejudice, Vince was her pet. He could do no wrong. She, like most of her Anglo-Saxon neighbors, was a closet bigot. She would only dare to refer to Italian immigrants as Wops behind their back. However, with Vince, it was totally different. She adored him. She'd gladly trade Grant for him anytime. Vince was a real American boy. "With the proper sort of guidance, a boy like that could achieve wonders," she'd tell her friends. And by "proper guidance" she, of course, meant hers.

Vince was not only an outstanding student. He was also a good athlete. At high school, he was the football team's star quarterback, and no one was prouder of him than Tessie. She rarely missed a game. She'd sit in the front row at the fifty-yard line and cheer loudly. "Hooray! Hooray for Vince," she'd shout. It didn't seem to matter to her that Grant was also a star athlete. He was the school's boxing champion. Ordinarily, Grant seemed so shy and quiet, but in the ring, he was like a raging bull. For the first couple of rounds, he would toy with his opponent like a cat with a mouse wearing him down. Gradually he'd work himself into a paroxysm. Suddenly exploding with rage, he'd tear into his victim; his fists pounding like pneumatic hammers. The spectators rarely cheered. They sensed that something was not quite right. Grant seemed distraught. He did not behave like a normal person. His face would take on a crazed expression. "You're just like your father," Tessie would charge. "So brutal." She had no idea how near the mark she was; that it was, in essence, his father that he was battering. At some time during the fight, his father's image would loom up before him. His opponent would assume the appearance of those sadistic brutal features. Grant would strike at the fearsome apparition until he had knocked his opponent unconscious. Nothing could stop the onslaught.

At the high school graduation ceremony, Grecco was awarded an athletic scholarship in Football at the San Francisco State. He enrolled in journalism. His parents were disappointed. They wanted him to major in business and become a corporate manager. However, Mrs. Olson told him that it was his life. "Do whatever you want. That's what you'll be best at," she said. For his graduation, Tessie gave him an expensive Swiss watch. He was her darling. Her all American boy. His parents didn't know whether to be pleased or angry. She was the strangest person they'd ever known.

Generating Refugee

Vincent Grecco stood in the doorway of the briefing room. He was pleased with it. As a foreign correspondent he had seen many briefing rooms, and they had always been the same – cinder block cubicles of pitch blackness with thick sound-proof walls and rows of fluorescent lights strung across the ceiling that plunged the room into a dazzling noonday desert brightness.

This room was different. It was small and rectangular. Large open windows enclosed three sides of the room. Maps of the province covered with patches of olive-green parachute silk hung from the walls. Grecco was pleased to note that there was none of the usual war paraphernalia strung about. No AK-47 assault rifles, Viet Cong flags, or catchy Rudyard Kipling quotes in ornate frames hung from the wall. There wasn't even a podium with an American flag to one side.

What a relief, Vince sighed. The others with their blinding lights and sound-proof walls awakened an inner horror. They trigger memories from the past. A reminder that occurred more than twenty years ago. It was World War II at the U.S. Marine Corps' Camp Pendleton. He was just seventeen. Sentenced to thirty days of solitary confinement in the military brig. For what? Being taken prisoner on a night patrol by Fox Company and surrendering his rifle. Some joker had hidden it. His platoon leader, a cocky second lieutenant just out of the Quantico Officer Training Center, was incensed. "You're an insult to the United States Marine Corps," he'd shouted leaving flecks of spittle on Vince's face. "You should be shot."

Instead, Grecco was locked up with his rifle in a five cubic foot box and fed bread and water for one month. The worst part were the lights that shown day and night. That month of incarceration had left its mark. He'd sooner climb ten flights of stairs than ride an elevator.

Vince sat down on a folding chair. They had been arranged in semicircles facing the cloth-covered charts. At the front were two rattan lounge chairs with foam rubber cushions. These were reserved for Hank Barban and Colonel Winters, thrones for their royal highnesses. Overhead three antiquated propeller fans clattered noisily stirring the hot moist air about.

Glancing about the rickety old structure with its open windows Vince had a second thought. It was a massacre waiting to happen. A sapper with a satchel charge of explosives could blow us all to bits, he thought. Either toss the explosive through an open window or better yet crawl beneath the floor to the center of the room. There wouldn't be a one of us left. Maybe the cinder block was better after all.

Grecco took a handkerchief from his pocket and wiped the sweat from his face and hands. The warm sultry air made him feel limp and listless. He had fifteen minutes before the meeting began and was tempted to sit and allow the heat to lull him into a pleasant stupor. However, he knew that he had better look over his notes. Barban was apt to ask him the usual pointless questions and look most annoyed if he was the least bit hesitant. Vince wondered what he should say about the napalm drop on the Son Thang Resettlement Camp. It had to be mentioned. There must be retribution.

Vince thumbed slowly through his pages of data. His eyes swept from one column of figures to the next until they blurred together. A thick smudgy smoke screen of statistics. Cloud after cloud of them numbing his mind. He imagined himself a mountaineer watching an avalanche of numbers cascading down upon him. He could not concentrate. Old Mr. Nguyen Van Throng's frantic features kept flashing before him. Flames billowing down over him. The job was getting on Vince's nerves. He could not remember ever feeling so useless. What could he possibly do for these poor tortured peasants? Another five minutes, and he too would have been consumed in fire. It would all have been covered up. Lies would have been told. The Viet Cong had killed him. That would be the official report.

For the past two weeks, Grecco had sat at a table with Vietnamese officials from the villages, districts and province headquarters. Outside a long line of peasants squatted in the dust. Their faces masked the anguish that they had endured for the past several months. Some much longer. They were the victims of the Communists' Têt Offensive. The Viet Cong had attacked while the nation was celebrating its Lunar New Year. However, it was our retaliation that had caused nearly all the death and destruction.

No province had been spared their attack and the Americans' devastating retaliation. The peasants were waiting for their indemnities, and Grecco was there to see that they got them. However, it was impossible to know how much they received, for they were quickly ushered outside before they could acknowledge the amount. Occasionally a peasant became angry and began shouting, but Vince never found out what it was all about. If he asked, the Vietnamese official would simply shrug his shoulders. If Grecco persisted, the man would smile at him as though it was all too trivial to bother about and tell him in a very off-handed manner a most implausible tale. Once he was told that a woman was angry because she had been told that the Communist would come to her house that night and take her money. "She wants protection," the deputy district chief said. "However, it is quite impossible for the soldiers to guard every home in the province," he added sighing heavily and shrugging his shoulders.

After each payment, Vince signed a ledger to the left of the recipients' thumbprint indicating that he had witnessed the transaction. When he complained about the sham, Barban told him not to make waves. Corruption was a way of life in the Orient. He'd have to learn to live with it. Barban had heard others use this flimsy excuse and adapted it whenever the occasion suited him. It was one of those clichés that made allowance for all sorts of corruption. No wonder the peasants were so keen on schooling for their children. If they were literate, they were not so apt to be cheated.

The payments were a mere pittance. They could not begin to pay for the damage. Most of the money was to compensate the victims for retaliatory attacks. U.S. aircraft and artillery would raze a village in order to drive off a squad of Viet Cong or North Vietnamese Regulars armed with nothing more than rifles and perhaps a mortar or two. However, the payments made favorable publicity and weakened the antiwar protestors' stand.

Grecco didn't like being used as a ploy for such collusion. What sort of confidence did that inspire? He felt like a simpleton. He was sure that the Vietnamese officials were all laughing at him. Lately, he'd been having dreams that he went about doing things that were contrary to his basic instincts. He worried about what might be happening to him. He imagined that he was a fool. An unwilling one, but a fool none the less. He was a marionette, and the Province Chief and his cohorts were pulling the strings this way and that making him dance to their tune, so to speak. Didn't all the Americans feel the same way? He supposed that they did with the exception of Max.

Grecco glanced at the statistics once more. People were beginning to arrive for the briefing. How could he memorize all these figures? He wondered. Eighty-three whose homes were fifty percent or more destroyed were paid the equivalent of six hundred and thirty-seven dollars. Fifty-seven whose homes were less than fifty percent destroyed were paid an amount equivalent of four hundred and twenty-eight bucks. Then there were the casualties. Those wounded or killed. How many were adults and how many children? The most difficult problem was keeping track of supplies. It was impossible to know just how many sacks of cement and sheets of roofing were being distributed to the refugees. The Province Chief always insisted that they sold it on the black market, and no one was foolish enough to contradict him. No one but the boldest, and they usually disappeared quite mysteriously the following day. However, it was common knowledge that it was Colonel Bo who sold the building material to Chinese merchants for high-rise apartments in Cholon and Saigon. It was so ironic, Vince thought. The building costs were being subsidized by the

U.S. Government to build quarters for its massive army of bean counters flooding into the country. But what could Vince do? What power did a Refugee Advisor have, or any American for that matter from the Ambassador on down? Who would listen to him? Who cared one iota? He was constantly being reminded that he was a guest of the Government of South Vietnam. His success depended on how popular he was with the local officials particularly his counterpart which generally amounted to ignoring all the corruption that swirled brazenly about him and occasionally required his assistance.

Billie Joe Webber, the Agriculture Advisor, sat down beside Grecco. Vince had found that it was quite impossible to speak with Webber about his work. Actually, there was very little that he was willing to discuss. The weather was one, and the marvels of his home state of Louisiana was another. If civil rights for blacks was mentioned, he'd hastily leave the room.

"Hot," Vince said dabbing at his brow with a damp handkerchief.

Webber glanced suspiciously at him for a moment before replying. "Yep, shore is, ah reckon. Ah do believe it's the hottest day we've had this year. Shore wish we'd get them air conditioners for the office that they've been a promising us."

"Barban's got three in his office," Grecco said. "Why don't you ask him for one of his? He doesn't need all three of them."

Webber looked fiercely at Vince for several seconds; then without so much as a nod began shuffling through his report as though he was searching for something of the most urgent importance.

Fucking peckerwood, Grecco thought. A hundred years and he's still fighting the Civil War. Even though my parents were born in Italy and didn't come to The States until 1908, I'm still a goddamn Yankee, an enemy, a threat to his way of life. To hell with all his bigotry and ignorance.

By now nearly all the seats in the briefing room were occupied. The military had changed into clean neatly pressed fatigues and polished boots. However, most of the civilians had come straight from work wearing the same clothing they'd had on all day. When the soldiers gave their reports, they stood erect staring earnestly at Colonel Winters and snapping off their words in a machine-gun-like staccato. One would guess that it was the highest point of their week, for many of them spent much of their time slouched behind their desks reading the armed forces newspaper.

The civilians, on the other hand, showed no interest in the briefing. It was just more busy work that cut into their free time. It was something to get over with and out of the way as quickly as possible. Most of them made no effort to stand erect and speak clearly and concisely. Some leaned back against the wall. Others slouched on one foot or let their large bellies droop out over loosened belts. They frequently mumbled running their words together so badly that Colonel Winters had to constantly ask them to repeat themselves.

Grecco stood with his feet placed wide apart and his head thrown back so that he had to peer over his nose at Barban and Colonel Winters giving, he hoped, an appearance of mild disdain. Whenever Barban questioned him, he would address him as Hank as he rocked up and down on the balls of his feet. He was pleased to see that it upset the coxcomb.

The CIA was always well represented. Three or four spooks gathered at the back of the room busily taking notes. As a matter of courtesy, Colonel Winters always asked their chief, Blaine Bruce, if they had anything to report. Bruce always emphatic but courteous would reply: "No, Sir." No one was the least surprised, for it was taken for granted that all their information was confidential. However, Grecco was annoyed by their secretiveness. It was a bit too theatrical for him.

Bruce had taken over many civic action projects in the province that the CIA had neither experience nor interest in. For example, it had taken over the Revolutionary Development Cadre Program because the Agency for International Development lacked sufficient funding to support it. On the other hand, the CIA had unlimited amounts of cash which it could do whatever it wished with and didn't have to account to anyone for the expenditures. The

The Idiot's Frightful Laughter

Revolutionary Development Cadre had been established to train Vietnamese youth as civic action specialists. They were experts in such disciplines as farming, sanitation, carpentry, and rural administration. They built community structures, such as clinics, schools, and public markets. Squads of young men were sent to villages throughout the country to live and work with the villagers. The purpose was for them to sow goodwill among the peasants and thus win government support. Of what interest could a spy agency have with such a program? It was all too clear to Vince. It wanted spies. With these RD cadre in villages and hamlets throughout the country, the CIA had a well-established network already in place.

Bruce was intent on keeping Grecco and other advisors out of the RD program. His cadre were not civic action specialists sent to the countryside to improve the peasants' standard of living and win them over to the government's side. The youth in the black-clad uniforms and bush hats were spies. That was their primary responsibility, and Bruce and his associates were doing their best to keep it a secret.

Well, as usual, Grecco figured that the spooks had outsmarted themselves. It was obvious to everyone that the Revolutionary Development Program was a miserable failure and would soon be abandoned. The peasants despised the cadre and made things as uncomfortable as possible for them. Who could blame them? Vince thought. No one likes to be spied on especially if it means being assassinated some dark night by a squad of tribal mercenaries.

The RD Program was phase one of the Phoenix Program. The cadres' job was to find VC suspects and target them for assassination or worse interrogation. The Phoenix Program was the brainchild of South Vietnam's CIA Chief, Bob Komer, nicknamed "Blowtorch", a nickname he loved. His old pal, President Lyndon Baines Johnson, had given him the special title of Ambassador of Pacification. It outranked that of the U.S.'s official ambassador to South Vietnam.

Grecco met Blowtorch Komer for just a moment when he was making one of his routine deliveries of refugee statistics to the colonel at the Little Pentagon. Komer had stepped into the office from a back room and began jabbing the colonel in the ribs with his elbow. Vince was surprised at how closely the head spook resembled his hometown butcher – red-faced, bald and beefy. The Ambassador of Pacification had been playful but rough. His jabs had thrown the colonel off balance, and he had to hold on to the edge of his desk for support.

Why Phoenix? Grecco mused. It was a symbol of immortality. The name of a mythological bird of ancient Egyptian lore. Every three or four hundred years the bird was supposed to be consumed in flame only to resurrect from the ashes. Was this supposed to be the symbol of Vietnam? Destroy it and then recreate it in our image? The American dream. What else? Grecco wondered.

The Phoenix Program was not especially new, Vince figured. The American Indians had faced a similar fate. In the late 1860's, the U.S. Cavalry had systematically slaughtered them one tribe at a time. The procedure was repeated in The Philippines at the turn of the century.

At Yen Chau as elsewhere in the Delta, The CIA was referred to as OCO, an acronym that stood for The Office of Civil Operations. In theory OCO was supposed to incorporate other organizations, such as the Agency for International Development and the U.S. Information Services; however, these agencies weren't a party to the CIA's covert operations. They were top secret, and the spooks preferred it that way; nevertheless, it enabled them to expand their operations and gradually absorb the other U.S. agencies' operations.

Grecco had a fairly good idea of what was going on, and he didn't like it. The revelation began to unfold at a hostess bar on Tu Do Street, Saigon's notorious red-light district. Vince was sitting at a bar alone when three rather unsavory characters wearing charcoal suits and black ties walked in. For a moment, they stood in the doorway, their hands jammed in their coat pockets looking about as though they might be casing the place.

"Who are you?" one of them demanded, thrusting his jaw out at Grecco.

The Idiot's Frightful Laughter

Gangsters, Vince thought. They reminded him of the thugs he'd come across as a police reporter for the *Chicago Tribune.* "I'm a tourist," he said not wishing to have to explain himself.

"We're with the embassy," the thug said. One of the others nudged him, and they moved to a table just behind Grecco.

"Fucking fuzz. I don't like them mothafuckers," the one who'd spoken to Vince said.

"You mean that Kike asshole, Jake?" One of the others said.

"Yea, that cocksucka," the thug said. "Yea specially him. He was a fuzz in L.A. before he came here. That's what he said."

"What are we doing working for dicks?" the third asked.

"Yea, it makes me feel like a fucking snitch," the first said. "We're supposed to be killing gooks. Not playing patsy to no fuzz."

"Hey, cool it, Nick," the other said. "The fucking tourist's listening."

"Fuck him," Nick said. "What the fuck can he do?"

"This ain't our turf, Nick," the other said. "We don't know who the fucker is."

"Hey Joker," Nick said getting up and placing a hand on Grecco's shoulder. "You didn't hear nothing. Get it?"

"Huh? Oh sure. No sweat," Vince said.

The next time Grecco met Nick, he was wearing black fatigues and a black bush hat. "The fucking tourist," he'd snarled as Vince stepped into the OCO office.

"You know each other?" Bruce asked.

After Nick had explained their encounter, the CIA Chief gave Grecco `a twisted sardonic smile. "You're in the wrong business, Vince. You ought to be with us. Tourist in Vietnam. That's rich."

Grecco never knew Nick's real name. That was all part of the cover. Nick like thousands of other hoodlums was hired because of his ruthless disregard for life. Killing was a piece of cake. Great sport! He like all the other criminals was hired for one year to carry out the assassination of Viet Cong suspects. The Central Intelligence Agency kept no record of him. Even Bruce didn't know who he was. He wasn't supposed to. It was better that way. If he was killed, and he most surely would be before his year's contract ended, no mention would be made of the death. Nick would be buried secretly in the jungle. No marker would be left to identify the grave. How many of these hoods had vanished? Grecco assumed that thousands, possibly tens of thousands had. Social cleansing, he mused.

Nick was a virtual prisoner. Vince never saw him walking about town or at the MAT Team's clubroom drinking a cool one. The Company, as the CIA was called, kept him hidden away inside their compound. Bruce knew that Nick's days were numbered, and he wanted his death to pass unnoticed. Having friends was apt to complicate things. However, Grecco had seen him on two separate occasions. One evening, Vince saw Nick with six Nung mercenaries. They all had grease guns with collapsible stocks. They wore the traditional black peasant pajamas and bandannas wound about their heads. Their faces were smeared with streaks of black and green grease paint.

The Nungs were descendants of Kublai Khan's Mongolian hordes that invaded Vietnam during the thirteen hundreds, some six hundred years ago. Greatly outnumbered, the Vietnamese had lured the warriors into the jungles and gradually chopped the indomitable army to bits. The survivors had mated with Mao Tribe women and thus survived preserving their identity. After six centuries, the Nungs still resembled their Mongol origin. They were short and stocky and walked with a swagger. Their broad flat features were fierce and defiant. Even the Viet Cong were afraid of them. They had a deep-rooted hatred for the Vietnamese that went back a long way, and they relished killing them. North or South, they showed no partiality. However, there was one thing that they made a special issue of – money. As much as they enjoyed killing Vietnamese, they expected to be paid for it and paid on time. They were tough negotiators. Americans had learned the hard way that they'd better not be late with the cash. It was apt to prove fatal.

Grecco noticed how much Nick's behavior had changed. He seemed unduly anxious as he spoke in broken English to the Nung commander. He kept nodding and grinning. The broader the thug's smile grew, the more scornful the Nung Chieftain looked.

The Idiot's Frightful Laughter

Blaine Bruce pulled up driving a pickup. Nick insisted that the Nung he was talking with get in the front seat with Bruce while he climbed in the back with the others. Vince figured that the Nungs had sized Nick up and felt insulted to be led by a piece of shit like that. Nick was in grave danger, and Vince could see that he knew it. Killing him would mean nothing to them, Grecco figured.

However, it wasn't the Nungs who killed Nick. He bought the farm so to speak while on a special operation with the MAT's team. Sergeant Rivera would not have told Grecco about it if he was not drunk. They were at a pick-up bar in Can Tho when the sergeant told him all the grisly detail. The team had been assigned the task of knocking out a Chicom 12.7mm machine gun that had knocked down several helicopters. No one knew quite where it was. The insurgents kept moving it about. However, recon unit claimed to have recently seen the gun and its operator. It was in a mangrove swamp about fifty meters south of the village of Go Duc where the gunner was believed to be staying. Nick was designated as the hit man. Bruce wanted to test his mettle. He was to slit the gunner's throat and anyone else who might stand in his way. In the meantime, the others were to knock out the gun provided they could find it.

"Nick was like a kid on Christmas Eve," Rivera said. "I never saw a guy so shitfaced happy about cutting a gook's throat. It was unreal."

According to the sergeant, the squad was taken by boat up a series of canals and then walked about four clicks to within about fifty yards of the village. They snaked along the ground an inch at a time. They'd move, stop, listen, move, stop, listen. They held thin strips of flexible aluminum between their teeth to check for trip wires. They'd move their heads from side to side and up and down, If the strip bent, they knew that they'd touched something, possibly a wire. It took about an hour and a half to get to the village. At the gate, they located a Claymore mine and disarmed it. Nick and Rivera entered the gunner's hut while the others set off with a member of the recon unit in search of the machine gun.

There were three people asleep in the hooch. As Nick was about to slit the gunner's throat, a girl of about twelve moaned. Nick moved to the child's side. Placing a hand over her mouth, he took his knife in the other hand and drove it up under a rib and through the heart. Then they heard a muffled explosion. The others had dropped a termite explosive down the gun barrel destroying it. As the gunner reared from his bunk, Nick slit his throat. The third, a girl, looked as though she was screaming, but no sound came from her lips. Rivera placed the barrel of his pistol against her temple and fired. As Nick stepped from the hut, his carbine thrust out in front of him, one of the team thinking that he was a VC, shot him. The automatic fire shattered his chest.

At the rendezvous point, no boatman was waiting for them, so they had to drag Nick's body an additional six kilometers through leech-infested swamp and razor-sharp reeds. When they were less than a click from Yen Chau two of Bruce's men showed up. Rivera had notified headquarters that Nick was dead. One of the spooks was carrying a plastic container. The two spies insisted on taking Nick's body. They told the team to go ahead. They'd catch up.

Curious, the sergeant crouched behind some brush a short distance from them. He saw the agents put Nick's body in a clump of bamboo and pile straw and sticks on it. Then one of them took the plastic container and poured its contents on to the corpse. The other lit a match and tossed it on the bier. It exploded into flame igniting the clump of bamboo.

Sergeant Rivera hadn't liked Nick, but that was beside the point, he told Grecco. Nick deserved better than what he got. The cremation outraged a sense of fairness deep inside the trooper. It screamed for some sort of rectitude.

Vince shared the soldier's wrath. Even war dogs were treated with more dignity than Nick. During World War II, Grecco recalled seeing a graveyard for dogs on Saipan Island in the Marianas. It was in a grove of palm trees. The grass was neatly cut, and each canine had a cross bearing its name. Nick had nothing.

Grecco wondered where The Company had found Nick. Probably in some federal penitentiary in The States. He'd no doubt

The Idiot's Frightful Laughter

been promised amnesty. All he had to do was murder a few Vietnamese in the dark of night for a year, and he was a free man. No questions asked. That was the line they'd fed him. Little did he know that he had signed a death warrant when he put his name to the dotted line.

Vince scrutinized Blaine Bruce and his two henchmen seated at a corner of the briefing room. He saw nothing mean or sinister in their countenance. Bruce might be mistaken for a small-town lawyer, full of righteous ambition. The other two were the sort one could find leaning on a working-class bar. They were brawny with sluggish dull features. Grecco had met their boss, William Colby, at the Refugee Division's headquarters in Saigon. He had just taken over Blowtorch Komer's job as Ambassador of Pacification. Colby was nicknamed the mole because of his deceptive behave. However, a casual acquaintance would never imagine that he was the brains behind anything so heinous as the Phoenix Program, for he was from all outward appearances a man of refinement and good breeding. Grecco recalled the time a Marine Guard had halted him at the entrance to Vietnam's U.S. Embassy and rudely demanded identification. Colby had been profusely polite. He had apologized for forgetting his ID card and agreed to go back across town for it. However, the following week, Vince noted that the guard was gone. Probably transferred to some combat unit on the DMZ.

At Colonel Edward Winter's briefing, Captain Percy Mendez, the team's intelligence officer, was always the first to give his report. He slid the cloth curtain away from the map at his left. It displayed the typography of Yen Bay Province overlaid with a sheet of clear plastic. Mendez circled large areas of the map using either red or black grease pencils and then filled them in with diagonal lines. Colored flags mounted on pins were stuck in the shaded areas.

The captain picked up a pointer and tapped at an arrow that swept across the upper left-hand corner of the map striking the largest of the four striped areas. "Sir," he said looking earnestly at the colonel. "Latest reports have it that the NVA's Fourth Division's

Twenty-Fifth Regiment is now in Yen Bay Province. Wednesday night its second and third battalions moved across the Hau Giang River and up the Tong Ton Canal," he said thrusting the pointer at a red flag in one of the striped circles. "As soon as we can be sure of the approximate coordinates, we'll call for the B-52's to saturate the area. We've already had Snoopy from Soc Trang working the area over.

Colonel Winters smiled. "I watched the fireworks last night from the tower at the airport," he said. "You got an estimated body count?"

"Yes Sir," Mendez responded snapping to attention. "The last figures show 32 KIA's and 78 WIA's. We've been getting a larger than usual number of civilian casualties though, Sir. It's been running about three for every NVA" The Captain pointed to a black dot to either side of the red flag. "There are two hamlets, Hieu Kinh, and An Phuoc, in this area, so large numbers of civilian casualties seem unavoidable, Sir. Any attempt to warn them is not recommended. Past experience has proved that Charlie is alerted and moves out of the area until the raids end, Sir."

"Let's round them up and herd them into a resettlement camp?" Barban said turning to Colonel Winters.

Captain Mendez shook his head. His eyes grew wide and more earnest. "Sir," he said ignoring Barban and looking intently at the colonel. "Charlie would become suspicious. To be effective, the raid must be kept secret. That includes Arvin and all Vietnamese counterparts. It's a known fact that at least half our Vietnamese officers are VC informants. Besides, Sir," Mendez added waving his pointer in the air, "these hamlets, as you know, have been reported each month for the past year and a half in the HES reports as Viet Cong hamlets." The captain looked at Bruce for confirmation. The CIA chief gave him a knowing wink. "So we are not likely to lose any friendlies from the air strikes," he concluded.

No, just blow a few dozen women and children to bits and cripple a few dozen more. That's all, Grecco thought. And we talk about the barbarities at Auschwitz.

The Idiot's Frightful Laughter

Lieutenant Berry Lefarge, the Air Force's forward observer, rose slowly and ambled up to the maps as Mendez returned to his chair. Eyeing Winters and Barban with a frightened-rabbit look, he sidled along the wall. With great care, he drew the curtain back over the map that Mendez had been using, and then with even greater care slid back the cloth covering the map to the right.

Several dozen jagged blotches of red had been carefully drawn on the map. "There has been more activity noted this week than at any time since the Têt Offensive Last February, Sir. Seventeen air strikes were called in at suspected enemy activities in these locations," he said tapping each of the red blotches with the pointer. "At these two locations, concrete bunkers were uncovered, and a secondary explosion occurred here. It was believed to be an NVA ammo dump, Sir."

"Where in the blazes are they getting the rock and sand for the concrete?" Winters asked.

Lafarge stood as though paralyzed; his mouth slightly agape, and his head shaking nervously from side to side. Captain Terrance Burk, the team's civil engineer, rose. "Sir, begging your pardon, Sir, but I believe I can answer your question, Sir."

"Have at it, Captain," Winters replied.

"Well, Sir, the Public Works Chief, Loi Lu, said that most of the crushed rock used on that marshy stretch of road between Xon Cho and Huyen Bao has been scrapped up and hauled off."

The colonel shook his head. "You've got to hand it to Charlie. He don't miss a trick," he said turning to Barban.

"No Sir, he certainly doesn't," Lieutenant Lafarge said nodding very earnestly. He then stood looking very intently at the colonel until Winters nodded for him to continue with his report. "Sir, night recon planes have picked up probable troop movement along this route," he said pointing to a red strip of plastic tape. "Snoopy has been called in to make strafing and flare drops along the trail."

"Have you coordinated this with S-3 to see if an Arvin patrol could lay ambushes?" Winters asked.

"Begging your pardon, Sir," Major Makhilovich said rising from his chair at a corner of the room. "I believe I can answer that question, Sir."

"Please proceed, Major," Winters said.

"Thank you, Sir," the major said. "I've spoken with my counterpart, Major Kim, but you know how slow he is to act?"

"I'll speak to Colonel Bo about it," Winters said writing on his notepad. A lot of good that will do, he thought.

A U.S. Information Service Chief and a Naval Lieutenant Commander took care of the propaganda for the team. The operation was termed "psyops", a contraction for psychological operations. An air force sergeant was assigned to drop leaflets and play tapes over a loudspeaker that was attached to the belly of an L-19 observation plane termed a "Bird Dog". The sergeant also saw to it that the TV sets at the more pacified villages were maintained and that movies were distributed weekly to the province's five district headquarters. Grecco saw one set fixed to the limb of a banyan tree in a village square.

Maynard Whitesides, Yen Bay's USIS Chief, took his turn on stage. He seemed oblivious to the scorn he aroused from the military. Whiteside, a middle age bureaucrat, stood swayback before the colonel, his stomach slopping out over a large low-slung belt. His long silver hair was combed back over his ears and bunched like a rooster's tail behind. A pair of bifocals sat perched at the end of his nose. His associate, Lieutenant Commander Lloyd Bernardo, once told Grecco that years ago, Whitesides was being groomed to head the agency, but alcohol had ended that. Now he was quite useless, Bernardo said. The chief could no longer perform the simplest task unless it was explained to him repeatedly in the most elementary terms.

"Sir," Whitesides said glancing down at a piece of paper clutched tightly with both hands. "Posters." He paused. A foolish gaping smile slowly transformed his features from dazed bewilderment to dull delight. "Sir, we have put up posters in one hundred and thirty-eight villages. They warn the people not to co…lab…or..ate with communists," he said reading from his notes.

The Idiot's Frightful Laughter

"Sir," he continued widening his smile. The lower lip was speckled with flecks of phloem. "The Viet Cong have stolen three of our television sets. New ones have been ordered from Saigon. We should have them in the next couple of weeks."

"I'll bet you'll find them if you search the district chief's quarters," Winters said with a chuckle winking to those behind him.

"Oh, no Sir," Whitesides said waving a finger at the colonel as though he was scolding a naughty child. "It was them VC, Sir. That's what everyone says, Sir."

The men broke into a fit of laughter. Such childlike naïveté was too much even for vinegar puss Webber. Whitesides gazed about in wide-eyed wonder; then covering his mouth with both hands, giggled. It took several minutes for him to regain his composure. "Sir," the Psyops Chief said. "One of our speakers was hit by rifle fire and is being repaired, so Sergeant Ross won't be making any flights for the next couple days." He paused as though to allow such profound wisdom to sink in. "Sir, two dozen copies of *Moby Dick* and *The Scarlet Letter* were translated into Vietnamese and have been passed around to the high schools.

"*Moby Dick* into Vietnamese!!" said the colonel scratching his bald head. "Whose numb skull brainstorm was that?"

"The United States Information Service, Sir," Maynard Whiteside replied rearing up and feebly attempting to throw his chest out. "That's who, Sir!" The USIS Chief was great fun, they all agreed. He was always worth a laugh or two, but this was without a doubt the best. His paramount performance.

Next on the agenda were the Public Safety Officers, a euphemism for Police Advisors. Although Officer Burl McDuff was their junior, the other three cops seemed pleased to have him brief the colonel. For them, it was a chore rather than a distinction. They were on leave from the Los Angeles Police Force. They could care less about protocol. If things go from bad to worse, they could always get their old jobs back. They were there waiting for them whenever they wanted them back.

When Grecco was a foreign correspondent, he must have asked several dozen of them at various times how law enforcement in a large U.S. metropolis qualified them for this sort of work. None seemed to know. "It's a whole different can of worms," a New York cop in Hue once told him. But then what qualified Vince to be a Refugee Advisor or that punk Barban as Deputy Province Advisor? Or for that matter, any of the other civilians, other than Gutschinritter, of course. What in the hell did they know about Vietnam?

It was evident that Officer McDuff was more articulate than the others. What's more, he was not ambitious. He had no intention of making a career out of the Foreign Service. One year was enough. He'd had all the military horseshit that he could stand. He was anxious to get back to the World. He thought about all the good pussy that was going to waste. He couldn't wait to make up for lost time. A different piece of ass every night. That was living.

The others were older. They liked the money. It was twice what they'd got walking a beat in The States, and then there was job security. Besides, it was easy. It only amounted to a couple hours of report writing a week and the occasional meeting with their counterpart. The rest was chickenshit. Watching the Viet cops slap the VC prisoners about until they loosened up and talked was low-class entertainment. They learned a lot about torture from their Vietnamese counterparts. The high point of the day was taking the VC prisoners up in a chopper and pushing them out. That was great sport. Would they ever love to do that to the junkies back in LA. That would solve the drug problem real quick. At least that was how they saw things.

What's more, the policemen could do whatever they pleased. They were free of responsibility. No one would blame them if their advice went unheeded. After all, ten years hadn't elapsed since these gook cops belonged to gangs of river pirates that controlled the Mekong Delta as far north as Saigon. Furthermore, they didn't have to bother with a prisoner's civil rights. If some gook got out of line, they'd beat the shit out of him and then shoot him. He was the

The Idiot's Frightful Laughter

enemy. That was that. No one questioned their authority. It was fun pushing people around. Letting them know who was boss.

As for Officer Burl McDuff, he liked being a stateside cop. He was different from the others. He wasn't running away from the growing hostility towards the police. He never took the protestors' taunts personal. He didn't see the peaceniks as his enemy. He understood their anger. Why they called him "pig". Controlling the demonstrators only made his job more challenging. "It separated the men from the boys," he'd say when a colleague lost his cool.

The year in Vietnam had broadened his horizon. It had given him a chance to travel. To work with police in other parts of the world and see what he could learn. How it compared with law enforcement in The States. On the other hand, he felt nothing but the deepest loathing for the Vietnamese Policeman. It wasn't simply because he was corrupt. McDuff was used to that. Los Angeles had its share of dishonest cops. It was the Vietnamese police's thorough lack of scruples that disgusted him. No matter how crooked an LA cop might be, he had some limits. He would not step beyond a certain point. However, as a Police Advisor in Vietnam, Officer McDuff felt that he was in league with a ruthless gang of criminals who plundered their country for all that it was worth. They served whoever paid the most.

Safety Officer McDuff wore neatly pressed khaki and polished boots. He stood erect, his legs spread wide apart; his thumb hooked in his belt. He had dark brown hair and icy blue eyes that looked as though they could penetrate steel. He was six foot, one and had a very engaging smile. Everyone liked Burl McDuff. He was the sort of guy that one could trust. "Sir," he said smiling first at Winters and then at the others about the room, "reports have it that the District Chief at Cau Ninh is dipping into the till. Twice during the past week, Colonel Bo has sent two jeep loads of police down there to investigate him."

"What do you know about that, Captain?" Colonel Winters said turning and nodding to Mendez.

"Sir, all the reports state that Major Suu is honest and cooperative. "That's more than can be said about any of the other

District Chiefs in the province." The Team's Intelligence Officer said glancing about the room as though he expected to be challenged. "Captain Andrini, the District's Senior Advisor, has nothing but the best to say about him."

Safety Advisor McDuff nodded. "Yea, we figured that the Province Chief's sore because Major Suu's spending the tax money on the people instead of splitting the loot with him. This is his way of getting the District Chief back in line. We've taken a neutral corner and are waiting for things to blow over," he said nodding to the other Safety Officers. They had their chairs tilted back against the wall; their heels hooked on the top rungs. Two were wearing shoulder holsters with snub nose 38's. The other had a 45 protruding from his hip pocket.

"How's Captain Andrini handling it?" Winters asked turning to Mendez.

"Sir, I believe I sent you a memo concerning the matter. Must have got misplaced?" Winters frowned and shook his head. "Anyhow," the Captain added shrugging his shoulders, "Captain Andrini said he's being pressured by Suu for support. If Colonel Bo figures we're solidly behind the District Chief, he's sure to ease off. Anyhow, that seems to be what Suu thinks. I advised Andrini to stall things until he heard from you, Sir."

"Yea! O'kay! I don't see what we can do," Winters said furrowing his brow and glancing about at the others with a very discerning expression. "This is strictly a Vietnamese affair, and no matter how much some of us might like Major Suu, we can't be getting mixed up in their politics."

Officer Burl McDuff grinned sardonically. 'If you like, Sir, I'll keep you posted on how things turn out from my end?" What a lily-livered sonofabitch, he thought. He hasn't got the backbone of a water louse. He's no George S. Patton. Not by a long shot.

The colonel nodded. From his expression, everyone knew that it was a dead issue. The District Chief was on his own. If he wanted to protect the people of his district from corrupt province officials, he'd have to do it alone. If he persisted in involving the Americans, he'd be marked down as a troublemaker unable to get along with his superiors. The task would be Major Andrini's responsibility. He could be counted on to close rank with the other members of the team; for he was keen on making Lieutenant Colonel. He had just one more chance. If he were passed over this time, he wouldn't be given another – not at the age of forty-five.

"O'kay Sir," McDuff said edging over between the maps and Winters, so he wouldn't have to face Barban. He was the only one on the team besides Grecco who dared stand up to the Deputy Senior Advisor. As a consequence, Hank has assured him of a poor performance evaluation. "Well, the piece of shit knew what he could do with it," McDuff had said. "He could wipe his ass with it. That's what he could do." No one back at his LA precinct gave one flying fuck for the shithead's phony fucking write up." McDuff wasn't about to kiss anyone's ass especially a smart-ass punk like Barban. That was about the gist of what he's told him.

"Our field forces made a sweep of eight villages in this area and picked up twenty-two suspects," the cop said pointing to a spot on the map to his left. "Eight of them are known VC. No one of any rank was apprehended. We also threw up roadblocks at six major intersections and on three canals. Charlie has evidently stopped using the roads during daylight." McDuff said. "However, we caught three VC cadre with a pile of propaganda and a tax collector with a sack full of dough. As usual," he added, "the money disappeared before we got back to headquarters. Police Chief Tan was sore because he didn't get a cut."

Gutschinritter stood up. "Begging your pardon, Sir," he said addressing Colonel Winters. "But I've been getting a lot of complaints lately about those roadblocks." He had such an earnest expression that Grecco had to grin. The Boy Scout with a chest full of merit badges came to mind. How oddly he stood out amid this gang of self-seeking ruffians, he thought. "Sir, the police have been keeping the merchants' ID cards and then making them pay to get them back. The shop owners say that after they pay off the police and the Viet Cong, they're too broke to stay in business."

"Well, that's Asia," The Province Senior Advisor said shrugging his shoulders and winking at those about him. "There's nothing we can do to change that." Barban gave Gutschinritter an angry look. He'd deal with the shit stirrer later.

Poor bastard, Grecco thought. Never tires of trying to get some sort of commitment from the Americans. Some indication that they aren't willing patsies for a gang of thieves. He'll never give up. That's not his character. Vince loved the sorry shit.

McDuff continued with the report as though he hadn't heard Max. "Things are still moving slow with registration. Only three hundred and sixty-eight ID cards were issued this week bringing the total for the province to eight thousand, six hundred and fifty-two, which leaves twelve thousand, three hundred and thirty-four still unregistered. At the present rate, it will take at least another year to complete the registration."

"What's the holdup?" Winters asked.

"Everything," McDuff said. "Corruption, lack of competent supervisors, too much red tape, a general lack of office facilities, a poor training program, recruitment of poorly qualified personnel, shortage of manpower, inadequate security throughout most of the province, low morale. You name it. If it's bad, the police force has got it."

The sweeping condemnation had startled not only Colonel Winters and Barban, but most of the others in the room. What he'd said didn't surprise anyone. Off-duty they were quick to admit that the South Vietnamese Government was a hopeless mess. However, officially they insisted that in spite of the difficulties, things were showing some improvement. To admit the truth officially was too demoralizing. To confess that their program or even a small portion of it was a failure meant that they had failed, and they didn't want that to go on record. It was like writing one's self a poor performance evaluation.

"Good man," Grecco muttered driving his fist into the palm of his hand. Three years on the *Chicago Tribune's* police beat hadn't left him with the most idealistic impression of cops; however, on the Vietnam scene, they'd assumed a much better image. Better at least than the bureaucrats and the military.

The Idiot's Frightful Laughter

There were other reports. Elmo Bledsoe gave the financial statement reeling off long lists of figures with such spit and polish that even the most professionally minded soldiers had to grin. However, they didn't resent him as they did Barban, for he'd served as a buck sergeant at the front for two years during the Korean War and earned a Bronze Star for leading a charge against a heavily fortified Chinese emplacement. Those were high kudos. He'd earned the right to behave like a soldier. Grecco could not understand why he wasn't Deputy Senior Advisor. He was superior to Barban in every way. Most likely racial prejudice, he assumed.

Reeling off long lists of statistic, Grecco ended his report by lambasting those who had napalmed the Son Thang Resettlement Camp. It was an impelling appeal for justice. It had been on his mind all week and had reached a boiling point. "Why in the hell are we here?" Vince demand waving his pointer about the room. "Is it our mission to indiscriminately incinerate innocent people? Is that why we are here? Is it? Where in the United States Constitution does it give us the right as Americans to roast others alive? Is it in our Bill of Rights? Our Declaration of Independence? Does the Geneva Convention provide us with this right? There are those among us who jokingly call it a Barbecue Run. Is it a joke? Is it funny? Is it fun to drop napalm on unsuspecting peasants; peasants who are under my care. My responsibility!" Grecco's gaze rested on the CIA Chief and his aides. They were staring at him with hooded-eyed wrath; looks of cold, sullen hate. He didn't care. He wanted retribution. "Is this how we represented that great nation of our, The United States of America? The greatest country on earth. There must be justice," he said jabbing his pointer accusingly about the room. "The culprits must be apprehended and punished. Punished to the fullest extent of the law."

What could anyone say? Everyone knew that nothing would be done. They had all known about it. They knew the rage Grecco felt. Few cared or even empathized. It happened every day somewhere in the country. If the Vietnamese officials didn't care, what business was it of theirs? Why should they bother? Barban had told him to cool off, to go soak his head in a bucket of shit.

Colonel Winters made the final address. He had a surprise for the troops. He reported that Retired General Clarence Corrigan, the new Deputy Commander for CORDS at IV Corps, would be making an inspection of province headquarters next week. CORDS was an acronym for Civil Operations & Revolutionary Development Support. Winters and the newly appointed Deputy Commander had been close friends when the general was the base commander at Fort Benning.

"He's quite a character," the Province Senior Advisor said smiling self-indulgently. "Very strict. Everything right by the book. One of the old school. No nonsense. A fine old soldier."

If it was the colonel's idea of how a commander should behave, why was he so lax when it came to military regulations? Vince wondered. Evidently, there were two Colonel Winters. One who sought to avoid controversy at all cost. The other who fantasized about being a tough fearless leader. Yen Bay Province's Walter Mitty, Grecco mused.

The army officers and noncoms responded with knowing nods and beaming smiles as Colonel Winters told of how the General had conducted inspections of the troops' quarters. "He'd stick one of his white gloves on a mop handle and rub it on the pipes behind the boiler or some such obscure spot checking for dust," he said. "Rarely did a unit pass his inspection without having at least a couple marks chalked up against it."

"Do any of you know what his nickname was at Fort Benning?" The Province Senior Advisor asked looking very pleased with himself. Several officers raised their hands. Winters nodded to Lieutenant Colonel Morris Palmer.

"He was known as 'Whitewash Corrigan', Sir," the Lieutenant Colonel said.

"Right!" Colonel Winters exclaimed beaming amiably about at everyone. "Whitewash Corrigan. Those of you who've been at Fort Benning may remember the coal bin just east of the old administration building. It has a long chute with high concrete sides that stand about this high from the ground." He held his hand about a meter from the floor. "During cold weather, they'd dump a truckload of coal down the chute every half hour or so. Every time the coal went down the chute, it was covered with grime. Well, General Corrigan had a detail standing by to whitewash the chute every time a load was dumped. Any hour of the day or night, you'd find a squad standing by with buckets of whitewash and brushes ready to turn to"

From the corner of his eye, Grecco caught Barban watching him. Vince had not laughed at the Colonel's anecdotes. Actually, he had sneered. It was most imprudent. Hank would surely tell Winters about it later. He would most likely say that Barban was not like the others. Did not have the proper attitude. That he should be replaced by someone more amiable. One who fit in better. A team player. One might imagine that the Deputy Senior Advisor had been a football coach, the way he was always telling someone to "get in there and carry the ball, pull together as a team, or show some team spirit. Grecco recalled how furious he'd made Barban when he'd said: "Sounds pretty Communistic to me. Giving the group more importance than the individual." Hank wasn't very good about taking a joke, especially when the joke was on him.

In spite of how absurdly childish Colonel Winters had made his old commander seem, it was evident to Vince that the soldiers seated about him greatly admired CORDS' new IV Corps Deputy Director. For them, Whitewash Corrigan was the tough old warrior whose petty antics were quite acceptable. They laughed about them as one might joke about the idiosyncrasies of a renowned scholar. The anomalies simply made Whitewash more human, more real. He had that common touch.

Grecco could well imagine what Whitewash Corrigan must look like – fierce, hawkish eyes, a mouth drawn down tight at the corners, a stiff erect posture, and a short, neatly trimmed crew cut. He was unimaginative, unwavering, intolerant, self-righteous, and opposed to any innovation proposed by a subordinate. A little Napoleon. Yes, little.

Grecco thought. He was probably short. A prototype of the little dictator. So, this was IV Corps' number one civilian potentate? A no-nonsense general who took an early retirement in protest to the desk jockeys' mollycoddling directives. If you fought a war, you fought to win. No holds barred. Drop the A-Bomb on Hanoi. That'd bring things to a screeching halt. That was the old war dog's philosophy. So now he was IV Corps' number one civilian chieftain? The one best qualified to understand the domestic needs of this war-ravaged land. It was always like this, Grecco figured. Either a master spy or a retired martinet. How distressingly ironic. The keystone of democracy, of political and social enlightenment. It was no wonder that the best-laid schemes of pacification experts at the national capital had crumbled into utter chaos, Vince thought.

"To show you just how human he is," Colonel Winters said, "he once signed a staff memo, 'Whitewash Corrigan'. I have a copy of it pasted in my scrapbook back at Fort Campbell." The Province Senior Advisor made no effort to disguise his pride at possessing such a coveted treasure.

Grecco could well imagine seeing the old general gloating over the effect the signature would so obviously have on his subordinates. His scowl contorted into a smug crafty smile. World leader. Designer of the nation's destiny. Vince felt ill. He could taste the bile burning in his throat. It was frightening. Such an absurd little man. Whitewash Corrigan was a child playing with lovely colored blocks. He hadn't the vaguest idea how to assist the millions of peasants that have inhabited this fertile delta rice bowl for the past two thousand years. He knew literally nothing of their culture, and that was obvious just how he liked it. Grecco shudder. To think, it was altogether possible for the American people to elect just such an imbecile as their president, or worse an older vainer Hank Barban.

Grecco thought of the bureaucrats whom he'd worked with at USAID headquarters in Saigon. They were so short-sighted, so content to flounder about doing meaningless tasks. He'd thought that things might be different in the field. Here they would have an aim, some objective; however, with the exception of Gutschinritter and Major Jack and possibly McDuff, he found the same bean counters spending the day tallying up their vacation time, sick leave, separate maintenance allowance, home leave, end-of-tour leave and all the other personal matters that bureaucrats are so preoccupied with.

"The general will be here a week from Tuesday," Colonel Winters said, and I think it's safe to assume that he's going to want a tour of all the facilities, and as some of you know from personal experience, there isn't much that escapes his attention." Widening his eyes and smiling smugly, the colonel gave the impression that he had let them in on something very extraordinary. "Hank's going to be in charge of things, so I expect you to coordinate any ideas you might have with him. You got anything you want to say, Hank?" he asked.

Barban flashed a radiant smile at the wall just above the men's heads. It was one of those that he practiced each morning before the mirror. He imagined that it had an electrifying effect on anyone caught in its path. He wore his khaki Jungle Jim suite; the kind big game hunters in Nairobi wore to impress their romantic-minded clientele. He stood there as though he was modeling for a fashion magazine. A civilian playing soldier. How that must gripe the soldier boys, Grecco thought.

"I want this inspection to be the best in IV Corps," Barban announced. The deadline for charts is noon Wednesday. When you've finished, leave them with my secretary. I want plastic overlays and at least three different colored grease pens, preferably red, yellow and black. The charts are the number one priority, so let's not have any excuses. Get started on them the first thing tomorrow morning."

"Ya all heard what Colonel Winters said about the Deputy Director of IV Corps," Barban continued, "so let's have everything shipshape. Furthermore," he added, "if there's anything hanging around on the wall that you don't think should be there, take it down." He thrust a fist above his head as though he were giving the Black Power Salute. "Men, let's make this the best inspection in

IV Corps. Let's show them who's got the best team." Then turning on the balls of his feet to face Winters, he asked: "Is there anything you wish to add, Sir?"

"Naw, I think you've covered everything, Hank," the colonel said. "We can go into more detail at the meeting Wednesday evening on just how it will be handled. In the meantime, let me repeat: if there are any problems, see Hank about them."

Barban was standing just outside the door as Grecco left the briefing room. "Vince, I want those charts at 1700 Wednesday," he ordered. Grecco pretended not to hear. As he went down the steps, Hank shouted: "1700 Wednesday." Barban was going to a lot of trouble to make him look incompetent. Was it a showdown? Was that what Hank wanted? Well, he'd taken just about all he could from the punk, Grecco figured. No job was worth this sort of crap.

Whitewash Corrigan

The evening before CORDS new Director of IV Corps was to visit Yen Bay Province, Hank Barban told Colonel Winters that no one was suitably prepared to brief Whitewash Corrigan, so he'd have to do it himself. However, he never bothered to inform his subordinates of the change. Each advisor was standing by his charts, pointer in hand preparing give his presentation when Barban would walk in followed by the great man and Colonel Winters. Taking the pointer from the advisor's hand, he'd brush him aside without a word of explanation, and proceed with the briefing. Colonel Winters was amused by the line of bullshit that his deputy was able to concoct on the spur of the moment. He wondered if the crusty old general suspected anything but assumed that he didn't. He was too absorbed in his own self-importance to notice that things were amiss.

Sensing what Hank had in mind, Grecco placed his pointer on the table beyond the coxcomb's reach. Just as Barban was about to edge him aside, Vince stepped forward placing himself between the charts and Hank. General Corrigan was so intent on displaying an image of the tough commander that he appeared quite oblivious to what was happening.

Whitewash Corrigan was just as Grecco had imagined him to be. His thick white hair was cut short and flat on top and very close to the skin on either side. His cheeks were deeply creviced like those of a bulldog. The eyes were intense but yet had no more life to them than a mannequin warrior's. There was no discernible meaning to their staged fierceness. Like the young popinjay, the old fraud had obviously practiced at it so lovingly each morning before his mirror, Grecco assumed. He could pass for his pal, Grant Olson's Uncle, Judge Edgar G. Hyde, the pompous old criminal judge. Chickenshit. That one word summed it all up so well, he thought. No other word fit the picture so well unless it was "asshole". A Chickenshit asshole. Yes, so apropos. Vince was pleased with his assessment.

Grecco could have carried the briefing off quite well if it hadn't been for Elmo Bledsoe. He grasped Vince by the shoulders and eased him aside. Then handed Barban the pointer. Grecco was so infuriated, he could barely keep from striking the bootlick.

That evening at supper, Elmo mentioned the incident. "Mr. Barban was sure mad at you, Vince. Couldn't you see that he wanted to give the briefing? The way he walked in and all, it was easy to see."

Grecco waited until he felt sure that he had his feeling under control. "Don't ever interfere like that again, Elmo," he said very softly and so quietly that he could hardly be heard at the other end of the table, but the tone left no doubt of how he felt.

"Sir, are there any questions?" Barban had asked once he'd finished. However, Whitewash had not been listening. A map of the province just to one side of the chart had caught his eye.

"Any VC in them mangrove along the coast?" he asked jabbing his swagger stick at the spot. Its bullet tip made tiny holes in the plastic overlay.

"Yes, Sir!" Barban said flashing his custom-made smile. "That's Viet Cong Country, Sir. We uncover bunkers there from time to time. We've been patrolling that area regularly, but rarely make any contact. Charlie only comes out at night, Sir. The mangroves are so thick you can step on top of them and not know it." Colonel Winters rolled his eyes at the ceiling. He was impressed with how Hank could manufacture such fiction on the spur of the moment. He's got a talent for bullshit, the Senior Advisor reckoned. A real talent.

Whitewash Corrigan nodded his head slowly stroking his chin. He looked as though he was pondering a very profound matter. "Is that a landing strip right in the middle of the swamp?" he asked tapping at it with his swagger stick.

"Yes Sir," Barban said, his smile resembling that of a villain in a melodrama. "That was built by the Japs during World War II.

The Idiot's Frightful Laughter

Used to make night raids on the U.S. fleet. However, only choppers can use it now."

"Is that a village to the left of the swamp, along the shore," the general wanted to know.

"That's an old French resort, Sir." Barban grew quite serious looking earnestly at the old commander. "The buildings are all demolished, Sir. Nothing left of it. However, at one time rich Frenchmen used to take their yachts there from Saigon for the weekend. I guess it was quite a place, Sir." Colonel Winters had to bite down hard on his tongue to keep from laughing. That boy's sure got a vivid imagination, he thought. How in hell does he come up with that horsecock?

So that's all the interest our number one civilian chieftain of the Mekong Delta has for the refugees, Grecco thought. An abandon Jap airstrip and a demolished French resort. A lot that has to do with winning hearts and minds.

Before leaving, Whitewash looked the room over, peering behind each desk and giving each occupant a long searching stare. Probably looking for expressions of adoration, Vince thought. Those simpletons will be remembered. "Them typewriters should be covered," he said turning to Barban.

"Yes Sir. That's right, Sir," Barban said gesturing to Bledsoe who began scurrying about looking in the most unlikely places for the nonexistent covers, afraid that the old general might suspect that there were no covers.

"It don't pay to be careless," the Director of IV Corps said. 'Things rust up fast in this here muggy climate." He looked about as though he were seeking confirmation for such an auspicious pronouncement.

"Yes Sir, they certainly do, Sir," Hank said with a look of great earnestness. Bledsoe nodded his head vigorously in assent.

"Toy soldiers," Grecco muttered into Major Jack's ear. But the major showed no reaction looking as though he had not heard. "Toy soldiers," he repeated this time to Air Force Sergeant Koffman. The airman's phlegmatic features broke into a large lusty smile.

Following Whitewash Corrigan from the room, Barban suddenly wheeled about and leaned down thrusting a finger beneath Lu Di's desk. A dozen or so tiny dots of paper made by a paper punch were scattered about on the floor. "Get them picked up," he ordered flashing a conspiratorial smile. Instantly Bledsoe was on his knees pinching them up.

"Toy soldiers," Sergeant Koffman said as the door closed. "Har, har, har, toy soldiers, har, har, har," He laughed jabbing Vince playfully in the ribs.

"Shuuu," Bledsoe cautioned waving a finger before his lips and then pointing to the door. "They might hear you."

Much to his dismay, Grecco found that beneath Elmo's sycophantic pretense lurked a black power militant. Bledsoe could be goddamn tough if there was no threat to his job security. He could be downright brutal.

It occurred late one Sunday afternoon. The two were in the living room of their bunkhouse playing cards when Grecco very casually mentioned how nice it would be to find a woman.

"You want a woman?" Bledsoe asked. "I'll show you one. You can meet my girl." Vince should have known better. The words "my girl" should have put him on his guard, but Grecco was not the cautious type.

It was downright cruel the way Elmo had set him up. Grecco couldn't figure it out. He'd never crossed the man. Not in the slightest. They'd always been on friendly terms except for that matter of briefing old General Whitewash, and that shouldn't have been anything to worry about. Vince had assumed that Bledsoe's girl would introduce him to a friend of hers. In afterthought, Grecco reckoned that Bledsoe may have once been a pimp for his rich college pals, and this had always rankled him. Vince's suggestion had quite possibly triggered those painful memories.

The woman in question was Mms Nhieu. She was one of the clerks at the compound. A very quiet person who rarely spoke to anyone. She sat at her desk all day; her face hidden behind a straw hat, calculating figure on her abacus. Nothing more than the most perfunctory sorts of greetings ever passed between her and Grecco.

The Idiot's Frightful Laughter

He guessed that she was probably in her early forties, very likely married and probably had children. She had a tired look, and Vince assumed that she might not be well. Being Bledsoe's lover would never have crossed his mind. He wondered if she'd been coerced into it. That Bledsoe had taken a cue from his boss. To the victor goes the spoils sort of attitude.

Bledsoe barged unannounced into her tiny room at the rear of an old ramshackle building. She was seated cross-legged on a reed mat reading a magazine. The room had no furniture. Just a bare floor. Some clothing hung on the wall, and a few utensils and a charcoal burner had been shoved into a corner. Ms. Nhieu's face turned crimson when Grecco stepped inside.

"He's looking for a woman," Bledsoe said gruffly standing over her, his hands on his hips. He looked as though he was very angry about something. He seemed to want to prove something either to her or to Vince or simply to light skinned people in general.

"I'm so sorry," she said looking beseechingly up at Grecco. "Please forgive me." He assumed that she was apologizing for Bledsoe's very rude behavior. But then perhaps she was begging his apology for the bad light that Bledsoe had cast her in.

Grecco saw Bledsoe as never before. His true character had emerged. A man to be reckoned with. The step-and-fetch-it routine was more than a cover. It was too deeply etched into the subconscious to be a calculated maneuver. Elmo was bipolar, but it was not a genetic malady. It was a conditioning. The bourgeois community he'd grown up in had pounded it into him as a child. Then the army had reinforced this duplicity. Never question your superiors even if they're a piece of shit like Barban. They are the law.

As a sergeant in Korea, Sergeant Bledsoe took his wrath out on the white recruits under his command especially the white trash from the Deep South. How he liked to see them squirm. It was sweet revenge.

Instinctively, Elmo shifted from one personality to the other. Grecco was on his way out. He was of no threat. Anything Vince might say against him would only strengthen his ties with Barban. The more he alienated himself from Grecco, the more secure his position would be. After all, Barban was the man, and one must kowtow to the man. That was all that concerned him. Nothing else mattered. Fuck these mothafucking honkies.

Grecco realized that Bledsoe was every bit as bad as Barban. He wanted to humiliate Ms. Nhieu. Make her more pliable and submissive. Nothing on earth would stop him from getting what he wanted. He'd sell a black brother down the proverbial river if it was to his advantage to do so. He knew where Vince stood on Civil Rights, and yet he chose to side with a blatant bigot. A peckerwood who'd do everything in his power to hold the black man down.

"You want him?" Bledsoe said smirking at his mistress. "Then take him." Turning to Grecco, he said: "You wanted a woman. Well, here she is. Go to it." Then Bledsoe left heading hurriedly down a narrow path that led to the town's main street.

For an instant, the two looked at one another in utter disbelief. "No, no, no," Grecco said shaking his head in bewilderment. He had never felt so mortified. Then he burst from the room running after Elmo. "Goddamn you," he shouted grabbing Bledsoe by the shoulder and spinning him about. "You cheap sonofabitch." The two stood eyeing each other for several moments. Vince was trembling so hard with fury, he was momentarily incapacitated.

"Cool it, man," Bledsoe said. He could see that Grecco was craving for a fight. He hadn't anticipated such a violent reaction. The dude was one crazy cat, he thought. A fight was the last thing he wanted. The whole sordid episode would be brought out in the open. It would not look good for him to get in a street fight. It would obviously appear to be over a piece of ass. Not even a good one at that. "Cool it, man. I was only jazzing you, ha, ha, ha," he laughed mirthlessly reaching out to give Vince a reassuring shake on the shoulder. Grecco spun away and walked off. "No hard feelings," Elmo shouted after him. "Still friends, okay?" He shook his head theatrically like a burlesque clown. Then he headed back in the direction of Miss Nhieu's quarters.

Friday Night Poker Game

It was at the Friday night poker games that Grecco learned what the troops were up to, or more specifically what the guys at OCCO, one of the many acronyms for the Central Intelligence Agency, were pulling off. The game was the high point of the week at Yen Chau. It was held in the rec room of Blaine Bruce's humble abode, a two-story, four-bedroom French villa and was restricted to officers and civilians with either FS or GS ratings of five and above. Miss just one time without a good excuse and your name was scratched. It was an unwritten rule to notify Bruce at least three days beforehand. The CIA chief wasn't beholden to anyone, not even the Province Senior Advisor. He did what he damn well pleased.

Bruce always had a case of Wild Turkey and barbecued steak on hand. They were the compliments of his pals at the Cholon Commissary. In return, the agency agreed not to interfere with their multimillion-dollar black market operation. It was a case of scratching one another's back, so to speak. However, in this case, "black market" was a euphemism for wholesale robbery.

The only Vietnamese present was Blaine's old pal, Colonel Tran Van Kha. The two had met in '64 at Fort Benning's School of the Americas, where the colonel taught methods of interrogation. His lectures were supplemented with Nazi training films with English subheadings. Kha and Bruce were great admirers of Hitler's Gestapo. They were the experts.

During the '50's and early '60's, the colonel served as a sergeant for the French Foreign Legion at Con Son Island, which was then a French Penal Colony in the South China Sea. He was in charge of the prison's torture chambers. Years later U.S. contractors would build the notorious "Tiger Cages" at the facility. The idea had long been a dream of Tran Van Kha.

Colonel Kha had loved his job. He took pride in extracting information from his prisoners. Those who didn't cooperate died a slow, agonizing death. The bodies were fed to tiger sharks that hung out at the cove at the opposite side of the island. If a visitor became too inquisitive, the prison commander would ask Kha to take the guest for a swim. He would urge the visitor to dive from a rock where the bodies were thrown to the sharks. He would disappear without a trace. "It was most regrettable," the Warden would tell those at the Saigon office. "I had no idea that he intended to swim there. It's dangerous, you know?"

If Grecco had not been told, he would have never imagined what a hideous monster Kha was, for he was one of the most amiable people Vince had ever met. The Colonel was a large robust man who appeared to be of Cambodian origin. Shave his head and put a saffron robe on him, and he'd easily pass for a Buddhist monk. His features were soft and blithe. Grecco could see that he and Bruce enjoyed one another's company.

Two of a kind, he thought. So erudite.

Colonel Kha was in command of the interrogation center adjacent to the province airfield. The buildings looked as though they had once been enlisted men's barracks. The complex was surrounded by a high wall of Ferro-concrete blocks crowned with strands of barbwire. Unlike the other military sites, it had neither sentries nor watchtowers. It was a CIA domain, and outsiders were not welcome. A half dozen Arvin did the softening up, and the Americans, the interrogating. Once they had gleaned as much as they could from a captive, he was thrown from the unit's white with blue trimming helicopter at three or four thousand feet into the South China Sea, or at an island in one of the Mekong River's many tributaries. Bruce referred to it as "making the bombing run". He dubbed himself the bombardier and insisted on doing the spotting.

The CIA Chief and the other interrogators were in awe of their Viet Cong captives and were quick to admit that they themselves could not endure such pain. However, they had found that humiliation was more effective. The Vietnamese were a proud people. They had been conditioned from early childhood to endure pain, but they had no defense against insult. If humiliated, they were taught that they must revenge themselves at all cost. Such abuse broke the captive's will. Made them vulnerable. Whereas the worst sorts of torture failed.

By ten that night, Bruce and Kha were both drunk. "Drowned in his own shit," Bruce said with a chuckle winking roguishly at Kha. The CIA Chief had a law degree from Yale and spoke with the gentility of a Back Bay Boston Brahmin. "You can't get much tougher than that," he added. Blaine loved his job. He couldn't imagine doing anything else. His only fear was that the war would end. What would he do then? He'd probably be sent to some horrid place like Saudi Arabia or Yemen and pretend to be a librarian at some American Culture Center checking out *Moby Dick* and *The Scarlet Letter* to the ragheads.

"Yes," the colonel said raising his eyebrows and nodding sagely, "The captain was, should we say, a true warrior." Kha had the soft melodic accent of the French aristocracy.

"Here's to Captain Bey," Bruce said raising his glass of whiskey. "May the fish have a good feast." He laughed loudly spilling liquor on his cards that lay spread out before him. "Shit," he said daubing them with his shirt sleeve. "Fuck a dirty fucking duck."

"You speak like an enlisted man," Colonel Kha said glaring at his friend with mock disdain.

"Better than talking like a goddamn frog," Burl McDuff, the Province Police Advisor, said.

"The French have a gentility that you Yanks would do well to emulate," Kha retorted bringing the corners of his mouth down in a smug reprimand.

"What's this about drowning in your own shit?" Major Makhilovich asked.

Bruce wagged a finger at the major. "It's a secret," he said in a stage whisper. "Big, big secret."

"We're among friends," Colonel Kha retorted. "Why not tell them?"

"I'm not sure of Vince," Bruce said looking quizzically at Grecco. "He doesn't like our little war. Do you, Vince?"

Grecco smiled disparagingly. What could he say to such a gang of warmongers? That yes, of course, he thought that mass murder, rape, and plunder were just great. A true test of manhood. Is that what the gentlemen wanted? "My lips are sealed," he said.

"They better damn well be," Lieutenant Berry Lafarge, the Air Force Forward Observer, said thrusting a finger at Grecco. "Or you'll find yourself floating face down in the Mekong River. I clue you not."

Everyone laughed. Ordinarily Lafarge was so shy; however just give him a few drinks, and he was a real bulldog.

"Easy Berry," Bruce said holding up his hand. "Remember what the colonel said. "We're among friends. Right, Kha?"

"Yes," Tran Van Kha replied. "No fighting in the ranks. United we stand," he added. Rising to his feet, he raised his glass and bending forward clinked glasses with each in turn. "Stand together through thick and thin," he said smiling reassuringly at Grecco. "No hard feelings, I'm sure, Vince," he asked sounding so deeply sincere.

"None whatsoever," Grecco said halfheartedly. You big fraud, he thought. How hypocritical can one get?

"You tell them, Kha," Bruce said. "You're the mastermind."

"No, no, no," the colonel said shaking his head in a slow methodical manner. "English is your mother tongue, Blaine. You are so much more articulate. In French, I am the master, but in English, I am like a pig in a pile of shit."

"Well, if you insist," the CIA Chief stretching back in his chair and clasping his hands behind his head. "I must say though that all the credit goes to Colonel Kha. He is an expert when it comes to the finer art of inquisition," Bruce added. "He has no rivals."

The colonel beamed. They could all see that he was truly touched.

"Well, actually the procedure is quite simple," Bruce said. "All one needs is a bucket of shit, a rope, and a pulley. The pulley is attached to the ceiling and a rope is threaded through it. The bucket

The Idiot's Frightful Laughter

of shit is kept in a warm moist place for a few days until it is literally swarming with maggots. Thousands of them. One has to stuff cotton up one's nose, for the smell will gag you." He glanced about the table. He could see that Maynard Whiteside, the USIS Chief, was turning green. Billie Joe Webber, the agriculture advisor, was the only one who seemed quite at ease; as though Bruce were discussing something as mundane as the distribution of food to the war victims.

"Well, you take a captive. Strip him bare and tie one end of the rope securely to his ankles" Bruce looked about to see if everyone was following him. Are you with us, Vince?" he asked.

Grecco seemed to be shaken out of a reverie. "Yea, yea, sure," he said. "No problem Blaine." The CIA Chief nodded his head towards Vince. A smile of weary disdain brought laughter from the others. It was as though he was saying: "Don't mind him. He doesn't know any better."

"Well you hoist him three or four feet off the floor and slip the bucket of well-ripened shit beneath his head," Bruce said. "You let him hang there for a while. Give him time to savor the delicacy we'd concocted for him. Which will it be? Drowning in a bucket of shit teeming with maggots or thrown from a helicopter? I know what I'd choose," he said. "Wouldn't you Kha? The Colonel and the spy chief laughed loudly. The others all sat stone still. There wasn't a murmur from any of them.

"Well, if he's hardcore VC, he'll take the shit and drown. The maggots will bury into his eyes and ears and crawl up his nose and into his mouth and down his throat, and he won't make so much as a wiggle." Bruce looked about at the others. There was not a stir. The graphic description had left a lasting image on their mind. They could imagine themselves in the same situation. The thought left them spellbound. Transfixed by the vileness of it. Suddenly Whiteside sprang to his feet knocking over his chair and bounded for the toilet. They could hear him retching. It broke the spell. They began to laugh self-consciously. The laughter brought tears to their eyes and their noses ran. Captain Mendez excused himself. He glanced nervously at his watch and said that he had a very important appointment.

"Hey, Percy, what sort of an appointment do you have at this hour? It's past midnight," Captain Burk asked. "She's probably found somebody else by now." Everyone laughed.

Whiteside came back to the table. He was white-faced and crestfallen. "I guess I drank too much booze," he said. It was funny, for he was the advisory teams' biggest lush.

"As long as we're on the subject," Colonel Kha said. "Why don't you tell them about the VC women? That should liven things up."

"Yea! yea! Right on, Kha," Bruce said thumping his glass on the table. "We kept running out of fresh ones until Sergeant Dzu came up with the plan to stage raids on hamlets in VC controlled areas. We have a squad of Rangers that does nothing else. They're our specialists. Their specialty is finding nice young cunt."

"Yes, they get the best. Twelve to fifteen years of age are very nice," the colonel said holding his thumb and forefinger a half inch apart. "Very tight pussy."

"But Sergeant Nghe has got to go," said the CIA Chief.

"I fire him tomorrow," Colonel Kha said. "I bust him to buck private. I was so patient. I talked to him many times about fucking the girls. Did he listen? Never. The French know how to take care of rouges like that. They'd back him up against a wall and shoot him."

"Good idea," Said Bruce. "I'll take it up with Bill Colby the next time I'm in Saigon."

"Never mind, Colby. I do it myself. Coup de grace," Kha said forming his fingers into the shape of a pistol and pointing it at the base of Grecco's skull. "Bang! One shot. All finished. No time wasted on Colby. As they say: 'What he doesn't know, won't hurt him.'"

"What exactly did the sergeant do to deserve a summary execution?" Major Jack asked. "It seems a bit severe."

"Insubordination," Kha said bringing the flat of his hand down on the table so hard, it sent his cards flying in all directions. "I told him time and time again, but did he heed my command? Never! There is a limit to just how much a commander can take."

"You see, it's like this," Bruce said. Sergeant Nghe and his men pick up three or four girls and keep them out the bush for three or four days." The heads began to nod in assent about the table. "You see what Kha is up against? The whole squad fucks them until their cunts are all torn and bleeding. It ruins everything. What's left for us?" he added pointing to the colonel and himself. "Nothing that either of us wants."

"Hey! When do we get some of this good stuff?" Captain Burk asked. "How about passing it around?"

"Yea, ha, ha, Hanks always hanging around when we get some fresh meat in."

Bruce said. "He's got a nose for pussy."

"Where's that shit for brains, now?" McDuff asked.

"Mr. Barban's in Hawaii with his wife on home leave," Whiteside said nodding very solemnly to everyone as if what he was saying was of utmost significance.

"I thought the State Department gave him a big villa with a swimming pool in Bangkok?" Lafarge said.

"They did," Bruce said, "but Hank's got pull at the Little Pentagon at Tan Son

Nhut. He's a wheeler and dealer, that boy is."

"I just hope that I run into that snot nose punk up some dark alley when I'm on beat with the LAPD," McDuff said. "That's my fondest dream."

"I wish you well," Captain Burk said giving him the thumbs up.

"So does everyone else," Major Makhilovich said. "He doesn't have a friend on the team."

"Oh, I wouldn't say that," Bruce said looking quizzically at Grecco. "You and he are great pals. Right, Vince?" Everyone laughed, for no one hated Barban more than he. And one might say the same for Hank.

"Tsk, tsk, he's still wet behind the ears," Colonel Kha said smiling consolingly. "Give the boy a little more time. He'll grow out of it."

Fire in the Hole

The refugee camp at Gia Hoa wasn't quite what Grecco expected. It was different from the ones he'd seen as a correspondent near the DMZ in I Corps. It was not enclosed with thick webs of barbwire and rows of pointed bamboo stakes. There were no watchtowers nor mud fortifications. Nothing separated it from the miles of rice paddies encircling it. It was unusual. Gutschinritter had insisted on it. His rationale was that if they wanted to leave, let them. If they returned to where their hamlets once were, they'd be shot. Proof as far as he was concerned that they pro-Communists. Better dead than red.

The camp amounted to two long rows of tiny thatched huts bordering either side of a dusty dirt road. Near the entranceway was a marketplace. It amounted to a large sheet-metal roof supported by slender concrete posts. It was deserted. There was no sign of food. Nothing whatsoever to sell. There was also a two-room schoolhouse built of scrap lumber and an adobe clinic. They were also empty. None of the structures looked as though they had ever been used. Evidently set up by the previous refugee advisor. The thatched shacks were about ten by fifteen foot in size. The palm frond was old and needed to be replaced. It looked as though it had been there since the camp was built over four years ago.

What alarmed Grecco most of all was how very quiet the people were. They squatted in their doorways staring at him with dull lifeless expressions. At the sight of an American, Vietnamese children usually ran after him shouting: "Okay, okay, you numba one. Gib me candy." If there was no candy, they'd chant: "O'kay, you numba ten. Fuck you GI." But these kids didn't budge from their doorways. They were as still and lifeless as their parents.

Where were the vegetable gardens? Grecco wondered. Usually, there were patches of taro and yams and a pig or two and some chickens scurrying in and out of the huts. But there was nothing. There weren't even any altars to the household God set before the entranceway. It's traditional for the Vietnamese peasant to have a simple shrine consisting of a board secured to the top of a bamboo post. A can or clay pot of sand was set on the board. At sunrise and sunset, joss sticks were stuck in the sand and lit. Offerings of food and cups of tea were made at least once a month. However, not a single home had an altar. Instead, heaps of trash littered the yards. No ancestors frequented this camp. It was a home of the living dead.

"See what I told you?" Major Marcelino, the district's Senior Advisor, murmured as he followed Grecco about the camp. "They have nothing," He was a tall, slender man with a lean lined face. He looked more like a farmer than a soldier. "They don't give them a thing. Stole it all," he said pointing at his Vietnamese counterpart, Major Coung, the District Chief and his three aids seated in a jeep. The soft sweet voice of a Vietnamese vocalist came from a radio lying in the chief's lap. She was singing a sad lament full of heartbreak and despair. The music added an eeriness to the camp of silent sullen captives.

"You tell them in Saigon what I said," Marcelino murmured as though afraid Coung might hear. "Tell them about the roofing and cement. All stolen. Tell them I'll show them where it is. That piece of pig shit used it to build his home," the Major added motioning to the District Chief. "Two hundred and sixty sacks of cement and three hundred sheets of roofing. Bring them here, and I'll show them the mothafucker's house."

Grecco peered inside one of the shacks. There was nothing there. Nothing but a couple of straw mats and a pit rimmed with a few stones for cooking. In one corner was an earthen mound. "Why the bunker?" Vince asked. "The Viet Cong has been shelling the camp."

"Fuck no," Marcelino said. "Why'd they shell a refugee camp? They got more important targets than this."

"Then why the bunkers?" Grecco asked squatting down to see inside the shelter. It was about five foot long and had a diameter of three feet. Hardly adequate for the man, his wife, and three children.

The Senior District Advisor looked as though he'd just swallowed a piece of shit. "Whenever that fat, slimy cocksucker gets tight, he and his pals drop a round or two in here. The next day the sonsabitches make these people clean up the mess."

"No shit?" Grecco said. "Did you report it?"

"Sure," Marcelino said shrugging his shoulders, "but what good's it do? That turd always gives the same excuse. There was a platoon of VC in camp."

"Was there?" Vince asked.

"Are you shitting me?" the Major said with a smirk. "Hah! How would they know who's out here? They're so stoned, they couldn't find their ass with both hands behind them."

"Anyone ever get hurt?" Grecco asked. He was standing stock-still and looking at the District Senior Advisor with rapt attention.

"Plenty," Marcelino said. "Made a direct hit a couple weeks ago. See that spot over there?" He said pointing to a bare patch of earth between to huts. "Scored a direct hit. Blew a family of six to pieces. Next day the bastards came out and made their neighbors fill in the crater."

Grecco walked over to the spot. There was no sign of anything. Just bare level ground. "Where're the bodies?" he asked.

"The pieces you mean? They're in there," The District Senior Advisor said pointing at the earth. "Everything was pushed into the hole and covered over."

Grecco felt as though a huge fist had taken hold of his stomach and was squeezing. No doubt Major Coung had blamed it all on the Americans, he thought. Probably told the refugees that he had been ordered to do it. That was standard procedure. Well, what more could you expect? No matter how one looks at it, we're accomplices. We chose this band of cutthroats. They didn't choose us. They've never tried to disguise the fact that they're anything more than unscrupulous opportunists. If we choose to be deaf, dumb and blind about it, it's not their fault, not in the least. There are good men in Vietnam – patriots. We could just as well have chosen to work with them. Why must we always side with the outlaws? Gangsters like: Marcos, Batista, Jimenez, Somoza, Noriega, Duvalier, Pinochet, Chiang Kai-shek? Why? "Does Colonel Winters know about this?" he asked.

"Sure, they all know," Marcelino said. "Surprised they didn't tell you."

"They don't tell me nothing," Vince said turning away and kicking at the earth. "I'm not on the team."

"What are you going to do about it?" Marcelino asked.

"Tell Saigon," Grecco replied. "Maybe send a copy to Ted Kennedy."

"Ted Kennedy! That Fink! You're shitting me?"

"Who else has shown the interest in the refugees that he has?"

"He don't give one tinker's damn," Marcelino said. "That's all politics. Same with Jane Fonda and Joan Biaz. Fucking publicity is all they're after."

Grecco walked off to a corner of the camp. He was getting tired of Marcelino. He could take a guy like that only in small doses. He'd already got a heavy saturation. Besides he wanted to think over what he'd seen and what the Major had told him. Something had to be done quickly, but just what, he did not know.

He unconsciously watched a woman picking lice from her daughter's hair and then crushing the parasites between her thumbnails. Why did they stay here? he wondered. It would be better to take one's chances in a free-fire zone. But then they had nothing to return to. Their hamlets had been burned and bulldozed off the face of the earth – ancestral tombs, coconut palms, clumps of bamboo – everything. And why had we done it? Because the hamlets had the misfortune of being situated near a VC supply route.

Grecco studied Major Coung's large bulk hunched over in the seat of the Jeep. He had never seen such a huge Vietnamese. Must be of Cambodian descent. But it wasn't likely that he'd admit it, Vince thought. He was Charlie's greatest asset.

Getting the District Chief to do something for these pitiful people wouldn't be easy. It was too late to get the roofing and

The Idiot's Frightful Laughter

cement for them. No amount of persuasion could get this barbarian to tear down his new house. And the food? That had no doubt been sold and eaten by now. As for the money, it was probably in a numbered account in some Swiss Bank. Four years is a long time. But the School building and the clinic? They had been built. Why couldn't they be used? What objection could the bastard have to that?

Major Coung didn't look up when Grecco spoke to him about the school and the clinic. His eyes were fixed on the radio lying in his lap. A thick roll of fat hung over his stiff military collar. "These people are Communists," the chief said. "Bringing them here hasn't changed them."

"Obviously not," Grecco said. "Why should it have? What has been done to win their respect?"

Major Coung stared at Grecco for an instant. The Chief's eye's told Vince nothing; however, he sensed that he had angered him.

"I would like the children taught something," he said studying the dials on his radio. "I want them to be taught to hate Communism. I'd also like them to have military training."

Grecco looked at the flat phlegmatic face. The eyes were a dull muddy color. "Sure, but all that comes later," Vince said. "Before you can get one to hate your enemies, you must first get him to like you. That is done by keeping the promises that no doubt were once made to these people."

Grecco saw the Cu Cat District Chief's jaw muscles tighten. Let him be angry, he thought. The fucking thief. It's time someone put him straight. "These people were promised that their children would be allowed to attend school. That was one of the promises. Another was that they would have medical care. There were other promises, but these two are no doubt most important to them."

"Who made these promises?" Major Coung asked smirking at Grecco. "I don't recall making such promises."

"Your government," Grecco said looking intently into the chief's mud-colored eyes. "The Republic of South Vietnam."

"No," he said. His smirk had spread into a cruel sneer. "Your government. I believe you call it Psyops?"

"What do you call it?" Grecco asked, his eyebrows raised in mock wonder.

"Nonsense," the chief replied smiling smugly at his two aides that understood some English. "Or as Major Marcelino would say: 'bullshit'." He smiled nodding at his counterpart who was scuffing intently at a tuff of grass with the toe of his boot. "Isn't that right, Major?" Marcelino pretended not to hear.

Hate Communism? Grecco shook his head. What did these poor peasants know or even care about Communism? About Karl Marx's Labor Theory of Value or his Historic Dialectics? All they wanted was to be left alone. That's why they were fighting. They were at war with the landlord and the tax collector and with Major Cuong. Yes, especially Major Cuong with his private garrison of soldiers whose kind had robbed and plundered the peasants for centuries.

And what about us Americans who speak in great glittering terms of liberty and freedom; democracy and equality? What are we doing? Yes, that's a good question. Making sure that thugs like Major Cuong and his cohorts stay in power. Is that what it's really all about? Grecco suspected that perhaps it was.

But why? Vince asked himself. So, the peasants, hundreds of thousands of them just like these refugees, can be trampled on? Is that what we are saving them from Communism for? Or isn't it all just a feeble joke? A cover that the host spreads over something that he doesn't want his guests to see? Are we Americans really interested in the fate of the Vietnamese peasants? Actually, isn't it a power struggle with China or more subtly Japan? Aren't the Vietnamese merely pawns? Isn't that what it's really all about?

On the way back to the District Office, Grecco thought of another resettlement camp that he'd visited just a month before. An elderly woman with lacquered teeth had invited him into her hut for a cup of tea. While he was sitting at the table that looked as though it would collapse at any moment, an elderly man stood very stiff and erect nearby. His thick white hair was combed carefully back in a pompadour. He had a long, neatly trimmed goatee. For a moment, Vince imagined that Ho Chi Minh was paying him a visit.

The Idiot's Frightful Laughter

There was a marked resemblance to the venerable old patriarch. However, this man was strong and burly. There was a sort of Napoleonic aura about him. One might imagine that he had just stepped off a movie set. Although small in stature, it was evident to Grecco that the man was a leader. It was easy to visualize him as the commander of a guerrilla brigade.

Grecco could not tell if he was angry or afraid, but he sensed that it was some of both. He spoke rapidly from time to time glancing nervously at the doorway behind him.

"We have received nothing. None of the things we were promised," he said.

Grecco was surprised at how earnestly his interpreter translated the old man's appeal. Ordinarily, an interpreter would have driven him off. "Go away old bitch full of fleas. The American doesn't care about your problems," one had once shouted at an old peasant woman. The interpreter then told Vince with a smile that she wanted medicine for a headache, and he had told her that they were not medics. However, Grecco was beginning to pick up the general gist of the language and knew that she was complaining about the water. It was brackish and could not be drunk."

"Let's have a look at the water," Vince had replied mimicking the interpreter's Giaconda smile.

However, on this occasion, the interpreter seemed to be making a very serious effort to convey the old gentleman's message as honestly as possible. Perhaps he suspects that I know some Vietnamese, Grecco thought. But then it may be because of the old man's bearing.

"We were promised resettlement payments. Where are they?" He looked firmly into Grecco's eyes. "We were promised subsistence allowances for sixty days. Where is it?" he demanded. "Where is the cooking oil, the Bulgur wheat, the corn flour, the white oats? Where are these things?"

Vince clasped his hands before his chest as though in prayer and bowed. "Sin loi. I'm sorry," he said.

The old man stared at Grecco for some time as though he was in deep thought. Finally, he said: "Sometime ago another

American, a very young man, came here and told us that our supplies were in the district warehouse. Our money was in the province safe." His eyes grew large. More intent. Two Arvin soldiers who'd entered the hut and sat at the table with Vince began to move their stools about and mutter to one another. Supposedly they had been assigned to guard Grecco. However, that was their secondary task. Their main job was to keep people like the old man from speaking with him.

"Later the young American returned," the old man said. "He told us that the provisions and money had vanished. He did not know what had happened to them."

Grecco only shook his head. What was there to say? What could be done?

The old gentleman spoke of his hamlet. He was its chief as his father had been before him and his grandfather before that. The lineage went back hundreds of years. The village was separated by a wide canal. A narrow suspension bridge connected the two sides. It was a prosperous community. Most of the homes were made of lumber with red tile roofs. Each family had a garden with mangos and bananas and areca palms. The soil was rich and plentiful. Unlike those in the neighboring villages, the people owned their own land. They were not troubled by absentee landlords. The ancestral tombs were as large and ornamental as any in the delta, and they had one of the most beautiful Buddhist temples in the province.

"Now," he said his eyes flaring out at Grecco, "there is nothing left." He told of how the Arvin troops had made a sweep through the village driving the people before them like pigs, shooting those unable or unwilling to leave. Looting and burning all that was left.

"Recently," the old man said, "some had slipped back to where the village had once been. They could find nothing, but the bridge that had once joined the two halves of the town." He was talking slower. The way people sometimes talk in their sleep. There was a sort of haunting hollowness to the tone. He explained that the site was now smooth and bare. Large tractors had dug trenches back and forth across the ground. Then they had shoved all the debris into the ditches and filled them in.

Later Grecco had asked Captain Percy Mendez, the Team's Intelligent Officer at Province Headquarters, about the trenches. "Tunnels," he'd said. "Underground rooms the size of soccer stadiums. Never can tell what you might find under one of them villages," Mendez added. "Might be an arsenal, hospital, weapons factory. Damn near anything."

"Had they found anything?" Grecco asked.

"No, not this time," the captain said. "But there's only one way to make sure.

Tear the shit out of the place. Then you know."

The former village chief had stopped talking. He hadn't said anything for several minutes; however, he stood very stiff and erect. Grecco wished to ask him to relax. To have a seat. But he wasn't quite sure how he would take the offer. Perhaps his stiff defiant posture was the old gentleman's way of assuring his people that in spite of what anyone might say, he was still their chief.

Grecco wasn't sure quite what to do; He could see that the old man wanted some assurance that justice would prevail. Justice? My god, here was Dostoyevsky's Prince Myshkin, Vince thought. That Russian aristocrat here on this desolate mound of earth in the midst of a vast sea of reeds; an aggroville initially settled in the 1950's by transplanting Catholics from the North. This idealist standing up for probity, rectitude, candor, honesty. This white-haired village chief in shiny black pajamas; the honest man in a dishonest world. After all the outrage that he and his people had suffered at the hands of these bandits, he still believes that justice would prevail. That good would triumph. A saint, Vince thought. Every bit as marvelous as Mahatma Gandhi and Nelson Mandela.

But then who would ever know? Grecco studied the village chief's seraphic bearing and felt the furor swell within him. How many such unknown heroes have been on this earth? He wondered. Thousands, perhaps millions. More than Vince could possibly imagine.

If he could do nothing more, Grecco thought, he could at least be honest with this brave little man. There must not be any more idle promises. He glanced at the two soldiers seated beside him. They were glaring bitterly at the frail old man. Their mouths twisted in sinister grimaces. Perhaps they had been among those who had driven him and his people from their homes? In any case, they would surely tell the district chief what he had said.

The old man's frankness troubled Grecco. He felt anxious about his wellbeing. His life could well be in grave danger. The two soldiers were so hostile. They appeared quite willing and able of killing him. It was a very plausible possibility, and it was all his fault. If he were a murderer, Vince could blame no one but himself. He had set the whole thing up. He never thought. That was his big problem. No foresight. It was a serious failing especially when a man's life was at stake. A very good man.

Grecco suddenly felt very tired. The hopelessness of all that he had seen and done for the past several months had quite overwhelmed him. Why had the old gentleman been so courageous? After all that he had been through, he was still so committed to his people. Was he doing this because of the trust they'd placed in him? Would place in anyone they might choose as their leader? Did he think that after all that had happened, any good might come of this? It was so foolhardy. Tomorrow his people might be looking about for new leader. This good honest man shot through the head, and the murder blamed on the Viet Cong. Always the Viet Cong. Charlie made such a convenient scapegoat.

Courage such as this troubled Grecco. He felt ashamed, for unwittingly he was to blame for this good man's pending doom, and there was no way that he could save him. Who in Saigon would care? "This is Asia," they would chant. "That's the way things are in Asia." They had told themselves this so many times that they no doubt believed it by now.

It was nearly a month before Grecco visited the camp again. No one seemed to know what had happened to their chief. He had vanished the night following Vince's visit. The District Chief said that he must have run off with the VC. His smile was smug and

The Idiot's Frightful Laughter

sinister. It was an expression that Grecco had seen all too often. It said so much.

Back at the District office, Grecco asked Major Coung if he could have a look in the government warehouse. The District Chief said nothing. Handing a key to an Arvin sergeant, he told him to show Vince the warehouse. The large corrugated steel building was more than half full of machinery – outboard motors, mobile generators, diesel pumps, etc. All stamped with the U.S.'s foreign aid symbol, two hands clasped together above a crest of the American flag. However, there was no sign of any refugee relief supplies. "No stay long," the sergeant said. "Three, four days then go."

That evening, Major Cuong had a party, and Grecco was the guest of honor. The food was as good as anything he had ever eaten – shrimp, crab, fish soup, pork and a dozen bottles of fine French Cognac. Vince wondered as he ate the shrimp and pork if they'd been fried with the refugees' cooking oil. He knew that, of course, they had.

That night Grecco dreamt of an incident he'd witness years before in India while on a special assignment for the Associated Press. It had occurred one morning while he was taking his usual walk before breakfast. He had not gone far when he saw a group of people dancing about a clump of bamboo waving sticks and throwing stones. Drawing closer, he saw that there were several dozen monkeys jumping about some thirty feet above.

It is a serious crime for a Hindu to kill a monkey, for like the cow, it is considered sacred. However, there is no law against abusing or even seriously crippling the poor sacred creature. As long as it didn't die, no sin was committed.

All morning Grecco had watched the monkey gods being driven from one field to another, and he imagined that this must go on eternally; that nowhere would they find safety. They would always be on the run; then his dream suddenly changed. No longer were monkeys scampering across rice paddies. They had become Vietnamese peasants. The refugees whom he had seen that day.

And the assailants were Major Coung and his soldiers. The stones had changed to hand grenades; the sticks, rifles.

Grecco awoke trembling. He imagined that a spirit was telling him something. He had no use for organized religion. Its history was one of murder and mayhem. However, he did believe in some sort of divine order. The idea that such a complex organism as the human body could come about by chance seemed absurd, Things like life, thought, reproduction, sense, perception, were miracles to him. He was sure that the most eminent scientists hadn't the vaguest inkling of how to create them. No one could create a living cell from dead matter. Darwin's *Origin of Species* was true as far as it went, but it was no closer to the truth than the *Book of Genesis,* and that was pure mythology. For Grecco, dreams were the most mystifying of all. They were a link with the divine, whatever that Omniscience might be. Thus, he took his dreams quite seriously. He would go over them trying to divine their meaning. He supposed that a supreme being was telling him something. Was it that the peasant was and always had been a victim of ruthless tyranny?

"BARROM!" An explosion shook the bunkhouse. "Outgoing," he said to himself and heaved a sigh of relief. Then he heard the American on radio watch mutter: "Fucking Coung's at it again. The drunk sonofabitch."

Coung? Drunk? The words ignited like phosphorus in his mind. It dawned on Grecco that Major Coung was firing the 105mm at the refugees. Springing from the top bunk, he landed flat footed on the concrete floor. In an instant, he was racing in his undershorts through the dark narrow streets in the direction of the artillery fire. Rounding a corner, Vince saw a soldier shove a long slender projectile into the breech of a howitzer. Major Coung was clutching the lanyard with one hand and holding his wristwatch close to his face with the other. He was speaking in Vietnamese. "How many seconds?" he asked the soldier. The district chief was swaying drunkenly from side to side.

"What are you firing at, Major?" Grecco asked trying to sound as casual as possible. He had run about three hundred yards and was gasping for breath. The District Chief took no notice of him. He was concentrating on the second hand of his watch and appeared oblivious to Vince's presence. The muzzle of the gun was pointed above the buildings in the direction of the refugee camp.

"What the hell are you firing at?" he repeated. This time much louder.

"VC," an Arvin lieutenant standing some distance away shouted. "Beaucoup VC."

"Where?" Grecco demanded. However, the lieutenant had clasped his hands over his ears, and in the next instant, Vince felt as though he had been lifted off the ground and then slammed back against it. Coung had fired a second round. Grecco could visualize the long spiraling arch of the projectile. It's downward plunge. Then the explosion. Striking a refugee family's shack. The one he'd inspected that day. Blowing the man, his wife, and three children into tiny bits.

"Kill beaucoup VC." The lieutenant was standing very near to Grecco shouting in his ear still ringing from the muzzle blast. "Kill beaucoup VC." His eyes were dancing with the alarm of a drunk. Still pretending not to see Vince, the District Chief turned and staggered towards his house. Three enlisted men busily secured the weapon.

"Where?" Grecco asked wheeling about and looking savagely at the lieutenant.

"Where VC?"

"In camp," the lieutenant said suddenly growing very sober.

"What camp?"

"Refugee camp."

"How you see?" Vince's voice grew more menacing.

"One soldier see."

"How many he see?"

"Beaucoup!"

"How many?" Vince shouted waving his fingers in the lieutenant's face. "How many?"

"Twenty, thirty, beaucoup VC."

"Beaucoup bullshit," Grecco shouted as he wheeled about and headed back to the district advisory team's compound. "Nothing but pure unadulterated bullshit."

Major Marcelino was stretched out on a lawn chair in front of the team's bunkhouse waiting for Vince. "Do any good?" he asked.

"Nope," Grecco said dropping onto a chair beside the District Senior Advisor. "Look. I'd like to go out there right now. I know it's risky, but I need an on-the-spot report. Maybe a couple of photos if anyone has a flash. What do you say we take the Jeep with the fifty-caliber machine-gun mount? I can fire it. I was a machine gunner in the Marines." Vince was not being heroic. Bravado sickened him. But the dream had shaken him. He'd been warned. He was responsible for the refugees. He couldn't stand by idly and allow them to be systematically massacred.

"No," Marcelino said. "Im-poss-i-ble." He enunciated each syllable very slowly and very emphatically.

"Why?" Grecco asked speaking quite softly. Abandoning all hope, but still compelled to press things to some plausible conclusion.

"Cause between sundown and sunup, the countryside belongs to Charlie." He spoke through clenched teeth. He was in command of the American outpost, and he didn't want there to be any doubt about it. Not for one split second. "They'd shoot the living shit out of us before we got a hundred yards out of town," He added.

Grecco leaned back in his chair and gazed at the Hydra Constellation that spread serpent-like across the sky. Was there anything in all the universe as contemptible as man? He thought not.

Scrounging

At the close of the week's briefing, Colonel Winter's expressed his disapproval of what he termed "Scrounging". Throughout the sermon, he wore a benign smile; a blend of infinite patience and sly embarrassment. He made a concerted effort to avoid looking at Grecco; however, Vince knew that the old reprobate was speaking for his benefit. There were others. Barban and Bledsoe were involved, but it was Vince who had taken the bait, for he had assumed that it was the Colonel's wish. At least he had said nothing to the contrary. Well, Vince had done all that he was asked to do. He had clinched the deal. The fault was that of a spineless vacillating commander. One who had no business in a position of command. One with all the qualities of a Benedict Arnold. In other words, a blatant coward. Vince alone must face any consequences that might possibly arise. The old reprobate was a master of subterfuge. The sort of politically adept martinet president's chose as their Joint Chief of Staff. One who could be trusted to shift with the wind.

Barban had initiated the scheme. It was his brainchild. The team was in dire need of a new generator. The one they had was too small and overloaded. Too many Vietnamese officials had plugged into it. Consequently, it was always breaking down. Something had to be done. For one thing, it was affecting the compound's security. It took lots of power to illuminate the perimeter. Winters had urged Barban to do something about it. It was Hank's responsibility. He was in charge of logistics.

Figuring that Grecco had connections in Saigon, Barban had ordered Bledsoe to urge Vince to see what he could do about scrounging a generator. The team needed at least 2400 KWs. However, it was a one-way proposition. Barban could think of nothing to swap for such an item as that. Vince told Elmo that he could promise nothing. The odds were slim, but he would see what he could do. Bledsoe was not nearly as forthright as Grecco. He told Hank that Vince felt sure that he could pull it off.

Grecco contacted his old Marine Corps buddy, Grant Olson. If anyone could scrounge up a generator, Grant could. After all, he supervised a vocational training center at a huge construction site. However, unbeknown to Vince, Olson had recently changed jobs and was now working for a service and maintenance company. Grant got Vince in touch with Nick Farrell, a shady character who had the inside track with the "Khaki Mafia"; a gang of NCO's who controlled the black market inside the military installations. It was well known among Saigon's expats that Farrell could scrounge anything within reason if the price was right. He showed Grecco several brand new generators at Orient Maintenance & Assistance's storage depot at the Saigon Port. They were big enough to generate enough power for the entire province capital of Yen Bay and then some. But Farrell needed bribe money. Lots of it. Something to swap.

Grecco had made it clear from the start that money was out of the question. Selling government property was a criminal offense. However, trading it was another matter. Soldiers had always done that. It was common practice, for one unit to swap items with another. It was a good way of bypassing lots of paper shuffling and thus saving much time and energy.

However, Nick Farrell was in it for more than that. He had made a fortune scrounging in Vietnam and prior to that in Korea and Germany. If Grecco wouldn't come up with the cash, he wanted nothing less than six Chicom AK-47 automatic assault rifles. Merchant seamen were paying a thousand bucks a piece for them. They had no trouble selling them to insurgents in The Philippines and Malaysia for double the amount.

When Barban told Winters how easy it would be to get a generator large enough to meet all their needs and more, the colonel was elated. Getting the AK-47's would be a snap. Blaine Bruce had hundreds of them that he used for clandestine operations. He

The Idiot's Frightful Laughter

armed his Nung mercenaries and their American counterparts with them for clandestine operations.

However, Colonel Winters was a cautious man. Gradually he began to grow wary of the scheme. Too many people knew about it. There was, of course, Grecco, Barban, and Bledsoe. Probably everyone on the team knew about it or soon would. It wouldn't be long before it reached IV Corps Headquarters. How would Whitewash Corrigan react? One could never tell about that guy. He had a split personality. His behavior changed from day to day. Colonel Winters had to think of his career. There's no telling what the old general might say. It may mar an unblemished record. He would have to give up any hope of making general, and Helen, his wife, and the kids had their hearts set on it. No, by God, he would not do it. They'd just have to make the best with what they had.

"I might be old fashioned," The Province Senior Advisor said addressing those at the briefing. "The apologist says that everyone does it. That it saves time. That it's a way of circumventing all the paper shuffling that we all hate so much. Well, by golly, if one dug deep enough, he'd find that there was a reason, a damn good reason, for all the red tape. For a system to work, people have to learn to work together and follow the rules. If we no longer have any use for rules, what would become of our country? Our civilization? We'd be back in the Stone Age."

Grecco felt the compulsion to do something quite childish like stamping his feet, sticking out his tongue, and going "blahhhh." The speech was what a father might tell his eight-year-old son, he thought. Colonel Winters was said to have graduated at the top of his class at West Point. Was this what thirty odd years in the army does to its superior minds? Vince wondered. A price paid for three decades of mental stagnation.

The Chieu Hoi Advisor

Aguinaldo Benavidez sat at his desk in the *Chieu Hoi* Compound writing a letter. He'd been working on it for several days now. This was his eleventh draft, and he was still not pleased with the tone. It had to have a certain firmness, and yet not so strong as to provoke anger. Confrontation with an American especially one with the rank of Lieutenant Colonel would be folly. I'm not only a foreigner, but I am a brown skinned foreigner, he thought. If I was white, I'd stand a better chance. One only had to read the newspaper to see what chance the colored man had in America. Benavidez was better off than the black man but not by very much. Colonel Bierhaus was obviously prejudiced or insane. Perhaps some of both.

Benavidez read the opening paragraph of the new draft aloud to himself trying to imagine how the Director of Pacification at Can Tho might take it. "In reference to your communiqué dated May 6, 1967, I should like to express my apology for any anguish suffered by Colonel Thornton D. Bierhaus. I assure you that I shall take every precaution in the future to prevent such indiscretion."

He made a gesture with his hands as though to crumple up the letter. "How maudlin," he muttered. "Have I no shame?" Shame, he thought. That's a very popular word among Filipinos. We are always so concerned with shame. Continually telling one another how ashamed we are for one thing or another. And yet we go on kissing the ass of the white man, our great white father, as though he were a frightful God.

Well, okay, so the opening sentence would mollify him. So what? There was nothing to be gained by being guileless. They would simply replace me with a more obliging Filipino. What difference would my sensibility make to them? However, the second paragraph must be more positive. The matter was really quite absurd.

He dropped his pen and walked to the window. Some twenty Vietnamese were squatting on their haunches cutting grass with long machetes. A month or so ago, they'd been the enemy. Insurgents fighting in the jungle. That was their story anyhow. Benavidez was not such a fool as to believe it. He was certain that very few of them were bona fide Viet Cong. Those who were had only been with the VC for a short time. Long enough to realize that it was not worth it. Life was too dear. Death too imminent. Some were nothing more than opportunists looking for a handout. Others were Arvin deserters in search of a place to hide. However, most had simply lost their identification cards. Frequently VC took people's cards. If they did not turn themselves in as Viet Cong defectors, they'd be picked up by the police for not having their ID cards and thrown in prison.

"*Chieu hoi,*" he muttered. He had a maddening urge to go skipping up to the grass cutters with his arms outstretch singing: "*chieu hoi, chieu hoi, chieu hoi,*" but he hadn't that sort of nerve. He thought of the millions of leaflets scattered by aircraft all over the countryside. Propaganda on expensive thick glossy paper with the picture of an Arvin soldier embracing a guerrilla fighter. "This is your pass to freedom," the leaflet said. "Show it to a GVN soldier, and he will greet you with open arms. Join the Government of South Vietnam in its struggle for a stronger freer nation. Bring whatever weapons you can, and you will be generously rewarded. Come now while there is still time to join in the fight for freedom."

How the Communists must laugh, Benavidez thought. "*Chieu Hoi*" quite literally meant "Open Arms". I am an Open-Arms Advisor, and my Vietnamese counterpart is an Open-Arms Chief. How impressive, he smirked. Quite likely some Advertising Agent in New York's Madison Avenue thought it up. How phony these Yankees are. Spin Doctors. No other people could possibly be so dull-witted. It's phony like their TV commercials, their Hollywood movies, their foreign aid, their Bill of Rights, Benavidez thought. The phonier something is the more flamboyant the title. Take "New

Sheridan Peterson

Life Development Hamlet" for example. It's a euphemism for detention camp, Public Safety Officer for Gestapo, and Revolutionary Development Cadre for CIA spies.

Benavidez returned to his desk and picked up a photocopy of Lieutenant Colonel Bierhaus' report. Boyish laughter floated in through the open window. The grass cutters were teasing a youth about his fiancée. That much the *chieu hoi* advisor could figure out. How could anyone think of these men as dangerous, especially a U.S. Army Colonel? If they were dangerous, they'd have chopped him into tiny bits. The Filipino felt more relaxed with these so-called insurgents than with other Vietnamese. They were the only ones who weren't openly scornful of him.

The Vietnamese, especially those with some authority, were as bad as the Yanks, he thought, nodding his head thoughtfully. His mouth was drawn tight at the corners. As a matter of fact, they're worse. During the past decade, the Yanks have made a half-hearted effort to help the black people. What have the Vietnamese done for their dark-skinned minorities? Nothing. Just look at the Montagnard? A French term for "mountain people". The Vietnamese call them "Moi", which is comparable to the term "Nigger" in The States. They consider the Montagnards no better than beasts. It has always been popular sport for Vietnamese soldiers to shoot these unarmed primitive people as though they were wild animals. They were fond of massacring whole villages. And how often has a Vietnamese pilot returning from a bombing mission saved a bomb or two for a mountain village? And here in the Delta, look how they treat those of Cambodian descent who'd chosen to live among them. They are third-class citizens. They have no civil liberties what so ever. Yes, the *Chieu Hoi* Advisor thought, the Vietnamese are worse than the Yanks

What about the Filipino? Benavidez thought, wiping the moist palm of his hand with a large bandanna. We are of Malaysian origin. The same as the Cambodian and the Montagnard. Benavidez's Vietnamese counterpart, Major Nguyen Van Hue, was as contemptuous of him as of the Montagnard. His racial bias was compounded by jealousy. Benavidez income was comparable to

The Idiot's Frightful Laughter

that of a Vietnamese brigadier general. That, of course, didn't include all the money the general got illegally which more than tripled his salary. However, that didn't matter, for the chief knew that the American judged a man's worth by the size of his salary. Thus, his counterpart felt that he was held in very low repute. This allowed him to rationalize his corrupt practices. It was his way of getting even. Getting less than his dark-skinned Filipino counterpart was a loss of face. The fact that Benavidez was better educated, spoke fluent English and had over sixty-years of exposure to U.S. technology made no difference. On the other hand, The *Chieu Hoi* Advisor thought, American expats earned three times what the Filipino did doing the very same work, so who should be losing face?

Aguinaldo Benavidez had been Yen Bay Province's Chieu Hoi Advisor for eight months, and not once in all that time had his counterpart visited the site. The *Chieu Hoi* Chief had made no excuses. He had been quite blunt. "I don't need your advice. I am Vietnamese. I know the Vietnamese. What can a Filipino tell me that I don't already know?" Several times after the confrontation, Benavidez had dropped by Major Hue's office to request an appointment. On each occasion, an aide had told him that the Major was busy and could not spare the time.

Benavidez read Lieutenant Colonel Thornton D. Bierhaus' report once again, moving slowly from word to word hoping to see something that he had failed to detect during the dozens of previous readings. Some subtle innuendo. An image of the colonel flitted through his mind. His fat flushed face. The gray carefully coiffured hair. The tiny nervous eyes. The pencil-thin mustache. The trim tailor-made uniform. The shiny black attaché case. The swagger stick with the brass handle and bullet. All that was missing were a pair of shiny black riding boots, and he'd be a perfect martinet, Benavides thought. The spitting image of a Prussian officer.

Lieutenant Colonel Bierhaus was one of the U.S. Army's top echelon advisors. His office adjoined that of the Ambassador of Pacification at the Military Advisory Corps Headquarters at the

Little Pentagon at the Tan Son Nhut Air Terminal. Thus anything Lt. Col. Bierhaus might say was taken very seriously at both the Corps and Province levels. He could make or break an officer's career with the flick of his swagger stick, so to speak. He'd made an unannounced visit at the *Chieu Hoi* Camp. Benavidez had been polite, but perhaps not as affable as the colonel had wished. The *Chieu Hoi* Advisor had not seen anything out of the ordinary in the colonel's behavior, so when he received a copy of the report, he was flabbergasted.

Colonel Bierhaus had accused Benavidez of ignoring him. Leaving him alone and unprotected amidst the Viet Cong defectors. He asserted that they had crowded about him grimacing and making threatening gestures with their razor-sharp machetes. He had taken care to back slowly away from them, his hand gripping the stock of his revolver. At the gateway, a group of them barred his path. For a moment he was indecisive. However, he knew that he must not let them think him afraid, so slapping his holster, he had strode through their midst staring defiantly at them. Benavidez slapped his hand down hard on the report. Shit, how could he answer such nonsense, he wondered?

"Why hell, these men wouldn't harm a flea," Benavidez told Grecco at the advisory team's clubroom the evening after receiving the report. "They're like children. Very curious about strangers, especially a squirrelly character like Colonel Bierhaus.

They want to be friendly. They saw that he was uncomfortable and tried to make him feel welcome. But hell, it's difficult when you can't understand their language. You're apt to imagine all sorts of things."

Vince advised him to forget it. The colonel was obviously paranoiac. It was a typical military behavior, especially among desk jockeys. But Benavidez did not forget. He finally drafted a reply that he felt would both spare Lieutenant Colonel Bierhaus' pride and mollify the Director of Pacification at IV Corps. He took each accusation in turn and pointed out most diplomatically the colonel's error. Grecco read it. "It's too good for that sonofabitch," he said. "The asshole is not worth such a thoughtful explanation. If

The Idiot's Frightful Laughter

it were me," Vince added, "there would only be three words – 'It's all bullshit.' That was all that horse's ass deserved."

Hank Barban had received a copy of the report from Whitewash Corrigan in Can Tho ordering him to check it out. Colonel Bierhaus was no one to trifle with. Driving over to the *Chieu Hoi* Camp armed with a Swedish K assault Rifle, Hank wanted to know what the hell was going on. He looked the alleged Viet Cong defectors over and left saying that the Colonel was a yellow fucker but warned Benavidez to be more careful with the brass from Saigon. They could cause the province a lot of trouble. That afternoon Barban wrote the Director of Pacification in Can Tho blaming Benavidez for immaturity and irresponsibility. Somehow or other, Benavidez got a copy of the report. This only confirmed what General Emilio Aguinaldo, The Philippines great liberator, had once told him years ago. "Never trust the Yankee. He speaks with a forked tongue. I surrendered on the condition that the vast estates owned by the Catholic Church would be returned to the people. That promise was never honored." There were exceptions, Benavidez thought. He felt sure that he could trust Grecco. However, the guy is a cynic. He obviously believes in nothing. Is loyal to no one. Is scornful of everything. It was uncomfortable being around such a negative guy. "Don't you believe in anything?" Benavidez once asked. "Give me one good reason why I should," he'd replied.

One thing puzzled Benavidez. He could not understand why he loathed the genuine defector so intensely. It ran counter to his task as a *Chieu Hoi* Advisor. Once it was clear to him that one was truly a Viet Cong turncoat, his feelings for the man changed instantly. And yet he had a sort of grudging admiration for the insurgents. It was probably because the man was a traitor. He had betrayed his comrades. Very likely given away their position causing some to be killed or wounded. That had to be why, for he did not believe that American troops had any right to be fighting in Vietnam. It was so obvious to him that the U.S. Government wasn't interested in helping the Vietnamese people. Take the Philippines.

Sheridan Peterson

Over sixty years ago Filipino patriots had driven the Spanish Colonialist from their islands. They had been armed and supported by the U.S. Navy. Then what had the United States' done? It had turned against them, driving the Filipino troops into the jungles. A guerrilla war had last for four year killing thousands of innocent peasants just as they were doing now in Vietnam. After the Filipinos helped drive the Japs from the Philippines, they were given their independence. But what has America done for them? Yes, they may have their own government, but the Yankees have a tighter grip on the economy than they had when it was an official colony of theirs. Now the ordinary people had nothing. They had none of the advantages of a U.S. Colony and all the disadvantages. Foreigners refer to The Philippines as a democracy, but the Filipinos know better. It is actually a plutocracy ruled by a few wealthy landowners and the church. These potentates take turns ruling the country and robbing the people. U.S. and Japanese corporations support these crooks helping them to exploit the peasants.

Aguinaldo Benavidez had taken the job in Vietnam because he was strapped for cash. Being solvent proved more important to him than all his lofty ideals which both his father and grandfather had fought for so fiercely. That was why he despised the genuine Viet Cong defector. Benavidez saw his own betrayal reflected in the renegade. Whenever he viewed the dilemma dispassionately, he could see that it was he who was the true traitor. He'd had a lifetime of exposure to Yankee exploitation; nevertheless, he had most willingly sought out this position as Yen Bay Province's *Chieu Hoi* Advisor. True there were thousands of well-educated Filipinos just like him in Vietnam for the very same reason – money. But that didn't ease his conscience. What had America done for The Philippines? Where was his national pride? His culture? His centuries of Malay Philippine heritage? It had all been swept aside for the American Dream. It was the mad pursuit of junk that most appalled him. Xmas toys broken before New Year's. Wash-n-wear suits that neither washed nor wore well. Appliances programmed to self-destruct the moment the warranty expired. Cars whose

The Idiot's Frightful Laughter

paper-thin bodies dented at the slightest pressure. Tires that frequently disintegrated without warning killing the occupants. His affluent friends, whose homes were packed with the latest Western gimmicks, acted as though every item they didn't own was a calamity. The Filipino was confused. The constant acquisition of junk was woven into the very fabric of his life. There was the feeling that without the junk, he was nothing. It was not only status. It was used to define the self and gave the Filipino the illusion of being a coherent part of the great American dream. He had an innate need to be wanted, connected, loved, and approved of by his great white father, America. His neighbors had them. His friends had them. Why didn't he? And so, Benavidez had followed the rainbow to Yen Bay Province in Vietnam's vast Mekong Delta in pursuit of that elusive pot of gold, the American Dream.

When Benavidez's son was six years' old, he'd become alienated from himself. He had begun to watch TV and was exposed to its American inspired commercials. The child was bombarded with images of pretty blue-eyed, blond-haired boys and girls playing with hundreds of toys. He became convinced that he had to have those toys. He would tell his father with an urgent and pained look that he must have a certain video game or GI Joe doll or such and such. He could not distinguish between what he dearly wanted and what he needed. A dilemma that most middle-class Filipinos both young and old had fallen into. They could not distinguish their needs from their wants. The industrial world's corporate conglomerates had them dangling from the proverbial hook.

What had become of the Philippine culture? It's ancient traditions? What did the Filipino child study in public school? He learned about America. It's history. It's economy. It's sociology. What did the average Filipino know about The Philippines? Who were his national heroes – Apolinario Mabini, Gregorio del Pilar, Andre Bonifacio? Of how bravely they had led the fight against the American imperialists from 1899 to 1902? What was ever said about them? They were all but omitted from the children's textbooks. It had been a war so similar to the Vietnam conflict. Benavidez recalled so vividly how as a child, he had sat at his grandfather's feet listening to him tell of the battles against the American soldiers. He had served as a colonel under General Aguinaldo and had insisted that Benavidez be named after their great leader; the first president of The Philippines. It had only lasted a few weeks following the defeat of the Spanish Conquistadors. American troops had driven President Aguinaldo and his supporters from Manila and into the jungles to fight a guerrilla war for three years. They'd had no Russia or China to look to for aid.

Much of what his grandfather had told him was what was happening right then and there in Yen Bay Province. He'd described how Yankee troops had burned all the villages along the west bank of Laguna Bay and then returned a month later to destroy those along the east shore. He told of how Caloocan, Pasig, and Malolos were razed. Not a stick was left standing. He introduced him to an old man whose bride was shot. American soldiers had fired into the wedding procession killing her and two guests and wounding three others. Two were children. There were the tortures. The same that were being used in Vietnam. He spoke of the "water cure". Water was forced down the throat and then forced out by kneeling on the bloated stomach. A worse torment was the "rope treatment" One end of a cord was tied about the victim's neck and the other about the waste. Then the rope was twisted with a stick. He told of how the Mayors of San Miguel and San Nicolas were beaten to death, and of the massacre of Jolo and Leyte Islands. However, the most dreadful tale was that of General "Hell Roaring" Jake Smith on Samar Island. The General had told his troops: "I want no prisoners. I want you to kill and burn. The more you kill and burn the better it will please me." Nothing had changed, Benavidez thought. There were lots of "Hell Roaring" Jake Smiths in Vietnam.

The *Chieu Hoi* Advisor's grandfather had taken him to visit General Aguinaldo many times. He was in his eighties, but his eyes had not lost their luster, and his voice was as sharp and crisp as a young man's. He once told Benavidez: "We Filipinos are a sentimental people. We let our feelings blind our reason.

The Idiot's Frightful Laughter

Unscrupulous politicians play on these sentiments in order to rob us of our birthrights. We must become canny like the Japanese. Agree to everything and give nothing. Pretend to be kind and compassionated, but instead be cruel and ruthless." Benavidez did not like the Japanese any better than any other Filipino. They had suffered horribly under the Japanese during World War II. However, he knew that the old general was right. The Japanese were the worst bigots of all. Worse than the Yankees. Someday they would stage another sneak attack more dreadful than ever. This time they would put ballistic missiles in orbit about the earth. General Aguinaldo had left him with a grim choice. Pattern his life after the Jap; his bitter foe. As a youth, he had fought them in the steaming jungles of Luzon. Was there not a third alternative?

That night the *Chieu Hoi* Advisor wrote a short crisp report to Whitewash Corrigan, IV Corps Director of Pacification, at Can Tho.

Dear Mr. Corrigan,

For the past eight months, I have lived among these defectors unarmed and unafraid. Never once during this time have they given me any cause to feel threatened. They are polite, cooperative and good-natured.

It would be most appreciated if you would pay the camp a visit and see for yourself how peaceful and tranquil these people are. I am sure that it would erase any misconceived notions you may harbor.

Most sincerely yours,
Aguinaldo Benavidez
Chieu Hoi Advisor

Benavidez packed his bags and bid the defectors farewell. The report was his swan song. He knew that he would be informed of his dismissal within a day or so. However, he felt good for the first time in weeks. Ever since he'd received that reprimand from the Director of Pacification. Well, Grecco had given him a letter of recommendation to give to his friend. Grant Olson. He was in search of teachers. He'd check it out.

Her French Gentleman

It was not long after his visit to the Gia Hoa Resettlement Camp that Grecco began to feel very tired. All he seemed interested in was sleep. Walking to the office became too great an effort. He began drinking large quantities of coffee for breakfast and took a thermos of it to work. He skipped lunch in order to take a nap. And still, he grew more exhausted. Even the simplest task required a great amount of effort. And so he soon fell behind with his reports.

One day he caught a cold, and it quickly developed into bronchitis. He stuffed his pockets with rags, for he began coughing up great gobs of phlegm.

One morning he went to the doctors' quarters before they'd left for work at the province hospital. The B-52 bombing raids kept them busy. They had no time to treat common ailments such as colds and sore throats. They gave him a bottle of Tetracycline tablets and advised him not to come back. He was not their concern. The civilians had a doctor in Saigon. If it got worse, see him.

Barban, seeing how ill Grecco was, increased the pressure. Moving up deadlines on reports and burdening him with added trivialities. On Sundays, Hank would find something extra. Something that he insisted could not wait until Monday.

Eventually, Grecco was too weak to get out of bed. He slept all day arousing himself for one and occasionally two meals a day. Barban insisted that he come to work and was continually sending Bledsoe over to aggravate him. Finally, one afternoon, Hank stormed into the house and bound up the stairs; however, when he saw how emaciated Vince had grown, he lost his hunger for a showdown.

"If you're sick, Vince, for christsakes do something about it. Just don't lie here. Go to Saigon and find out what in hell's wrong," Barban said. "We don't want you dying on us."

The Idiot's Frightful Laughter

The next day Grecco climbed aboard a chopper for Can Tho. From there, he took a plane to Saigon. Doctor Elias Younger was a short, plump man with a round reddish face. When he smiled, his face radiated with pleasure. He looked more like a small-town tavern owner than a U.S. State Department physician.

"You're having a nervous breakdown," he said. "All you need is a little rest." He handed Grecco two small bottles of pills. "These large ones are sleeping pills. One should be plenty. However, there's a possibility that you may need two after the third or fourth day. Take one every twelve hours." Then he held up the other bottle. "These blue ones are tranquilizers. Take one as soon as you wake up."

Grecco handed the pills back to Doctor Younger. "You don't understand," he said. "Getting to sleep is not my problem. It's staying awake. I sleep all the time. And as for tranquilizers, well I'm too tranquil already."

"Trust me," Dr. Younger said smiling. His face seeming to shatter into a thousand pieces. "I deal with this all the time. You're not getting the right sort of sleep. These will restore your energy. You are suffering from thorough exhaustion. The machine has worn itself out."

Grecco smiled. It was a weak condoning sort of grin. If he only knew the devastation I've faced, he thought. Having so much responsibility and no authority whatsoever. Seeing innocent people terrorized and slaughtered by cold-blooded killers, and me, powerless to lift a finger. How courageous these peasants are. Facing death with stoic resignation. These poor brave people are my responsibility, and I can do nothing," he recollected. It was too horrible to imagine, and yet he must imagine it day and night for as long as he lived.

What would Walter Van Tilburg Clark have said? Grecco wondered. Clark had been his teacher at the University of Montana. He had written *The Ox-bow Incident*, a Western classic. Clark's protagonist had said that there were two kinds of sin – the sin of commission and the sin of omission. Clark would have considered Major Cuong's guilt the sin of commission. He had committed the sin of commission by willfully slaughtering the defenseless peasants. Only two things meant anything to the District Chief – power and cruelty. He did the only thing he'd ever dome – kill.

On the other hand, Clark's protagonist would have had great scorn for Grecco. He would have said that Vince was guilty of the sin of omission. He had let the refugees die because he was too timid to stop Cuong. Too cowardly. Grecco's behavior was that of a whipped cur. He had stood by passively and done nothing to stop the bloodshed. In essence, he'd given Major Cuong his passive consent. He'd known it was wrong and yet had done nothing. According to Clark, this was the worst sort of sin. A burden Grecco found so unbearable. It was no wonder that he'd had a nervous breakdown. The human psyche can take just so much. When it's on overload, the safety switch snaps off. It takes time to reload, Vince thought.

The introspective man cannot fool himself. That's the one person who will not be fooled. He'd had no intention of getting involved. That's what Grecco thought. It was just a job. Someone else would do it if he didn't. He was no crusader. Who was he fooling? As always Vince invariably let his feelings get involved. It was the same with everything he'd ever done. No matter how cynical he'd pretend to be, the shell always cracked open, and the slush oozed out sticking all over everything. That's how Grecco pretended to saw.

It was different with others, Vince thought. They genuinely did not care. Oh sure, they pretended to, but beneath it all, they were utterly indifferent. There's was the sin of commission.

"Do you have a place that's quiet?" Doctor Younger asked. "Somewhere where you won't be disturbed?"

Grecco nodded. When he'd been transferred to the Delta, he had not given up his apartment. It was in the center of what looked like a giant concrete bunker. The rooms had no windows, just drapes covering patches of bare wall. It gave one the illusion of having them. If the air conditioner ever stopped during the night, he'd surely suffocate.

The Idiot's Frightful Laughter

"Good," Doctor Younger said. "I want you to stay there for four or five days. Longer if need be."

Sleep for four or five days. How tremendous. Perhaps he could stretch it out to six or seven. A week of utter oblivion and no Bledsoe or Barban to hassle him. But what about Barban? He'd have to tell him, or better yet, Colonel Winters. Barban would insist he never got the message. And yes, one to Simoni, just in case.

"My boss is a hard man, Doctor," Grecco said. "He'd have little sympathy for one so weak as to have a nervous breakdown. I'm absolutely certain that he would not believe me."

"I'll tell him," Doctor Younger said looking suddenly very serious, and a good deal older. "And I'll send a note to your regional office if you like?"

"Great," Grecco said, taking a notebook from his pocket and scribbling down Colonel Winter's and Simoni's addresses. "Thank so much, Doctor."

"You come and see me again in four or five days," He said. "We'll decide then what to do." He took Grecco's hand and shook it warmly. "Take it easy, lad. I'm afraid you take things a bit more to heart than most."

"Afraid you're right, Sir," Vince said shaking his hand.

The apartment had not been touched since he'd left it four months ago. A magazine lay open on the dining room table. A frying pan with scorched egg yolk was still in the sink.

Everything was new and modern. There was a huge fridge and freezer and a six-burner gas range in the kitchen. The furniture in the dining room was Thai teak. There were two lounge chairs and a sofa. In the bedroom was a king size bed with innerspring mattress. However, the most appealing thing was the shower. A huge water heater provided an inexhaustible supply of scorching hot water.

After setting his rucksack on the dining room table and turning on the air conditioner, Grecco went into the bathroom and closed the door. He turned on the shower, and while he was undressing, the room became like a steam bath.

After showering, Grecco heated a can of ham in the oven and boiled several potatoes, however in spite of not having eaten since early morn, he had almost no appetite. Turning up the air conditioner and putting an extra blanket on the bed, he took a sleeping pill and crawled beneath the covers. He did not have to wait for the sedative to take effect. Within minutes, he was sound asleep.

No one. Absolutely no one knows where I am, Grecco thought with a sigh, as he slipped off into oblivion. Before leaving Saigon for the Mekong Delta, he was told to vacate the apartment, and it had been taken for granted that he had.

Awakening, he checked the time. It was 2:35. However, unless he went outside, he'd have no way of knowing if it was night or day. What's more, he had no idea how many days had slipped by. It must have been quite long, for he was very hungry. After taking a tranquilizer and searing himself lobster red in the shower, he reheated the ham and potatoes and heaped two cans of diced pineapple on top. Then without bothering to find out what day it was, he took another sleeping pill and went back to bed. After reading an old issue of *The Nation* for a half hour or so, he decided that one pill was not enough. A second one took effect almost immediately, and he slipped off into a drugged slumber. Again, when he awoke, he had no idea what day it was, nor how long he had slept. He repeated the same process as he had done the time before. The next time that he awoke, he dressed and went outside. It was dark. His watch said 10:20. It's twenty-two hundred hours, he thought. Still plenty of time for a couple beer.

The bar was only a block away down a narrow alleyway littered with garbage and pools of raw sewage. It was upstairs above a steam bath and massage parlor. A year ago, the boiler had exploded, and it had only recently reopened.

Grecco stood in the doorway allowing his eyes to adjust to the dimly lit surrounding. It was like any of several thousand hostess clubs scattered throughout the city that catered to foreigners. A bar with a brass rail and stools stretched down one side of the room. Booths lined the other wall. One of the latest rock n' roll melodies

The Idiot's Frightful Laughter

blared from a stereo amplifier at the rear. Some two dozen girls dressed in white waitress uniforms stared with bored indifference at Vince as he moved hesitantly towards the bar.

Grecco had been there a number of times before. Remembering Vince, the manager walked towards him with a broad smile and outstretched hands. It was rare to find a club managed by a man. Most were run by stout middle-age madams.

"Where you been hiding?" he said pumping Grecco's hand vigorously. "You're a sight for sore eyes." He had a crew cut and a pencil thin mustache. His name was French; however, he claimed to have fought against them at Dien Bien Phu with the Viet Ming. Now he was intent on getting rich. Vince heard that he ran a number of illicit businesses on the side and was always having to buy his way out of jail.

"Pierre! How in the hell are you?" Grecco said trying hopelessly to match the manager's enthusiasm. "I've been in the Delta. Yen Chau."

"No kidding?" Pierre said grimacing and snapping his head back and forth. "Lots of VC, eh?"

"Yea, lots of VC," Grecco said frowning. He felt somewhat annoyed by Pierre's aggressiveness. He was the most Americanized Vietnamese he'd ever met. The metamorphose was so contrived. "Why the ugly uniforms?" Vince asked pointing to the bar girls.

"Oh, I know. I know. Terrible! Disgusting! No sex appeal! But what can I do?" Pierre said holding up his arms in despair. "It's a new law. Since last Sunday there are no longer any bar hostesses. No more bars. Puff! All have vanished. This is now a restaurant. See the sign there on the wall? 'Sandwiches'," Pierre said spitting it out as though it was much too foul a word to adorn such sacrosanct premises. "Only don't order one. You'll be wasting your time. We have just sold out. We have always just sold out. Hah! Hah! Hah! Such a crazy law. Hey! Want to talk with the waitress?" he said leading Grecco to a vacant table.

"Has Saigon tea been outlawed?" Grecco asked with mock enthusiasm.

"Hah! Hah! Don't you wish?" Pierre said. Then wagging his finger at Vince, he added: "Do not joke. Tomorrow they might."

"What do you like? Whiskey?" Pierre asked as Grecco sat down. "We've got the best – Old Forester, Wild Turkey, Black and White, Johnny Walker Black Label."

"How about a beer?"

"Sure. Pabst, Budweiser, Schlitz, Hamm, Millers, all fresh from the PX."

"Naw," Grecco said. "Just give me a bameba."

"Ba Muoi Ba? You got to be kidding. That shit ain't fit for pigs."

"No really. I've got so I like Vietnamese beer."

"You've got to be shitting me?"

"If you want to get in with the people, you've got to drink what they drink," Grecco said.

"Oh sure. Ha. Ha. Hearts and minds. Ha. Ha," Pierre said pressing out his lower lip and widening his eyes. "This is how to win hearts and minds," he added rubbing his thumb across the palm of his hand. "Lots of the good old green stuff. Ha. Ha." Then wheeling about and making a sweeping motion of the room with his hand, he said, "See anything you like? No blondes or redheads. Ha. Ha. Just brunettes tonight. How do you like the one in the corner? French-Cambodian. Real stacked," he said bringing his hands down in an hourglass motion. "Like a brick shithouse."

"I'm not up to it tonight. I've been ill." Grecco said.

The manager peered down at him. His eyes full of mock disdain.

"Hey, no shit, I'm serious," Vince said.

"You got the clap?" Pierre asked. "Where'd you get it?"

"No! No!" Grecco said shaking his head. "It's not VD. It's my nerves."

"Screwing is good for the nerves. Nothing more relaxing than a good piece of ass," Pierre said smiling sheepishly.

"No, I'm not nervous. It's just the opposite. I have no energy," Vince explained. "All worn out."

"Well, hell man, you haven't been getting enough," Pierre said nodding his head like a doctor reassuring a patient. "That's all that's wrong with you. Nothing like a good fuck to give you energy. Make a new man of you."

Grecco gazed helplessly at the intrigant. He'd never met such a persistent pimp. Without a doubt he was the whoremaster's whoremaster, he thought.

"How about that tall one with the long hair? French Cambodian? She's a real hot number. I'll send her over, okay? Maybe she'll change your mind?"

Grecco shrugged his shoulders. He was still too weak to put up any further resistance. In a way, it was a welcome change. Pierre's hard sell gave Vince a sense of acceptance. It gave him the feeling of being wanted in a society that hadn't the slightest use for him or any foreigner for that matter. At any of the thousands of hostess bars in the city, the manager wouldn't have so much as looked at him. And if Vince did not buy a bar hostess a glass of tepid tea for about two hundred and fifty piaster within at least five minutes, the girl would call him a "Cheap Charlie" and walk away. He'd then be ignored by all the others. It was not always quite that bad, he thought; however, that was the general pattern.

"Hi Joe. Can I sit down?" The girl standing before him looked nothing like a Vietnamese. She was about five-foot, nine and well built. Her face was round and golden brown. However, the most unusual thing about her was her radiant smile. She must be the French-Cambodian who'd been sitting in the dark at the far corner of the room, Grecco thought. The one Pierre had pointed out to him.

"Sure," he said sliding his chair over to make room.

"My name is Susan," she said. "What's yours?"

"Vince," Grecco said smiling amiably.

"You American?"

"Yeah," Grecco said nodding.

"Oh, I thought you Français? You not like American."

"I'm just not feeling well. I'm really loud and ugly when I'm not ill," Grecco said with a playful wink.

"You joke, I think?" she said smiling very sensually as though she was posing for a picture for some erotic magazine. "I no like that," she said pointing to a GI who had both arms tightly wound about a tiny Vietnamese girl and was kissing her most ardently. "That number ten. It okay you home. Nobody see. Then can do everything. But not where every people see."

"Americans like to show off," Vince said. "They want everyone to see what great lovers they are. It's an old tradition of ours."

"You like?" Susan asked pointing again at the couple.

"Naw. I'm not a good American," he said smiling.

"That good," Susan said squeezing his hand.

"She like?" Grecco asked motioning to the Vietnamese woman.

"Yes, she like. She beaucoup like," Susan said looking very grave. "Some like. Some no like. I no like." Craning her neck about, she scrutinized Grecco very carefully. "How old you?" she asked.

"Forty-one," he said.

"Oh! I don't think so," she said shaking her head vigorously. "I think maybe thirty."

"Ah ah," Grecco said waving a finger at her in mock severity. "Mustn't flatter."

"No! That true," Susan said. You no look forty-one. I think you joke."

"How old are you?" he asked.

"I nineteen," she said. The bar was beginning to fill up with all sorts of foreigners. Mostly servicemen on leave. Some waved to Susan. They looked disappointed. Others gave Grecco an angry look. Evidently, they'd come too late.

"I thought you were twenty-two or three," he said appraising her well-developed figure.

"Why you think?" she asked.

"You act older," Vince said motioning to her voluptuous breasts."

"Yes, I think so," she said nodding gravely. "Not so silly like her," she added turning her gaze on the Vietnamese girl. "Why you come here?"

"To find a beautiful Cambodian girl," he added.

"Oh! You joke," Susan declared. "How you know I Cambode? Too black, yes?"

The Idiot's Frightful Laughter

"No! No!" Grecco protested waving his hands before him. "It's because you have a very lovely figure," he added motioning to her breasts.

"Ah yes. True! True! Vietnamese girl too skinny. American no like skinny girl. Like big teats. Big ass. I know," Susan said smiling very self-satisfyingly. "You like?" she asked pointing to her large bosom that pressed tight against the stiffly starched uniform, as though it would burst out at any moment. The teats reminded Grecco of ripe luscious melons.

"Very much," Vince said. He no longer felt so tired. He'd been rejuvenated.

"Oh! I happy you like. You play with them tonight?" she asked looking at him anxiously.

Grecco smiled. Why not take her home? He thought. It would be a long time before he found anything quite as nice as this. And like Pierre said, it would relax the nerves. He had used the last of his pills. Sleep would not come so easily tonight.

"When Vince did not answer, Susan said: I like you play. Make me feel good." She looked at him most earnestly. Her eyes full of expectation. "Why you no talk?"

"Sure," he said patting her on the knee. "I would like very much to play with them." He was not good at pillow talk and was afraid he might not sound convincing. It embarrassed him to speak so frankly about such things.

"Oh! I happy," Susan said with childish glee. She ran her fingertips lightly over his lips. "You have nice mouth. Not fat like mine."

Grecco looked at her mouth. It was full and sensual. So different from the Vietnamese's thin taunt lips. "You have lovely lips, Susan." He said. "They're the kind a man loves to kiss."

"You make joke?" Susan said looking at Grecco very seriously.

Grecco laughed. "The Vietnamese girls are jealous. That's why they make fun."

"They no make fun. I have mirror. I see," she said. "My nose flat. My lips big."

Like minorities everywhere, Susan was suffering from a feeling of inferiority, Grecco thought. No doubt, she hungers for reassurance, but he'd have to be careful not to overdo it. "What's wrong with your nose, Susan? It's an Asian nose."

"I no like. I like big long nose," she said. "Some day I go Hong Kong get nose fixed. You like?"

"I like it just the way it is," Grecco said. "It's very cute. A big long nose just wouldn't suit you."

"Oh! No! No!" Susan said shaking her head vigorously. Her eyes popping with excitement. "It no good. It flat like monkey."

Grecco couldn't help laughing. She was as vain about her appearance as a New York fashion model. "American women do not like big noses. They'd be happy to have your nose, Susan. Movie Stars often have their noses bobbed."

"Bobbed? What you mean bobbed?" Susan asked.

"Snip the end off," Grecco said snapping at the end of his nose with his fingers as though they were a pair of scissors. "The famous writer Norman Mailer had his nose bobbed," Vince added. "I must say, he looked a good deal better. He had a long crooked nose like a Caribbean Pirate."

"Oh! They crazy. I think so," she exclaimed.

"It's true, Susan," Grecco said shaking his head reassuringly.

"I no believe," she said.

"What's your real name, Susan?" he asked hoping to change the subject.

"Attopeu," she said. "You like?"

"Yes, much better than Susan," Vince said. "Attopeu. It's quite pretty."

"You very nice to me," Attopeu said squeezing his bicep. "I think you no American. I think you French, maybe?"

"I was born in America, Attopeu," He said, "However, I've been in Asia for six years now, and I like to think of myself as Asian."

"You Asian?" Oh! No! You no Asian," Attopeu exclaimed. "You too big. Too white. You very handsome. Asian man no handsome."

The Idiot's Frightful Laughter

"But my heart is Asian, Attopeu," Vince said.

"Yes, I think so. I think maybe true," she said smiling wistfully.

"The GI and the tiny Vietnamese girl, who had been necking so ardently at an adjacent table, were now dancing. Their arms wrapped about one another. The soldier had bent his legs so that his pelvis was pressing hard against her crotch. They were rotating slowly to the music as though copulating. It was very erotic to watch, and Grecco began to grow quite restless. "Shall we dance?" he asked Attopeu preparing to rise.

"Okay, but consat no like. Lights go out mean consat come," she warned. "We stop dance."

What a paradox, Grecco thought. Things that were socially accepted throughout most of the world like dancing were against the law, but things like massage parlors, where any sort of sexual perversion was permissible, were scattered all over the countryside. They were thinly disguised whorehouses.

The dance floor was quite small. Only large enough for half a dozen couples at the most. Grecco caught Pierre's wink as they moved on to the floor. You foxy ol' pimp, he thought. If I'd appeared more willing, you'd have sent me a less desirable one.

Attopeu kept an inch or so of space between them. Remembering what she had said about the spectacle that the GI and his girl made earlier in the evening, Grecco felt it wise not to draw Attopeu any closer. He was her French gentleman. It was best to keep it that way. He was sure that when they were alone in bed, things would be different. He thought of her firm golden-brown body with the wide hips, the slender waist, and the large, firm breasts that longed to be kissed. The expectation of what awaited him made his flesh quiver. He'd have to calm down, or he'd ruin everything, he cautioned himself. It must be made to last a long time. All night if that was possible. It would be his crowning assignation. How many times had he made that promise to himself? Dozens no doubt. But this time he was in earnest. He would not tire. He would stay the course.

"How do you like Susan?" Pierre asked sidling up to Grecco, his eyebrows wavering up and down rakishly.

"Magnificent," Vince said.

"I thought you would," he said. He was so sure of himself, Grecco thought.

"What do you mean 'mag..ne..fi..cent'?" Attopeu asked.

"Magnificent means very nice," he said.

"Number one, yes?" she said with a wide mouth smile.

"Yea, number one."

At closing time, Grecco gave Pierre 2,500 piaster which figured out to about twenty U.S. dollars on the black market. The procedure was for Vince to leave first and wait at the gate of his apartment complex. Attopeu would arrive about five minutes later perched on the back of a 90cc Honda. Grecco was told not to worry about the driver. He was a friend of Pierre. He would not tell the police, but it was wise to tip him a hundred piaster none the less.

In exactly five minutes, a motorcycle pulled up in front of the compound. Vince's heart skipped a beat when he saw Attopeu seated side-saddle behind the driver. She had changed her clothes and was now wearing a bright red mini skirt and a tight fluffy white sweater. She looked as fresh and full of vigor as a college cheerleader.

At the apartment, Grecco lay in bed listening to the water running in the shower. Attopeu had made it quite clear that she preferred to take her shower alone. It was all part of a ritual with her. There were certain steps that had to be followed. She was singing one of those soft tonal Vietnamese laments.

Vince wondered if he should use a condom. He held one in his hand. The kind that are soaked in oil and sealed in a square plastic capsule. All he had to do was press it between the thumb and forefinger, and the case would crack open. He'd spoiled things before by insisting on using a rubber, and he was anxious that nothing go wrong this time. He was not afraid of gonorrhea. Anyone who'd been around as much as he had was sure to get it a couple of times, and he'd never had much trouble curing the infection. A week or two of tetracycline tablets had always wiped it out. But he was terrified of contracting syphilis. The consequence was grim. Nothing would cure it. Yea, penicillin would hold it in check for a while, and that was it.

But it was so hopeless trying to get an Asian girl to let a guy use a rubber. They were usually much too sensual and intimate to tolerate any sort of impediment. And moreover, it insulted them. It implied that they were not clean. That, like a leper, they had some ugly disease. Of course, it was a different matter if they didn't like you. However, Attopeu was obviously very fond of her French gentleman.

He gazed questioningly at the square capsule with the three X's on it. Even so much as a suggestion might place a barrier between them. Lessen her desire. And then very likely, he'd have to take it off anyway. She'd insist on it, so it'd be a lot of fuss for nothing, he figured tossing the capsule beneath the bed.

When Attopeu came out of the bathroom, she had a towel about her. Slipping between the sheets, she unwound it and dropped it on the floor. Then she rolled up tight against Grecco. Her hand slipped down and felt his cock. "No rubber. Oh! I happy" she said smiling innocently up at him.

She pressed her teats up against Vince's face. "Kiss, kiss," she coaxed. "No, no," she scolded. "Like baby-san," She made a slurping sound. Then she was on top of him easing his cock inside her. She moved very slowly up and down on bended knees. "Don't come," she whispered. "I not ready. You wait."

Grecco nodded. "My darling," he murmured quite beside himself with ecstasy. It was difficult to hold back, for it had been quite some time since he'd had such a seductive lover. He felt her cunt grow taut squeezing firmly about his prick. He tried desperately to think of other things. The memory of an outhouse in a village. The heap of shit swarming with maggots and flies. He recalled how the smell caused him to gage and vomit. It was hard to concentrate on such a revolting scene, but it worked. His cock began to relax somewhat. Oh, the things we do to please, he thought.

"Now. Now I come," she panted moving faster. Her face wreathed in a look of utter rapture. "Quick. You, me, we come" she gasped. They grasped each other tightly and rocked madly about on the bed moaning loudly. Vince felt all the poison and anxieties of the past six months gush out of him. He was awash in a sea of tranquility. Attopeu's hot sweaty body pressed heavily down upon him. This is the closest anyone ever gets to heaven, Grecco thought. How marvelous it would be to lie like this forever.

Soon Attopeu fell asleep cuddled next to him. Vince placed a hand on her pussy and felt how soft and warm it was. He lay awake for a long time, his fingers massaging the tender lips of the vulva. Then he bent down and kissed them rubbing the tip of his tongue back and forth between them. Of all the gifts that the Gods had given man, this was the most precious of them all, he thought.

The next morning Grecco slipped a five hundred piaster note into Attopeu's hand as she was leaving. She had been worth every cent of it, and he wondered if she did not expect a more sizeable gift. How much had others given her? Surely some had given her more.

"You come club tonight?" she said standing just inside the open doorway.

"Sorry, Attopeu. I can't. Leaving for Yen Chau today," he lied.

Grecco was tempted to keep her for a few days. It had been a long time since he'd had anything nearly so nice. If he were younger, things would be different. He thought back to '44 when he was a seventeen-year-old Marine on leave for the first time. A hostess at the famous Hollywood Canteen had picked him up. When she found that Vince was a virgin, she sent his uniform to the cleaners with instructions to keep it until she called for it. She wouldn't let him leave the hotel room for two weeks. When Grecco finally got back to Camp Pendleton, he was locked up in the brig for ten days. After that his appetite for pussy was insatiable. For the next few years, he could never get enough.

But that was twenty-four years ago. And besides, Grecco was still recuperating from his illness. It may not be a good idea to tax his strength too much. Attopeu was one hell of a great lover, Vince thought. One of the best.

"When you come back?" Attopeu asked.

The Idiot's Frightful Laughter

"One month." Another lie, he thought. It may be three or four months before he got back to Saigon. But he couldn't tell her that.

"You come see me?"

"Of course. The first minute I'm in town," Vince said.

"You no forget?" she asked.

"Never," he assured her. He had trouble looking her in the eye.

"I think you lie," she said squeezing his hand. "American all time tell lie."

"I don't lie," Grecco said looking about nervously. "I'm different."

"I hope so," Attopeu said. Then she turned and was hurrying off down the corridor. Her high heels clicking rhythmically on the concrete floor.

Grecco felt a pang of guilt. He had fucked a nineteen-year-old. Probably seventeen or even sixteen. Young enough to be his daughter. In The States, he'd be charged with statutory rape and tossed in jail for seventeen years. Oh, sure, she was a hooker. It was for sale. If he hadn't done it, someone else would have. But whose fault was it? Why was the country teeming with teenage whores? The reason was so obvious. It was the same wherever American troops went. They were fucking for the Yankee dollar. Attopeu could make more in one night screwing; then she could in a month doing anything else. It was a matter of economics. There Grecco went again rationalizing. One could rationalize absolutely anything, couldn't one?

A Jungle Ambush

The sun was setting, casting streaks of red and gold across the tropic sky. Tufts of cloud lay black against the radiant horizon. Twelve figures strung one behind the other were seen silhouetted against the dwindling rays of sunlight. They crept quietly along a narrow trail, their weapons held out before them. And then like the setting sun, they were gone. Disappearing into a triple canopy of foreboding jungle.

For a while they moved blindly along the trail, their feet sliding in the slimy thick mud. Up ahead the point man felt about cautiously for trip wires that would set off a booby trap. An explosion, that could if it were large enough, blow him into tiny fragments of flesh and bone. A small one might blow off a leg or perhaps just a foot.

After a while, One-Zero, the squad leader, motioned for the point man to stop. Then each, in turn, touched the one behind him. They moved off the trail and selected a spot to lie in wait for the enemy to pass. Each took a Claymore mine from his pack and pressed its two front prongs into the soft earth so that the explosion was set at the proper angle along the path. A fuse was then screwed into a well at the top, activating the mine. Then the man stretched a wire back to where he would lie in wait. The end was fixed to a clacker, an electric cell detonator. Ideally, the Claymores would all detonate simultaneously on command, each firing a hundred and fifty BB-sized pellets ripping the hapless enemy troops to shreds. It was "overkill", the squad leader thought. Two would be sufficient. One facing back down the trail and the other in the opposite direction would be adequate. However, it was a morale booster, and that was always important. Sometimes one just couldn't go by the book.

The Idiot's Frightful Laughter

The machine gunner moved in among the troops with his M-60 in search of a wide, unobstructed field of fire. He noted the other men's positions. Calculating just how well his fire could best cover them, and at the same time, not hit anyone. He and his assistant set several logs on top of one another hacking out a slot for the barrel to rest. Placing it in the groove, he set an aiming stake at either side of the weapon, so that he would know just how far to swing it without shooting any of his teammates.

In total darkness, the gunner cautiously inspected his weapon by feel. He pulled the operating handle back twice easing it forward carefully to be sure it had cleared. Then easing the buttstock, the buffer yoke, and buffer free, he slid the rod and bolt assembly back until they dropped into his hand. The gunner then sprayed the receiver and bolt with a thin coat of oil. Re-assembling the weapon, he fed a 250-mm belt of ammo into the cartridge feed. And finally, he ratcheted the operating handle. The M-60 was now loaded and ready for action. The weapon spit forth a rain of death. It fired a salvo of six hundred .308 caliber slugs per minute. "That's my sweet fucking baby," he murmured caressing its stock fondly.

Moving about cautiously in order not to disturb the Claymores, One-Zero crept some distance back down the trail and set up a trip flare at the edge of the undergrowth. He could activate it when the enemy was in flight. Each grunt picked up several empty C-rat cans and dropped a handful of pebbles in them. He then hung them from low hanging limbs and bamboo twigs about his position. A rattling sound would alert the man that Charlie was slipping up on him.

However, the men had more to worry about than enemy troops. The jungle was alive with all sorts of annoying creatures. Some were deadly. There were poisonous snakes and swarms of fire ants and leeches as well as scorpions and centipedes. And zillions of malaria-carrying mosquitoes swarmed all about them. However, the worst nuisances were the horse flies that the grunts called "banzai bugs". Hundreds of these wide-winged insects would appear at dusk darting about biting off chunks of skin and flesh.

The troops cut away the undergrowth with shears wrapped with cloth to muffle the noise. The ground, tree trunks and overhanging branches were sprayed with a very light film of kerosene. In the close humid air, the fumes were strong, but this could not be helped, for no one could endure the leeches and ants for long. And a snake bite could kill one in an instant. The men spread their ponchos on the ground. They covered their boots and pant legs with insect repellent and also rubbed it on their hands, face, and neck. The pungent odor permeated the air. How could the enemy not help but smell it? But then the jungle was foul with the stench of decaying leaves and rotting logs.

They lay quietly throughout the night. No one dare sleep for fear he might snore or moan. It was the monsoon. It rained constantly. Their clothes were soaked, for the ponchos did little to ward off the downpour. Their skin turned white, wrinkled and cracked. The rain would wash away the kerosene and repellent, and then the insects and varmints would move in leaving them to suffer in silence. There was the tremendous monotony; plenty of time for a multitude of ghoulish premonitions. A dense foreboding jungle pressed in upon them. There was a symphony of strange exotic sounds. The shrill screeches of night birds. The imbecilic cries of the orangutan. The gnawing, rustling about of rodents and weasels. The men lay numb with fear shivering in the chilly dark drizzle. They relived in vivid detail the vision of the bloody shattered stump of a comrade. His leg suddenly blown to bits by an unsuspected booby trap, dying in shrieks of pain and fright. The torn and shattered body zipped up inside a black Vinyl bag and heaved into a chopper. Lying alone in the damp decaying undergrowth, these youth relived such horror again and again. It drove some to homicidal madness. They hungered for revenge. The enemy was everywhere, or so they thought. They hated all Vietnamese. They were to blame. They'd caused it all.

One-Zero peered along the trail probing the gloom with the help of a starlight scope attached to his rifle. When the sky was clear, and there was no overhead canopy, it amplified the light of the stars enough to detect an enemy soldier's silhouette slipping silently through the dense undergrowth.

Suddenly the field radio came alive. "Deadeye. Deadeye. This is Macho Man comm. Check, over," it hissed. One-Zero reached for the handset and pressed it to his ear turning down the squelch.

"Macho man. This is Deadeye. Hear you five by. How am I? Over," he whispered.

"Deadeye. This is Macho Man. Hear you same same. What's your position?"

Cupping both hands over the speaker, One-Zero gave his map coordinates in code whispering as softly as possible.

It was mid-morning before the sunlight penetrated the luxuriant tropic growth giving the bivouac area a shade-drawn appearance. The grunts ate unheated cans of spaghetti and meatballs, stew or whatever C-rats they might be carrying in their rucksacks. They applied camouflage grease paint to their faces and then carefully shouldered their gear. Loaded magazines went on the left side so that a guy could instantaneously drop an empty one with the right hand and insert a full one with the left. The maneuver took less than three seconds. Grenades were on the right. The pins were straightened and then wrapped with tape, so if one arm was wounded, the grunt could pull the pin with his teeth. A compass was strapped to the left wrist so that the GI could extend his hand away from the magnetic pull of his steel helmet and weapon.

The squad left the trail and moved out into the thick tangled undergrowth in order to avoid any possible booby traps. The jungle floor was stiflingly hot, for no breeze could penetrate the dense foliage. Vines wound about them pulling their rifles from their hands making their movements slow and arduous. Thorns two to three inches long tore the clothing and ripped deep gashes in the flesh. Patches of razor-sharp reeds towered several meters above their heads. Overhanging branches often bore hives of fire ants that would cascade over the men dropping down the collar and on to the bare chest and back. They were so named, for their bite burned like fire. And whenever the grunts waded through a swamp or crossed a stream, dozens of huge black three to four-inch leeches would attach themselves to the legs, groin, and abdomen. The blood-bloated parasites were removed with care by pressing the embers of a lighted cigarette against them. One could not simply pull them off, for the head would break away beneath the skin causing infection.

Drenched in sweat, they edged forward stopping frequently to check their bearings on the map. A greenish-gray mold began to appear on everything. First, it was noted on the plastic rifle stocks and metal gear. Then it was seen on clothing, canvass jungle boots, inside helmet liners and on ammo clips and bandoleers. It coated the radio, and this was a critical problem. Then the men themselves became moldy. The fungi covered their arms and neck. The skin began to shrivel and peel. Warts emerged frequently on the fingers and in the crotch. Some found them on their cock. The cuts and scratches from the bramble became infected, grew inflamed, filled with puss and throbbed with pain.

The patrol came upon a small thatched hut hidden in the undergrowth. Inside were several dozen sacks of rice, sign that the enemy was nearby. One of the grunts doused the sacks with kerosene, and before One-Zero could stop him, set them aflame. It was a mistake, for the smoke would give their position away.

An enemy unit watched the twelve figures strung out one behind the other skirt a grove of rubber trees. The Yanks crept quietly through the undergrowth; their weapons held out before them. And then in a flash, they were gone. Blown to bits by a half dozen Claymore mines placed along the row of rubber trees. A cheer went up from the bluff above. The Viet Cong had scored a joyous victory and so cheaply. They'd bought the mines from an Arvin soldier guarding a resettlement camp. The Claymore had cost one hundred piaster each. Less than one dollar. The Arvin was pleased to be of help. Both his father and brothers were VC.

Suburbia, U.S.A.

Doctor Elias Younger was surprised that Grecco had slept so long. He'd figured on four days. No more than five. Eight seemed a bit excessive. This was Vietnam. A War was going on. The longest in U.S. history. The situation was growing worse by the day. Those, who had chosen to be here, must bite the bullet, so to speak. Show the Communist that they meant business.

"I wired your boss and said that you'd be back in five days, so your three days late, and four by tomorrow," Doctor Younger said, "Want me to wire him again and try to smooth things out?"

"No, thanks anyway. I'll explain when I get there." Grecco saw that Doctor Younger was not the compassionate physician that he'd thought he was. His message may not be all that supportive, possibly one of disillusionment or worse betrayal. He could do without that. Besides he wasn't all that anxious to get back just yet. Not for at least another day. Tomorrow was Sunday. He had to see Grant Olson and find out how things were doing at the Saigon Sport Parachute Club since he left. He'd reluctantly turned over its operation to Grant and had his doubts about Grant's managerial skills.

It was nine a.m. when Grecco left the doctor's office. Too early to see Olson. He wouldn't be home from work until after 6 p.m. To kill time, Vince decided to make the rounds of the post exchanges. There was a large one in Cholon and an even larger one at the Tan Son Nhut Air Terminal. There was also a small one in downtown Saigon. Alongside the Cholon PX was the commissary; a stateside supermarket for Americans and their allies. Officially it was off limits to the Vietnamese.

But first, there was a matter of money. He could cash a check at the lobby of USAID's main office building; however, most everyone got theirs from the black market. The rate was much better. Grecco knew an Indian from Madras who he'd dealt with at times. No one knew his real name. Gene was all he ever went by. One could get at least one hundred and forty dollars in cash for a hundred-dollar check. A profit of forty dollars in U. S. military script.

"You're only making things more difficult for the average Vietnamese," Olson once told Grecco.

"You're looking at it all wrong, Grant," Vince replied. "I'm helping to bring this war you so despise so much to a quicker end."

"Rationalizer," Olson said. "The worst sort of hypocrite."

"The only kind," Grecco replied smiling sardonically. What made some people so puritanical? He wondered. He'd known the Olsons as a child. Grant's mother had been his teacher. They were so sanctimonious.

Grecco rang the bell at the ornate gate of an antiquated French villa. He held his finger on the button for several minutes before the concierge came and pulled open the latch. Vince climbed a narrow staircase at the rear of a garage and then walked along an outside corridor. Gene's apartment was at the end of the ramp. His door was open. At Grecco's appearance, two Caucasian youths wearing denim jackets and pants got up and without a word edged past him and hurried along the corridor. They were not Gene's usual clientele.

Gene was a stout dark man with large gazelle eyes. He wore slacks and a neatly pressed white nylon sports shirt. He was intensely shy, and his voice was very soft.

One never asked Gene for money, not right away. That always came later. One must first enjoy his hospitality, smoke a cigarette or have a beer or coke. After discussing the current state of affairs in Vietnam and elsewhere, Gene would most discreetly ask: "How much would you like to cash?" He spoke with a clipped upper-class British accent.

Grecco asked for two hundred U.S. dollars in MPC (Military Payment Certificates) and one hundred dollars in Vietnamese piaster.

The Idiot's Frightful Laughter

"I say, the rate is a mite low just now," Gene said looking most apologetic as though it were somehow his fault. "Would you want to wait a bit?"

Grecco was hesitant about asking the rate. He felt that it might be considered indiscreet. "May I ask just how much it is?" he asked trying match Gene's solicitude. However, he felt that he sounded more maudlin than discreet.

"Only a hundred and forty-five," he replied looking most apologetic. "Last week it was a hundred and fifty. Piasters are three hundred and eighty. That's not so bad."

"That'll be fine," Grecco said beginning to feel a bit disgusted with the whole crooked deal. Oh, the lies we tell to deceive. He's a phony sonofabitch, but a high-class phony sonofabitch, he thought.

"Are you quite sure?"

"Quite," Grecco said. "I'm leaving for Delta either tomorrow or Monday." He wrote out a check with the Bank of America for three hundred dollars and handed it to Gene. The line for the payee was left blank. Vince would get the canceled check back in a month or two, the back covered with a half dozen stamps. Logos of clandestine banking firms from places like Hong Kong, Singapore, Switzerland, and New York. The check will probably earn ten times its true value, Grecco though. But how? Why? It was a great mystery.

Gene went into the bedroom and returned with a thick bundle of piaster. Then he slipped off his belt. There was a zipper on the inside. He unzipped it and pulled out a wad of MPC. He counted out fourteen twenties and a ten. Recounting them a second time, he handed the bills one at a time to Olson. In such a sleazy business, one couldn't be too careful, Vince figured. One never knew.

Grecco knew better than to rush off after getting his money. That would be most indiscreet, he assumed. It was best to have another beer and talk a little more of current events or encourage Gene to tell him of India. Ask about things to see, the transportation, the best time of year to visit, and such. Then earnestly promise to be his guest in Madras at some unspecified time, and finally shake hands and depart; suddenly recalling that he had a pressing engagement. One that could not wait.

As he hurried down the corridor, Vince thought of the two lads in denims. Quite likely they had not known how to behave and thus had been refused. Gene was unquestionably a gentleman. Just as the American Mafia, Indian gangsters lived by a code. Self-respect was a cherished commodity, a top priority. Gene would not allow the degrading nature of his work to lessen his self-esteem, not for a moment.

On the boulevard outside the villa, Grecco stopped a tiny blue and yellow taxi. They were everywhere throughout the city. They were said to be owned by a wealthy Chinese merchant. They all had meters, but Vince had never known of a driver to use one.

"Cholon PX," Grecco said.

"Okay," the driver said. The tiny man looked angry; however, Vince knew that it was a bluff. They had learned that Americans especially civilians were more apt to agree to a higher fare if they were troublesome.

"One hundred pee," Grecco said trying to match the driver's fierce countenance.

The driver laughed scornfully. "No way, GI," he growled. "You pay two hundred. Cholon beaucoup far. Okay?"

They eventually agreed on a hundred and fifty piaster. They each edged towards the fare ten piaster at a time. Not until the price was fixed at one fifty did Vince get into the cab, for the driver was apt to roar off saying: "Okay, you pay one-eighty," or whatever the figure was that he was holding out for.

The Military Policeman at the post exchange's main gate was in full battle dress. He stood just to one side of a concrete bunker. Looking scornfully at Grecco, he carefully scrutinized his ID card. "Yea, okay," he snarled with a toss of his head.

"REMF," Vince muttered to himself. The acronym stood for Rear Echelon Mother Fucker. They're always the most gung-ho, he thought. Probably have a guilt complex. They'd shit their pants if Charlie took a shot at them. Seventy percent were REMF.

The Cholon PX Compound covered all but a tiny portion of a huge city block. The thick wall that surrounded the complex was crowned with jagged chunks of broken bottle. They looked as though they'd been there for a very long time. Within the barricade was a slice right from suburbia USA. Just inside the main gate was a branch of the Chase Manhattan Bank, the lodestone of the Rockefeller Dynasty. A huge one-story concrete warehouse dominated the center of the compound. The PX occupied a major portion of this building. It resembled Costco only larger. It had everything from women's cosmetics, diamond rings, and women's fur coats to full-size refrigerators, portable typewriters, and Bermuda shorts. The building also had a barber shop, a liquor store, a recording shop with every conceivable type of tape recorder and stereo set, a curio shop with Thai souvenirs, an army clothing store, a repair shop, an automobile agency, and the commissary.

Across from the entrance way to the PX was a shed where canned beer and soft drinks were sold by the case, and next to it was a shoe repair shop and gift-wrapping counter. There was also a snack bar that not only served foot-long hot dogs, hamburgers and French fries, but also such full course meals as Southern fried chicken, roast beef, barbecued ribs, mashed potatoes, and Kentucky baked ham. At intervals throughout the day, a mobile unit served frozen custard, ice cream and milkshakes made its run. At the rear of the compound was a U.S. post office where one could mail these PX items to friends back in The States at half the price. An irony that never ceased to amuse Grecco.

First of all, Vince went to the liquor store and bought three fifths of Scotch for Tan. He would have liked to buy a couple of bottles of Napa Valley wine, but he'd used up all the liquor coupons on his ration card for the month. The Social Welfare Chief took his entire liquor ration each month. Grecco wondered why he didn't hate the little chiseler. Most Americans despised their counterparts. Perhaps it was because Vince had never really had the tiniest particle of confidence in the creep. How could he hate someone who was so hopelessly insignificant? Nevertheless, out of habit, Vince was always trying to get him to take the initiative. Just do something for once. Show that somewhere in that petty self-serving heart of his, he had a tiny speck of compassion for his people.

Next Grecco went to the music shop. A shipment of large stereo tape recorders had just arrived from Japan. The room was jammed with Korean and Thai troops busily buying as many of the electrical appliances as their ration cards would allow. The items brought high prices at the hostess bars and strip joints on Tu Do Street.

In the main PX, Vince found more Korean and Thai soldiers lined up at the checkout counter. Their shopping carts were heaped with items to sell at the public market. Grecco was amused at how it outraged the American shoppers. Not long ago a Korean captain had shot a reporter for photographing him at the checkout counter with a cartload of electronic equipment. He had very casually drawn his pistol and shot the man in the shoulder. "The next is your heart," he said easing the weapon back into its holster. Now there was a large sign taped to the main door forbidding anyone to take photos in the PX.

What about the weapons? Grecco thought.

A short stocky American with a bulldog face and a cigar butt crammed in one corner of his mouth edged over to where Vince was standing. "Doesn't that gripe your ass?" the man said motioning to the line of Korean and Thai soldiers. He had a Brown & Root logo on his cap.

"No, not in the least," Grecco said glancing down at the angry man. "It's all part of a clever scheme of our marketing experts to wipe out French competition. American businessmen learned back in World War II that if you lock things up inside a compound and tell people they can't have them, they'll do almost anything to get them. The Vietnamese think they're outwitting the stupid Americans, and that makes them happy, Vince said. "But then this is just a sideline. It's actually aimed at whipping the Communists," he added.

"Oh yea," the bulldog said taking the cigar butt from his mouth; his small pig eyes boring into Grecco. "You wouldn't be shitting me?" he said bristling.

The Idiot's Frightful Laughter

"No, I'm quite serious," Vince replied. "The main reason for all this," he added motioning to the long line of Koreans, Thais and a smattering of Filipinos, "is to change South Vietnam into a consumer society. Just as long as the Vietnamese are dependent on the U.S. and Japan for all these luxury items, the less apt they are to embrace Communism."

"You're a smart cocksucker, ain't you?" The bulldog snarled throwing his cigar butt on the floor and grinding it to a pulp with his shoe.

Grecco wouldn't be deterred by the little man's ferocity. "Hey, look at it this way," he said. "What would become of the hundreds of thousands of Japanese motorcycles choking the streets and highways if this country went Communist?" Vince asked gazing down at the bulldog whose teeth were bared looking as though he were about to bite him. "You can bet your sweet ass that China and Russia are in no position to assume such responsibility nor would they want to."

"You got all the answers, don't you?" the little man snarled. "Well, all I know is my tax dollars go into buying that stuff, and I don't like to throw it away like that." He walked off several paces; then turned back and took a good look at Grecco. "Listen, smartass, I ain't forgetting this. See," he said.

Grecco wandered aimlessly about the huge warehouse. It was so old. Must have been built by the French a hundred years ago. Nice how they left all this for us? He thought. There was nothing that he needed. Why had he come? He wondered. However, after more than an hour of ambling back and forth between the three and four tier shelves, his cart was heaped with an odd array of items. He'd picked up a battery for the light meter in his camera, copies of *The New Yorker* and *The Nation*, several yards of Thai silk, a red polka dot ascot, a coffee percolator, a tube of Duco Cement, and a box of decongestant pills for his sinus. At the commissary, he picked up three cans of ham, six frozen tenderloin steaks, a can of Yuma coffee, a quart jar of mayonnaise, a bag of marshmallows, a can of grape juice, six cans of crab, and a sack of Stark Delicious apples. Then he stopped at the snack bar for a cheeseburger, French fries, and a malted milk.

When he'd finished eating, he poured the apples into the carton with the rest of the purchase. Then he tore the sack open and spread it out over the top of the box tucking the edges in about the contents. Next, he took his wristwatch and wallet and put them in his front pocket stuffing a handkerchief down on top of them. Twice before a group of small children ranging in age from six to ten had surrounded him only a few yards from the compound. The little ones had shouted and tugged at his arms and clothing while the older youth grabbed whatever they could get hold of and ran off. The MP guarding the main entrance laughed heartily. He thought that it was great sport. "What goes around comes around," he told the flabbergasted Grecco.

This time there were no children lying in wait for him, only the usual throng of cyclo and taxi drivers who made a habit of harassing foreigners. Grecco placed the carton box on his shoulder and moved in among the drivers walking at a rapid pace, knowing that if he stopped, it would be difficult to shake them off. Several planted themselves squarely in his path, thus he had to pivot about them trying not to shorten his stride.

After walking several blocks, well out of reach of the hustlers, Grecco stopped and hailed a taxi. "Ky Dong," he shouted. That was where Grant Olson lived. It was a short street, only three blocks long.

The Proletariat Dictatorship

Victoria, Grant Olson's Filipina wife, met Grecco at the door. She had a *Betty Crocker Cookbook* in one hand. "What's cooking, Vicky?" he asked.

"Mr. Grecco! Long time no see," she giggled as though she had said something quite witty. She was tiny. No more than five-foot-two standing just even with Vince's chest.

"Been looking for a Filipina girlfriend," he said pinching her playfully on the cheek.

"Vince! Goddamn, it's good to see you!" Olson said leaping to his feet and coming to the door. He'd been seated at a round wicker table with a glass top correcting a stack of test papers. "When'd you get to town?"

"I've been here more than a week," Grecco said taking the carton box from his shoulder and placing it on the floor. "Look! Tenderloins. A half dozen of them. What do you say we have a feast?" he said holding up a package of frozen steaks.

"Great!" Olson said leading Grecco into the room. "But what's the idea of hiding out from me?" I could have sure used your help last Sunday. The club's getting to be more than I can handle."

"I've been sick," Vince said glancing about the tiny room. Except for a few knickknacks, it hadn't changed much. An ugly metal bed with a gauzy-looking mosquito net occupied nearly a fourth of the space. Lacquer vases with inlaid mother-of-pearl, a large ceramic lamp and wood carvings, all gifts of appreciative students, were scattered about everywhere. Shelves crammed with books lined the walls, and there was still the Buddhist shrine with the joss sticks and food offerings. Victoria's vanity table loaded with PX cosmetics stood near the window. Two huge temple rubbings from Angkor Wat graced the wall. A half dozen vases of flowers from Dalat, once a popular French resort in the central highlands, set on shelves in the window. Overhead an ancient propeller fan creaked noisily.

"Sick?" Olson said. "Nothing serious, I hope?" He took the stack of papers from the table and set them on the bed.

"The doctor said that it was a nervous breakdown," Grecco said sitting down at the table.

"You! A nervous breakdown? Impossible!" Grant said looking aghast at his old friend. "Nothing ever bothers you. Why I remember when Sergeant Murphy changed padlocks on us and wouldn't let us have our rigs. Said they were property of the U. S. Government. You were as cool as a cobra."

"That's a pretty poor simile, Grant," Vince said laughing. "Cobras aren't very cool. At least not the ones I've seen." Then raising his finger, he said "I know. Can't bear to use a cliché. Still the same old pedant."

"Yea, I suppose," Olson said frowning. "But a nervous breakdown? Are things really that bad in the province?"

Victoria brought in two frosted glasses of limeade and set them on the table. The juice was made from limes about the size of large marbles. "Calamansi juice," she said nodding to Grecco. "You like?"

"You bet, Vicki," he said taking a sip and smacking his lips. "Magnificent! You're a lucky man, Ollie. I must go to The Philippines," Vince said turning about and winking at Victoria.

"Good idea," Grant said smiling rakishly. "Vicki's got a good-looking sister and tons of cousins, don't you, Vicki?"

"I don't think so," she said frowning with mock severity. At the kitchen door, she leaned back and made an impish face at Grant.

How's the club doing?" Grecco asked. He could hear the grease popping in the skillet. A cloud of rich meaty aroma billowed from the tiny kitchen cubby hole and hung in the still air. She's cooking them much too fast, Vince thought. They'll be tough as leather.

"Terrible," Ollie exclaimed. We're in bad with Colonel Meo again. Can't use the choppers."

"Why?" Grecco said looking intently at his friend. One eye was cocked derisively.

The Idiot's Frightful Laughter

"You remember Bob Brady?" Grant asked. "That red-headed airman you grounded for making a low opening."

"Yea, how could I forget< Vince said. "Nearly killed both of us."

Olson took some tissue from his pocket and wiped the sweat from his brow. It was hot. Must be over a hundred, he thought. "Well, the dumb punk called Sergeant Chao a gook. Mad because Chao hadn't modified his canopy."

Did you run the sonofabitch off?" Grecco asked. Outside a youth was gunning the engine of his motorcycle. Even though they were on the fifth floor, the noise was deafening. They had no windows to shut out the sound. Vince leaned forward cupping his ears.

"Can't. Sergeant Murphy won't let me touch any of the military," Olson said.

"What?" Grecco shouted leaning further across the table. The wicker creaked beneath his weight, and the glass tabletop flipped up spilling the lime juice.

"Murphy won't let me," Grant shouted. Vince shook his head and made a face as though he had tasted something foul. "We're renting a Dakota from Constellation," he added. "It's costing us three hundred bucks an hour."

Vince fixed his gaze on the angry features of black power poet Roi Jones on the dust jacket of a book. It was propped up on the top of the bookshelf across the room from him. "Three hundred bucks an hour for a lousy DC-3. Incredible! Ab-sol-ute-ly incredible," he enunciated.

"Yea, it averages out to more than twenty bucks for a single jump per jumper," Olson said. Victoria placed the steak on large ceramic plates before the two men.

"Oh boy!" Grecco said beaming up at Victoria. "They look exquisite."

"I don't think so," she said teasingly.

"Have you really had a nervous breakdown, Vince?" Ollie said looking gravely at him. "You look great. Doesn't he, Vicky?"

Grecco picked up his knife and trimmed a piece of fat from an edge of the tenderloin. "Well, I slept for eight days. Now I believe I know how Rip van Winkle must have felt when he woke up to find his world turned upside down.," he said placing a piece of fat in his mouth. "Can't we have a little chat with Colonel Meo, Ollie? Give him a couple fifths of Johnny Walker Black Label?"

"Not as long as that redhead asshole is still with the club," Grant said. "It's a matter of face."

"Well, I guess I better have a little chat with my ol' pal Murphy tomorrow," Grecco said with a sinister smile.

"Now you're talking, Vince," Olson said extending his hand across the table. "Shake. Now you sound like your old self again," They both leaned back in their chairs, for it suddenly occurred to them that they needn't shout. The youth was no longer revving his motorcycle.

Victoria set a large bowl of salad and a platter of fried rice on the table. "Well, let's eat while the meats still hot," Grant said picking up his knife and fork. "Won't you join us, Vicki?"

"Later," she said. "I'm busy."

Next door the television had been turned on full volume. The staccato of machine gun fire chattered through the wall. "*Combat*," Olson said. "The Vietnamese love our war movies. Strange, isn't it? War and Westerns."

Grecco looked up at Grant and nodded gravely. "Incredible," he said. "Absolutely incredible."

Vince gazed intently at LeRoi Jones' book of poetry. The poems were a rallying cry for revolution. "Kill the honky. Burn the country," they screamed. Grecco wondered just how far Grant was willing to go. Was he simply one of those Ivy League Radicals, all mouth, and no fight, or was he a rebel burning for a scrap with the military-industrial complex? Just how deep did his anger go? "Look, Ollie, let me be the Devil's Advocate, okay?"

"Fine, what's the pitch?" Olson

"A straight one right over home plate," Grecco said. "You're a liberal, right?"

"Right," Olson said. Same ol' Vince. Always picking some guy's brain, he thought.

"Might even say you're a radical, to some degree, right?"

"To some degree, yes."

"Do you believe in the Bill of Rights?"

"Some of them. Not the one to bear arms. That's outdated," Olson said.

"Take freedom. You know. Freedom of speech. Freedom of religion. Freedom of the press."

"Freedom of the press? Give me a break, Vince. Who has freedom of the press? The CEOs of some thirty blue-chip corporations? NBC's a subsidiary of General Electric. CNN has been swallowed up by Time Warner. CBS is Westinghouse, and ABC belongs to Disney. The mass media is owned by big money. That's where your so-called freedom lies," Olson said slapping down hard on the table.

"What about freedom of speech, freedom of religion and freedom of assembly? They're still in the hands of the people, aren't they? We can still vote although the choices are somewhat limited, can't we?" The discussion was heating up. Grecco seemed to be taking his role quite seriously.

"I suppose," Olson said. He was growing troubled. Sometimes he wondered who this guy he'd known all his life really was.

"Then how can you support the VC, Ollie? How much freedom do they have? Zero," Grecco said making his thumb and forefinger resemble a circle.

"Yea. Sure. That may be true. It's a so-called proletariat dictatorship," Grant said. "But look at the alternative. What about the clowns running things down here. What do they believe in? Looting the nation's coffers. They're nothing but gangsters."

"But there's a parliament. The legislators have something to say about what the president does," Grecco said noticeably enjoying the role of agitator.

"Come on, Vince. They're nothing but pawns. They say whatever they're told to say. Take Nguyen Cao Ky, the American brass's pride and joy. He was their pick for Prime Minister and Air

Force Commander. He was groomed by the CIA's Saigon Bureau Chief, Bill Colby. Ky's an avoid Nazi. Considers Hitler the greatest. History's most emanate. Is that freedom, Vince? Come on. Get real. You can't be serious?" Olson was quite beside himself.

Grecco noticed that Grant's hands were trembling. "So, which is worse: a compassionate dictatorship that can only go so far, or a Communist dictatorship which is absolute?"

"Compassionate? You sound like Tricky Dick," Olson said. "At least it seems clear that the Viet Cong are not corrupt. As a matter of fact, they give every indication of being quite puritanical."

"Nevertheless, they're still Vietnamese," Grecco said smiling his sinister twisted lip grin.

"That has all the marks of a racial slur. Are you saying that the Vietnamese are genetically corrupt?" Olson said slapping his hand on the table. It made a face-slapping sound that brought Victoria scurrying from the kitchen.

"Why you fight?" she demanded. "You old friends."

"It's an old American tradition," Vince said smiling reassuringly. "Then we kiss and make up." Then turning back to Grant, he said: "Not genetically, environmentally."

"It's the Viet Cong's hope to change the environment socially, economically, and ah," Olson paused.

"And politically," Grecco said leaning back and laughing loudly. "Don't take things so serious, Grant. You'll have a heart attack."

"Or a nervous breakdown," Olson said.

"Touché," Vince said pretending as though he'd been stabbed through the heart.

Smokejumpers

That night after Grecco had left, Olson lay awake for a long time thinking about skydiving. He no longer liked it, but he could not tell Vince. It would be too hard to explain.

It wasn't that he'd lost his nerve. That he dreaded making free-falls. Pummeling towards earth at over a hundred miles an hour. It wasn't that. It was all the work and responsibility that was suddenly thrust upon him after Vince had been transferred to the delta.

There were innumerable things to worry about prior to a jump. The equipment had to be in order. There was the plane and pilot to negotiate with. The reserve chutes to repack. Things like wind-drift indicators, smoke signals, and first aid equipment at the drop zone. And then there was the manifest. That was the most unpleasant task of all. It was up to him to decide who was qualified to jump and who wasn't, especially who wasn't. Whether or not to use a static-line. And from what height a novice could make a free-fall. Always there were bitter arguments. Beginners insisting that they were ready to make their first jump, and the neophytes always wanting to go higher and higher. Make longer and longer delays. And to top it all off, there was Sergeant Mike Murphy, the club's safety officer. A mere sergeant who behaved like a battalion commander. He waited until they were in the aircraft, all suited up and ready to take off before scratching a half dozen or so names from the jump list. Invariably they were civilians.

During the jumps, it was Olson who had to spot for everyone. Dropping one crepe paper streamer after another until he knew the strength of the wind and was certain of the exit point. He was the one to give the students last minute instructions. Tell them to be sure and check their canopies. See that they weren't tangled, that there were no lineovers. Advise them on how long to hold into the wind and to be sure and keep their legs together and not to look at the ground prior to landing.

All Sunday afternoon there was training. Teaching them how to leave the aircraft. How to guide their chutes. How to touch the ground and roll. If anything went wrong. If anyone broke an ankle or even twisted it, Sergeant Murphy would blame Olson. Threaten to send a report to the U. S. Parachute Association's central headquarters in Monterey, California, and get Olson's instructor's license revoked. Mike Murphy swung a lot of weight with the USPA. He was not only a member of the Golden Knights, the Army's elite skydiving team but had taken first place in international competitions. He was someone to be reckoned with.

When Olson had threatened to resign, the civilians had pleaded with him not to leave. Who would train and qualify them to jump? Murphy would take control and force them from the club. They promised to help Grant. Give him whatever assistance they could. Several actually did help some. Ron Starkey, an accountant at Brown & Root's main office, was a licensed rigger and spent Saturday afternoons and occasionally during evening hours mending parachutes and repacking reserves. However, most of the members hastily forgot their commitments. After all, skydiving was just a Sunday morning activity. It wasn't one's lifetime career. And then there was all that good pussy on Tu Do Street to consider.

For years, skydiving was all Olson had to look forward to. It was an escape from a bad marriage and a classroom full of contentious adolescents. But it was more than just that. Those thirty, forty-five, and sixty seconds sailing about in space was the sort of freedom that only a bird with human awareness might know. He liked to tumble backward from the plane and float on his back watching the aircraft seem to zoom upward and disappear. He'd feel himself accelerate for thirteen seconds and then stop and float about on a foam mattress of air as pliant as water. He'd flip over and gaze about at the earth a mile or so away and feel the stillness. A sense that he and the world were transfixed. That for those few moments, everything had paused as though a pantheistic god had stopped to meditate.

The Idiot's Frightful Laughter

Olson could tumble and twist and spin about as freely as a skylark. But there was fear. And that was important. It started the moment he climbed aboard the aircraft. As the plane rose, he'd feel it surge through his limbs. His breath came faster and stronger. The heart thumped harder and harder. The legs grew weak. All this he relished. It was reassuring. Reminding him that in spite of everything, life was the ultimate. But the moment he'd leap into space, the fear would vanish as though it had clung to the plane, too timid to follow.

Now all this was gone. There were none of those feelings of tranquility, stillness, exhilaration and especially fear. That had all been ruined. Circumstances had made a drudgery of the sport. Jumping had become so routine. He'd leap quite automatically thinking of the students. How had they landed? Were there any injuries? He was so totally oblivious of his own freefall. He no longer bothered to try any acrobatics or hook up with other skydivers. He fell in a flat relaxed position. His knees slightly bent. His hand held at either side of his head as though he were pressing against a glass door. His eyes were fixed on his altimeter prepared to pull the ripcord at twenty-five hundred feet. Preoccupied with what might have happened to the novice jumpers.

Grecco also had trouble falling asleep that night. He was thinking of all that Olson had told him, and he was angry. He'd put so much hard work into building up the club, and now Grant was letting it fall apart. Vince had liked being club president. It was the only thing he'd regretted leaving. The tasks that Olson despised so much were what he'd enjoyed the most especially the showdowns with Sergeant Mike Murphy. He'd savored those moments over and over again in his mind.

Seldom had anyone complained to him about the manifest; however, when one did, Grecco would smile at him as though he were a naughty child and say quite matter-of-factly: "Things are rough all over," and walk off.

What's more being president made his own jumping more meaningful. He'd select those he wanted to jump with, and it wasn't long before everyone wanted to be on his stick. It was partly status, but mainly because each jump was different: a new challenge.

He'd showed them how to form a cartwheel. As many as six would lock arms and spin about like a Roman candle. Then there was the six-man baton pass, and later they had all piled on to an air mattress. But the hula-hoop was the ultimate. Grecco would jump holding a hoop made of bamboo. The others would make passes at it like fish hawks. They would plunge straight down at the hoop, their arms and legs pressed tightly together. At the last moment, they'd flare out and try to slip through. Usually, they'd misjudge and either hit it with an arm or leg or miss it all together.

These team jumps formed strong bonds of camaraderie. He rarely had trouble getting a guy to take charge of some tedious task and do it without being reminded. On the other hand, Vince wouldn't hesitate to ground a skydiver for making a low opening. He kept one jumper grounded for three months for pulling another's ripcord at seven thousand feet. The man landed several miles from the drop zone on a river bank that was considered Viet Cong territory.

Grecco had expelled only one jumper. Rusty Piper was an impulsive young airman who would listen to no one and thus was always making careless mistakes, some quite serious. The showdown occurred the day Piper came within an inch or so of killing both of them. Vince often wondered how he could be so stupid as to allow the punk to jump with him. One day short of experienced jumpers, Grecco had allowed him to join a five-man stick. He needed someone to complete a five-man baton pass. Vince knew that he was going against his better judgment but had taken the risk. He had no idea just how grave the gamble was. Not until it was too late.

They had jumped at ten thousand feet from an old battle-scarred Sykorsky chopper that had seen better day during the Korean War. It had a huge doorway so that they were all able to jump in a string holding hand. Grecco was at the end. Piper was to make the last baton pass to him. By four thousand feet they had completed the fourth pass to Piper. He had plenty of time to make the final one to Vince; however, Rusty overshot dropping several hundred feet below Grecco. By then they were too low to make the final pass, so Vince waved Piper off and tracked out of range of anyone who might still be above him. At twenty-five hundred feet, he pulled his ripcord. As his canopy slipped free of its sleeve, he saw Piper diving straight at him. Grecco felt a surge of panic, as the youth's canopy popped open next to his. Another foot or so and the chutes would have tangled together, or Piper would have plunged into his parachute, killing himself and quite likely Grecco. The cord connecting Rusty's pilot chute to the sleeve tangled with Vince's. Piper began to rotate clockwise about Vince. When he saw Piper reach up to press his capewells that released the harness to the canopy, Grecco screamed: "Don't break away. You're too low." He was in near hysteria yelling the command a half dozen times. They were well below a thousand feet. There was no time to deploy his reserve. Besides, the two canopies would tangle, and he would also have to break away.

"Pull your left toggle," Grecco shouted holding tight to his right steering toggle. This stopped the chutes from oscillating about one another; however, Piper's chute was only partially inflated and was pulling Vince's canopy to one side. He tugged hard on his right risers to stabilize the parachutes. Fortunately, they struck a clump of bamboo that broke their fall lowering them gently to the ground.

Grecco didn't catch up with the youth until they were back at the drop zone. "You've made your last jump with this club, kid," He said trying to make his voice sound casual and indifferent, as well as tough and final. If Piper had said so much as one word, Vince would have smacked him hard in the teeth. The kid no doubt sensed it, for he could see the rage in Grecco's eyes.

A year later, Vince heard that Piper had been killed at a skyport near Chicago. Defying death, he'd attempted to throw out his reserve chute at no more than a hundred feet from earth. Lucky it was he and not someone else, Grecco had thought, remembering with a shiver of his own narrow escape.

Grecco thought back to the summer of '53 when Olson and he had first become interested in Parachuting. He had graduated with a degree in journalism and was studying creative writing from Pulitzer Prize-winning novelist Walter Van Tilburg Clark at the University of Montana when he learned about the Smokejumpers. They were an elite group of U.S. Forest Service firefighters who parachuted into remote sectors of the national forest to suppress fires before they got out of control. Vince had notified Grant, his old Marine Corps pal, of the job and coaxed him to come. It would be great fun. Lots of thrills. Olson, who was attending the University of Missouri, hitchhiked to Missoula in time for training.

The Nine Mile training site was a long abandon CCC camp. On weekend the two men double dated. They frequented the Big Foot Tavern about ten miles north of Missoula. The road snaked its way along the Clark Fork River blazed by the famed explorers, Lewis and Clark. Kuba, the proprietor, was a big personable Flathead Indian who passed himself off as a Hawaiian, for being an Indian in Montana was the equivalent of being a Negro in Mississippi. Kuba and Tillie, his platinum blonde girlfriend, switched off running the bar and dealing at the blackjack table. If the price was right, Tillie did a trick or two on the side.

Grecco and Olson usually managed to leave camp early Friday afternoon and get to Montana State University before classes ended. The student union was usually packed with young elementary and secondary teachers attending summer school. Once they got to know the two men, making pickups were easy. It was partly because for nine months these young women lived as strangers in remote mountain or prairie towns where the gossips watched their every move twisting and stretching the most trivial sorts of dalliances into wild orgies. These teachers were in rebellion against the tyranny of small-town bigotry.

Throughout the summer, Kuba reserved the same two cabins for them. The setting was most idyllic. The cabins were hidden from sight by a beech grove. Fern grew waist high about the cabins and wild strawberries could be gathered in a meadow only some twenty yards away.

The first thing every morning, the two men and their girls would make a ritual of scampering down the bank and plunging into the icy waters of the Clark Fork. The last one in would have to cook breakfast. The first Saturday morning that they were there, they didn't tell the women what the consequences were; until they were racing ahead of them down the path to the river, so Saturday morning one of the women had to prepare breakfast; however, Sunday the two women were splashing about in the snow-fed river before either Vince or Grant had awoke.

The Smokejumper training had been fun; however, Olson was nearly washed out. The instructor said that his reflexes were too slow. One must begin his roll the instant his toes touched the ground. Olson was taking all the shock in his ankles. He was sure to bust an ankle on his first hard landing.

Vince worked with Grant for hours every evening having him repeat the rollover and over again. Olson would mount a platform, grab hold of a rope and swing out over a sawdust pit. When he was directly above the pit, he would let go of the rope and drop, feet together, toes pointed downward, arms above the head, eyes on the horizon. Vince would crouch at the edge of the pit in order to watch the impact. No matter how hard Grant tried, the result was always the same. Grecco would shake his head disparagingly. "Nope," he'd say. "Too slow. Try it again." So, Olson would climb back on to the platform more determined than ever. However, the reflex just wasn't there, and no amount of practice would change that. Nevertheless, Grant's persistence impressed the supervisor. Anyone with that much grit was entitled to special consideration. Driving off an able-bodied man wasn't what he called good horse sense.

There were certain kinds of people the supervisor couldn't tolerate. He had no use for Jews, Communists, conscientious objectors, faggots and laggards, but Olson was none of these. He was a Marine who'd stormed the beach at Iwo Jima, so the supervisor had told the instructor to let Grant make a couple of practice jumps. They'd be able to tell more from that than anything else.

On his first jump, Olson landed ankle deep in mud, so all he could do was fall on his side. However, there was no one near enough to see. The important thing was he didn't suffer any ill effects.

The Jumps had begun in a marshy meadow and progressed to a hard stony plateau. Their final jumps were in timber, huge hundred-foot Ponderosa Pine and Douglas Fir. The canopy would drape over the top of a tree leaving the firefighter dangling high above the ground. To get down, he would take a hundred-foot coil of rope from a pants leg pocket and fix it to the parachute harness. Then he would release himself from the straps and lower himself to the ground.

On the last practice jump, Grecco and Olson left the plane together. Vince was behind Grant as they stepped from the doorway. They landed on a mountainside of loose shale tumbling more than thirty yards down a steep incline and finally coming to rest against a large outcropping of rock. The landing left the two badly shaken and bruised. They lay against the rocky ledge for some time before they felt like moving. They were unharmed. However, that could not be said for the other men. A number of them had broken something – a wrist, an ankle, an arm or a leg. One man had snapped his back crushing a disc in the lower lumbar. After that, no one worried about Olson's reflex.

For three summers, they jumped throughout the northwest as far south as the Trinity Alps in Northern California. They parachuted, fought fires, double dated and made plans to save their money and in two years' time buy a boat and sail around the world. They were each to save four thousand dollars, go to Scotland and buy a sailboat. However, long-range plans such those have a tendency of getting short-circuited. It was ten year before the two saw one another again. They met quite unexpectedly at the Tan Son Nhut parachute loft. They'd both got married, and the money that they'd been saving for the around the world boat trip went for payments on home, car, kitchen appliances and such. Now here they were after all this time jumping together in Vietnam, of all places.

The Saigon Sport Parachute Club

When Grecco arrived at the parachute loft the next morning, Olson and Ron Starkey had opened the huge steel connex box and laid the rigs out on the ground. A dozen men were standing about in groups of three and four talking. No one had offered to help. Sergeant Mike Murphy had not yet shown up. He was supposed to have gotten a truck for the drop zone. It was he who had insisted that at least four men be on hand at the DZ prior to the jump.

"Murphy is a fuck up," Grecco said loud enough so that everyone, especially the military, could hear. He had rehearsed just what he intended to say to the sergeant and was anxious to get it over with. However, now that he had nothing to do with the club, he didn't figure that he'd have much influence on the airborne advisor; however, someone had to take a stand before the civilians were squeezed out. Murphy was a ranger advisor and also a member of the Golden Knights. He was held in high repute by skydivers worldwide. However, he was also an ignorant man with a swelled head. Six years of international renown had badly inflated his ego, and his hatred of civilians only complicated the matter.

For some time, Grecco had Murphy believing that the Saigon Sport Parachute Club's founder, General Dick Stillwell, had made it a civilian club in order to keep it out of the clutches of any military commander averse to skydiving. However, Mike Murphy found a copy of the charter. He waited for a regular meeting in order to blow Vince's hoax apart. He announced that according to an old military directive, civilians could not jump from military aircraft. What's more, their gear was U.S. Army issue, and if they could not produce receipts showing that the rigs were purchased from army surplus stores, they would be confiscated. Furthermore, he had removed their padlock from the connex box and replaced it with his own.

It was Major Lon, the Vietnam Paratroop Battalion's adjutant, who saved the day. Like most Arvin, he despised U.S. servicemen. Their arrogance and condescension annoyed him, and many were racists. He'd never forget the time a truckload of Marines called him a fucking gook. The civilians, by and large, were no better. Many looked as though they might be ex-convicts and probably were. However, the civilian skydivers, on the other hand, were more amiable and easier to deal with. He especially liked Vincent Grecco and Grant Olson. They were true gentlemen. Recently Olson had collected money from the other civilians to buy him a state-of-the-art altimeter.

The gift couldn't have come at a better time. Major Lon was seated nearby in his jeep when the confrontation occurred. He intervened just as Grecco was telling Murphy to take a flying fuck. Olson was standing behind Vince ready to step in if he were knocked down. Neither thought that they had the slightest chance against the sergeant and his Ranger pals, but someone had to stand up to the prick. After all, they'd been running things long before Murphy showed up.

Major Lon told Sergeant Murphy in no uncertain terms that the aircraft were Vietnamese, not American. That the civilians were his friends and were welcome to jump from the choppers just as long as they respected Vietnamese authority. As for the equipment and facilities, well, they were Vietnamese property as well. The rigs had been bought from Arvin paratroopers.

While all this was going on, Bernie Sutton, a spunky little Australian who'd been a CIA mercenary in the Congo, found a steel crowbar and was prying at the connex door's padlock. "That's my fucking rig, you bloody fucking Yank," he was shouting.

Sergeant Murphy sprang to attention and gave Major Lon a snappy salute. He was more than a foot taller than the Vietnamese paratrooper and glowered down at him as though he might plunge on top of him at any moment. "Yes, Sir," he said saluting him once again. Then wheeling about, he marched down the aisle between

The Idiot's Frightful Laughter

the packing tables, unlocked the connex box, placed the padlock in his pocket, and took the one belonging to the civilians and handed it to Major Lon.

Without a word to anyone, the world-renowned Golden Knight left walking ramrod stiff across the Vietnamese Airborne parade ground. His red beret was set jauntily on the side of a closely shaved head. His camouflage fatigues were starched, and the creases pressed to razor sharpness. His black jump boots shined to mirror brightness. There was no doubt about it, Grecco thought. No matter how much he might dislike him, Murphy was a real soldier.

Major Lon appeared to enjoy the opportunity to put the cocky ranger in his place. He gave the civilians a thumbs-up salute. "If you have any further trouble, please let me know," he said. Sergeant Mike Murphy kept clear of the parachute loft for nearly a month.

"Thanks to Bob Brady's big mouth, there'll only be one jump today," Olson said giving the airman a hard look.

"Take a flying fuck, Dad," the acrimonious youth said.

"Thirty bucks is probably all any of you will want to pay anyway," Olson continued ignoring Brady's insult. "Besides the drive from the DZ takes more than an hour. By the time you get back for a second jump, there won't be any time left over for training, and a number of you expect to be jump qualified today."

Ollie's too thorough. Too long winded, Vince thought. He's too anxious to avoid criticism. Always sounds as though he's giving a prepared speech. Shows a lack of self-confidence.

"Would you take charge of this, Vince?" Olson said handing the manifest to Grecco. "It's all complete."

"Sure. Why not?" Vince said scanning the roster. He noted that Grant had placed red checks after those who were apt to be troublesome, and also reasons for those being held back. "Trouble with you, Ollie, is you're too damn sympathetic. Most of those guys don't understand. Think it's a sign of weakness. Got to be hardcore," he said giving Olson a friendly jab in the ribs with his elbow.

Grant nodded thoughtfully. "Maybe so," he said. "But it isn't likely that I'll be able to change now, is it?"

"Only you can answer that, Ollie," Grecco said turning and walking over to the connex box. He saw his bamboo hoop hanging from a wire hook inside the container. "What do you say?" he said pointing to the hoop and winking at Olson."

"Sure," Grant laughed. "It'll be great. Just like old times."

Vince shook his head. Olson was too much. It was he who should have had the nervous breakdown, he thought. Just as he was preparing to swing the heavy metal door closed, he saw a pair of striped coveralls crammed back in a corner of the box. "My bat wings!" he exclaimed nudging Grant. Grecco had had cloth webbing sewed to the sleeves and along the sides of the waist and between the legs. One evening when Vince was absent, Murphy had made a big show of ripping the wings off.

The following day, Grecco had waited for the sergeant outside his quarters. Murphy appeared with four other airborne advisors, so Vince thought it best to restrain himself for the time being. Murphy showed him the USPA's list of rules that he'd folded up inside his wallet. "The association forbids the use of wings of any sort," he said.

"It doesn't say anything about destroying personal property, does it?" Vince said.

I'm warning you, Mike, just leave the jumpers' equipment alone. Is that clear?"

"You better shape, Grecco, or I'll write the USPA and get you kicked out," Sergeant Murphy threatened, waving the paper in Vince's face. "It's SOP." He said. "Standard Operating Procedure, if you didn't know."

Murphy had won the upper hand, for now, Grecco thought. Being a top echelon Golden Knight no doubt gave him a good deal of clout with those at USPA headquarters. Vince could quite possibly lose his instructor's license. The thought infuriated him. He'd made three jumps with the bat wings at the Issaquah Sky Port near Seattle, and the safety officer had signed them off in his logbook. Surely the USPA officials had seen them when they

The Idiot's Frightful Laughter

checked his log to verify his eligibility for expert. He had that to his credit.

"You know four good jumpers excluding Murphy?" he asked Olson. "Let's get lined up for the hula-hoop jump. But no goof-offs. I've had all I want of that."

Grant nodded. "Sure, but the important thing is to get the plane in the air by seven. By eight the aircraft are backed up ten deep at all the approaches at Tan Son Nhut, and it takes an hour to get airborne. And that's all tac time."

"You mean we pay to wait?" Grecco asked as he adjusted his parachute harness.

"The moment the plane leaves the hangar, it starts costing us at the rate of five bucks a minute," Olson said looking most distressed.

"Well, shit, let's get the show on the road," Vince said. "What's the holdup?"

"Murphy," Grant said shrugging his shoulders in hopeless exasperation.

"Fuck that sonofabitch and fuck all his equipment," Grecco said kicking a windsock mounted to a metal tripod. "Load a half dozen smoke grenades, the target, and first aid kit in the back of that jeep, and shag ass," he added waving his arms about at the men who had huddled about him and Olson. Within a few moments, the gear was piled in the vehicle, and it had disappeared in a cloud of dust for the DZ.

Vince climbed in behind the steering wheel of a weapons carrier. "Let's get a move on, troops," he shouted gunning the engine. The skydivers tossed their rigs on the bed of the truck and climbed in on top of them. As Grecco was pulling out of camp, Olson spotted Murphy from the side view mirror. He was stepping along as though he was marching in review. His red Ranger beret set jauntily on the side of his freshly shaved head.

"Here comes Murphy," Olson said nudging Vince.

"Sorry, Ollie, I couldn't hear you," he said giving his old pal a wink.

At Constellation's airdrome, Grant climbed aboard the DC-3 to secure the anchor cable for the static lines. In the meantime, Grecco checked the jumpers' rigs, as they snapped on their harness. He then gave the neophytes a last-minute briefing. Occasionally a man was apt to forget everything just prior to his first jump. Vince could well remember his first one. Nothing is quite so traumatic, he thought. It's a little like facing a firing squad, he supposed.

The men climbed aboard according to the height they were slated to jump from. The skydivers, who were going to seven thousand feet or higher, got in first and moved to the rear of the fuselage. They were followed by those authorized for five thousand and so on down to the beginners whose chutes were opened for them as they left the aircraft at twenty-five hundred feet. One end of a line was tied to the apex of the canopy. The other end was fixed to the aircraft. At the moment it inflated, the canopy broke free of the strap

"If you don't mind, Ollie, I'd like to spot and put the beginners out. Got to stay in practice, Vince said flashing a big smile. He was beginning to get that giddy sensation that he always had prior to a jump. It's like taking a deep drink from the fountain of youth, he told himself. He felt more alive than he had in months. "Resurrection" was the word that always came to mind. Great therapy for a nervous breakdown, he thought, smiling to himself. He wondered what Doctor Younger would think if he could see him now.

"Fine," Olson said trying not to show his delight. For once he could concentrate on his own jumping. Learn to enjoy skydiving for a change. Let Vince worry about the students. 'I'll work the intercom for you, Vince," he said.

"I never spotted from a Dakota before," Grecco said. "What do you line up on, Ollie?"

"The fuselage is curved like a chopper's, only more so. It's damn deceptive," Olson said. "Stand straight and sight along the edge of the doorway." He demonstrated by standing very erect and peering down over his nose at the tip of his boots. "The first time I put the students out a half mile from the DZ. It was damn

The Idiot's Frightful Laughter

embarrassing. Murphy was all over my ass for it," he said shaking his head.

Grecco wedged the bamboo hoop behind a seat. Then he took three drift streamers from an ammo box and stuck them in his right pants leg pocket.

The plane taxied out onto the runway approach and lined up behind three other aircraft. "Seven thirty," Olson said. "It'll be a half hour before takeoff."

"Yea, at five bucks a minute, Grecco said frowning.

"Afraid so," Grant said. "It'll probably cost thirty bucks a man."

Vince took off his helmet and wiped his brow with the back of his hand. "Whew, anyone who'd pay that kind of money for a jump's got to have holes in his head," he said.

Olson unzipped a side pocket of his jumpsuit and took out a pocket book. He sat on the floor using his rig for a backrest. Grecco looked at the cover, *Existentialism from Shakespeare to Sartre.* That's part of Ollie's trouble, Vince mused. He doesn't read the GI's comic books. "Say, Ollie, before you get too deeply engrossed in that, let's rounds up the other four men and work out the hula-hoop routine." "Sure, Vince," Grant said holding out a hand to Grecco and swinging to his feet.

Grecco picked up the book and opened it to where Olson had left his bookmark. He read an underlined passage: "King Lear is a good example of the existential hero. He passes from the state of simply being to that of nothingness. It is here that he finds existence." I'll bet Willie Shakespeare would be surprised to know that, Vince thought setting the book back on Olson's rig. Why can't people just leave a great work alone?

Let it speak for itself. Why must they pollute it with a lot of pedantic bullshit?

The four men came and squatted about Grecco. "Hi, I guess I don't know any of you guys. I'm Vince" he said shaking hands with each of them. "I want you to make the last pass, Ollie. Don't attempt it below thirty-five hundred. If you're too far away, I'll wave you off before that." Grecco hadn't picked Grant for the anchor man because he was any better than the others. He supposed that a couple of the others were better. It was because of his dependability. Olson never took chances.

"I'm not so sure I'm the best man for the last pass," Grant said. "I think Erick . . ."

"That's not very existential of you, Ollie," Vince broke in with a laugh.

You've been reading my book," Olson said trying to look indignant, but instead breaking into a nervous giggle. "Okay Vince, the last pass it is."

"As for the rest of you guys, let's not bunch up," Grecco said looking at each of them to make sure they were listening. "Hold back until the man in front of you has cleared the hoop. I'd like to avoid any danger of a collision," He glanced at the manifest and then back at the men. "Which one is Guy Shievers?"

A slender youth with horn-rimmed glasses held to his head with a thick elastic band raised his hand. "Yo," he said.

"Okay, as soon as you're stable start your dive for the hoop. Get in there as quick as possible," Vince said looking the youth over. "You're pretty light. It's best that you go first. No doubt I fall faster than you. By the time you're stable, I'll have dropped way below you."

"I don't know," Shievers said shaking his head. "You may never catch up with me."

"The odds are I will. Remember, I'll be right behind you. Besides I like playing favorable odds," Grecco said. Shievers seemed a bit disconcerted. He looked as though he'd been rebuffed. Is this guy for real, he seemed to be thinking? "Okay, any questions?" Vince asked.

"Yea," a fat angry-looking man with jowls that bulged out about his chin strap said. "I never dove through no hoop before. Could you sort of give me the skinny on it?"

"Sure," Grecco said laughing good-naturedly. He pulled the hula-hoop out from behind the seat and handed it to Olson motioning for him to hold it out "Flare out of your dive directly even with the hoop," he explained crouching before it and

The Idiot's Frightful Laughter

spreading his arms as though he was making a swan dive. "If you flare out above the hoop, you'll miss it and have to take another pass. As soon as you come out of your dive, go into a tight frog." He brought his hands in flat above his shoulders as though someone had just stuck a gun in his back. He then brought his knees up tight against his chest. "Some lose their momentum and get hung up in the hoop. Then they have to wiggle out of it. Right, Ollie?" he said smiling sardonically at Olson. It was mean of Vince to remind him of the difficult time he'd had getting free of the hoop. "However, provided you have enough momentum, a tight frog should get you through the hoop without any difficulty. Think you have it?" he asked looking at each of the four men.

"Yea, it don't sound too hard," the angry looking man said. "I reckon one can do no more than try."

It was hot outside, and inside the metal fuselage, it was a good twenty degrees hotter. Well over one hundred degrees Fahrenheit. Most of the men had stripped of the upper half of their jumpsuits.

"We've got quite an assortment of people here," Olson said pointing them out to Grecco. "Fred there. He's a logistics man for US AID," he said motioning to a sour looking youth thumbing through an issue of *He-Man Magazine*. Thel's a private secretary for the First Secretary at the US Embassy. Sort of scatterbrain," he said pointing at a very slender young woman with short cropped hair.

"Why Ollie, I had no idea you were a male chauvinist pig. I must report you to Woman Lib," Grecco said in a falsetto voice.

"Horseshit!" Grant said. Nothing made him madder than to be accused of anything right of center. "I'm all for equal rights. Was involved in the movement back in The States. Attended a workshop at UC at Sonoma." He was angry enough to fight. "No shit, Vince, I'm telling it like it is. Female or not, she's a scatterbrain. She's continually making low openings and doesn't seem to realize it."

"Why the hell haven't you grounded her?" Grecco said looking questioningly at Olson.

"Waiting for you to be the male chauvinist," Grant said smirking at his pal.

"A very sick joke, Ollie," Vince said. You could very well be waiting for her to be carried off in a plastic bag. What's her name?"

"Ms. Tisdale. Thelma Tisdale."

Grecco walked over to where she was seated. She looked very fragile and timid. No one would ever have taken her for a skydiver. Never underestimate the power of a woman, he thought. They can be damn deceptive. That was certainly the case with the Vietnamese women. "Hi Thelma," Vince said trying to look as amiable as possible. "I'm Vince, Vince Grecco. Murphy isn't here today, so I'm acting as safety officer." He waited several seconds for the information to sink in.

"Yes, of course," she said offering her hand. "I've heard of you." Her voice was so soft that he had to strain to hear her above the drone of the plane's engines. "You were the club's former president, weren't you?"

Grecco nodded smiling with mock boyishness. "How's it working, Thelma?" he asked pointing to an aircraft altimeter strapped to the top of her reserve.

"Fine, just fine," she said looking up at him suspiciously.

"I want you to have your chute open at twenty-five hundred feet, Thelma," he said looking down at her as a teacher might look at a mischievous pupil. "Make your pull at three thousand feet. I'll be checking you with my stopwatch," he added.

Ms. Thelma Tisdale nodded. Her lips were pursed, and her eyes were wide with alarm.

"Okay?" he said breaking into a smile and winking good-humoredly. When he got back to where Olson was, he saw that Ms. Tisdale was still staring at him with a fixed dazed expression.

"I think you sized her up about right, Ollie," Vince said. "She has all the symptoms of a scatterbrain, and frankly it worries me. People like her aren't apt to have full possession of their faculties. They're only half present. The other part is in a world of fantasy. At a very crucial moment, that world might have more hold on them than the one that tells them that it's twenty-five hundred feet and time to pull the damn ripcord."

The Idiot's Frightful Laughter

"You sure it's as bad as all that?" Grant said smiling satirically. "You should have been a psychiatrist."

"Psychology was my major before I switched to journalism," he said nodding gravely. "I actually have a minor in it."

Olson raised his eyebrows as though impressed. "Well, doctor, what do you prescribe as a remedy?"

"Get rid of her, and I say that in all earnestness. I don't care how you do it, but it must be done."

Why me? Olson thought. Why always me? "I'm not very good at this sort of thing," Grant said suddenly looking very depressed. "Well, you're the Saigon Sport Parachute President. That goes with the job."

"I'm not like you, Vince. I don't have your leadership abilities, nor the joy that goes with it." The thought of kicking Thelma Tisdale out of the club frightened him. "You're still the presidents. A position to be proud of," he said sincerity.

"I've tried to resign several times. The civilians won't let me. Murphy and I are the only ones with instructor's licenses. If I resigned, he'd take full control and force the civilians to quit." It was a dilemma. If only Vince would come back to Saigon.

"Yea, I know," Grecco said with a sign. He rose and walked over to the doorway and leaned out. Suddenly his ears rang with the piercing sound of sirens as a fire engine and ambulance raced past. Above he saw a single-engine A-1 Skyraider come rocking from side to side towards him. A thick dark cloud of smoke poured from the engine's cowling. Only the right landing gear was extended. The left was stuck up in the aircraft's fuselage. Stopping just above the end of the runway, it dove and then flared out at the last moment making a full stall landing. It seemed to Vince that it had missed them by just a few meters.

The plane struck the asphalt hard taking the full impact on its one landing gear. It bounced several times and then pivoted around on the tip of its right wing facing back up the runway.

"It's going to hit us," Grecco shouted moving away from the door. The momentum caused the fighter to skid across the runway, onto a taxiway, and into the Dakota's parking area. Sparks flew from beneath the fuselage and smoke poured from the engine. It skidded to within twenty meters of the C-47. The screeching sound of metal on concrete reverberated through the Dakota's fuselage causing the jumpers to bunch up at the tail end of the aircraft.

Coming to a halt, the pilot slid back the Plexiglas canopy and leaned out. Black smoke enveloped the Skyraider. He scrambled out onto the wing. Dropping onto the ground, he ran towards the Dakota. Soon firemen were spraying the fighter plane with great gushes of billowing white foam.

"Christ! That was a close call," Grecco said gripping the pilot's shoulder.

"Piece a cake," he said smiling, but Vince noted that the airman's hand was trembling, as he took a white scarf from about his neck and wiped his face. Good man, Vince thought.

Grecco jumped back aboard the Dakota and gave the fighter pilot a thumb's up salute as the plane began to move. A giant four-engine C-130 Hercules transport just ahead of them taxied onto the runway. Well, it won't be long now, Vince thought, as he watched a truck resembling a snowplow push the wreckage off the airstrip.

The plane crash seemed to have unnerved the jumpers somewhat especially the beginners. Some were bunched together near the door while others sat quite rigid staring at the fuselage's bare metal wall. Their coveralls were soaked with sweat. Shit, Grecco thought, they've been suited up like this for nearly an hour. I should have had them relax.

Well, it's kind of late now. He knelt down in front of them. "Any of you making your first jump?" he asked. Three raised their hands. "Are you all on the same stick?"

"Yea," a tall redhead GI named Danny Cogswell said. He was making an effort to appear jaunty. He looked as though he was the toughest of the three, Vince thought. I'll put him at the door and line the other two up behind him. Standing there looking off into space can chill a veteran's blood.

"This waiting is tough," Grecco said. "It's best getting it over with as quickly as possible. You've had too much time to think. Too much time for the anxieties to build up." The three nodded.

The Idiot's Frightful Laughter

"Yea, I guess so," Cogswell said trying to sound matter of fact about it.

Vince glanced at the insignia on his shoulder. The Fifth MP's. A cop, he thought. He had that hard, no-nonsense look of one accustom to putting unruly servicemen in their place. Quick to wield a club if the need arose. Well, he'd see just how tough this kid was.

"Garrison, Patrick Garrison," Grecco read the name from the jump roster.

"Yes, Sir," a youth who appeared to be about eighteen said. He was a Marine assigned to guard the U.S. Embassy and one of Ambassador Bunker's special bodyguards.

Grecco was taken back by the Marine's military discipline. Vince was no officer. Not even a sergeant. Just an ordinary civilian. "Well Pat," he said trying to put the lad at ease," What do you do as soon as your chute opens?"

"Check the canopy, Sir. See if there are any line-overs, Sir."

Vince couldn't help smiling. The youth was so earnest. It reminded Grecco of when he was a Marine boot more than twenty years ago. He'd changed a lot in what seemed like such a short time. Where had all his faith, his idealism, his devotion gone? He was such an inveterate cynic. The change had happened quite suddenly. One might say instantaneously. It happened the day the process server handed him his divorce papers ordering him to abandon home and family. From that moment, he hadn't cared about anything anymore, or at least that's what he had told himself. He'd tried to wipe the blade clean. Well, it wasn't all that easy, was it? Down deep inside one never really changes, Does one. From the age of seven, one's marked for life.

Ralph Mendoza was third on the stick. He was a maintenance repair supervisor for Transport Limited. "Ralph, what do you do in case the wind is carrying you past the DZ?" Grecco asked. The Latino smiled. He had a kind amiable face. His smile was heartwarming. "Turn and hold into the wind," he said. "If that doesn't work, pull down on the front risers somewhat."

Grecco was about to ask another question when the co-pilot stepped back to say that they were preparing to take off and to buckle up until they got the "No Seatbelt" signal.

As the plane sped down the runway, Vince saw long lines of jet fighters, each housed in a concrete revetment. When the jets revved their engines, the roar could be heard eight miles away in downtown Saigon. Suddenly the DC-3 was airborne skimming above row after row of barbwire and bunkers that surrounded the airbase. Then came the clapboard shacks – whorehouses, bars, gyp joints, opium dens – that ringed its perimeter.

The Dakota gained altitude leaving it all far below. Tan Son Nhut looked like an amusement park with hundreds of tiny toy airplanes. The landscape changed to a patchwork of green, yellow and brown severed here and there by the silver threads of rivers and canals. "We'll be there in a minute, Ollie," Vince said. "Check the first stick over and line them up. I want to concentrate on the spotting." Hurrying back to the doorway, he saw the jump spot just ahead of them. Ap Don Village was just to the south of it. It amounted to a half dozen thatched huts. The DZ was a reddish mound of earth poking up out of a checkboard of rice paddies like a half-submerged football. Vince motioned for Grant to hurry. The sooner he got on the intercom the better. He tightened the elastic band on his goggles and pressed them up tight against his helmet. If they blew off, it would be hard to see the drop zone. He glanced down at his altimeter fixed to his reserve. Thirty-two hundred feet. Much too high. He saw that Olson had placed the earphones on his head and was testing the mike. The ground crew had unfurled a large white cross. It was easy to see against the red earth; however, their jeep was too close to the DZ. It was a hazard.

"Tell the pilot to drop down to twenty-five. Ollie," he shouted.

"What?" Olson said removing the headset and leaning forward, a hand cupped to his ear.

"Twenty-five hundred," Grecco repeated jabbing a thumb downward. Grant nodded and within a few minutes, the plane was losing altitude.

The Idiot's Frightful Laughter

Vince pulled a wind-drift indicator from his pants leg pocket and unwound about two feet of a strip of yellow crepe paper that was wrapped about a piece of wire. Holding it bunched in his left hand, he shouted: "One right," to Olson jabbing his thumb out the door. The Dakota veered slightly to the right. They were still too far away to be certain, however, it looked right on course. The aircraft suddenly shifted again to the right and he lost sight of the DZ. "One left" he called to Grant, however, Bob Brady was standing between them apparently talking to him. "One left," Grecco repeated shoving Brady to one side. Grant picked up the headset and relayed the message. When they were back on course, the plane had already passed over the DZ. Nevertheless, Vince knelt and threw the stream beneath the plane away from the prop. "Okay, turn," he shouted. Brady was once again standing so that Grecco could not see Olson. "Turn," he repeated taking hold of the airman's shoulder and pulling him aside.

"Watch it, asshole," Brady said twisting loose of Vince's grasp.

Grecco looked at the punk's sour bellicose face. No one should be cursed with such an ugly mug, he thought. He was about to say something when he thought of the drift streamer. He stepped back to the door and scanned the horizon. It was several minutes before he saw it fluttering above a grove of trees at the north end of the drop zone. It was still too high to tell just how strong the wind was. He couldn't be sure until it touched the ground. Keeping track of it with one eye, he motioned for Olson to line up the first stick at the door. However, once again Brady was blocking his view.

"Get the fuck out of here, Brady," Vince shouted. The airman didn't budge. "Bug off, goddamnit," he screamed. Brady turned slowly and stared insolently at Grecco for several seconds; then turned back to Grant. "The sonofabitch," he muttered. I imagine he figures Murphy and his Ranger pals will defend him, he thought watching the strip of crepe paper land at the edge of a dirt road that ran down the center of the mound of earth. It was about five hundred meters northeast of the target, so he'd have to drop the students out an equal distance southwest of the drop zone. He measured the distance from the DZ to the streamer with his thumb and forefinger as though they were a draftsman's compass, then pivoting his thumb about plotted an equal distance to the other side of the white cross. Brady had messed up his calculations, but it would have to do. A hole that looked as though it might be an old artillery crater would make a good exit point, he thought.

"You call me?" Olson said shaking Vince by the shoulder.

"Yea, only about ten times," Grecco said. "Would you mind getting rid of that fucking Brady, and line up the first stick?" He gazed for several moments at Grant's startled anxious face and felt a sudden impulse to be cruel. To attack his old friend. Tell him how thoroughly worthless he was. His vulnerability aroused Vince's sadistic instinct.

"Where's the streamer?" Olson asked as though in apology. Ever since he'd landed up to his waist in a huge cesspool of shit in the midst of a slum bordering Manila's International Airport, he no longer trusted anyone to spot for him.

"By the side of the road just past the intersection," Grecco said letting Grant sight along his arm. "I'm putting them out at that hole," he added swinging his arm in an arch to the crater. Olson studied both distances from the DZ carefully.

"I'd put them out a little before that, Vince," Grant said. "If they overshoot, they're apt to land on the jeep."

"Good point, Ollie," Grecco said. "Better safe than sorry."

While Olson was lining the men up in front of the doorway, Grecco took their static-lines from their rigs and hooked each to an anchor cable that ran along one side of the fuselage. As Vince had arranged, Grant placed Danny Cogswell in the doorway. He was amused by the youth's change of expression, for during ground training, he was so cocky and brazen. Now he was no longer bubbling over with self-assurance. His ruddy complexion had turned chalky, and his eyes were glazed over as though in shock. When Olson gave him a friendly nudge and asked how he felt, he got no response.

"Perhaps we ought to put one of the others out first?" Grant said. "Cogswell doesn't look too good."

The Idiot's Frightful Laughter

"He'll be okay," Grecco said smirking. "Them MP's are tough. Cream of the crop. This is a piece of cake, right Cogswell?" he said giving him a good-natured jab in the ribs.

Vince did his best to ignore Brady. He couldn't afford to be distracted. He needed to focus all his attention on managing the students' jumps. However, he couldn't block the jerk from his mind. Brady sat glaring at him, his mouth twisted in an ugly sneer. Grecco sensed a showdown germinating. He liked getting such matters over with as quickly as possible. He hated the youth's surly pampered features. The mouth was what bothered him most. The lips were loose and swollen hanging open in a sullen smirk. And the hair. It was the color of moldy straw lying down over the eyes. Vince had an overwhelming compulsion to smash him in the face, flatten that large bulbous nose.

The C-47 banked turning about for the jump run. Grecco checked his altimeter. Good, he thought. Right at twenty-five hundred feet. Then he looked out the door. Shit, they were way off course. "Hard right," he shouted to Olson. The plane turned sharply overshooting the jump run.

"One left," Vince shouted. Another ten seconds and they'd be over the exit point. The plane veered left, but it wasn't far enough. "One left," he shouted again. As the plane turned, he saw the shell hole loom out beneath them. "Holy shit, the exit point," he said aloud to himself as he slapped Cogswell across the rump. "Go man go," but the MP didn't move. He looked as though he was hypnotized. His wide-eyed gaze was fixed on the horizon. "Go goddamnit," he shouted shaking Cogswell roughly, but still there was no response. Grecco pulled the MP to one side and motioned for Garrison to jump. Instantly the Marine bounded from the plane followed immediately by Mendoza. Vince looked at the ground. They were nearly over the target. He was furious. Cogswell had ruined his spotting. They'd probably miss the target by a good four hundred meters.

However, Grecco's anger softened some. The big ruddy-faced kid sat bent over, his teeth clamped tight to the knuckles of a clenched fist. He was batting his eyes to force back the tears.

However, Vince felt no urge to console him, for Grant had told him that all through training Cogswell had been a loud-mouth, know-it-all. Grant hadn't been able to tell him anything that he didn't already know. There wasn't anything he couldn't do. Well, maybe this would sober him up. Take some of the arrogance out of him, but Grecco doubted it. His type never learned. If anything, the humiliation would only make him more overbearing. Well, one thing was certain. He was no he-man MP. He was a fraud. "Jesus H. Christ!" Olson shouted. "Mendoza hit the jeep!" Vince could faintly see that someone was being lifted from the vehicle and laid out on the ground. The parachute lay draped over the jeep.

"Yea," Grecco said nodding in a slow deliberate motion. "If Cogswell had jumped this wouldn't have happened." He felt a surge of bitterness for the brash young policeman. Sergeant Mike Murphy would use this against the civilians, and it was a serviceman's fault. He and Mendoza would be blamed. He had done the spotting, and Mendoza had been injured perhaps critically. That was all that would be considered. From all outward appearances, the civilians had fucked up. They were a menace to the club, to the professionally minded military airborne, to the sport in general. This is in essence what Murphy would surely say. Irresponsible civilians or rather "fuckups" was more in harmony with his vocabulary.

Grecco glanced back at Cogswell. The MP was still seated hunched over, a fist jammed in his mouth. The poor bastard, Vince thought. He needs a pacifier to suck on. He was taking it pretty hard. A moment of truth. Perhaps he realizes that he's not nearly the god almighty the thought he was.

The next has got to be on target, he thought. "Look, you guys," he said waving his arms to get their attention. "If you're holding into the wind and are being carried backward, look behind you from time to time." He paused for the advice to sink in; then making a downward thrust of his arms, he added: "Don't go banging into a tree or jeep or something."

Brady was back talking to Olson blocking the view again nearly causing a second stick to miss their point of exit;

consequently, Grecco wasn't able to tell the pilot to cut the engine, so the jumpers had a hard opening. The backblast had flung them about twisting their suspension lines.

"What the fuck does that sonofabitch want anyway?" Grecco asked.

"He's mad because he's not on the hula-hoop jump," Olson said.

Vince looked at the recalcitrant who had moved back to the middle of the plane and sat down. He was staring at Grecco with the same open-mouth sulkiness. "The hell he is," Vince said. He wanted to run back there and hit him square in the mouth. Smash those fat swollen lips. Keep pounding at his ugly mug with both fists until it looked like a lump of raw hamburger. He could see the brawl building up between the civilians and the military. It might be for the best. Sort of clear the air. Then they could start devoting their full attention to skydiving again. There was the distant chatter of automatic rifle fire and the flat thudding sound of mortar shells exploding. Grecco looked out the door. A battle was being waged less than a mile from the drop zone. Three tanks with 106-millimeter recoilless cannons were advancing on a treeline. Then suddenly the artillery opened up, and the trees disappeared in clouds of dust and debris.

Well, he couldn't worry about the war, Grecco thought. Not with three hundred dollars an hour at stake.

The third stick was termed "clear-and-pull". Vince had Ron Starkey take notes for him. He stood beside the jumpmaster with a clipboard and pencil recording each jump.

"Don't forget," Grecco said glancing at each man in the stick, "as soon as you clear the plane, go into a hard arch." To illustrate, he spread his legs and arms wide apart arching his back. "And the moment you're stable, grab a hold of your ripcord and pull," he said bringing his arm into his chest and then flinging his arm out in a wide arch.

The first one to jump flipped over on his back. The canopy unfurled between his legs. His left foot caught in the suspension lines, and for an instant, he hung upside down before being jerked upright.

"Ass over tea kettle," Vince told Starky. "No arch. Bad exit."

The next jumper went into a dive flapping his arms and kicking his legs as though he were trying to fly. The chute jerked him upright throwing off his helmet.

"Unstable. No arch. Head down," Grecco said.

The last man rolled on his side but recovered his balance by spreading his arms and legs and arching his back.

"Weak exit. Good arch. Stable. None of them are ready for a five-second freefall," Vince said. Turning to Olson, he asked: "Why didn't you have the pilot cut the engine. The prop blast is throwing them off balance."

"We've only been doing that for static-line jumps," Grant said. "But I guess you're right. We'll do that for the clear-and-pulls from now on."

The plane turned and climbed to thirty-five hundred feet for those making five-second delays. Far below, Grecco saw the tiny pale green canopies. Two of the men had turned and were holding into the wind. They looked as though they might land on target. The third jumper was letting the wind carry him. He had already passed over the white cross and would probably land a good five hundred yards beyond it in among the tombstones of an ancestral graveyard. Very hazardous, Vince thought, but it was the guys own goddamn fault. No reason why he couldn't have turned into the wind like the other two.

"You take this next stick, Ollie," Grecco said. "Ron can run the intercom. I thought I'd have a nice little chat with my old buddy, Bob Brady," Vince said with a knowing wink.

"Oh yea! Sure! Fine!" Olson said nodding vigorously. "Glad to."

The airman watched Grecco as he approached. "I hear that you're unhappy with the way I'm running things, Brady," he said sitting down next to him.

"No shit," Brady said speaking from the corner of his mouth. "Like how'd you ever figure that out, Daddy-oh?"

The Idiot's Frightful Laughter

Vince looked at the punk until he dropped his gaze. "You don't like the way things are being run?"

"Yeaaa! Like now you're grooving, man."

"You want to run things to suit yourself? Is that it, Brady?"

"Man, like fucking wow. Now you're radiating with rocket fuel," the malcontent said. His thick lips were twisted into a grotesque sneer.

"Well you better get one thing straight, Buster," Grecco said thrusting a finger at the youth's chest. "And you better get it straight now. You're not on the hula-hoop jump. You're not on it because I said so. Olson has nothing to do with it."

"You're a real tough daddy-oh, ain't you?" Brady said baring his teeth.

"If I were you, Brady, I'd be goddamn careful what I said. Your big mouth is costing the club three hundred bucks an hour to jump," Vince said feeling the anger mount. It was all he could do to restrain himself. "If I were running the club, I'd have kicked your ass out for calling Sergeant Chao a gook."

"So like what's all the jazz, Daddy-oh? That's what he is, ain't he?"

"And I'm a Wop, eh, Brady? Is that how it is, eh? And you? The white Nordic superman? Is that how it is, eh, Brady?" Grecco felt his blood pressure rising. He'd have to watch it. Much more of this and he'd clobber the punk.

"That's the breaks, Daddy-oh. Some got it. Some ain't."

"Look, smart guy, we'd be making free jumps from a chopper if it weren't for you." He raised his voice so that everyone could hear. "You can be goddamn sure that I'd have kicked your ass off the base if I'd been here."

"Shit," Brady said spitting at Grecco's feet, "like you scare me, Daddy-oh."

"Just try making the hula-hoop jump, and we'll see how tough you are, smart ass," Vince said as he rose and walked away.

Back at the doorway, Olson was having Starky time the five-second freefalls. "Make sure that no one opens below twenty-five hundred feet." Grecco cautioned finding it hard not to curl his lip.

He had once liked Ron. Considered him a fine upstanding young man of the very highest caliber. One he'd relied heavily on. Now he had nothing but the deepest contempt for. Behind those boyish earnest features lurked a lurid fiend. A ghoul. The most putrid scum on earth. A piece of pig shit.

Grecco had assumed that he was a good judge of character. Starkey was the last person on earth that he'd have thought was a pedophile. The idea would never have crossed his mind. The revelation was something he could never reconcile. Not for one instant.

Starkey was a country boy, who grew up on a large wheat farm in Nebraska. He had that wholesome corn-fed look of the Midwest farm boy. The sort of guy you'd trust your best girl with. From all outward appearances, he seemed to be a man of unquestionable virtue. He'd graduated from Tulane with a BA in business management and had been an accountant at Brown & Root's Saigon office. Olson had unwittingly recommended him to his boss at Universal Education as office manager.

One Sunday evening after jump training, Grecco and Olson had had a beer with Starkey at a nearby club. He told them quite matter-of-factly that he had been frequenting a children's brothel. Quite oblivious to the alarm he'd ignited, he went on to explain that the children were from seven to twelve. They were little pests always trying to wheedle more money from him. One had to be firm. "Give them an inch, and they'll take a mile," he'd said. He spoke of infants no more than three or four who ran about with hot washcloths wiping off guys cocks. "They'll give you a blow job and lick your ass for fifty piaster," he said "Greedy little buggers. They keep after you for more. Have to slap them around to make them behave. Can't take no for an answer."

Starkey's French friends introduced him to the brothel. When Olson asked if he could see it for himself, Starkey grew cautious. He didn't want a bunch of freewheeling Americans spoiling a good thing. He told Olson that he'd assured his French friends that he would not bring anyone else. When Olson insisted that he didn't want so much as to touch the children, Starkey became suspicious and tried to downplay the whole thing. Olson told Grecco that he wanted to take a camera and catch the scumbag red-handed. He was out to get the degenerate. String the cocksucker up by his balls. That's how he felt about pedophiles. Unfortunately, he'd been too eager and blown his chances. Starkey pretended that it was all a sick joke.

Olson kept the nightmare deep within, gnawing like a serpent at his guts. It was too awful to tell. Who would believe him? Starkey's friends would hate him. He'd tried tailing the ghoul, but the entranceway to the infant whorehouse was guarded by a large Cambodia armed with a longshoreman's meat hook. He was no one to trifle with.

Olson ran across Starkey years later in San Francisco. He had become enormously fat. He was on his way to Thailand. He had a job in Bangkok, the pedophiles' paradise.

One thing that trouble Grecco was that the students were forgotten once they were in freefall, and that's when they needed help the most. Captain Bruce Gomez was a case in point. Being a paratrooper with eighty-seven static-line jumps had not helped in the least and was probably a hindrance. Grecco had noticed how intense Gomez looked as he stood at the doorway preparing to jump. Vince had tried to get him to relax. "It can't be as bad as all that, Captain. Just imagine that you're about to leap into bed with some beautiful blonde," Vince had said squeezing his shoulder good-naturedly. However, Gomez's face grew even tauter. Skydiving might be a recreation for some, but for him, it was serious business. When Grecco signaled for him to jump, he sprang into space like a sprinter at the sound of a starter's pistol. Every muscle was taut, as he plunged from the door at the jump master's command.

Everything went well until he hit terminal velocity at nine seconds. That was when the trouble began. Grecco could see how rigid he was. His arms spread wide apart. When he stopped accelerating, he would begin to spin slowly at first. By twenty seconds, he was out of control. By twenty-five, he was rotating so fast on a vertical axis that all Grecco could see was a blur of arms, head, and legs. It was a terrifying spectacle. Vince knew just how frightening it was, for he had gone through that himself. Captain Gomez would check the spin temporarily by tucking into a tight ball and then flaring out again. However, the second time he tried this, he flipped over and began to tumble head over heels. Unable to check the somersaulting, he pulled the ripcord. Grecco sighed with relief when he saw the canopy blossom out with Captain Gomez swinging serenely beneath it. It could have been bad, very bad, he thought. The captain could have wound up inside his parachute.

"How long has this been going on?" Grecco asked turning to Olson.

"He does it every time. Can't seem to relax."

"Well, put him back on fifteen-second delays for christsakes and keep him there until he stops spinning."

"The Captain's pretty touchy about his jumping, Vince," Olson said. "He's a paratrooper, you know? Doesn't like anybody to tell him anything about jumping."

"So you're going to let him keep right on spinning until one of these days, he spins right into the ground?" Grecco said.

"Look, Vince, so far the captain hasn't taken sides. He's stayed neutral. However, if I start bugging him about his jumping, he's sure to team up with Murphy, and then it's all finished."

"Maybe," Grecco said. "I don't know Captain Gomez; so I can't say, but what are you going to be thinking about when you see him roll up in his canopy? What's going to be on your mind for the next fifteen or so seconds as you watch that bundle of nylon plunge to earth? Murphy? The civilians? No, you're going to be thinking about how you wished you'd taken my advice and put Gomez back on fifteen-second delays. That's what you'd be thinking about. And you wouldn't stop thinking about it, either. It'll be on your conscious for the rest of your life."

"Christalmighty, Vince! You're the most righteous sonofabitch I've ever met. What about other hazardous sports like hang gliding and scuba diving? They don't have anyone looking after them. If you want to hang-glide, you go up to the top of a mountain and jump off. There's no jumpmaster or safety officer checking your logbook. You're on your own. Why should skydiving be any different? Do you think there are lifeguards all along the coastline checking on scuba divers? Fuck no. They do whatever they like. No one gives a shit. What makes skydiving so special? Besides, what training or experience have I had to qualify me to wield the whip over this gang? The mere thought is ridiculous."

"What's there to be afraid of, Ollie? You're as big and rough as any of these birds. If it means kicking ass to get control, well then, kick ass and keep kicking until they straighten out," Grecco said. Then turning to Starky, he said: "Make a note to put Captain Gomez back on fifteen-second delays. And just in case Ollie forgets about it, be sure to remind him," he added looking back at Grant with a consoling wink.

"You just don't get it, Vince," Olson said shaking his head. "You blockhead, you just don't get it."

The plane climbed to twelve thousand feet for the hula-hoop jump. All the others had jumped, or at least Grecco thought they had until he spotted Bob Brady at the end of the stick. "The only thing to do is to have him jump first," he told Olson. "Well, wait for a second or so. By then he'll be too far off to catch us. This is not the time or place for a showdown with a smartass punk like him. You pass the word along to the others. I'll take care of the rest."

The Dakota turned and began the jump run. Grecco glanced out the door to see if they were in line. It was difficult to tell from such a height. More than two miles below, the earth looked nebulous, ineffable. Keeping the aircraft on course was very exacting both for the jumpmaster and the pilot. The turns had to be made with great care. Shift the plane a fraction of a degree off course, and they were apt to be over the next province or out in the heart of Viet Cong country. The slightest move compounded itself a hundred-fold at the ground; however, once they were out of the plane, it was easy to orient themselves. If they were too far off target, they'd have to forget about the hula-hoop and track for the jump spot. By forming an airfoil of one's body, a good tracker could make one foot forward for every foot down. However, first Grecco had Brady to deal with. He'd have to move fast if he hoped to get rid of him.

Looking as though he had conceded defeat, Grecco motioned Brady to come to the front of the stick. "Olson's our anchor man, so you'll have to make the first pass," he explained. "The winds picking up, so we'll have to get out over that shack with the red tile roof," he added giving Shiever's a conspiring wink.

"You wouldn't be shitting me none, would you, Daddy-oh?" Brady said with a sickly smile.

"If you'd seen where the others landed, you wouldn't be so suspicious," Vince said trying to sound matter of fact.

"There's the hut," Grecco said giving Brady a nudge. The kid spun sideways trying to grab Vince as he fell, but he had stepped back. Brady rolled over on his back and shook his fist, as he fell away from the plane. Pushing someone from an aircraft was a crime, and he may be faced with serious consequence. However, the danger of jumping with that hooligan was worse. On the other hand, Brady may be looking for a fight. Well, he couldn't think of anything he'd enjoy more.

Some distance from the crater, Grecco tapped Guy Shievers on the shoulder. The youth posed for an instant at the doorway, pressed his horn-rim glasses up against his helmet with his thumb, and then sprung straight out from the plane as though he were making a racing dive. Vince stuck the hoop out into the prop blast letting it pull him from the plane. He fell bent-kneed, his other arm held wide to compensate for the weight of the bamboo hoop. He tumbled about clumsily for several seconds moving his free arm about before him feeling for the point of balance. Once he was stable, he grasped the hoop with both hands and spread his elbows and knees to steady himself. While he was still groping for balance, Shievers plunged through the hoop. It happened so fast that Grecco wasn't sure what had happened until he saw him turn and wave both hands. The next man flared out too soon and swept above the hoop grabbing it as he went past, throwing Vince into a loop and causing the third man to drop past him. It was a treat to see the fourth jumper maneuver his huge bulk through the hoop. He was the fat angry looking one, and he looked even angrier with his plump red face pressed inside a crash helmet. It seemed to Grecco that he stopped for a moment to look the situation over and then began very slowly to edge his way through moving his arms and legs as though he were a fish. The maneuver seemed so relaxed, so effortless, so very smooth. It was masterful, Grecco thought. If only he could have filmed it.

All the time this was going on, Vince was aware that Olson was lying just above and a little to the left waiting. He glanced at his altimeter. Fifty-five hundred feet. Still lots of time, he thought.

The moment the angry appearing man had cleared the hoop, Grant dived squeezing himself into a tight ball and bouncing through striking it with an elbow. Grecco looked about for the other jumpers. They were all far below him. Shiever's canopy was already open. Converting his body into an airfoil, Vince glided out of the way of the others. Holding the hoop with one hand, he grasped hold of a pant leg pocket, so the hoop would not jerk up inside the canopy when the parachute opened.

Nearing the ground, he saw a half dozen small boys running directly beneath him. *"Di di mau*, get out of here," he shouted pivoting to one side to keep from clobbering one of them. Without a word, the ragged little urchins began to field pack his parachute. One stretched the rig out on the ground while a second daisy-chained the suspension lines. Then they stuffed the canopy into the sleeve, folded, and fastened it inside the container with the bungee straps. Then still paying no attention to Grecco, picked it up and headed for the DZ. Another urchin placed the reserve on his shoulder and a fourth put the goggles and ripcord in the helmet and carried it over his shoulder by the strap. The rest of the children clustered about Grecco eyeing him solemnly, as he struggled to his feet and lumbered towards the waiting vehicle. When he reached the jeep, those who had field packed the rig, pressed up against him. "One hundred pee! One hundred pee! Okay GI? You give me money!" they demanded. Unable to remember which children had packed his rig, he handed twenty piaster to the oldest boy indicating for him to divide it up.

"No way, GI!" the little boy shouted. "Tee tee money. You give one hundred pee."

"*Di di mau*," Grecco said pressing through the ring of urchin and climbing into the back of the jeep. He held one hand on his watch and the other on his wallet.

"You number ten," the children shouted running after the jeep as it sped off in a cloud of dust.

"What's been keeping you, Vince?" Olson asked. "We've been waiting for you for a good twenty minutes." Then he noted Grecco's haggard features. "You okay, Vince?"

"I told you last night that I'd been ill. Well, it's hit me again. I feel as weak as a kitten," Grecco said looking about. "Where's everyone?" Only the ones that had made the hula-hoop jump were there.

"They hooked a ride in with a duce-and-a-half a good half hour ago," Grant said.

Grecco felt a surge of relief. It had occurred to him when they were in the plane that there'd be no transportation at the DZ. And then there was the trouble with Brady and Sergeant Murphy. There was a possibility that they'd be waiting for him at the loft. Well, he was in no shape to deal with them now. It would have to wait.

When they got to Tan Son Nhut's main gate, Grecco handed Olson a check for his jump. "Look, Ollie," he said lowering his voice. "Brady maybe waiting for me. If so, tell him that I had an urgent engagement and will be glad to settle the score at a later date." Olson didn't look at all pleased. Running out on his friend like this was cowardly, but the way he felt he couldn't punch his way out of a wet paper bag. Brady would stomp his ass right into the ground.

Grecco took a taxi straight to his apartment. He got there around noon, turned up the air conditioner, took a hot shower, and fell asleep almost the moment he touched the bed. He awoke early the next morning. He'd slept about sixteen hours and felt good. Just take it easy, he told himself, and I'll be okay. Don't let that shitass Barban bother me. He's nothing. All I've got to do is keep reminding myself of that.

Vietnam's Voltaire

When Grecco got back to Yen Chau, Barban was in Bangkok. Every twenty-four days married civilians employed by the State Department were permitted to visit their wives at such places as Bangkok, Manila, or Hong Kong referred to as "safe havens". Hank never missed a leave no matter how pressing the work might be. He always took the five-day maximum usually extending it to a full week. His wife was the sole occupant of a deluxe villa with a swimming pool and tennis court compliments of the U.S. taxpayer. She had a cook, housekeeper, and gardener to maintain a luxuriant tropical garden. A chauffeur driven limousine was at her command. Barban had left the previous day and wasn't expected back for at least four more days. As a consequence, everyone seemed relaxed and cheerful.

That evening, Grecco learned that Barban was angry with him. Bledsoe said that Hank had informed Colonel Winters that the whole thing included the letter from the doctor had been faked. Vince wasn't ill at all. Just an excuse to waste time.

Seeing that Elmo was enjoying his role as the bearer of ill tidings, Grecco gave him a deadpan stare. "So what's new?" he asked.

Nonetheless, it bothered him. He'd had too many setbacks in his life to shrug it off so lightly. It had all the markings of a dismissal or at least a transfer to another province accompanied by a poor efficiency report. Of course, he hated working for the shithead. Who wouldn't? However, he was tired of being run off. Every time he was fired, he lost something. Call it self-esteem, will, ambition. Whatever it was, it always left him more cynical. It wasn't that he didn't know why. He did. It was an attitude problem. Like Voltaire's *Zadwig*, he had the impulse to tell people what they didn't want to hear. Truth was not a saleable commodity. He was too willing to say whatever he thought. However, lately, he had tried to be more circumspect, not so god almighty righteous. He thought that he'd finally got things under control. Held his ego in check. He was no longer so candid with his boss, certainly not Barban. And yet it hadn't helped. He had made a superhuman effort to comply, but it had made no difference. The defiance was etched too deeply in his psyche. It could no longer be disguised. He was forty-one. Much too old to start being someone else. But surely someone must have a need for an honest man even if he was a bit abrasive at times. Was guile, deceit, cunning the only marketable qualities these days? He thought of the guy at the commissary. Why had he given the jerk that long lecture? The guy had hated him for the unsolicited advice. He seemed to go out of his way to antagonize people. He thought of the redneck from Hattiesburg, Mississippi. Why had he told him that he had serviced with the Student Nonviolent Coordinating Committee in Mississippi? The bigot had wanted to kill him. Called him a nigger lover every time they met.

The next day, Major Jack was waiting for Grecco at the chopper pad. "It's about time," he said. "Thought you'd never get back."

Vince had forgotten all about the arrangement he'd made with the major. They'd planned to furnish a school room at a new refugee camp with lumber. Like nearly everywhere in the province, the only way to get to the camp was by helicopter. It was no longer safe to travel by jeep. The Viet Cong had taken over the surrounding area.

They loaded the aircraft with boards that Major Jack had salvaged from ammo cases. The lumber was to be used to build desks and benches for the classroom. They knew that if they left the task to the Social Welfare Chief, it would never be done. He'd have sold the boards at the market and pocketed the money.

Although they had not expected Tan to show up, they had, nevertheless, waited. Miracles did happen. Sure, he'd agreed to visit the refugee camp with them, but then he'd promised countless other things and never kept them. Always he'd give a very feeble excuse. The sort that he could not expect anyone to believe. But there he was standing at the edge of the landing pad. Grecco was elated. Perhaps all his efforts had not been in vain. Maybe Tan would do something? After all, he wasn't as greedy as the others. His bribes were more a token gesture. It may be his way of asserting himself. Showing that it was he who was in charge, not Grecco. Now that this matter had been settled, perhaps he was ready, even eager to help his people.

Filled with optimism, Vince crossed the chopper pad at a run. He grabbed Tan's hand and shook it vigorously. He wanted to grasp the little man in his arms and hug him. Months of disappointment washed away. He'd show Barban and Simoni. Things were going to start happening now. Tan wasn't such a bad guy after all.

While the Huey hovered a foot or so off the ground, the pilot had shouted to Grecco, but the roar of the engines was too loud to hear. Then the pilot had signaled to the door gunner and pointed at Tan. The man had stepped quickly from behind his weapon, caught Tan by the arm, and flung him from the chopper. Tan's agility had surprised Vince. He landed on the balls of his feet, his arms outstretched as graceful as a ballerina. There was no expression of any sort on his face.

Grecco had sprung to his feet and waving awkwardly in the doorway shouted apologies to Tan. Then shaking his fist at the pilot, he demanded him to land. What had bewildered Vince more than anything was Major Jack's utter indifference. He had not appeared the least bit alarmed. Later when Grecco had time to reflect, he figured that it must have had a lot to do with being a black man from South Carolina. He was all too accustomed to seeing the white man abuse the colored.

When they landed at the resettlement camp, Grecco took a notebook from his pocket and went around to the pilot's side window. "I want your name," he shouted above the roar of the engine.

"It's SOP," the pilot said. "I ain't allowed to haul no gooks. Its general's orders." "He's not a gook," Grecco said. "He's the Social Welfare Chief for the entire province," Then giving the pilot a hard look, he added, "We're here to help these people.

Not intimidate them."

"He's still a fucking gook, the pilot said.

Taking a camera from his pocket, Grecco backed off and snapped a picture of the pilot. Then jotted down the aircraft's number painted on the fuselage. He had left Major Jack to unload the boards by himself. Well, it served him right, Vince thought. Uncle Toms have no business being majors. What earthly good is he to the black race?

Grecco submitted a report of the incident to Barban the following day. A week later, Bledsoe said that the pilot and the door gunner had been reprimanded; however, he didn't know what sort of punishment if any had been administered. Vince doubted if the report even got beyond Colonel Winter's desk. "A reprimand won't do it, Grecco said. "What's needed is for those two bigots to go over and make a personal apology to Tan. A real heartfelt apology.

"You're right. Yes by God, you're right," Bledsoe said. "I'll tell the Colonel what you said."

"However, that was the last Grecco ever heard of the issue, and as a consequence, his relationship with the social welfare chief grew worse. After the chopper incident, Tan made it very clear that he would never visit the resettlement camps. Vince ceased pressing the matter. This is so obviously the Americans' war. The Vietnamese aren't even allowed on the sidelines.

Doctor Hiram Finley left for The States the day Grecco got back to Yen Chau. He left six huge cartons of discarded bowling jackets with instruction for the Refugee Advisor to pass them out to the war victims.

Doc Finley was a general practitioner who had been coming to Yen Chau for two months each year for the past four years to help out at the province hospital. The discarded bowling jackets were donated to the Vietnamese by the Kiwanis Club at Melbourne, Nebraska. Doc Finley was a past president and ardent booster of the association. He had been quite emphatic about who should get the castoffs. "None of them refugees," he said. "They're all Communist. Make sure they go to the Têt war victims."

The Idiot's Frightful Laughter

It didn't surprise Grecco that the doctor had wanted a story and pictures sent to the hometown paper. Vince had been a reporter for too long not to know a publicity hound when he met one. They had that nickel-plated goodwill that never ceased to disgust him. The doctor had been very specific about the photos. Shots of recipients wearing the jackets were not enough.

"Be sure you take them so that the sponsors' names show," he said handing Grecco a list of business establishments he wanted pictures of. "That'll s sure make the boys happy." And there were other poses like those of the village chief passing out the jackets to the victims. "Anything that's got a lot of human interest. That's what the papers like," he said slapping Vince on the back like a football coach sending in a substitute. "And give the story some punch. You know, something about how thankful the Vietnamese were. That sort of stuff always goes over big. Makes them want to send more the next year." Then giving Grecco a knowing wink, he added: "Get a plug in for the Kiwanis. Great bunch of guys. Got hearts of gold. Don't get a nickel out of it. Just get a big kick out of helping people."

That evening after Doc Finley had left for The States, Grecco opened one of the cartons and laid a half dozen jackets out on the floor. They weren't exactly the ordinary Vietnamese peasant's latest fashion, he thought. Bright luminous reds, yellows and orange jackets with names like; "Pearl's Pizza Parlor" or "The Piggly Wiggly Supermarket" emblazed in bold shiny letters across the backs. They were a far cry from the peasants' austere black or white pajamas. They weren't apt to win many hearts and minds, Vince thought. But then that wasn't the doctor's aim, was it. He was after another merit badge from the good old boys at Melbourne, Nebraska's Kiwanis Club. Who knows, maybe he'd be the town's mayor someday?

Grecco left the cartons stacked in an anteroom for a week before mustering enough nerve to distribute them. If anything, it would give the Province Chief and his cronies something more to laugh about. More reason to hold the infantile Americans in contempt. If Doc Finley could only see what a fool he'd made of himself and his hometown cronies. And me too, Vince thought. I'm the unwilling fool. That's got to be the worst kind. Well, he'd give the hometown paper a story they'd long remember. "The Vietnamese of Buu Dinh Village dance with glee when handed bowling jackets donated by the members of the Melbourne's Kiwanis Club." How was that for a lead? That should have enough punch to make the old boys delirious with joy, Grecco thought.

Actually, Grecco probably would have forgotten all about the jackets if it hadn't been for Bledsoe. Doc Finley had asked him to assert pressure on Vince, if necessary, and so Elmo had done so every morning and evening for a full week. On the seventh day, he had threatened to inform Barban if the matter was not settled promptly. The thought of being fired for neglecting to distribute a half dozen cartons of discarded bowling jackets struck Grecco as the touchstone of the whole Vietnam fiasco. He could see his performance evaluation: "Dismissed for neglecting to distribute discarded bowling jackets to Vietnamese War victims."

Passing out the clothing proved more difficult than Grecco had envisioned. For One thing, the village elders were reluctant. They thought it some sort of trick. That someone, probably the Americans, did not like them and was trying to humiliate them. The peasants were also hesitant. They did not like the bright colors and strange designs. However, it was the lettering that troubled them most. They supposed that the strange words might be a jinx that would cast evil spells on them. It was the deputy district chief, a rotund jolly little man, who finally solved the dilemma. He told the people not to hurt the foreigner's feelings. They must take them and pretend to be pleased. Later they may do whatever they pleased with them. Vince caught the gist of what the deputy had said. The credibility gap had just been widened another thousand miles, he figured, but then what did a mere thousand matter one way or the other when the void was countless billions.

Some even agreed to pose for the camera, but hastily removed the jackets as soon as the picture was taken. Most rolled them up in tight wads and stuck them somewhere out of sight. Not once did Grecco or anyone else for that matter see a peasant wearing one.

The Idiot's Frightful Laughter

Vince supposed that they'd tied them to stones and thrown them into the river. He wondered what some archeologist might think when he dug one out of the mud thousands of years from now. Pearl's Pizza Parlor? A ceremonial costume, no doubt, the renowned professor might think.

Passing out bowling jackets was only a minor part of Grecco's troubles. He was more concerned about the large number of war victims who had not received their reparations. When Barban returned from Bangkok, he found the following report on his desk concerning the matter.

Sheridan Peterson

TO: Harold Barban, Deputy Senior Advisor
FROM: Vincent Grecco, Refugee Advisor
SUBJECT: Corruption

    The sum of 386,000 VN$ allotted as indemnities for Têt War Victims at Tay Chi Village is unaccounted for. There is substantial evidence that 100,000 VN$ of this for 200 specified recipients is missing. Mr. Vinh, The Deputy of Administration, informed me that they were each to receive 12,500 VN$ instead of 13,000 VN$ that was clearly recorded on each of their receipts that five Vietnamese officials and I signed. Mr. Vinh claimed that soon after the Têt Offensive, the Province Chief lent these 200 war victims 100,000 VN$ for their immediate needs from a personal fund and that this was how the emergency fund was repaid.

    Mr. Vinh informed Major Pifer, District Senior Advisor, and me that the Social Welfare Ministry in Saigon was not informed of this transaction; however, he assured us that just as long as the war victims got the indemnity, the ministry was not concerned about the payment procedure. Major Pifer pointed out that the emergency fund was intended for such immediate needs as food and clothing, not to rebuild their homes and such. He added that the Province Chief was obligated to report all such transactions to the ministry.

    Mr. Vinh disagreed with Major Pifer. He insisted that the 100,000 VN$ was a personal fund and that the Province Chief had been authorization to lend the money to those in dire need of it. He did not have to account to anyone for such expenditures.

    Nonetheless, several of the war victims complained that they had been short-changed 500 VN$. Mr. Vinh told me that they were lying. That they slipped the cash into their pockets. He said that an unidentified guard had seen them do so.

    That evening, the Deputy of Administration let it slip that 100,000 VN$ had inappropriately been withheld. He showed me one of the receipts where 500 VN$ had been subtracted from the 13,000 VN$. The deduction had not been made when I signed the receipt, nor was it on the copy given to the war victim.

Barban's first impulse was to throw Grecco's report in the wastebasket. He could care less what happened to the war victims' money. "It's no skin off my nose," he'd said to himself. "I'm not about to rub the Province Chief the wrong way." Then an idea struck him. Have Grecco make the complaint directly to Colonel Bo. That'd fix the mothafucker. He'd run Grecco off the province before he knew what'd happened.

"Hey, Willie," Barban said leaning back in his chair and swinging his feet up on the desk.

"Yes, Sir, Mr. Barban," Major Jack said rising to attention.

"Get Grecco."

"Yes Sir, Mr. Barban," the major said standing very stiff.

When Major Jack returned with Grecco, Barban was leafing through a burlesque magazine. The cover depicted a girl wearing a pair of black lace panties and hip boots. She held a bullwhip in her hand. The heading read: "Lover Beaten to Death." Hank kept Vince waiting as he thumbed casually through the porno publication.

Finally setting the magazine down, he picked up Grecco's report and handed it to him. "Nail these sons of bitches' ears back. It's time we put a stop to this sort of shit," he said picking up his bullet tipped swagger stick and striking it on the desk. "Write it up for Colonel Winters. He's meeting with the Province Chief this evening. He'll want to show it to Colonel Bo. And yes, don't forget to sign it," he added giving the desk a "rat tat tat" beat with the stick. "Make it look official."

"Is this SOP?" Grecco said looking first at Barban and then back at Major Jack. "Look, Hank, you've always been very emphatic about going through channels?"

"This doesn't have anything to do with me, Vince," he said flashing one of his Colgate Toothpaste smiles. Rising to his feet, Barban leaned forward and thrust his fists down on the desk. "According to the date on the report, it occurred while I was out of the country. When I'm gone, you are directly responsible to Colonel Winters. Is that clear?" He sat back down and picked up the girlie magazine. The matter was closed as far as Barban was concerned.

"I was under the impression that it was Bledsoe," Hank said. What a copout. I should have known the chintzy bastard would worm his way out of it, Grecco thought. He's ordered me to go over his head, and he's the one who's always harping about going through proper channels. He's a Dick Nixon pragmatist. Does whatever suites him at the moment.

"That's only in matters of administration," Barban said peering scornfully over the top of the magazine. "This matter does not come under Elmo's jurisdiction. Isn't that right, Willie?"

"Yes Sir," Major Jack said. "That is correct, Sir."

"Yea," Grecco said nodding his head trying not to show his rage. "Yes, of course." It's bullshit, pure unadulterated bullshit, he thought. Just another chance to pull the noose one notch tighter about my neck.

"All right, let's get the lead out and have it on my desk in thirty minutes," Barban said.

Grecco sat glaring at the report. "The phony prick," he muttered beneath his breath. "The phony fucking prick." If it was a trap, he'd set it himself, he thought. They had him no matter what he did. Well, at least he could tone it down a bit. That might ease things somewhat.

TO: Col. E. K. Winters, Province Senior Advisor
FROM: Vincent Grecco, Refugee Advisor
SUBJECT: Misappropriation of Funds

A sum of 100,000 VN$ was deducted from indemnity payments to some two hundred war victims at Tay Chi Village last Monday and Tuesday. According to Mr. Vinh, Deputy for the Administration Chief, the former Province Chief gave these war victims 500 VN$ each soon after the Têt Attack. It was given with the understanding that the amount would later be deducted from the reconstruction payments, he said. The District Chief is the only one who has a record of those who received the 500VN$. Major Pifer, District Senior Advisor, has agreed to bring it to the Province Headquarters this coming Monday. He stated that he would attempt to collect the receipts of those who had received their 500 VN$ payments.

Major William Jack, Civil Action Advisor, informed me that he remembered when the payments were made. However, it seems to me that there is also an emergency fund. Immediately after the disaster, war victims are entitled to this fund in order to purchase such emergency items as food, clothing, and medicine.

On page 39, section 5 of the *Refugee Relief Operational Handbook*, it mentions that if above-mentioned commodities are not available, a sum of 500 VN$ may be made to war victims. I would like to know if this is a separate fund or part of the resettlement fund? It appears as though it is separate.

If it is designated as a separate fund, then why was it deducted from the war victims' indemnity fund? Was this simply an administrative error? If so, then why wasn't 12,500 VN$ in addition to the 13,000 VN$ written on the receipt that four Vietnamese officials and I signed? Was it an oversight? The former Province Chief should be asked to clarify this matter. Has Saigon's Ministry of Social Welfare been made aware of this? Mr. Vinh said that they were not. He pointed out that the Ministry was not interested in such discrepancies so long as the war victims receive the full amount allotted to them. This is a misnomer. I suggest that the Ministry be informed of this matter.

Reading over the revised edition, Grecco felt that although it was still incriminating, it did assume that a former Province Chief had taken the cash enabling Colonel Bo to save face. The overall tone had been softened somewhat. It's so bizarre, Vince thought. What did America hope to accomplish by being led around by the nose by a gang of thieves, former Binh Xuyen River Pirates to be more precise. It was a comedy of the absurd.

That evening after supper, the phone rang. It barely had a chance to ring a second time before Bledsoe had dashed across the room and grabbed the receiver. "Yes, Sir. Yes Sir, Mr. Barban. Yes Sir, I'll get him, Sir," he said wagging his head up and down. Then laying the receiver on the table as though it was a very precious piece of porcelain, he motioned urgently to Grecco. "Vince! Vince! It's for you. Mr. Barban wants to speak to you." He had that eye-popping look of disdain that he reserved for those who had fallen out of favor with the boss.

Suddenly Grecco felt very tired, as he picked up the receiver. Barban was on his back sucking his lifeblood. A fucking vampire. A fucking Hollywood vampire, he thought with a wry smile. "Hi Hank," he said. "Something wrong?"

"Something wrong?" Barban bellowed. "You can bet your ever-loving sweet ass, something's wrong. Colonel Bo jumped all over Colonel Winter's ass after he read your fucking report. You're at the top of the Province Chief's shit list."

"So what's the problem?" Grecco asked trying to sound very innocent. "Remember? It was you who ordered me to address the report to Colonel Winters. You wanted no part of it. Besides no one forced Winters to give it to the Province Chief. He surely must have read it first. Colonel Bo's reaction couldn't have come as any great surprise to him, now could it?" Vince noticed that he had an audience. Everyone even Elmo was grinning, spurring him on.

"Colonel Winters thinks that you made the whole thing up just to embarrass him," Barban said.

"Aw give me a break, Hank," Grecco said giving his audience a thumbs up gesture. "He's too intelligent for that. He knows what a crook Bo is. I'll be damn to hell if I'll be the patsy."

The Idiot's Frightful Laughter

"Now listen here, Vince. I'm fed up with your fuck ups. Everything you touch turns to shit." Everyone crowded in about Grecco so that they could hear. "You haven't been able to do anything right; since you got here. You even screw the reports up. We're here to help the Vietnamese, in case you didn't know" Grecco put his finger to his mouth. Cautioning Coffee Koffman not to laugh. "How far do you think we're going to get if you're constantly antagonizing them?" Barban screeched. "If your charges were right once in a while, it wouldn't be so bad, but they're all bullshit. I'm warning you for the last fucking time. You better shape up if you want to stay here." Grecco handed the receiver to Max and pretended to play a soulful tune on an imaginary violin. "If you ever, and I repeat ever accuse a Vietnamese of anything. I don't give a shit what it is, you better have proof," Barban stammered. "Willie told me the money had already been passed out. Why do you ignore him? You think he lies?" Grecco widened his eyes and shook his head causing everyone to laugh. "Or is it trouble you're after? Is that what you're after? Is that what you want?" Vince nodded his head vigorously. "If it is, Vince, you can bet your ever-loving ass that you'll get it. Is that clear?" Again Vince nodded even more clownishly. "I want to know, is it?" Barban demanded. He had worked himself into a state of hysteria.

"Hank," Grecco said.

"Yes," Barban said.

"Let's go through all of that again, Hank, only this time more slowly. Let's take one point at a time. If I recall correctly the first charge had to do with me turning everything to shit. Is that literally or figuratively?" Then he looked about at the crowd and posed his finger as though he had just thought of something. "On the other hand, if I remember correctly, this matter is between me and Winters. That was your order. Major Jack is my witness or as you would say Willie is."

"Don't get so fucking cute, old man," Barban said "You'll go through channels. And it's Colonel Winters to you."

"Oh! We're back to that again?" Grecco said "Now we go through channels. It's so convenient, isn't it? We go through channels when it suits you. That's the way it is, isn't it?" Vince added winking at Koffman. "Summer soldier," he said holding his hand over the receiver.

"Heeeeee aaaaah, summer soldier," Koffman brayed. "Heeee aaaah"

Although Grecco had covered the mouthpiece to muffle Koffman's loud hyena laughter, Barban had heard a fragment of it. Sensing that something had been said about him, he exploded. "Look, Vince, you're not fooling anyone," he snarled. "We've got your number."

"My number? What do you mean my number?" Grecco looked aghast.

"You're a fucking Commie," Barban said in a very confidential tone. "'Oh yes. Don't deny it. The FBI's been checking on you. Ask anyone. Max knows. He's told us all about it. Saw your Commie books by Chomsky and Dellinger and Tom Hayden, that mothafucker. He and his wife, Jane Fonda are up there in Hanoi fucking over our POW's. Bruce has got you marked, Vince. Not letting you out of his sight."

Grecco glanced at Gutschinritter and smirked giving him a knowing nod. "Is that true Max? Hank says that you have my number. What's my number, Max?" Gutschinritter looked very earnest and a bit miffed. Barban had blown his cover. The fanatic, Vince thought. Should have known that he'd do something like that. Alert the FBI. Now Bruce has his spooks tailing me. God almighty, where does all this end? "That's what American's all about, isn't it, Hank? Grecco cooed. "Freedom of speech. That's what we're here for. Freedom to say whatever one wants."

Barban was speechless for a moment. Grecco had turned the tables. "Your days are numbered, Vince. I've put up with all the bullshit I can."

"Now listen, Hank..." Grecco said forcing each word out in a slow halting cadence. He'd taken all the abuse he could stand. He'd tell the sonofabitch to meet him at the soccer field in ten minutes. They'd settle their difference there once and for all.

"Yea," Barban said. His voice was taut and ugly.

The Idiot's Frightful Laughter

"Look, just how much . . . . ?" Grecco thought of his position. The efficiency report. Beating the Deputy Senior Advisor half to death. How would that look to a prospective employer? There had always been Barbans as far back as he could remember, and there always would be. Halfass Hitlers thirsting for power. But why had it always had to be him? Why couldn't someone else have stood up to them? What was it about him that these tinhorn dictators disliked, distrusted, felt so threatened by? What possible danger had he been to Barban? He'd certainly been more careful than he'd been with previous bosses. It was so obvious that Barban was baiting him. Well, he wasn't so dumb as to bite.

"Yea, how much what?" Barban snarled.

Grecco noticed that the room had grown very quiet. Everyone was listing. Noting how harassed he looked. Expecting a showdown. They'd like nothing more than to see Barban knocked about a bit. But would any of them dare defy him? Not on your life. It had always been that way. He was always the one to stand his ground. Say what he thought. And what had the consequence been? He had always lost. Fired. Unable to find other work because of a former boss's reference. Making Grecco out to be incorrigible. Unable to get along with others. That sort of thing. Well, he was through being the sacrificial lamb.

"Yea, what?" Barban demanded. "Speak up, man. Let's have it?"

"Nothing. Forget it," Grecco said setting down the receiver. "We'll meet in some dark alley someday when it's just you and I, you mothafucker," he muttered giving those huddled about him a rather pathetic look.

As Grecco slunk from the room, Hank Harvey said, "Don't let it get you down, Vince We've all had our ass chewed by Barban at least once." He nervously pushed the long strands of gray hair from his brow. "It's par for the course."

"You know it, man," Bledsoe said chuckling and rocking his head up and down. "You can sure say that again."

That evening Grecco wrote IV Corps' Deputy Director of CORDS about Barban.

Sheridan Peterson

TO: Mr. Percy Corrigan, DEPCORDS, IV CTZ, Can Tho, VN
FROM: Vincent Grecco, Refugee Advisor, Yen Bay Province
SUBJECT: Unsolicited Evaluation

I am forty-two years old and have worked under many trying circumstances, but never have I worked for a more exasperating, overbearing, arrogant individual as Harold Barban, Deputy Senior Advisor of Yen Bay Province. I spent three years during World War II with the U.S. Marine Corps. I've worked for years as a reporter for large city dailies. I have also been a foreign correspondent making eyewitness coverage of the Korean War as well as here in Vietnam. I have suffered abuse and ridicule, but always there was some reason, some explanation. However, working for Mr. Barban is like working for a madman. He raves and shouts, badgers and insults everyone, and for some very strange reason, we have taken these abuses stoically – all except Burl MacDuff, Public Safety Advisor. He stands his ground, a man among men.

Mr. Barban not only abuses his American staff; he also harasses the Vietnamese and Filipinos. It outrages him because the Deputy Province Chief prefers to meet with me. The deputy is terrified of Mr. Barban. What's more, Mr. Barban only hires obliging secretaries. Competing applicants are turned down if they refuse his advances.

He has driven off a lot of highly competent men. Melvin Flannigan, who is now attending Columbia University's Law School, was one of the ablest men in the Refugee Division if not in CORDS. Lowell Holmes, an agricultural specialist, also left because of Mr. Barban. Within less than three weeks after Max Gutschinritter, the New Life Development Hamlet Advisor was assigned to the province, Mr. Barban threatened him with a poor performance evaluation. Gutschinritter is one of the most conscientious, industrious men that I've met; since I came to Vietnam, and I've been here for thirty months. What's more, Mr. Gutschinritter is the only one on the team that speaks Vietnamese. As a matter of fact, he speaks it fluently. The Vietnamese adore and trust him. That's more than I can say for any of the rest of us.

The District Senior Advisors are all too aware of how ruthless Mr. Barban is. Whenever I visit their outposts, they pump me for information about him. Their questions go like this: "Has he said anything about me?" "What did

The Idiot's Frightful Laughter

he think of me?" "Did I think he might give him a poor evaluation?" Mr. Barban has no qualms about ruining a man's career. What seems most alarming is how afraid all of us have become of him. Elmo Bledsoe, the most able administrator in the province, is miserably abused by Mr. Barban, and the irony is that Mr. Barban could not manage his job without him. He literally does absolutely everything for Mr. Barban and gets nothing but contempt in return. His tour of duty ends soon; however, Mr. Barban has forced him to extend it by another six months until he can find a suitable replacement.

No one person could possibly have caused more harm and alienated more Vietnamese than Mr. Barban. Men like him are a very serious menace to the war effort and the pending peace.

The next morning Grecco read the letter, and then tore it into tiny pieces and dropped them into the wastebasket. He had never written anything with such fervor and so quickly before. It was so effortless that the typewriter seemed to write the report itself. Pure catharsis, Grecco thought. If old Whitewash Corrigan had seen it, he'd have thought I'd gone mad, stark raving mad. Vince did not trust the arrogant old general.

The Photos They Took

Tommy Lewis hadn't killed the Viet Cong. He wasn't even a combatant. He was a cook's helper at the enlisted men's mess and only left camp occasionally to look for pussy in the nearby village.

The corpses were badly mutilated when he found them stacked behind a connex box in the supply depot. He had gone there to get a sack of beans. Their ears had been sliced off, and they were in advanced stages of decay. Flies were swarming over them, buzzing in and out of their nostrils and mouths. He picked up a cleaver in the kitchen and chopped off two of their heads. It was not easy. He'd had to strike at the neck with both hands as though he were chopping wood. His pal, Bernie Lopez, took pictures of him holding a head by its hair in either hand. He had jammed lit cigarettes in their mouths. "It was fantastic." That's what his buddies had said.

The photos showed a smug teenager sneering at the camera. At his side was an AK-47 assault rifle. Sally will really be impressed, he thought. Would he ever feed her a load of shit. He'd really spread it on. Tell her how he'd charged a machine gun emplacement and thrown hand grenades at a platoon of VC blowing the living shit out of them. Ripping them open and watching their guts spill out. That ought to impress her. Show her how rough and touch her guy was. Not like those draft dodging wimps back at school.

The war hadn't brutalized Tommy Lewis. You might say that it was in his blood. He had grown up on a three-hundred-and-eighty-acre farm in Northern California's wine country. Zachariah Baines Lewis, Tommy's great-great-grandfather, had seized the land from a Mexican family in 1848. He had come west in search of gold but instead had joined a gang of outlaws who were terrorizing the countryside. They would ride into a settlement in the dark of

The Idiot's Frightful Laughter

night and kill everyone. It was rumored that Zachariah had murdered those who owned Tommy Lewis' farm and buried their bodies in the barnyard. General Fremont showed up the following year and granted Zachariah title to the farm, for it was assumed that the rightful owner had abandoned the land. At any rate that's what the deed stated.

When Tommy was only five, he watched his father bash in the head of an old horse with a sledgehammer. Instead of turning it out to pasture after years of toil, it was killed in the most savage manner, and the carcass sold to a fertilizer plant. Lewis and his playmates romped up and down on the nag's stomach while his father pounded it to death. This sort of thing went on all through Tommy's childhood, so the Vietnam War came as no shock to the youth.

Trading Photos was the cool thing to do. Nearly all the guys had some in their wallet. They liked to show the FNG's (fucking new guys) and the missionary types. Watching their reactions was a real gasser. Vince Grecco, the gook loving civilian, was a little too much. Whenever he was lodging at the camp, he'd spend the all day at some refugee camp fretting over the slopes. He claimed to be an ex-Marine, but the guys had their doubts. He was a real bleeding heart. When Tommy showed Grecco his photos, he really got an earful. He reported Lewis to his CO, but nothing came of it. Colonel Jones was a good guy. He cautioned Tommy to be more careful whom he showed his photos to. Some civilians were real assholes. They could stir up a lot of shit.

Jake Tracy, a mortar-man with Fox Company, gave Lewis a snapshot of a teenage gal with a piece of bamboo jammed up her snatch. He'd dragged her out of a family bunker. She was the only survivor. Once the squad had finished gang-raping her, he'd shot her at close range through the nipple of either teat. Tracy called the photo "double jeopardy". It was a classic. Lewis had it blown up and framed. He set it on his nightstand beside his bunk. However, he figured that he'd better not send Sally a copy. "You know how women are?" he told his pal Bernie. "You never can tell how they'll take it." Bernie agreed.

Bernie traded Lewis a necklace of ears for a fifth of Johnny Walker Black Label. It was his last ration coupon for the month, but it was worth it. There were eight pair hung by their lobes. They were dry and withered and looked really weird. He liked to wear the necklace to the village. It really shook the slopes up. They'd stare at him as though he were an alien from outer space. One mama-son tried to tear them off. She was an old withered hag with black enamel teeth. He wished that he had a photo of that. How the guys in the hooch would howl.

Joe Slocum from Easy Company was one crazy mother. He had a collection of cocks. They were little shriveled up things. Didn't look anything like one's pecker. More like a pan full of chitterlings. He must have had a couple dozen. Slocum was the company clown. Always doing weird stuff to get a laugh. The FNG guys were shocked; however after they'd been there a while, they no longer gave a royal fuck. Bill Karen, his squad leader, said that Joe didn't have all his marbles. However, he was the only guy in the squad who'd been to college. He had an AA from some junior college in the Midwest. "Goes to show you what an education will do," Sergeant Karen said.

There were others. Photos of all sorts of mutilated corpses. There were those of old people and of women and children. Some were infants only a week or so old. One corpse had its face blown off. Tommy had a manila envelope marked "Barbecue Party". It was full of pictures of charred bodies. There were photos of whole families burned alive by napalm. Some victims had been stopped in midflight running for their lives, their hands outstretched. Lewis had a C-rat box full of grisly photos he'd devoted considerable time collecting. It was a prized possession. He planned to sell them to some publishing house and make a bundle of money.

However, when he left for The States, they were confiscated at the airport. A military policewoman tossed them into a garbage can of some sort of chemical. The container was full of photos and necklaces and stuff such as that. "You're a sick mothafucker," she told him.

The Idiot's Frightful Laughter

Tommy was thunderstruck. It was a momentous loss. "Aw, give me a break, will you? I wasn't the only one," he pleaded. "Everyone does it. The officers don't care. They'll tell you."

"You're a sicko," she said. "They ought to lock you up in a psycho ward. That's what they ought to do."

The Precocious Young Lawyer

The day after Barban's phone call, Grecco found a cable lying on his desk when he returned from lunch. It was from Chuck Simoni, IV Corps' Refugee Chief at Can Tho. Vince was ordered to pack his things and report there immediately. He was being transferred. No explanation given.

Just as he'd suspected, it was a trap. Barban had no doubt radioed Simoni that morning. Told him that the Province Chief was angry with him. Wanted him out of the province. The sooner the better. That was the gist of it. He'd wager his life on it.

However, getting out would not be so easy. He had his motorcycle to think of. The Viet Cong had closed the roads surrounding Yen Chau, and there was no convoy going to Can Tho, not for several weeks. His only alternative was to go to the airport and wait for a C-130 Hercules to land, and that may take several days or longer.

He fantasized of having a showdown with Barban. Spitting in his face. Pissing on his desk. Filling his desk drawers with shit. However, he quelled the impulse, for he could well imagine what the retaliation would be. He consoled himself with the thought of how he would track him down at some later date and settle the score. Only he and Barban alone facing it off on some deserted beach. A fight to the finish. He would show no mercy. Give no quarters. He would have his sweet revenge. Such nonsense, he thought. He was truly a Walter Mitty in every sense of the word.

Grecco waited at the airstrip all that afternoon. At sunset, there was nothing left to do but return to his quarters. He anticipated the sort of reception he would get. It was always the same. People whom he had worked with for years carefully avoiding him. Acting as though they hardly knew him. In this case, he did not care, for he had not been there long enough to make any close friends.

However, there were jobs where there had been very strong bonding. After working together all week, they'd go off on fishing or skiing trips for the weekend and often longer. And in the evenings, they'd be at one another's home. One of them would always be giving a party for some reason or other. The humbug had left him feeling resentful. His colleagues never actually said that they sided with the boss, and they had rarely said anything to the contrary. There was seldom a show of sympathy. They were very careful not to say anything that might in any way put them in an unfavorable light with management. It was as though all of a sudden, Grecco had not existed.

The conversation at supper carefully avoided any mention of Barban or anything alluding to Grecco's termination. Even Koffman was rather circumspect. If Vince was going to say anything at the IV Corps Headquarters against Barban, they didn't want to be mentioned as sympathetic supporters. They wanted that to be made clear without having to say anything. If Grecco involved any one of them, they'd close rank and firmly deny it.

The cowardly bastards, Vince thought. They can kiss my rosy red ass. He'd seen this act before. It aroused memories of slights he'd endured. How neat it would be to pick up the soup bowl and shower them with the hot sticky broth. The cheap cowardly sonsofbitches.

After supper, Grecco was left alone in the house. Most of them went to the clubhouse at the military advisory team's compound. Anywhere just to get away from the outcast. The mood a breakfast was the same, and when he left for the airstrip, only Koffman shook his hand and wished him well.

It was late that afternoon before a transport finally landed. The huge C-130 Hercules was big enough to haul a medium-sized tank. Two sergeants had been waiting all day to load several two-and-a-half ton trucks aboard. The plane was Australian with a large red kangaroo painted on either side of the fuselage. Grecco drove his Suzuki up the ramp and parked it beside one of the trucks. After fixing the vehicles to the floor with webbing and cable, an Aussie airman tied Vince's bike to the wheel of one of the trucks. When they landed at Ben Tray, five miles east of Can Tho, there was a platoon of grunts waiting to board the aircraft. As Grecco rode his bike down the ramp behind the trucks, he was greeted with handclapping and laughter. A motorcycle roaring out of the whalelike gaping mouth of the huge transport plane behind the large trucks was a memorable sight.

Vince didn't expect much help from Chuck Simoni. He and Barban were one of a kind. Callow youths. Simoni had come to Vietnam straight from the University of South Carolina's Law School. Like Barban, he was very sure of himself and greedily ambitious. However, he was shrewder than Hank. More calculating. He knew that it was more advantageous to be coolly polite especially to those he chose to dislike. He treated them with a condescending good humor. It made them less troublesome. Easier to manage. Law school had taught him how to be deceptive. He could appear genuinely sympathetic. Give them all the rope they needed and then strangle them with it. Twist their words about so deftly that they ended up incriminating themselves.

That was life, he told Grecco. Just as long as Colonel Winters approved of Hank, what could he say? He had to follow policy. Simoni had once intimated that Vince wasn't cut out for that sort of work. That this was a young man's job. It required enthusiasm, dedication, and unlimited energy. It was his observation that older men were inclined to be jaded. The accusation had come in response to a remark Grecco had made. He had complained about how futile it was to expect most Vietnamese officials to do anything for the peasant. Simoni had won his confidence. Got him to open up and say what he thought, and then hit him square in the solar plexus, so to speak.

It was during an inspection tour of a refugee site at Rach Gia on the shore of the Gulf of Siam that Grecco saw just how mean-spirited Simoni was. The Refugee Advisor and a member of the International Voluntary Service had achieved the impossible. They'd inspired the refugees to build their own homes. The IVS volunteer was a skilled craftsman. He had taught them how to make their own cinder blocks from clay and build a kiln to fire the

The Idiot's Frightful Laughter

bricks. He had a large role of blueprints, which he explained to the peasants encouraging them to pick out whichever design they liked. He worked from sunrise to sunset leading them step by step through the construction of thirty-four modern Western-style homes. Vince was amazed. With a little Yankee ingenuity, the youth had accomplished what experts at the U.S. Agency for International Development and other American conglomerates had failed at. These refugees were immensely proud of what they'd achieved. They'd lay down their lives defending their domains.

The houses were the envy of the town folks. The youth had set a trend. Everyone wanted a house just like the ones that the displaced peasants had built. Grecco noted that the people did not crouch in their doorways glaring at him with mistrust and hostility, as they had in camps at Yen Bay Province. They were friendly offering him tea. They were anxious to show him about their dwellings. Pointing out how the roofing was fixed to withstand a hurricane. How the brick had been glazed to make tile floors.

However, Chuck Simoni was not impressed. Instead of praising the two men, he pointed out that they were going counter to policy. Vietnamization, that was the policy. "We're advisors," he said. "Not directors. It's our job to urge the Vietnamese officials to take command and run thing their way. You should be striving to restore their faith in nation-building. It's their country, their culture, their people, not ours." Grecco was outraged. How crass can one get? The two men were stunned. They had worked so hard, and now this kid was telling them that they had wasted their time. "Teaching the refugees to build American style homes is undermining the Vietnamization program," Simoni continued. "The people must look to their officials for leadership, guidance, national solidarity. These people," he said pointing derisively at a group of refugees, "have grown lethargic. They've washed their hands of everything. They want nothing to do with the war. We must give them back their country," he added pointing accusingly at the two men. "Awaken an interest in their culture. Encourage them to take part in the war." Simone told Bruce Pallette, the IVS volunteer, that he and the refugee advisor were not allowing these refugees to take the initiative. They were corrupting the culture with Western concepts. The idea was to gradually withdraw leaving the Vietnamese in control of their destiny.

The two Americans were deeply wounded. For a moment Pallette could say nothing. Then he threw a hammer he was holding on the grounds. "You're as full of shit as a Christmas goose," he said stomping off. The new policy was an about-face. Getting the Province Chief and his cohorts to take an interest in anyone but themselves was futile. The refugees were alarmed. Their benefactor was angry. The stranger had abused him. Who was this outsider to come here and cause disharmony? They would have nothing to do with this foreign devil or any of his associates.

The Refugee Advisor, an army captain, saw a career that had looked promising a moment before now in serious jeopardy. He tried to mollify Simoni. It wasn't as bad as that, he explained. Of course, the Vietnamese officials were involved. He had made sure of that. He had the full support of the Province Chief. Colonel Tu was very supportive.

Simoni smirked. How disgraceful, Grecco thought. To force such a good man to have to lie to save his career. The sadistic sonofabitch loved making the captain grovel at his feet. This punk kid had not been in the field. He had no idea of the frustrations advisors had to endure, Grecco thought.

What a dilemma, Captain Dirk Bruno thought. It was a Catch-22. The new policy was a reversal of all that he had been instructed to do. When the Province Chief and his pals had bluntly refused to do anything, he and Pallette had taken charge. For the past year, they had made great sacrifice struggling to raise the refugees' standard of living from dire poverty to an acceptable lifestyle only to be told that it ran counter to the new Nixon Doctrine. How were they to know that they were undermining the Vietnamese Government's self-determinism? Why hadn't someone told them? Why hadn't Simoni called a meeting and explained the new program to them before they'd wasted so much time integrating the refugees into society? Supposing that they were making them an

The Idiot's Frightful Laughter

integral part of the government of South Vietnam? A foe of the Communists?

The captain had endured great danger and hardship but never before had he regretted joining the army. Never before had he felt as though he was supporting the wrong side. That he had duped the refugees into embracing a false cause. For five days during the Tết Offensive Captain Dirk Bruno had single-handedly fought off a squad of Viet Cong guerrillas from the rooftop of his three-story dwelling. Armed only with an M16 assault rifle, two cases of ammo, and a box of grenades, he had held a dozen VC at bay killing six of them. On the fifth day, they had tried to launch an assault on the roof. They had charged up the staircase at either side of the roof; however, the captain had rigged booby traps with grenades at the stairs leading on to the roof. As they lifted the lids opening onto the roof, they triggered the grenades beneath them blowing them to shreds.

In the chaos that followed the Tết Offensive, Captain Dirk Bruno's heroics had gone unnoticed. He was a modest man and expected nothing. He had simply been doing his duty. However, the months of hard work and frustration that had gone into building thirty-four Western-style homes deserved recognition. He felt a strong bonding to his friend Bruce Pallette. The IVS Volunteer had put a career in architecture on hold to come to Vietnam and help these poor unfortunate peasants. Pallette did not deserve this nasty whelp's sarcastic abuse. The military had taught Bruno discipline. He had learned to take unwarranted ridicule, but Simoni had gone much too far. What did this young callow punk fresh from law school know? What experience had he had? Captain Bruno would somehow right the wrong no matter how long it took. Pallette would get his just reward. He'd see to that.

"I know you knew," Simoni said raising his eyebrows in mock wonder. Don't you read the circulars sent out from the main office in Saigon? It's your responsibility to keep abreast of newly enacted policies."

Simoni didn't let it go at that. He was a lawyer. The best in the business, or so he thought. He had warmed up to the case. He would drive his verdict home. Win at all cost.

He saw the captain as a culprit. He'd broken the code. He had not followed headquarters' directives. He must be made to feel shame for his transgression. "What is the advantage of all this?" Simoni asked waving his arm about at the newly constructed homes. "How has it helped win support for the Republic of South Vietnam? If anything you have only widened the gap between the government and its people. The U. S. advisor's sole purpose for being here is to help make its leaders stronger. More secure. It's up to you to get your counterpart to do this," he added. "If you can't work with them then you've failed. You're just wasting your time and mine."

"Who do you know who's got his Vietnamese counterpart to do anything?"

Grecco broke in. "Anything at all."

Simoni was annoyed with the intrusion. Vince was out of order. Where was the judge banging his gavel? It had been made clear from the start that he had been brought along to simply observe. Get a better idea of what it meant to be a Refugee Advisor. "I know of plenty," Simoni replied. "I'd say that most of the Refugee Advisors in IV Corps have a good working relationship with their counterparts." He made no attempt to hide his displeasure with Grecco nor to provide proof to support his pronouncements. Be seen and not heard. That was his edict, Grecco assumed.

"Hank tells me that you set the pacification program back two years in Yen Bay Province, Vince," Simoni had said once twisting about in his swivel chair and nodding to his assistant, Horace Harvey. He was a man in his late fifties who had recently transferred from CARE International where he'd been assisting refugees in I Corps near the DMZ.

"I swear it was three years," Harvey said winking good-naturedly over his bifocals at Grecco.

The Idiot's Frightful Laughter

The sonofabitch," Grecco said realizing how in earnest Simoni was.

"Barban's the best man in IV Corps," Simoni said looking quizzically at Grecco. "Just ask the Depscords Director. He has nothing but praise for Hank."

"Whitewash Corrigan?" Grecco asked smirking slightly.

"General Percy Corrigan to you," Simoni said. "It's a safe bet that Hank will make Province Senior Advisor when Colonel Winters leaves," he added rocking back in his chair and folding his arms behind his head. "Yep, the youngest PSA in Vietnam."

"Oh my aching ass," Vince said slumping down in his chair. "Is there no justice in this world?"

Simoni sat studying Grecco for several moments. "Let's be honest about it, Vince," he said. "You may not like Barban, but you've got to admit, he's doing a damn good job."

It was too nauseous. All this hypocrisy, Grecco thought. Simoni was too smart to believe his own bullshit. It was his way of having fun. A special brand of sadism. "You're putting me on, Chuck?" he said. "You can't be serious?"

"I am," Simoni said nodding his head sagely. "I was never more serious in my life."

Grecco felt as though he were suffocating. He took a deep breath, then a second and a third in quick succession. "Well, he does nothing! Absolutely nothing!" he blurted. "When he's not riding about in his jeep with Suu playing hero, he has his feet propped up on his desk reading porno magazines."

The mask of good humor faded from Simoni's face. "Then why's he rated as having the best pacification program in IV Corps? Just why is that?" He had that look of the prosecuting attorney cross-examining a witness.

"Bledsoe," Grecco said. "Elmo Bledsoe and Major Jack. Sure, they may be Uncle Toms, but they're damn good administrators. And Max. Max Gutschinritter. The Vietnamese love him. Those three are holding the province together."

"And Grecco. Don't forget Vincent Grecco," Simoni said with a sinister laugh.

Vince caught the subtle implication and said nothing. He looked down at his hand and nodded his head. Yes. There was Grecco. There had always been Grecco as far back as he could remember. He felt as though he was watching a very dull movie for the umpteenth time, and if he didn't leave, it would start all over again. Ever since he could remember, he'd been watching it. The characters and setting would change, but the main character, Vincent Grecco, was always there. And the plot? That was invariably the same. For a long time now he had been anticipating the ending, almost before the drama began. He'd hoped that going abroad would break the cycle. But it had made no difference. Not the slightest.

Working for the Yankee Dollar

It would be more than a month before Grecco was reassigned to another province. In the meantime, someone needed to unravel the bureaucratic irrelevancies at IV Corp's refugee office that had accumulated over the past months. Vince was handed a stack of mail that had been gathering dust on Simoni's desk. The letters and circulars were chiefly inquiries from the Refugee Division's main office in Saigon and the Military Assistance Command of Vietnam (MACV) at Tan Son Nhut's Little Pentagon. When Grecco finally answered the last of Simoni communiqués, Horace Harvey handed him another stack. He made a game out of it doing what he could to downgrade Yen Bay's achievements and omitting Barban's name whenever possible. Simoni didn't appear to care. He simply wanted the burden off his shoulders.

Grecco also served as their receptionist informing visitors that Simoni and Harvey were off inspecting some such resettlement camp. However, he soon learned that that was seldom the case. Usually, they were with their Vietnamese girlfriends at the CORDS' swimming pool, a kidney-shaped ceramic pool surrounded by the homes of civilian VIP's. Since the Secretary of Defense had stayed there a year or so ago, the pool had been renamed the CORDS' Reservoir. McNamara had informed the IV Corps Deputy Director that the taxpayers might be displeased if they learned that this was how their money was being spent. His displeasure was deepened one evening when he stepped outside for some fresh air to find a nude Vietnamese woman swimming in the pool. It was discovered that she was the mistress of the Deputy Director. That might explain why the Director was dismissed two months later.

In another sector of Can Tho, CORDS had a large compound enclosed by a high wall. Within the enclosure was a private clubhouse and first-class restaurant with attractive provocative waitresses and barmaids wearing translucent hot pants. There was also a commissary loaded with stateside groceries and liquor, a theater which showed a different newly released movie nightly and high-rise apartment buildings. Each two-bedroom flat was furnished with state-of-the-art appliances and glossy Thai teak furniture.

Grecco rarely visited these golden ghettos. He found the Vietnamese culture far more alluring. There were the Chinese restaurants. One served braised turtle and another roasted snails. Then there were the honky-tonk bars that catered to Americans, mainly GI's straight from the boondocks with muddy boots and sporting trench knives and pistols slung at their hip. Some of the clubs were sturdy concrete structures with ugly plastic furniture and up to date jukeboxes. However, there were hundreds of clapboard shacks with nothing more than a few rickety chairs and tables. It was at the latter that Vince spent many an evening slumped in a dark corner watching tiny Vietnamese cuties bully their GI boyfriends. "Shut up, Joe. Don't talk so much. All time yap, yap, yap," one would say as her six-foot, two-hundred-pound soldier smiled sheepishly down at her. "Okay honey. No sweat," he'd murmur. Grecco's favorite hangout was a tin roof hut where a couple GIs took turns playing boogie-woogie on an old fashion piano which hadn't been tuned in years. The sheet metal roof reverberated in rhythm to the stomping of soldiers' army boots as they disco danced the evening away.

When he traveled throughout South Vietnam as a war correspondent, Grecco had seen thousands of these shacks. They sprang up wherever there were Yanks. These tenderloin quagmires usually included steam bath massage parlors and whorehouses. Many of the latter were nothing more than a reed mat spread on the dirt floor of a lean-to behind a bar. Some shacks were built on stilts over foul smelling cesspools littered with trash. Swarms of flies frequently covered table tops and the beer was hot. However, the whores were always young and attractive. Rarely had he seen an ugly or even plain one. In spite of the filth and heat, the girls were always clean and neatly dressed. Those, who had been

The Idiot's Frightful Laughter

whoring for very long, lost their shy demure and grew loud and coarse. It was the way most GIs like their women. They reminded them of home, of the tough mom, the assertive sister, the no-nonsense wife.

Can Tho was by no means the worst that Grecco had seen. On average, it was better than many. The shacks were generally snugger and cleaner and most served cold beer. Some with chunks of ice bobbing about in the glass. A good many had stateside whiskey bought on the black market or gifts of GIs in exchange for lots of free pussy.

The military police made their rounds several times throughout the evening, looking for GIs hiding in the back, for the joints were officially off-limits to U.S. military personnel; however, no one worried much about it. The bars hired small boys as spotters. They would warn the GIs in ample time.

For the first day or so, the MP's would ask to see Grecco's ID, but soon they got to know him and would simply nod and say: "You fucking civilians got it knocked."

Whenever the Vietnamese Rangers and Special Forces were in town, the bars would usually lock up, for these soldiers had no qualms about blowing up a bar and killing everyone in it just for kicks. One of their tricks was to set a grenade on the bar with the pin partly drawn. Grecco soon realized that they weren't bluffing. If the bartender didn't serve them free drinks all night, they'd pull the pin and drop it behind the bar. If they were drunk, they were just as apt to be killed right along with everyone else. What did it matter to them? Their life expectancy was so short anyhow. Sometimes they'd bring along a Viet Cong they'd captured still carrying his AK-47's. Who gave a shit? He might very likely be a brother or father.

These counterinsurgents traveled in gangs of six or more, for most of the bars had a thug or two referred to as "cowboys". If a Ranger wandered into a bar alone, a "cowboy" would slip up behind him and either jab an ice pick into the kidneys or garrote him with a wire. The body would be seen at dawn floating face down in the Mekong River. The murder was invariably blamed on the VC. What's more, these guerrilla fighters would much rather fight one another than Charley, especially if they were drunk. It was not unusual for Rangers to spray a club full of Green Beret with automatic rifle fire killing indiscriminately. Grecco was once in a bar in Cu Chi when a drunken Arvin opened fire on the shack. Vince dove under a table. The bar hostess seated across from him was hit three times, twice in the head and once in the chest. Her body had shielded Grecco from the onslaught.

Occasionally Vince took a bar girl to his room; one usually young enough to be his daughter. The routine was to point out the one he wanted to the "mama-san". She invariably sat at the bar guarding the cash box. A price was agreed upon, and the payment made before anyone else could claim the girl. She seldom knew until closing time that she had been purchased for the night. She quite likely spent the evening with someone else urging him to buy her drinks intending on fucking him. As a result of this procedure, fights frequently broke out between the Yanks.

Grecco soon learned that "mama-san" was the boss, and whatever she said was law. By dealing directly with her, he saved a lot of money on drinks that were never anything more than glasses of tepid tea.

The next morning, Vince usually felt uneasy about the assignation. It was worse if she wanted to stay which was often the case. Most of the civilians had Vietnamese mistresses, which they generally changed once or twice a month.

One Sunday morning as Grecco was strolling along one of Can Tho's pleasant Tree-lined streets, he was confronted by an old woman with ragged hair that looked as though it had been clipped with a pair of sheep shears.

"You like young girl. She cherry," the woman chanted pulling at his arm. "Number one cherry girl, okay?"

Vince was led through a confusing maze of alleys wading through mud and garbage. They wound in and out among shacks, patchworks of cardboard, scrap lumber, and sheet metal. Some dwellings were made of flattened beer and soft drink cans. Finally,

The Idiot's Frightful Laughter

the old hag stopped before a thatched hut. The interior was divided with gray tattered sheets into four cribs.

Pulling aside one of the ragged drapes, Grecco found a pallet covered with soiled straw mats. While he was waiting, a child that looked to be no more than ten or eleven lead a huge burly sergeant with a bulldog face into the crib adjacent to his. Several minutes later another child entered the crib to the other side of him with a tall black GI. She was just an infant, younger than the other child. Soon the procuress returned with a child for Vince. She looked smaller, frailer and younger than the other two. Probably seven or eight, Grecco thought with horror.

"Number one cherry girl," the hag said standing with her arms folded preparing to haggle for a price. The little girl climbed on to Grecco's lap and kissed him tenderly on the cheek. He lifted her from his lap and set her gently on to her feet shaking his head nervously.

"Too young?" the hag asked in Vietnamese. At that moment the burly bull-dog face sergeant let loose with a loud lion's roar followed by a series of snorts and teeth clenching growls mingled with the tiny child's whimpers.

Grecco rose from the pallet. He'd begun to perspire profusely. Outside he heard the angry voice of the old hag and the sobs of the child he'd rejected. At the doorway, the woman barred his retreat. He must stay, she insisted. She would get another. An older one. Very nice. Cherry girl. No bullshit." She was babbling partly in Vietnamese and partly in pidgin English. She would not be deterred. The customer was always right. She aimed to please. It was not simply business. It was a matter of face.

Pressing past her, Vince set out at a frantic pace through the maze of muddy garbage littered alleyways. He'd broken the code. Thugs might pursue him and beat and rob him. He wandered blindly about for more than an hour before coming out on a narrow street that curved along the bank of a foul-smelling canal that cut through the center of Can Tho. He was on familiar terrain. "Home free," he gasped.

The day Simoni told Grecco that he'd been transferred to Than Uyen Province, he got a letter from Forest Huff, his backup officer at Personnel in Saigon tersely informing him that he would not be rehired when his eighteen-month appointment ended January 31st. Less than four months left, Vince thought. He'd have to hand it to Barban. When he set out to get someone, he didn't waste time. And it was evident that Simoni had sped it along. He'd obviously given the prick his full support. Jaded, that was the indictment. Guilty of showing jaded perversity. No doubt his new boss, the Deputy Senior Advisor at Than Uyen had been forewarned. Keep a tight rein on this bird. He's sure to fuck things up. He knew that Vince had only four-month, one hundred and eleven days to be exact. That may have been the condition on which he'd agreed to take him?

For the following couple of days, while Grecco waited for Personnel to straighten out his records, he dreamt bitterly of revenge. He would return to journalism. Get a job as a foreign correspondent. Be assigned to the Mekong Delta. Expose USAID, CORDS, the whole IV Corps debacle. He'd target Yen Bay Province. Depict it as the most deplorable example of inefficiency, corruption, and incompetence in South Vietnam. And why? All because of Hank Barban specifically, and the Refugee Division in general. It would all be Barban's fault. He'd heap it on so thick that he'd never be able to wiggle free. Flies in the honey pot, he mused. Barban would be notorious. He'd be pointed out by historians of what happens to a nation when an ignorant, greedy, power-mad person takes control. He'd fix that sonofabitch.

His Kind of People

Grecco was anxious to leave Can Tho. He was looking forward to a small quiet town with tree-lined streets lush with shrubbery and flowers. Consequently, he was quite unprepared for what he found. Lang Son, the capital of Than Uyen Province, was as filthy and desolate as Yen Chau was neat and pleasant.

At one time, Lang Son appeared to have been a pleasant provincial city. The main street was very wide, and Grecco could see where a park had once stretching down its center. There were the ruins of stone benches, tile fountains, and oblong spaces with rock and mason borders where flowers once must have grown. Now all this was strewn with filth and rubble.

For the past forty years, Lang Son had been the site of many battles. During World War II, the Japanese had occupied it, building an airport to guard their supply route on the Mekong River that passed west across Cambodia and north through Laos along the Thai border. Later the Viet Ming had taken it from the French. A year ago the Viet Cong had captured Lang Son and held the city for several weeks systematically destroying all the fortifications. What they didn't destroy the Americans did. For six straight days, U.S. aircraft and artillery bombarded the province capital. Mementos of the senseless onslaught lay everywhere protruding from the dirt and rubbish. Bulldozers had scooped the rubble of pillboxes, barricades, and buildings into large ugly heaps at intersections and vacant lots.

The thought that Lang Son had once been a picturesque capital city like Yen Chau was disheartening. The sight of scarred weather-stained buildings, some still with large gaping shell holes; pools of greenish foul sewerage; the absence of trees or any other sort of vegetation; the thick layers of dust and cobwebs that covered the merchandise in the stores depressed Grecco. However, it was the people that distressed him the most. They were so sullen, so very different from the smiling courteous people of Yen Chau. Obviously, they were demoralized by what countless years of war had done to their once picturesque city and their lives, especially those six days of aerial bombardment. It was so unnecessary, so insane. What possible advantage could be gained by such indiscriminate destruction? If they hated Americans, Grecco could hardly blame them. Who would not resent anyone especially those from the other side of the earth bombing one's town into oblivion in the name of such misnomers as democracy and equality; concepts that they had probably never heard of and couldn't possibly relate to. As Wild Bill O'Hara, the Province Senior Advisor had told Grecco" "Shit man! Can't you get it through your fucking head? We had to destroy Lan Son in order to save it." The paradox was quite beyond Colonel O'Hara's comprehension. Tunnel vision, Vince thought. The American military were all alike. They had such a narrow point of view. As a sergeant major once told him: "We ain't paid to think." And that went for generals, especially generals.

Grecco wasn't overjoyed about living among the enemy for the next four months when one considered how truly just their claims for retribution were. His job would not only be more difficult but a good deal more dangerous. The CORDS offices and living quarters were all in the same building. A two-story rectangular structure built on a pile of crushed stone in the midst of a foul-smelling slough. Vince's room had two cots with foam-rubber mats. There was a large refrigerator and an air conditioner. His bathroom was equipped with Western fixtures including a hot water shower. It was his, all his. He didn't have to share it with anyone. That was a big plus, he thought.

The following day Grecco met Greg Kalick, Than Uyen Province's Deputy Senior Advisor. That day he had driven a new minibus from Saigon. It was covered with a thick coat of dust. Kalick, a former air force major, was a year or so older than Vince; and as pleasant and natural as Barban was obnoxious and pretentious. What's more, he had none of Barban's bravado. He wore a white sports shirt, khaki slacks, and a pair of badly scuffed

The Idiot's Frightful Laughter

loafers, and although he'd traveled some two hundred miles through Viet Cong controlled territory, he had no pistol slung at his hip. "What would I do with a pistol against a half dozen AK-47's?" he said when asked.

One could not help liking Greg. He never got angry. He was always polite, sympathetic, a perfect gentleman. There was never the slightest evidence of insincerity. He was the very antithesis of Barban. They had nothing in common, nothing except a love of killing Viet Cong. That they did share although Grecco had never known of Hank actually killing a VC. For Barban to want to kill seemed natural. Vince would have found it incongruous for him not to. However, with Kalick, it was a different matter. To imagine him crouching along some jungle trail, his automatic rifle poised and ready to fire, preparing to riddle some unsuspecting little man in black pajamas full of holes, troubled Grecco. He wondered if deep inside Major Kalick lurked a Barban carefully camouflaged over the years. What could Greg have been like in his twenties? Had he been an arrogant, self-centered narcissus? Had a series of setbacks taught him to assume a humbler, more tolerant guise? Was he a chameleon? If he was, it would not be the first one Grecco had encountered. He had best be aware.

Vince got his first clue when he visited the major's quarters the following day. It was a virtual arsenal. Rifles, machine guns, mortars, and grenade launchers were stacked about an empty room. An in one corner were six locker boxes of ammunition. On the roof of the compound, Greg Kalick had built four bunkers; one at each corner where machine guns could be mounted quickly.

It never seemed to occur to Kalick that the civilians might be averse to killing. That some might prefer to die rather than kill another human being. As for Grecco, it was a different matter. He had blood on his hands. As a teenage Marine, he'd killed a good many Japs on Iwo Jima. During the final day of battle, his company had mowed down hundreds of them when they threw a suicidal Banzai attack against them. Vince had felt ill-used. If the Japs were so keen on killing themselves, why should he have to do it for them? It would be best for all concerned if they killed themselves.

The slaughter had scarred him. It had hardened something deep inside, so Kalick could count on him to defend the compound if it was absolutely necessary. However, he was not going out in search of people to ambush and murder. That was definitely out of the question. Such conduct was against the articles of war set down by the Geneva Convention. Civilians were classified as noncombatants and were not supposed to take part in combat. The enemy had the right to execute anyone who did. A humanitarian pledge signed by fifty-eight nations and the Vatican was a step in the right direction, and Grecco had no intention of violating it if he didn't have to.

Kalick held regular meetings to discuss how the building was to be defended in case of an attack. He'd given up on the Arvin guards. They'd slept through two mortar attacks. Vietnamese soldiers had grown immune to war. Death and destruction were all they'd ever known, and they saw no end in sight. They had ceased to care. Kalick assigned each American a weapon and required that they fire them at least twice a month at the Special Forces' rifle range. The instructors turned in quarterly reports on their progress. No one gave a damn, for they knew that they could not be included in their annual performance evaluation. In case of an attack, everyone was to go to the roof and man a designated spot. Although Grecco had none of Kalick's killer instinct, he enjoyed firing the Green Beret's wide assortment of weapons at their firing range. It was a pleasant diversion. During World War II, he'd fired a Browning Automatic, an M1 Rifle and a 45 Pistol in the Marine Corps. That was the extent of it. He learned to operated and maintain a variety of weapons, such as: the 9mm Swedish K Submachine Gun, the 45 caliber M-3 "Grease Gun", the M-79 Grenade Rifle, the Colt CAR-15 Survival Rifle, the M-16 Assault Rifle, the 60mm Mortar, the M-60 Machine Gun, the .380 Walther PPK Automatic Pistol, and the Uzi Submachine Gun. He was a crack shot scoring expert in marksmanship. Not bad for an old geezer.

After a few drinks, Kalick enjoyed telling war stories. He'd been a Marine Corps fighter pilot in the Pacific during World War II and in the Korean War. As a teenage pilot, he claimed to have shot down twelve Jap Zeros and was angry for not getting recognition for his valor. Grecco, on the other hand, never spoke of his combat experience. He hated to even think about it. For the first couple of days on the beach, he'd been sick with fear. However, his dead comrades had driven him mad with remorse and hate. He became intent on revenging their deaths. Nothing else seemed to matter. Now after a quarter of a century, he still couldn't bear to think about all those thousands of young kids killed for a useless piece of volcanic rock in the Pacific. Now that pile of foul-smelling volcanic sandstone soaked with their blood had been returned to Japan. It was heaping insult on top of injury, he thought.

Gene Nakamura, the Administrative Assistant, wasn't the least bit offended by Kalick's war stories, and Greg would have been surprised if he'd shown a flicker of resentment. Nakamura was a first-generation Nisei, but was in no way Japanese, no way except perhaps in appearance; however, he was tall and muscular, over six foot, and built like a Greek wrestler. He was at least a foot taller than either of his parents. His face was more elongated and his eyes rounder than theirs. An American high protein diet may have had something to do with altering his appearance.

He'd visited Japan several years before and didn't feel the slightest kinship with his ancestral homeland. He had not received the prodigal son's reception that he'd somewhat anticipated. Here he was, the son of a poor immigrant farm laborer visiting his parent's birthplace. He was the fulfillment of the American dream. A graduate of Cornell University, one of the most prestigious universities in the country. He was a U.S. Foreign Service officer. He'd served two years in France as a vice council and another two in Mexico. He was fluent in both French and Spanish; however, he couldn't speak a single sentence of Japanese and didn't particularly care to.

Nakamura was surprised, genuinely amazed, and a bit offended by the way the Japanese had so pointedly shunned him. He was treated like a renegade. They had so much as said that it was shameful for a Japanese to turn his back on his homeland. No matter what the circumstances might be nor wherever he might live, he must never forget that he was Japanese, a descendant of the Sun Goddess Amaterasu.

Nakamura had never mentioned the visit to his parents, and they had not asked. They knew all too well what such an encounter would be like. One could not go home again, not if he were Japanese. For them to return would have been to lose face. They could not have endured the shame, for one spoke their local dialect anymore.

Kalick had no reason to feel embarrassed. Nakamura made no association with the word "Jap". It had nothing to do with him. It had to do with a people on some tiny islands that he had visited for two weeks. He didn't care for their excessive politeness. It seemed insincere. He liked people who were straightforward and frank. The kind that let you know where you stood. People who weren't afraid to say "no". Those were his kind of people.

To End a Feud

Nguyen Thi Tu loved Americans, especially the GI's in hooch #33, most of them anyway. Her official job was cleaning their quarters and washing their clothes. It paid twenty piaster a week. That wasn't much. However, it was the side jobs that were so profitable. For one thing, she sold all sorts of drugs to the guys – hashish, heroin, cocaine, LSD. You name it, she had it. She got the drugs from a Hong Kong Chinese guy in Cholon and sold them on commission.

However, what she liked best was the fucking. It was all pure profit, and besides it was fun. She simply couldn't get enough. At first, the grunts tried to bully her, insisting on paying four or five piaster at the most; however, she soon found out that the going rate in Can Tho was twenty piaster for a short-time and ten for a blow job. Being right there in their sleeping quarters all day, it was easy for her to control things. If a guy didn't want to pay the going rate, there were others who did. Some came all the way from MAT outposts in other provinces. They considered her a great fuck. Unlike the Saigon whores, she put her heart into it. Occasionally a GI was so horny, he'd come before he could get it in. In that case, if she liked the guy, she'd give him a discount. It was good for business.

Tu soon realized that American men weren't like the Vietnamese. They liked strong, assertive women. A domineering gal gave them a sense of security, reminding them of their women back home. The tougher she was the better they liked her. She got a lot of her clues from the GI's' porno films. "How's it hanging. Joe?" she'd say grabbing a hold of his cock. "Been getting much lately?" They loved it. "You number one fucker," she'd tell them off to the side, as though it was very confidential. "You got beaucoup cock." They knew that it was pure bullshit; that she said the same to all of them, but nevertheless they loved it. She was like mom, an out of the ordinary sort of mom; yet someone they could rely on and confide in. No matter how trivial a problem might seem, she took it seriously, or at any rate appeared to. It bonded them. They'd do anything within reason for her. Tu knew what those limits were and was careful not to stretch them. The grunts would bring her gifts like hairspray and cosmetics from the Post Exchange. And when they went on R&R, they'd bring back stuff like pantyhose and lingerie. They were always giving her boxes of chocolate. This made her fat, so she sold it at the market or used it to bribe children to run errands for her.

Tu hoped that the war would never end. It sure beat sloshing about knee-deep in the mud planting rice. She was rich and getting richer by the day. She had two hundred thousand piaster and five thousand U. S. dollars in a plastic sack buried three feet beneath a manure pile at the back of her nepa hut. Someday she'd buy a hostess bar on Saigon's notorious Tu Do Street. That's where the money was.

However, Tu had trouble with Gutschinritter. Max told Colonel Winters that the GI's were corrupting her. The colonel laid it on the line. Either stop messing with that hooch girl, or she'd have to go. Tu tried to get Max killed, but none of the Arvin wanted to do it. She could hardly believe that an Arvin would turn down two hundred piaster. That was her highest offer. It was easy money, very easy. Just bring her his ears. That was all the hitman would have to do. However, it wasn't that simple. Gutschinritter was well liked by the Vietnamese. That in itself wouldn't have mattered much. What did matter was a warning from the Province Chief. He and Max were great pals. Colonel Bo considered the other Americans simpletons and wanted nothing to do with them and that included his counterpart, Colonel Winters. However, whenever he had business with a member of the advisory team, he'd ask for Gutschinritter. He was the Province Chief's liaison. Colonel Bo made it clear to the Vietnamese that Max was not to be bothered. Anyone who harmed him would be skinned alive. He wasn't joking. He pointed out that Gutschinritter was their friend. He loved the Vietnamese.

Tu finally had a talk with Max. She told him to mind his own business. No one was corrupting her. She liked it, and besides, she needed the money. She even offered to pay him off. Name your price, she had said, but he wanted no part of it.

Each afternoon after Tu had finished her chores, she'd position herself at the edge of the pool table in the middle of the hooch. If a guy was short, she'd place her legs over his shoulders. If he was tall, she'd press her feet against his chest. There was often a dozen or so standing in line. "Okay, let's rock and roll," she'd say.

However, like everything, there was always some oddball who loused things up. One day Corporal Timothy Skinner, an expert sniper, rammed a broomstick up her snatch. The wood was rough, and slivers tore her uterus causing it to bleed profusely. It took more than a month to heel.

No one liked Corporal Skinner. Ask anyone. They'd tell you that he was a real asshole. However, they were a team and had to stick together. It was the law of the pack. They had to cover one another's ass. But that wasn't the half of it. If some grunt got in a fight with Skinner, it'd be all over Four Corps that he'd been fighting over some whore. He'd never be able to live it down.

Tu refused to let anyone fuck her while the corporal was in the hooch. One night while he was staggering home drunk from the NCO club, an Arvin garroted him with a piece of packing wire. Tu paid the soldier a hundred piaster. As always, the murder was blamed on the Viet Cong. They got a lot more credit than they deserved. If the truth were known, Americans would be amazed to know that the number of GI's killed by their Vietnamese comrades far exceeded those killed by the enemy. And the longer that U.S. troops were in Vietnam the greater that number grew. It was a well-guarded secret that the Viet Cong's most courageous warriors were former Arvins who'd served alongside U.S. troops.

One day while Tu was scrubbing clothes, a GI told her that a guy from the embassy in Saigon wanted to see her. Burt Hardwig was a small-town cop from Weeds, Kansas who'd joined the CIA at the start of the war. His job was to target members of the Viet Cong infrastructure.

Tu was taken aback by Hartwig's dissipated features. He had large dark bags beneath his eyes, a red bulbous nose, and a patchwork of fine crimson veins that spread out across his cheeks. A lifetime of heavy drinking had taken its toll. He spoke a kind of pidgin Vietnamese that he'd probably picked up talking to bar girls. Spreading a blown-up aerial photo of Tu's hamlet on the table, he wanted to know if there were any Viet Cong sympathizers living there. "Check around, and if you find any, circle their homes," he said pointing to the photo. "I'll pick it up in a couple of days."

This was the Phoenix Program that Sergeant Rivera was always talking about, Tu figured. A hit squad would slip into a village at night and kill the suspects in their sleep, by slitting their throats. She had heard how villagers had used these cut-throats to settle old scores. Get rid of longtime enemies. Her family and the Buu's had been feuding for centuries. It started so long ago that no one had any idea how it began. But every so often, one of her relatives or a Buu would disappear, buried somewhere in the Wang Du Swamp; the body eaten by muskrats. There was her Aunt Lu's three-month-old son, Ky, burned alive last year. He was left in a thatched shelter nearby while his parents thrashed rice. Someone had set fire to the reed hut. Although no one had seen the arsonist, everyone assumed that it was a Buu.

Tu's maternal grandmother had two holes where her nose had been. Long before Tu was born, she had caught a Buu stealing their rice. She was cutting the kernels and tucking them beneath her blouse. The two women fought to the death with their sickles, slashing at one another, probing for a vital spot. Tu's grandmother drove the point of her sickle down hard into the other's heart. During the fight, her nose was hacked off. The villages nicknamed her piggy or pig face.

Tu took a grease pencil and drew circles around the Buu's eight thatched huts at the northwest corner of the hamlet. "Beaucoup VC," Hardwick said examining the circles on the aerial photo. "Good work, Tu. You number one," he said. One night a few days later a fleet of helicopters fired missiles at the huts. Nothing remained but craters where the shacks had been. That marked the end of the Buu clan. The feud was brought to an abrupt halt.

Six months later, Tu bought the Eden Rock hostess bar on Saigon's notorious Tu Do Street across from Prime Minister Nguyen Cao Ky's swanky Maxine Night Club. She had the best looking, most expensive whores in town. That was the consensus among Saigon's rear echelon GI's. Tu fucked a bird colonel and a naval captain on alternate nights. Yes, Nguyen Thi Tu had come a long way from the rice paddies of Yen Bay Province.

Lieutenant Hank Hesse's Best Shot

Grecco had only been in Than Uyen Province three days when Kalick asked him if he'd like to go on an ambush at night. He an Otto Kramer, a Special Forces Captain, had organized one. Greg had asked Vince as casually as though he was being invited on a hayride or a wiener roast.

Captain Kramer, who'd been a Hitler Youth in Germany during the Second World War, fought with the French Foreign Legion in Vietnam prior to joining the Green Beret, the military arm of the CIA. He was a few years younger than Grecco, and a naturalized citizen. He had risen from the rank of platoon sergeant with the French to Captain with the Special Forces and was in line for a promotion to Major at the end of that year's tour. Here was a guy raised from birth to believe that he was a Nordic Superman, Grecco thought. Ruler of the world. An ex-Nazi with the rank of Major in the U.S. Military. Grecco wondered just how many race hating ex-Nazis were high ranking officers in the U.S. armed forces? Plenty, he figured. Fascism wasn't new to America. It had been around for a long time. During the Great Depression of the thirties, Governor Huey Long set himself up as a virtual dictator of Louisiana by exploiting the bias of the downtrodden farm workers and sharecroppers. He was popular among the working class nationwide and might have become president of the United States if he had not been assassinated. Fascism was a real threat in the U.S., Grecco surmised, like a geyser rumbling just beneath the surface ready to erupt if the economy was ever to collapse and the masses grew unruly. Hate, he thought. How easily it could be nurtured. How devastating its effect.

Captain Kramer had learned of the Viet Cong's infiltration route from a paid informer. However, it was risky business trusting a Vietnamese, for he was very apt to be a double agent; thus,

Kalick's squad might be the ones ambushed. But that wasn't Vince's reason for declining the invitation. "I'm here to save people, not kill them," he said and meant it. At Yen Bay, he'd assumed the role of cynical indifference, and what had it got him? A proverbial kick in the ass. So from now on, or for the next four months anyhow, he intended to be candid. What could he possibly lose? Kalick did not seem to care; however he never asked him again, and Vince had not asked him how the ambush had turned out. He hadn't wanted to know.

The evening prior to the ambush, Grecco had looked closely at Captain Kramer. At the round fleshy face, the small suspicious eyes, the closely shaven head. Where had he seen this man before? Then he remembered. No, it was no Nazi, but a close facsimile. The same features. Those same broad shoulders and thick wrinkled neck. Ten years younger, no doubt and raised somewhere in Midwest America, he supposed. And yet they could be brothers. Identical twins for that matter if it weren't for the age difference.

The encounter had occurred five years before at an after-hours club in Seattle. Grecco recalled how he'd been sitting at a long picnic table talking with a pale complected blonde when the man, a second lieutenant, sat down next to him. He was with two other young officers who were dancing with the blonde's companions. The lieutenant said nothing; however, Grecco felt that the soldier was watching him. That he was sizing him up.

Vince had met the blonde at Boeing Aircraft where he worked as a technical editor. Whenever he passed through the shop area where she worked cutting fiberglass patterns for airline fuselages, she would call out: "Hey lover, come here," beckoning to him with her finger. She always had a spicy joke or two to tell him. Grecco had never laid her; however, he was hoping that he would before the night ended. It was past three in the morning when the lieutenant sat down beside him.

For the past half hour, Vince had been trying to get the blonde to go home with him. She hadn't wanted to abandon her friends but seeing how enamored they had become with the officers, she seemed on the verge of consenting. While they talked, she rubbed the inside of Vince's thighs brushing her hand lightly over his cock. Half mad with lust, it was all he could do to keep from dragging her from the room.

A few moments after her two friends and their companions had left the dance floor and returned to their table, Grecco felt a tap on his shoulder. Turning about, he was startled to find the lieutenant's fat face just inches from his. He could well remember the expression. He wore a mask of bored disdain. His voice was low and menacing. "Beat it," he said.

"What? Why?" Grecco had said with alarm.

"Beat it or I'll twist your fucking head off and jam it up your ass," he snarled, but so quietly that only Grecco had heard. All this time the blonde continued to caress his thigh moving closer and closer to his cock.

"But why?" Grecco said struggling to get control of himself.

"Step outside and I'll show you, you sonofabitch." The Lieutenant said motioning towards the doorway.

"All right, let's go," Vince said struggling to his feet. Pausing at an adjacent table, he said to his friend, a Korean exchange student: "Joon, I'm going to kick this dogface's ass. I'll be back in a minute." Joon Pak had been waiting patiently for Grecco for the past couple hours. He had a seven o'clock class at the university the next morning and was anxious to go; however, he had not thought it appropriate to leave at such a propitious time.

Grecco was afraid of losing his nerve. He hadn't fought since he was a Marine some fifteen years ago. He walked quickly across the ballroom weaving in and out among the tables and leaped three steps at a time down the stairs. He was trembling. His legs felt rubbery and lifeless. He hoped he'd feel better outside; that the fresh air would somehow restore his energy. He stood at the entranceway taking deep breaths and rocking up and down on the balls of his feet.

After several minutes, he realized that the lieutenant was not coming. That it had all been a ruse to get the blonde. His fear turned to rage. He felt the fury mounting, as he sprang back up the stairs.

The Idiot's Frightful Laughter

Crossing the ballroom, Joon Pak stepped before him. "No! Stop!" he said. "I fix everything."

Vince pushed past his friend. He grabbed the lieutenant and shook him roughly. "Come on," he said. "You want to fight. Let's fight."

The officer turned about slowly and looked at Grecco out of the corner of his eye. "Go away. You bother me," he said.

An older woman, one of the Blonde's friends who worked with her at the fabrication section, tugged at Grecco's arm. "Come on over here," she commanded. It's strange how docile American men are around older women. Foreign men notice it immediately. It annoys them. "Come on over here," she demanded. "I want to talk to you." Her face was heavily coated with make-up, and her gray hair was dyed an Oriental black. "Come on now," she insisted. She sounded like a manly sort of mom speaking to a naughty child.

Grecco allowed himself to be led to a corner of the ballroom. "Look, I'd advise you not to make no trouble. That security guard over there at the door is Patrolman Erickson," she said pointing to an off-duty cop perched on a stool at the entranceway. He was drinking beer and chatting with two hookers. Large black bags hung beneath his eyes. His nose was swollen and covered with a patchwork of red veins. "He's a very good friend of mine," she said. "Known him all my life. Went to school together. If you cause the lieutenants any trouble, I'll have him throw you out on your ear. I'd have done it the moment you caused this ruckus, but then you and Dorothy and me all work for Boeing, and I don't think it's a good idea for people at the same company an all making trouble. It looks bad for the company, don't you agree?" Noting that he wasn't buying her bullshit, she wagged her finger in Grecco's face, "I won't have you making trouble for them lieutenants. They're officers and gentlemen, and they don't go around brawling like ruffians. And after all, this is a free country, isn't it? I think it's up to Dorothy to decide who she's going home with, don't you?' She added puckering her face up into a look of utter repugnance.

"Shut up. Just shut up," he said moving in the direction of the security guard.

"Just where are you going?" she demanded, pulling at his arm.

Jerking loose of her grasp, he said: "thought I'd have a chat with your old schoolmate. Tell him what you told me. Bring him up to date. Have a feeling he and I may have lots in common. Believe we may have served in the Marines together. Marines hate dog faces, especially smart ass second louies."

She was stunned. This wasn't how she supposed he'd behave "Okay," she said shaking her head as though to clear her mind. "Just don't mention me,"

"Why not," he asked smiling sinisterly. "You two grew up together. Next door neighbors. Went to school together. Isn't that right?"

"My name ain't Erickson," the off-duty cop said. "It's Vinetti. Who told you that?"

"The elderly lady over there," Vince said pointing her out.

"That two-bit whore," Vinetti said, "She ain't no friend of mine," Grecco told the patrolman what had happened. He was right. The cop had spent twenty years in the Corps retiring after twenty years as a Gunny Sergeant. "I'll throw them shave tails out of here if you like?"

"It's not necessary," Vince said. "Just as long as you understand the situation. That's all that matters." As he approached them he noticed that Dorothy's head was resting on the lieutenant's shoulder, and her hand had slipped up between his legs. Vince felt very hot and then very cold. He could have killed the blonde. The fucking prick teased. The humiliation of having been dumped for that animal infuriated him. "Fuck you," he said to the Lieutenant. Then directing his attention on Dorothy, he said: "Fuck both of you." The old woman was watching Patrolman Vinetti. Grecco noted that he, in turn, was watching her. It was not a friendly look.

On the way home, Joon Pak explained why the Lieutenant hadn't followed Grecco outside. "Three men come after you. Too many, I think," the Korean said. "So I push chair in front of them," he said making a kicking motion with his foot. "'You stop!' I say. 'Shut up! Go! Sit down!'" Then Joon Pak stopped and took a martial arts stance. His feet slightly apart. His hands held flat and stiff at

The Idiot's Frightful Laughter

his side. Then with slow precise motions, he moved them out before him. "'I karate expert. I kill you' I tell them. They sit down. No more trouble," he said throwing his head back and laughing a deep mirthless laugh. "They three big guys, but they too scared."

It was obviously a bluff, Grecco thought. A very daring bluff, for during all the time he'd known Joon, he'd never seen him exercise, as he knew any karate expert must do daily. This little man had bluff three burly bullies who were set on beating a man fifteen years their senior. They might have dragged Vince into an alley and beat him to death. However, this Korean exchange student who wasn't an inch over five foot had frightened them off. He'd probably saved Grecco's life.

The more Grecco observed Otto Kramer, the more certain he was that they were cloned from the same cell. The same mean beady eyes and thick bull neck. The shaved scalps and dull gross features. It was so paradoxical. How could two individuals from two totally different cultures be so much alike? It just went to show that every country had a potential Gestapo on standby ready and waiting. All that was need was for a Hitler to emerge and legitimatize their sadistic impulses. What was considered criminal became laudable. Craven miscreants were transformed into national heroes, both feared and honored. Brutality was universal. Every country had its sadists. Look at Israel, Grecco thought. Was the Israeli's treatment of the Palestinian so very different from what the Nazi had done to them? Lust and brutality, Vince thought. Those were the hallmark of the human race.

At the mess hall the next day, Otto told Grecco that Kalick had killed four VC. "He's a true German. An Aryan Superman. They would have loved him. He leaped out in front of the slopes firing from the hip," the Nazi said. "It was magnificent."

"You're mistaken, Otto," Vince said. "Greg is a cowboy. He loves John Wayne movies. Last night he was Gary Cooper in *High Noon*." Well it's all the same, isn't it, he thought.

Four members of the International Voluntary Service were Grecco's next door neighbors. Two were farm boys from the

Midwest who helped Rufus Burns, The USAID Agriculture Advisor. The other two were young women who taught English at a nearby high school. Jeanette Hackworth was strikingly beautiful. She spent her weekends in Saigon with her boyfriend, the Naval Attaché at the British Embassy. During the weekdays when she wasn't teaching, she'd be on the roof of the compound in her Bikini tanning herself with an aluminum reflector.

Prior to coming to Vietnam, the other woman, Candy Templeton, was an anti-war activist. She'd been arrested a half dozen times for protesting the war. Now here she was right in the midst of it and being hustled by Green Beret fresh from battle.

She was an easy lay and fucked the two farm boys when nothing else was at hand. However, Grecco couldn't touch her. She considered him a hypocrite. "You're always telling everyone how much you hate war, and then you go around kissing these fucking fascists ass. That was her term for the Green Beret.

"You're the one who invites them over here," Vince would reply. "If you hate them so much, why do you ask them over?"

Candy waved a fifth of Jack Daniel at him. "How the hell else can I get any liquor in this fucking hole?" she asserted.

The more despondent Candy grew, the more she drank. She was drunk to some degree most of the time. The civilians all wondered why she stayed.

Of all the GI's that hung about the compound, Candy detested Lieutenant Hank Hesse the most, and she didn't want there to be any mistake about it. However, her animosity didn't deter him in the least. In fact, it only whetted his lust. Whenever he wasn't out on patrol hunting Viet Cong, he'd be at the compound with a bottle of Jack Daniel.

He never tired of bragging about killing VC. He'd go into the most grisly details. "You fascist fucking murderer," Candy would say. "You baby killing mothafucka." She'd glare at him with wide-eyed disbelief, her hands clutching the arms of her chair.

Late one night, Grecco found the two fucking in the rec room. He had got up from the bed and gone to get a cold beer. He found Candy lying on the pool table, her legs held wide apart in a V formation. Standing before her outstretched limbs, Hesse was looking down at his limp cock. The warrior did not seem so belligerent at the moment, Vince thought.

"Is that your best shot?" Candy asked. "How is it when you rape those VC chicks?

"Come on, show me. Do it, killer," she demanded. "Just do it."

"I hope I'm not intruding?" Grecco said as he opened the fridge and took out a can of Schlitz.

"It's your turn," Hesse said pulling up his pants. "Be my guest."

Vince heard Candy's cruel taunting laughter, as he left the room. Lieutenant Hank Hesse knew when he'd been had.

A few days later, Candy Templeton was gone. The IVS Director in Saigon figured that she was drinking too much. She needed to go somewhere and dry out.

The Sea of Reeds

Grecco was pleased to know that he need not give Tan Van Xuyen, his new counterpart, a fifth of whiskey each month or anything else for that matter. However, it didn't take him long to realize that this Social Welfare Chief was just as poorly motivated if not worse than the previous. As far a Kalick knew, no one had ever been able to get Mr. Xuyen to visit a resettlement camp or even venture beyond the city limits of Lang Son. Xuyen was a shy portly little man who appeared to be in his early fifties. He had taught English at a private school in Saigon for years, and so Grecco had no trouble communicating with him, Whenever Grecco spoke with the Social Welfare Chief about visiting a refugee camp, he was always amiable and willing. A date would be set, and the helicopter flight scheduled, but at the time of departure, Grecco could find no trace of him and ended up going alone. So what's new? He thought shrugging his shoulders. It's par for the course. However, the reason was clear. Now Vince knew why? His time at Yen Bay had taught him that. Xuyen, an English instructor, was better able than most Vietnamese to detect the contempt that the Americans had for the Vietnamese.

By the end of the first month, Grecco had visited all the resettlement sites in Than Uyen Province spending the night at Military Assistance Teams' outposts, Special Forces' enclaves, and Vietnamese District and Sub-District Compounds. Most of the province was swamp, which was inundated six months of the year. Under French colonial rule, some effort was made to reclaim the rich alluvial soil. However, President Ngo Dinh Diem had mapped out an ambitious plan and dug a network of canals finishing much of the project just prior to his CIA instigated assassination. With his death, the Land Reclamation Program came to a halt.

The Idiot's Frightful Laughter

Diem had transplanted a dozen villages to the marshlands called the Sea of Reeds. The peasants built thatched huts along the canals' levees. Diem's country home was partly completed at the time of his murder. It was situated at the intersection of two major waterways. Late one night soon after the assassination, the partly built home was blown into a pile of rubble. An act that delighted the displaced peasants. The destruction was blamed on the Viet Cong, but no Vietnamese believed it.

Grecco first saw the Sea of Reeds from the side door of a Huey Helicopter. For hundreds of miles, all he could see was a vast plain of dark green grass swaying in the wind. The canals that bisected the marshland at precise intervals like the grids on a surveyor's map were a coffee-cream muddiness. On the horizon, he saw tiny specks that he assumed were boats, but drawing near, realized that they were houses. He supposed that they were tiny thatched boathouses. The idea of floating about in a hut through this mammoth mash of reeds miles from shore fascinated him. However, as the aircraft dropped level with the shacks, he saw that they were perched on tiny islands often no larger than the base of the hut.

The tiny islands were piles of earth dug from the canals and heaped along their bank. When the water receded during the dry season, the thatched huts looked very strange perched on top of from ten to twenty-foot mound of earth.

Phong Tho, the district headquarters, was different. It was built on a long levee that stretched some two hundred meters back into the swamp. Huts built on stilts leaned out over the canal. These constituted an open market, a clinic, a primary school, and a Catholic church. A U.S. Military Advisory Team had its compound at the west end of the village. Whenever Grecco was at Phong Tho, he stayed there.

Grecco visited a number of Military Advisory Units know as MAT Teams throughout the province. Of all the U.S. Outposts, Phong Tho was the worst. All they had was a thatched hut with a dirt floor. The other teams had either taken over concrete structures abandon by the French troops or built them of scrap lumber and concrete cinder blocks with sheet metal roofs. However, the Phong Tho team's isolation made it difficult to scrounge building material.

Actually, MAT teams weren't supposed to build living quarters. They were in VC country. The idea was to dig in. Burrow underground. Fortify themselves with sandbag bunkers. Lots and lots of sandbags piled one on top of another. Post sentries. Be on the alert for sneak attacks in the dead of night. That's how to survive in a war zone. A Viet Cong sapper team could wipe out the Phong Tho outpost whenever they chose. Just one guy with an AK-47 automatic rifle could kill everyone. The outposts were calamities waiting to happen. Grecco felt fatalistic about staying overnight at them. It was suicidal. On Iwo, they'd dug two-man foxholes and took turns as lookout throughout the night. However, things had changed. Discipline was weak. Troops were soft. Comfort took priority.

The Phong Tho team was understaffed. There was only a captain, a lieutenant and three sergeants. The noncoms were old enough to be the officers' fathers. The lieutenant was only twenty; however emotionally he seemed no more than fifteen. He'd gone directly from high school to officers' candidate training. The captain was twenty-four and behaved more like a college sophomore than the commander of an advisory team. As for the sergeants, one was a combat veteran of World War II. He'd made the landing at Normandy. All three had fought in the Korean War. The captain felt threatened and thus was defensive and critical, taking issue of trivial things. No one paid any attention to him.

Grecco soon found that getting to the refugee camps from Phong Tho was a difficult task even during the dry season, for there were no roads through the marsh. Transportation was confined to crudely constructed boats.

Captain Hung Dao Kheim, the District Chief, had a large unwieldy sampan. Generally, the plan was to borrow the MAT team's outboard motor which they might just as well have given to the District Chief for all the good it was doing them. For nearly a year the Americans had been promised a fiberglass outboarder. Every month or so, the captain had submitted a requisition.

The Idiot's Frightful Laughter

However, the team's chances of getting one were slight, for no matter how often a boat was sent, it would invariably be stolen en route. There was always someone along the supply line that needed a boat.

Captain Kheim had spent several years at Fort Benning, Georgia. Although he made no attempt to disguise his contempt for the MAT team, he was proud of his U.S. military training and always dressed as though he was standing inspection. His ramrod stiff bearing, the flattop haircut, the pressed fatigues with the sharp military creases, the spit-shine boots, the swagger stick, the bleached white pistol belt, the set jaw, the steely-eyed stare were all so reminiscent of a parade-ground martinet. However, he was also a combat commander. His troops were not like the run-of-the-mill Arvin. They were well disciplined and fought aggressively.

What must his Vietnamese colleagues think of him? Grecco wondered. He was certainly unique. It wasn't that the Arvin were sloppy. On the whole, they looked trimmer than the GIs. The difference was psychological. It was the Arvin's casual lackadaisical behavior that was annoying. It was the first thing that the Americans noticed. However, there was nothing casual or lackadaisical about Captain Khiem's troops. They were ready for action. Grecco realized that with the right kind of leadership, the Arvin would make excellent combatants. The problem was officers. Most had bought their commissions. It reminded Vince of a shop in Bangkok where copies of degrees from prestigious universities from throughout the world hung about the wall. One could buy a degree from the Harvard Law School for two hundred dollars. The workmanship was flawless. Imagine a high school dropout passing himself off as a Harvard Law Student. In essence, that's what the Vietnamese officers right up to a four-star general were doing. They were impostors and the troops knew it.

Although Captain Kheim only came up to Grecco's chest, he was in awe of him. And the .45 pistol that hung from the hip had a lot to do with it. Kheim was quick to use it on the slightest impulse. Once when they were en route to Aggroville 12 at the end of one of Premier Diem's unfinished canals, the Captain suddenly whipped out his pistol and fired across the bow of a large junk that was passing by. Grecco had protested. The weapon had been fired too quickly for him to have taken aim. Vince figured that the bullet must not have missed the boatman at the prow by more than a few inches, possibly less.

"Don't! Don't do that!" Grecco said in a shrill voice.

When the boat pulled alongside the junk, Kheim told its skipper that the American had ordered him to fire at them. He wanted to come aboard. The sampan was too slow. The District Chief did not know that Grecco knew some Vietnamese. None of the MAT team understood more than a half dozen words. Captain Khein assumed that all Americans in Vietnam were either too lazy or too stupid to learn the language.

Why Grecco wondered as he watched an Arvin sergeant tie the sampan to the stern of the junk. Why would anyone who aped the U.S. military as arduously as Captain Khein did want to disgrace him, a bona fide American? What a paradox, he thought. The whole Vietnam fiasco was one big hoax. Next time he'd remember to bring his recorder; the small one that fit inside his shirt pocket.

The junk sped along at more than twice the speed of the overloaded sampan. Grecco looked at a mother and three children squatting on the floor of the cabin. Then he glanced about at the seamen. A younger one was at the stern working the rudder and another stood at the bow watching for obstacles in the water. Only the children looked at him. How many enemies had the Americans acquired by such diabolical acts, he wondered? Hundreds, perhaps thousands, he assumed. Slipping quietly up beside the youth at the stern, he held his finger to his lips and whispered in Vietnamese: "I did not tell the captain to fire the pistol at your boat. I am your friend."

The young man smiled and nodded knowingly. "I believe you," he whispered, his dark eyes glistening. But did he? They were a canny people, Grecco thought. Perhaps he did not.

Americans were quite capable of alienating their allies. They didn't need Captain Khiem's help, Grecco thought. Not whatsoever. Not when there were so many Barbans running loose.

The Idiot's Frightful Laughter

Aggroville 12, once an experimental farming village managed by a French agronomist, had in recent years been converted to a refugee camp and abandon to its own fate. It was the furthest from Phong Tho District Headquarter, and that perhaps accounted to some extent for its neglect. None of Than Uyen Province's resettlement camps could be classified as adequate. The South Vietnamese Government had long ago forgotten them. The officials right up to President Nguyen Van Thieu and Premier Nguyen Cao Ky had stolen the refugees' supplies and sold them on the black market. The tiny clinics and school buildings were ramshackle huts on the verge of collapse. They had not been built to last long.

As for Aggroville 12, it had neither a school building nor a clinic. Not that it would have mattered, for where would these poor peasants get medicine for the clinic or textbooks for the school let alone a medic or a teacher? But then these things were the least of the peasants' worries. Grecco wondered how they'd managed to survive. Where was the food?

The refugees had been driven from a prosperous village. Most had either concrete or wooden homes and an abundance of fertile land. It was a picturesque place. Coconut trees formed an archway across a narrow canal that cut through the center of town. Most of the families had artistically designed ancestral set at the corner sections of open fields and rice paddies. The graves had been there for hundreds of years, ever since their forbearers had driven the Chams from the land and claimed it for their own. The peasants worshipped their ancestors' spirits. It was believed that they guarded the village and the surrounding farmland from interlopers.

However, Aggroville 12 was a much different world. It had been built on two large mounds of earth scooped from the canal. The nearest palm frond and bamboo grew some thirty miles away, so the huts were made of woven bulrushes. The French had sought to reclaim the land by reducing the level of alkali in the soil; however this venture had been abandoned when they left, and the original settlers went elsewhere. The peasants ate what few catfish and crawdads they could catch in their wicker-basket traps that they hid in among the reeds. They gathered watercress and aromatic leaves that flourished in the stagnant ponds. This was supplemented by an occasional muskrat or snake.

"Why do you stay?" Grecco asked the village chief, a tiny frail old man who wore baggy black pajamas.

"Our village has been razed. Nothing is left," he said. "Now it is a free-fire zone. Anyone seen there is shot. The few that returned were all killed." He was a dignified old man, who stood very erect, his hands pressed at his sides. Grecco was reminded of the white-haired village chief in Yen Bay Province. The story is always the same, he thought. Nothing changes. Every resettlement camp has a tale of woe to tell. The senseless cycle of death and destruction. We promise them democracy, freedom, liberty, and what do they get? Bomb! Napalm! Agent Orange! George Orwell in his novel, *1984*, expressed the dilemma so well. In a fit of rage, the protagonist said: "War is peace, freedom is slavery, ignorance is strength." It summed up the Vietnam War so well.

Noting how afraid the refugees were of the District Chief and his troops, Grecco figured that he would have to get away from them if he wished to learn anything. He dropped to the rear of the group; and then while Captain Khiem was preoccupied chiding a distraught widow, Vince slipped behind a reed hut. "You have killed my husband and my son," he could hear the grief-stricken woman chant over and over again in a mournful monotone.

"They had no business fishing in that area, Kheim snarled. "They knew that it was off limits." The terse clipped tone of his voice angered Grecco. How different the bastard would feel if it was his son or father who'd been shot down unexpectantly from the air for having wandered into a forbidden area. And why? Vince asked himself. Simply because they were starving. There were no more fish nearby. They had to take the chance. Risk their lives and fish in a so-called pacified area or starve. Die of malnutrition. They'd chosen a rain of machine gun fire. It was quicker, less agonizing.

Grecco hadn't been out of sight of the soldiers long before a crowd pressed in about him. Their small emaciated bodies and

The Idiot's Frightful Laughter

gaunt features troubled him. They made him unduly aware of his own physique. How bulky and well-nourished he looked. He tried to appear concerned, interested in whatever they had to tell him. He assumed that he must appear repulsive to those who see only anguish and despair in one another's eyes.

Vince had no sooner knelt down to speak with an old man squatting in his doorway when the crowd suddenly surged in about him, everyone shouting at once. It was impossible for Grecco to converse with them individually. However, he caught such words as "water bad." "No food." "Helicopter shoot." "No medicine." "Children hungry." Those at the perimeter began to shove forcing the other up against him. Then the woman, the one who had been pleading with the District Chief, rushed at the crowd tearing and clawing the others aside. Her small frail body seemed to possess superhuman strength. "You kill my son. You kill my husband," she screamed.

Before Grecco quite knew what had happened, she was sprawled face down in the dust. A soldier stood over her holding his rifle by the barrel. He had struck her at the back the head with the butt plate of his weapon. Blood spread out about her hair and soaked into the thick reddish dust. Then other soldiers waded into the crowd knocking the stunned refugees about with their guns.

"Stop it! Stop it!" Grecco screamed in Vietnamese, but the Arvin paid no attention. "Stop this," he shouted grabbing for their weapons.

It wasn't until the people had fled and were cowering in their huts that the soldiers stopped. Vince ordered two of them to carry the injured woman to her hut.

"Don't touch her," Captain Kheim shouted as a soldier began to raise her. The District Chief had stepped from between two shacks. Grecco suspected that he had been secretly watching the onslaught from there.

"I asked them to," Grecco said.

"She's not to be moved," Kheim said in English pivoting about and marching off.

Vince raised the tiny old woman in his arms and took her to her hut. Then he found a pail of water and washed away the blood placing his handkerchief over the wound. She was still breathing when he left.

Later that evening, Hien Van Coung, the MAT team's interpreter told Grecco that the District Chief was very angry. "You must never wander off by yourself again," he said. "It's very dangerous. The people in these camps are Communists. They will kill you. The Americans agreed. Vince had been goddamn stupid.

"Well, what can you expect of a fucking civilian?" Grecco overheard the Captain tell one of the sergeants. "He has no business out here."

"Shit Sir," the Sergeant said. "He ain't no fucking desk jockey, Sir. He was a fucking Gyrene on Iwo Jima. He's one tough mothafucker, Sir."

A Volunteer

Nguyen Van Mung was working in the field when the people from the National Liberation Front came to see him. He had been expecting them. His father had told him the previous week after the festivities at the village that they wished to speak with him. He was not surprised. He'd been expecting them ever since he'd turned eighteen last month. They'd be after him to join the guerrilla forces fighting Americans and their Saigon lackeys.

He'd been working all morning knee deep in the mud harrowing the rice paddies and welcomed the break. Dung, His carabao, was just two years old and very hard to handle. It was continually trying to break loose of its harness. The other day it had bolted breaking four wooden spikes in the harrow. It had taken Mung and his father all afternoon to repair it.

Mung ran to the well and tossed several buckets of water over his legs and feet washing away a thick coating of sticky silt. As he approached his home, he saw the two NLF cadre seated on a bench sipping glasses of hot tea. Seeing him, they smiled cheerfully. They were dressed in black; the same as the peasants. From a distance, a stranger would not know that they were high ranking officials. They were so different from those of the puppet government. Major Phan Van Linh, the District Chief, wore an American uniform and drove about in a new jeep with several heavily armed bodyguards. He was fat and had harsh bloated features. The major was often seen drunk staggering about his compound. He was formerly a feared river pirate with the Binh Xuyen Gang.

"This is Comrade Cau Ngoc Xuan" Mung's father said motioning to a short slender man with thick-rimmed glasses and long gray hair." "And this is Comrade Le Thi Dieu, he added. She was younger than the man, and although middle age still quite attractive.

Comrade Xuan clutched Mung's hands firmly in both of his. "My but you're the very image of your father," he said. "So strong and rugged."

"And so handsome," Madam Dieu added winking jovially. "I'll bet he has many girlfriends in the village?" she said nodding to his father. Ming felt his face grow hot.

They all laughed good-naturedly at Mung, for his face had turned quite red. "Do not feel shy with us," Xuan said. "Comrade Dieu was only teasing you."

"My son is a good boy," Mung's father said suddenly looking quite serious. "He's much too busy to think of such things."

'Yes, of course," Xuan said nodding vigorously. "We can see that he is a very industrious young man. However, Comrade Dieu and I feel that it is our duty to warn your son," he added. He'll soon be drafted by the puppet government and be made to fight for the American Imperialists. He'll be made to fight against his own people." Then turning to Mung, Xuan said: "You have little time. You must decide quickly. For you will either be conscripted or shot as an enemy of the American invaders and their puppet regime.

Madam Dieu smiled warmly at Ming, for he looked quite perplexed. "Please sit here," she said motioning to a space on the bench beside her. "Your father is an old friend of ours," she added placing a hand on his knee. "He served bravely and faithfully with the Viet Minh against the French devils." Mung could see that his father was deeply touched. He was proud of his father. He knew that he was highly respected by the neighbors.

Nguyen Van Mung had lived all his life near the village of Dong Xoai. He'd attended school for only four years and was literate. He would have liked to have had more schooling, but his family was poor, and his father needed his help on the farm.

Mung had once been to Lang Son, the province capital some fifteen kilometers from home, but otherwise, he had not traveled much. A couple of the villagers had radios, and on several occasions, he had seen a newspaper published in Saigon. However, he had little interest in politics that took shape at the nation's capital. He had never seen an American and could not imagine why

The Idiot's Frightful Laughter

they were fighting the Vietnamese people. As yet there had been no fighting in his district; however it was a contested area, and he knew that someday soon it might become a battlefield.

"What is the revolution?" Mung asked.

"It is to drive the foreign devils from the land," Comrade Xuan said.

"And it is to take the land from the rich lazy landlords and give it to poor peasants like your father," Madam Dieu said. "The land will be divided equally among those who farm it. That is the revolution," she added thrusting her tiny fist into the air. "Power for the people."

No one liked Saigon's garrison troops quartered at the nearby village, Mung thought. They were rude and slovenly. The villagers called them mercenaries or more derogatorily "running dogs of the Yankee devils." Once several of them beat up Mung's friend, Chu, for strolling about the village after dark. The villagers were careful not to look at them for fear that their stare might be misinterpreted

"The puppet soldiers are laggards," Comrade Xuan said. "We wouldn't trade one of our men for twenty of theirs." Mung had to agree. The National Liberation Front's soldiers were different. They were polite and spoke kindly to the people. They had not joined the NLF for money. They had enlisted to free the people and unite the country. They were fighting for a free and independent nation, or so they thought. Mung had no reason to doubt their leaders' sincerity. The insurgents were young and idealistic. He hoped that they might be right. However, one could never be sure. Dissenters had a way of disappearing.

For the next several months, the two cadre came to see Mung quite regularly. Usually, they would complain about being busy and could only stay for a few moments. However, one day they dropped by at siesta time and invited him to join them for a picnic at the gravesite of his ancestors. Madam Dieu spread a reed mat among the roots of a large banyan tree that shaded the ancient tomb and put some fruit on the mat.

"Have you ever wondered what the foreign devils might do to these?" Comrade Xuan asked pointing at the family's ancestral graves.

Mung was bewildered. What possible reason would the Americans have for disturbing his forbearers? What harm could their spirits cause the white demons?

Madam Dieu took several joss sticks from a bag and stuck them in a clay bowl of sand before the tomb. She struck a match and lit the incense fanning the flame with her hand until the tips glowed brightly. "They're barbarians," she said. "They care nothing for our ancient culture. They not only want to destroy us. They want to wipe away our great heritage."

"What Comrade Dieu says is true," Xuan said. "Only last week the Yankee scum destroyed the hamlet of Vinh Tai just fifteen kilometers west of here." Mung had never seen the old man look so angry. A vein in his temple began to throb. "After rounding up villagers like cattle and herding them to some detention camp many kilometers away, they set fire to the hamlet burning it to the ground."

"That isn't the worst of it," Madam Dieu declared. "The worst part was the tractors. The profane bastards had a half dozen tanks equipped with enormous blades. They ran over the ancestral graves crushing the tombs beneath their great steel tracks." Mung gazed mutely at his forbearers' tomb. He could not imagine such a terrible thing ever happening. "Then," she added, "the tanks dug a deep hole and shoved the debris along with the bones of their ancestor into the pit and covered it over."

Mung shook his head in disbelief. "If you do not believe, go there and see for yourself," Comrade Xuan said. "All that remains is a flat bare field. No trace of life is left. Not a single blade of grass."

"No," Madam Dieu said, "He must not go. He'll be shot down like a dog."

"Mung, my boy, you must not allow such a dreadful thing to happen to your forbearers," Xuan said pointing at the ancient rococo fashioned wall that surrounded the gravestones. "It is your

The Idiot's Frightful Laughter

duty to do everything in your power to protect this hallowed ground."

This was their last visit. It was time to lay it on the line. Tell Mung that they had done all that they could. It was up to him now. They were sorry to say so, but it appeared to them that he did not care about his country and its proud history. "Will you run away and let others fight the foreign dogs for you?" Xuan demanded to know.

"Is it fair for young men like you to stay at home with your families?" Madam

Dieu asked. "I joined The Front to fight the foreign beasts when I was just sixteen."

Mung was embarrassed. His manhood was brought into question. Vietnamese men were raised to believe that they were stronger and braver than their women. He could not allow her to be better than he. He'd show her. He'd be more courageous and persevering than any woman. She'd see.

Mung's father had been careful not to pressure him to join The Front. It was not wise for a parent to be too forceful with a child. It was apt to make the sibling stubborn and resentful. However, when Mung announced that evening at supper that he intended to fight the enemy, his father could not suppress his joy. Although he would not be able to farm the land alone, he was proud that his son was following after him.

The day that Mung was to leave, his father invited a few old comrades to celebrate the occasion. He told the gathering that the boy had given him the greatest honor a son could bestow upon a father. Mung would carry on the family's proud tradition. During World War II, His grandfather had been beheaded along with hundreds of other insurgents by the Japs, and his great-grandfather was imprisoned on Con Son Island by the French. It was an illustrious past.

That evening his parents went with Mung to the field some distance from the village where he was to join his unit. Comrades Xuan and Madam Dieu were on hand to wish him a warm farewell. "We are all so proud of you," Madam Dieu said. "We know that you will bring great honor to your ancestors. So many of your forbearers gave their lives for their motherland. They were too proud to be slaves of foreign scum."

Mung was issued a pair of sandals made from slabs of rubber cut from U.S. truck tires, a bag of rice, a canteen of water, a slender home-made knife with a bamboo handle, and an AK-47 automatic assault rifle with two bandoleers of ammo that crisscrossed his chest. He would need training, for he had no idea how to operate the weapon. He'd never fired a gun. A red checkered scarf identified him as an insurgent. Comrade Xuan cautioned him not to tell his comrades anything pertaining to his identity. His family and hamlet must be kept secret. "Someone might betray you," he said. "The Yankee dogs may force a comrade to tell them who you are. They may torture him until he talks. It could bring great danger to your parents and others in the hamlet. Terrible things could happen. Napalm might be dropped on your village burning everyone alive."

Mung's father gave him a jade Buddha to wear about his neck. "May our God protect you," he said. "And make you a great warrior; the pride of our fatherland." Mung's father had worn it as a Viet Ming. It had been given to him by his mother after his father's execution. It was a family heirloom; a sacred memento.

"Like your father," Madam Dieu said, "I am very proud of you, younger brother." She pressed his hands in hers and kissed him lightly on the cheek.

Later that night, Mung joined up with a squad of guerrillas in a bamboo grove nearby. They had been waiting there for darkness. Each of the insurgents had a code name. The squad leader was Con Tran, The Buffalo. Mung was Con Doi, The Bat. The squad leader greeted Mung warmly. "Meet your brothers," he said pointing to the others. We are a brotherhood. All for one and one for all. You must swear a sacred oath to defend your brothers with your life and theirs for you." He handed Mung his knife. "Prick the palm of your right hand and then pass the knife on to the brother nearest you," he ordered. "Each will draw blood in like manner. Fine. Now press your palms together and mix your blood." Once they had all done

The Idiot's Frightful Laughter

this, he said: "Good. Now we are blood brothers. Our lives are one. My life is your life and yours is mine." He held a clenched fist in the air. The others did likewise. "Repeat after me," he ordered. "We are the brotherhood. Under no circumstances will anyone of us ever betray another brother whether alive or dead. We'll fight the enemy and defend our fatherland as though we were one. We will fight for the honor and glory of our country, a united free Vietnam."

"My brothers, it is now dark," Con Trau said. "We must hurry, for our destination is quite far. We have to be there before sunup." Only the Squad Leader knew where they were heading. "It's a secret," he explained. "However, if I am killed or captured, look beneath the strap of my left sandal. You will find the route on a piece of paper rolled in plastic. If this is not possible, return here and wait for instruction."

They crept through the thick jungle. "Never follow a trail," Con Trau said. 'It is too dangerous. The foreign devils often lie in wait beside well-worn paths. After dark, they will shoot anyone. It doesn't matter to them."

Con Trau hadn't been named Buffalo because of his build. He looked nothing like the great lumbering carabao. He was small and slimmer than any of the others. He was so lean and resilient that he could slip through the coils of razor-studded concertina barbwire without so much as a nick.

Mung felt fortunate to be led by such a seasoned warrior. Con Trau's twenty years of guerrilla warfare had made him both fearless and cautious. Whenever there were signs of danger, he would slip quietly ahead of his comrades scouting out the terrain. If he came upon an enemy encampment, he'd withdraw his men to a secluded spot where he would construct a model of the enemy outpost. He'd then assign each a specific target. The men would run through a mock-up of the ensuing attack. They'd quietly assault the replica again and again until Con Trau was satisfied that even the dullest of them knew his assignment by heart. The timing was of utmost importance. They would attack under cover of a mortar barrage striking each target simultaneously. The first couple mortar rounds were aimed at the command post knocking out radio contact throughout the compound. Thus it was easy to confuse the enemy, picking them off one at a time. However, more important, it would eliminate the danger of air and artillery attacks.

During the very early hours of morning, the guerrillas would crawl up to the perimeter of the encampment. Some would turn the Claymore mines about, so that they were aimed back at the machine gun emplacements while others slipped long bangalore torpedoes beneath the barbwire entanglements. Blowing bugles and firing flares, they would charge the bunkers. Instinctively the Yanks would trigger their Claymores, killing or maiming themselves. Then the bangalores would explode clearing passageways through the concertina and across the minefields. The insurgents would head for their targets lobbing grenades into the bunkers and spraying them with automatic rifle fire.

However, Mung, The Bat, would not learn all this until later. The squad's mission was a simple one. They had to reach their destination before sunup. Nothing must deter them. All night they cut their way through the tangled vines and razor-sharp reeds. They waded waist deep in muddy leech-infested swamps and squeezed through thick clumps of bamboo that would bend and then swing back with the force of a horse's hoof striking one across the face and chest. Con Trau moved swiftly never pausing to rest. The men held to one another's shirttails in order not to become separated and thus lost. The squad reached their destination just before dawn.

"This is your home, The Buffalo said. All Mung and the others saw was jungle. Clusters of bamboo and tangled undergrowth. Some distance to their right was a grove of rubber trees; once part of a Michelin Rubber Plantation. That was all.

"Where is our home?" Mung asked rather timidly.

Con Trau laughed. "You are standing on it," he said pointing to the earth beneath Mung. "Con Doi is standing on it."

It was the first time that they had heard their leader laugh. Moving Con Doi, The Bat, aside, The Buffalo tapped several times on a stick stuck in the earth nearby. Within seconds, a square of

The Idiot's Frightful Laughter

earth rose in the midst of them and a man's head appeared. "Quick. Get inside" the man said. "You may be seen."

"This shaft goes straight down for about three meters," The Buffalo said. "Then it levels off. Watch how I brace my feet and back against the sides, he explained lowering himself into the hole. Once Con Trau had reached the bottom, he called out: "Now one of you try it. Remember, brace your back firmly against the side and move one foot at a time. There are groves in the wall for your feet. Be careful not to let your ass slip beneath your knees, or you won't be able to move. You'll be stuck like a rat in a trap," he added. "Who wants to be first?"

Con Doi, The Bat, volunteered. It was more difficult than it looked. However, the earth was firm and did not crumble beneath his weight. He edged down slowly several centimeters at a time. The Buffalo did not press him to move faster, for he knew that The Bat must develop his own special method. Each person's body behaves differently. However, they would have plenty of time to perfect their tunnel climbing skills. "Practice makes perfect," he told them.

Reaching the bottom of the shaft, Mung saw that a tunnel a meter or so square zigzagged at a gradual incline for about thirty meters. At the other end, a man was holding a flashlight and motioning for him to follow. They crawled on their hands and knees for what seemed like kilometers. Arriving at a dead-end, their guide tapped on a bamboo pole at the end of the tunnel. Once again, a trapdoor opened, and the same man's head appeared. "What took you so long?" he asked. He spoke softly; however, the tone was that of one who commanded obedience.

This time the shaft was less than two meters in depth. It opened into a large smoky kitchen. The pungent odor of *nuoc mam* permeated the air. The rotten fish smell was nauseous even in the open air. In the confines of an earthen tomb five or six meters beneath the surface of the earth, it was insufferable. The men covered their noses and mouths with their red checkered scarves. Mung felt as though he would vomit.

What's more, the kitchen was unbearably hot, and the smoke made their eyes and lungs burn. However, most of the fumes from the stove were defused through a dozen or so bamboo vents that were spread out about the jungle's thick undergrowth. Con Doi, The Bat, and his comrades were given several balls of rice and some boiled fish. After the all-night hike through the jungle, nothing had ever tasted quite so good.

The squad's quarters were down another shaft directly beneath the kitchen. A nylon parachute covered the ceiling, preventing chunks of dirt from falling on them. They were each given a cord-knit hammock that they hung from hooks cemented to the hard laterite clay walls. The air was hot and stale, filled with the nauseous fumes from the kitchen. Their toilet was an earthen jar sunk in the floor at one corner of the room. When it was full, it was covered over with a layer of moist clay.

That evening they attended a briefing in a bare room down another shaft to a third level. There were large drawings of an intricate subway system on the wall. One map was a cobweb of pencil thin lines. They represented some four hundred and fifty kilometers of tunnel spreading some seventy-five kilometers from Saigon to well inside Cambodia's Parrot Beak. Years later it would be known worldwide as the famed Cu Chi Tunnels.

The first speaker was a captain. He introduced himself as The Mole. He was in his late forties and had lost a side of his face fighting the French. He had been in the caves some twenty-five years. He joined the Viet Ming at seventeen, and since then had dug countless meters of tunnel. He spoke of the National Liberation Front's glorious victories, the number of helicopters and planes shot down, the tanks, trucks and armored personnel carriers destroyed, the foreign devils killed and wounded, the supplies captured. Next, a woman, whose body was horribly burned by napalm, described the great agony she and others had endured. A sergeant recently released from prison told of the torture he had suffered. He showed them the wounds the fiendish puppet soldiers had inflicted on him and stressed the importance of keeping one's personal identity a secret even from one's dearest friends. "What a comrade doesn't know; he can't tell," he said. "Yes, everyone has a breaking point," he confessed, as though admitting to own shortcomings. "Some sooner than others, and then there are the truth serums. One has no defense against them."

A scholarly old man with horn-rimmed glasses explained the drawings to the recruits pointing out where the subterranean city's living quarters, storage depots, ordinance factories, hospitals, radio rooms, temporary cemeteries, and command headquarters were located. He showed how the tunnels connected with specific villages, district compounds, and province capitals. He also pointed out where each recruit would work. Mung, for example, was assigned to the munitions factory making grenades. The instructor advised the recruits to study the drawings carefully. They must memorize their immediate surrounding, for no one was allowed to carry a map about with him. It may get into the hands of the Yankee swine. At present, a team was setting up signs at key intersections. They were using Hanoi's street names. He was not pleased with the idea. Numbers and letters would be so much easier to remember. "It is very easy to get lost," he said pointing to the maps vast network of tunnels zigzagging in all directions. "So learn the names and the general layout of this bewildering maze. People have disappeared."

The recruits' basic training began early the next day. It was assumed that the best way to become accustomed to cave life was by digging one. Their task was to build a room for the radio equipment recently taken from damaged enemy aircraft and tanks. Organized into three-man teams, they set out to see which group could remove three cubic meters of soil first. Armed with short-handled garden hoes, they took turns hacking at the thick laterite clay. The blades had been ground down to the size of small bowls.

To begin with, a two-meter shaft had to be dig from the surface. One man, Skunk, would remain at the mouth of the pit. Skunk had a long bamboo pole with a wicker basket attached to one end. His job was to lower the basket into the pit. Once the basket was filled, Skunk would raise the container of loose soil and pour it into a nearby stream. Meanwhile, Bat jabbed at the loose soil while the third teammate, Cat, scooped up the dirt and packed it in the basket. After an hour or so, Bat's arms and shoulders ached. He wished that he was home with his carabao plowing in the soft dark earth. He was accustomed to working outside beneath a bright sun and blue sky. He missed the fresh air and green spacious landscape. He enjoyed the monsoon. The heavy downpours that made him feel fresh and clean. How could he endure these dark dank tunnels? Living like a mole in the ground? Some of the soldiers had been there for years. They were hard-bitten men full of hate, thirsting for revenge. They never smiled or laughed. Their eyes were hard and fierce. Killing was all they ever talked about. It was an obsession. They seemed to him like characters in horror stories he'd read; demons conjured up by sorcerers. Bat's thoughts were shattered by a clattering sound. It was the muffled clatter of a helicopter's rotor blades followed by a burst of machine gun fire. Skunk fell into the shaft, his body riddled with bullets.

A hole at the side of a tunnel was dug, and Skunk's corpse was buried. The body was shoved in a fetal position into the small enclave in the wall set aside as a makeshift mausoleum. A coded aluminum tag cut from an enemy aircraft was fixed to the spot to marking Skunk's location. Sometime later, his remains would be interred at the family's ancestral grave site.

It was all so sudden, so unexpected, Bat thought. Death from above. The earth had saved Mung's life. Mother earth. So appropriate. She had shielded him from danger, from the evil foreign giants and their machines of mass destruction.

It took more than two weeks to dig the radio room as well as a series of adjoining passageways. The man, at the surface, now hid beneath a straw mat whenever aircraft were nearby. Another mat was tossed over the mouth of the shaft. Leaves and weeds were stuck into the coverings. Two other teams dug shafts some distance from Bat's. Once the shafts were three meters in depth, the teams dug towards one another. A woman with unusually sensitive hearing guided the excavators with pinpoint accuracy. It was uncanny. Rarely was a cut more than a meter or so off course. Once the operation was completed, most of the shafts were filled in such a way as to be easily reopened, for heavy rain would solidify the clay. Hatches of enemy tanks and armored personnel carriers were used as lids. A few centimeters of earth would easily hide them from sight.

To protect the telecommunication equipment from seepage, a concrete roof was laid beneath the floor above. Until the cement hardened, the form was covered with tarps bought from Arvin for a couple piaster. Radio and TV antennas were threaded among vines that wound about the great teak trees that towered some fifty meter above ground. The transmitters could reach as far off as Hanoi. Translators, fluent in many languages, intercepted radio messages, tapped phone conversations and broke secret codes. Thanks to Yankee technology, The Front had achieved state-of-the-art telecommunication. The scheme was nothing new. A wily Chinese General, Sun Tzu, had written over twenty-three hundred years ago: "Know the enemy as you know yourself, and your victory will never be endangered. A successful general avoids strength and strikes weakness." The NLF was doing just that with considerable success. What's more Arvin officers as high ranking as generals kept the operators posted on military maneuvers. The Yanks could no longer trust their Vietnamese counterparts. The very ones they were assigned to train to take their places were betraying them.

During the early morning hours just before sunup, Bat's team performed tactical maneuvers. They would move as quickly as possible from one spider trap to another pausing just long enough to take careful aim at others posed as enemy soldiers. His team was also taught how to operate the Soviet 122mm-rocket launcher. It was most effective at night against aircraft making surveillance, especially when a helicopter with seven powerful landing lights flew low overhead. One simply could not miss. However, it was dangerous, for the chopper was usually followed by a couple Cobra Gunships armed with rockets and miniguns.

During the afternoons when the Yanks had withdrawn to their outposts, Bat learned how to make grenades. The workshop's only light was one battery operated bulb. The workshop had a hand-cranked drill press and a small forge. Mung's job was to pedal a bicycle that operated a bellows heating the charcoal to a fiery brightness. Scrap metal was melted in a pot and new casings made in clay molds. Smaller grenades were made from beer and soft drink cans. First, they'd drop a handful of tacks and scraps of metal into the can. Next TMT or C-2 was packed on top of them. Then a detonating cap was fixed to a six-second fuse and stuck in the explosive. The handle was made of wood. A small firing chain was attached to eye screws on the handle. One had only to pull the chain to activate the grenade.

Those with more experience made mobile mines. They molded them from crudely shaped pieces of steel resembling dishpans. These explosives were packed with hundreds of steel pellets and from three to six kilo of powder taken from an enemy bomb or artillery shell that had failed to explode. They either stood the explosive up on bipods or buried it a few inches underground. The explosion was equivalent to firing simultaneously seventy twelve-gauge shotguns loaded with double-o buckshot.

Frequently at night during an artillery barrage, Bat's team would watch for rounds that did not explode. They would mark the general vicinity of where the duds had hit on a grid. When the bombardment had ended, they'd race to the spot and remove the shell's explosive. One of the other teams was blown to bits when a round that they were attempting to disarm exploded. Nothing was left of them.

Operation Flaming Dragon occurred just as they'd been told. An informant from Saigon's Ministry of Defense had told the radio operators that night that thousands of Yankee troops would converge on Cu Chi's subterranean city at a quarter past eight the following morning. The foreign troops were right on time. At eight fifteen, Bat saw a dense reddish cloud on the horizon. Then dozens of tanks, bulldozers, and armored personnel carriers emerged from the dust. It was an eerie sight. They were heading straight for Mung. All he had were two anti-tank mines and a sack of grenades. His rifle was slung across his back. As instructed, he hid the two mines on the ground between the approaching vehicles and his escape route. Then setting off a yellow smoke grenade, he ran for the trap door. The lead APC sprayed the area blindly with its fifty-caliber machine gun. However, the bumpy terrain caused the bullets to fly in all directions. Climbing inside the spider trap, Bat waited until a tank had run astride of one of the mines. Pressing two wires together, he triggered the explosion blowing the tank apart. An APC came alongside the crippled tank running over the other mine. Mung ignited it killing a dozen American soldiers inside the vehicle. Then an armada of Huey Cobra helicopters burst from the sky firing rockets and spraying the earth with machine-gun fire. Other troop transport choppers landed nearby. Soldiers leaped from the aircraft and fell to the ground firing blindly in all directions. Those moving towards Bat looked to him like giant orangutans. Half appeared to have shiny reddish complexions and the others, various shades of black and brown. He'd never seen such dreadful monsters before. It was like tales he'd read of aliens from outer space. However, they seemed quite helpless, unsure of just what to do. They wandered here and there in the undergrowth like carabao. Bat set his rifle on semi-automatic and fired a single shot hitting a huge black man's steel helmet right between the eyes. He teetered for a moment and then pitched forward on his face. The others stood about looking down at him. They appeared stunned, not knowing what to do. Next, Mung aimed at a tall lean man with hairy arms and faded blue eyes. The bullet struck his chest piercing his heart. He spun around and sat down, then lurched forward his head dropping between his knees. Bat killed a half dozen foreign devils before they found his spider trap and pried open the lid. By then he'd moved to a new location fifty meters to the left. As the Yankees opened the trap door, they triggered several grenades killing three of them and critically wounding two others. Mung shot two more in rapid succession. He'd had no idea how easy it would be to kill these foreign devils. In spite of all their modern war materiel, they were so helpless, so vulnerable.

 Later that morning, a chopper load of Yankee soldiers no large than Vietnamese arrived. They were armed with .38 caliber pistols, short slender daggers, flashlights and gas masks. They wore skull caps, T-shirts and knee pads. It was evident to Bat that these were the "tunnel rats" that he had seen on TV in the radio room the previous night. Some were true warriors. Men who knew how to fight and loved a good scrap. However, Mung also knew that they were at a disadvantage. They were on his turf. He called the plays, not them. They were on the defensive, subject to surprise, unsure of what was apt to happen.

A lead tank's cannon pivoted about and aimed at Bat's emplacement. They've got me spotted, he thought, as he scampered to the bottom of the three-meter shaft. A moment later a 90mm round blasted the trap door off bringing a shower of dirt down on top of him. He pressed into a cubbyhole at one side of the tunnel. There was a pit for grenades in case one bounced into the shelter. He pressed his hand hard against his ears as several grenades were dropped down the shaft. The explosions reverberated through the long twisting passageway. The concussion nearly knocked him unconscious causing his head to throb. He retched violently unable to vomit. After the smoke and dust had cleared, dirt fell from the opening warning him that a "tunnel rat" was descending. The soldier moved slowly; his flashlight scanning the pit below. Reaching the base of the shaft, he wiggled awkwardly forward to where Mung waited, a knife with a slender pointed blade held ready. As the white devil came abreast of Bat's alcove, he stabbed him over and over again in the groin and abdomen. The man's agonizing screams made Bat laugh. Only a craven coward would cry like that, he thought.

Mung had plenty of time to move to another defense. The body stuck in the narrow passageway prevented others from entering. They must first pull it out. Although it had a rope attached one leg, still it wasn't an easy maneuver.

After the passage had been cleared, several more grenades were dropped down the shaft. However, by this time, Bat was well on his way to a third outpost. Another, "tunnel rat" pursued Mung dropping nimbly down the shaft and scurrying along the passageway to a second shaft. He then dropped down to the next level and along the tunnel to a third shaft where Bat lay in wait

The Idiot's Frightful Laughter

above him. When the Yank shined his flashlight up at Mung, he dropped several grenades down the pit. Bat then slammed the trapdoor door weighing it down firmly with a sack of dirt. He had just enough time to sit on the sack before the grenades exploded blowing the foreign devil to bits. The explosion shattered the door and tore apart the sack of dirt; however, Mung was unscathed except for a bullet in the foot. The "tunnel rat" had time to squeeze off a shot before Bat slammed the trap door.

Mung was a hero. Everyone from his village turned out for the award ceremony. Madam Dieu pinned the Valiant American Killer Citation on his chest. Colonel Nguyen Van Quot, commander of the tunnel complex, promoted him to the rank of squad leader. In just one morning he had killed thirty-two Yankee soldiers and knocked out a tank and an armored personnel carrier, and he was only eighteen years old. It was a proud day for the people of Dong Xoai Village.

Sneaky Little Fuckers

A five-meter-high plaster-of-Paris statue of the Madonna holding baby Jesus stood near the MAT team's compound at Phong Tho. She wore a blue shawl and had a very large gold rosary. She stood on the bank of a canal peering out across the vast Sea of Reeds. The idol looked as though it was in search of something. There was a smaller one in the market in the center of the village. Although those at the resettlement camp nearby were Hoa Haos, a very recent offshoot of the Mahayana Buddhist sect; those at the district town were Roman Catholic. They were refugees from the North.

The late Prime Minister Diem, a religious zealot, had promised them administrative posts in the province if they moved south. They were to manage Diem's huge track of swampland that he was in the process of reclaiming. They'd been handpicked for the venture and assured wealth and power, so it had been a crushing blow for them when he was assassinated. Had they had any premonition of what their plight might be, they'd have stayed in the north and taken their chances with the Communists.

The Hoa Haos, on the other hand, had been moved there as menial labor, for they were noted for their industriousness and honesty. They were also chosen because of their deep-rooted hatred of the Viet Cong. They had once been on friendly terms with the insurgents, and on occasion joined forces with them. That had all changed when the VC were alleged to have murdered their spiritual leader. He was worshipped as the reincarnation of the Lord Buddha.

Why then, Grecco wondered, did Captain Hung Dao Kheim insist that the refugees were the enemy? What did he have to gain? Was it because Kheim was the same sort of medieval Catholic Diem had been? Did he imagine that he was carrying on the Prime

The Idiot's Frightful Laughter

Minister's holy crusade? Was his ruthlessness spurred on by religious fanaticism? So then Grecco surmised, it was really the Buddhist pagans that this zealot and his troops opposed? The French colonialists had put the Vietnamese Catholics in positions of power, and that was where Prime Minister Diem and his cohorts intended to keep them. Maintain the status quo. It was the case of North Ireland in reverse, or was it?

One evening Grecco took a swim in the canal and then stretched out on an upper bunk pulling the camouflage mosquito net down about him. He hadn't been there ten minutes when Cuong, the team's interpreter, came in. He went to the fridge and took out a can of beer. Flipping off the snap up top with his thumb, he set it on the table that stretched down the middle of the hut and sat down.

In spite of the outpost's primitive conditions, the advisory team did have a small generator and a fridge that was usually loaded with stateside beverages. Cold beer was first priority at any U.S. installation.

"Stealing beer again, eh, Cuong?" an advisor said as he stepped into the hooch. He was Sergeant Les Shaw, a large burly man with a small round head set on a pair of large shoulders.

Cuong bared his teeth as though he might be trying to smile but found the gesture too troublesome. The grimace remained frozen on his face, for what seemed to Grecco like an unusually long time.

"Stealing! That's all you fucking dinks know," Sergeant Shaw said taking a beer from the fridge. Snapping off the top with his thumb, he blew the foam at Cuong, covering the youth's face with flecks of white froth. The interpreter made no effort to wipe it away.

"There isn't one of you fuckers I'd trust as far as I could throw a bull over my left shoulder," The sergeant said wiping the brew from his lips with the back of his hand. "You'd steal your own grandmother's gold teeth if you had the chance."

Cuong sat very still and straight, his head held back. His face was blank. Sergeant Shaw leaned forward on an elbow and thrust a finger in his face. "I'll tell you right here and now, Cuong. You better never take nothing of mine, or I'll cut your fucking balls out. Is that clear?"

The interpreter reared back and bared his teeth again. "Laugh you sonofabitch," the sergeant said standing up and shaking his fist at the youth. "You won't think it's so fucking funny when you get a mouthful of knuckle." He doubled up his fist and shook it in Cuong's face. Then he snapped his head back and drained the last remaining drops from his can of beer. Pivoting about, he threw the empty can at the wastebasket as though he was shooting a basketball from center court. It bounced off the rim and onto the floor. "Shit," he muttered picking it up and dropping it in the container as he stomped outside.

A few moments later, Lieutenant Leonard Anderson came in. "How's it going, Cuong?" he said smiling cheerfully. "Having a cool one, eh?"

The interpreter shrugged his shoulders and took a long drink. The Lieutenant stood smiling at Cuong for some time as though awaiting a reply. Then shaking his head, he got a beer from the fridge and went outside.

"What's bugging Cuong?" Grecco heard Lt. Anderson ask.

"Beats me," Sgt. Shaw said. "Never been able to figure them gooks out. You can never tell what they're thinking. Sneaky little fuckers."

The Swiss Bank Account

Grecco laid it on the line the day he returned from his inspection tour of the Aggrovilles. At the Long Son Province Senior Advisor's briefing, he told Colonel Wild Bill O'Hara and his staff just how things stood. Fuck them. He could give a shit what they thought. He wasn't there to mollycoddle the brass. They could kiss his ass if they didn't like it.

It was no wonder that the Viet Cong were winning, he told them striking the podium with his fist. The refugees had nothing, absolutely nothing. They were promised everything – schools, clinics, farmland, resettlement allowances, subsistence pay for sixty days and surplus commodities. Where were they? he demanded. Sold, and the money is in some Swiss Bank accounts.

Grecco paused and glanced at the civilians in the back row. Only Gus Cassari, the CIA chief, seemed unmoved. Kalick was in Penang, Malaysia, visiting his family, and Rufus Burns, the agriculture advisor, was in Can Tho in search of chickens for a new project. However, the others were there – Brad Giddings, logistic; Gene Nakamura, Administration; Chris Zaccaria, New Life Development hamlets and education; and Buck Millons, public safety. They were watching Colonel O'Hara. They looked as though they'd been beneath water for some time and were nearly out of breath, Grecco thought.

"What about that?" the colonel said turning to three solemn-faced majors seated beside him on a large rattan davenport, as he gestured at Grecco with a slow roll of his head. Then cocking his hands behind his head, he leaned back on the sofa and crossed his legs. "Why Swiss? Why not Hong Kong?" he asked. He took a large cigar from his mouth and smiled a broad side-of-the-face grin that said: "Just try to squeeze your way out of this one."

"I saw it," Vince blurted out.

"Whose for christsakes?" Colonel O'Hara said rearing upright in his seat. His green beret dropping in his lap.

"Captain Khiem's. The District Chief at Phong Tho. He showed it to us. It was one of those numbered accounts," Grecco said. "No name. Just a number." He spoke rapidly in short gasping phases as though he was finding it difficult to breathe.

"Why? Why would he want to show you? Is he nuts?" The Senior Province

Advisor asked raising his eyebrows and clamping down hard with his teeth on the cigar.

"We were in the market. He offered . . ."

"Who offered?" Colonel O'Hara broke in looking highly indignant. "Who the fuck is 'he'?"

"Kheim. Captain Kheim, the district chief. He offered to buy us all a beer. Those large bottles of La Rue." Grecco was out of breath. His heart was pounding hard. He realized that he'd stepped into a minefield.

"Who the fuck is 'us'?" The colonel's face had grown bright red.

"Captain Burke, Lieutenant Anderson, Sergeant Shaw," Vince said. "Captain Burke said he'd buy the beer. He was making more money than Captain Kheim. That's when Kheim pulled out his Swiss Bank Book. Wanted to show Captain Burke that he had more money." Grecco looked winded as though he had just finished running a hard race.

"I'd have torn the fucking book up," O'Hara said turning to look at the Major to the right of him. "I'd have torn the living shit out of it." Then turning back to Grecco, he said: "How much fucking loot's that cocksucker got?"

"I didn't see inside, Sir. He only let Captain Burke see."

"Why the shit didn't he tear the fucker up?" O'Hara demanded.

"That's what Lieutenant Anderson said later. He said that Capt. Burke should have destroyed it," Grecco said. "Anderson was mad, but Capt. Burke said that Anderson didn't understand the Asian mind. That you just had to live with that sort of thing if

The Idiot's Frightful Laughter

you wanted to get by in Vietnam." Vince took a handkerchief from his pocket and wiped his brow. Although the briefing room had ten air conditioners protruding from the wall, sweat was streaming down his face. His shirt was soaked.

"Horseshit!" Colonel O'Hara said rearing up from the couch. "Horseshit," he shouted at Grecco. "That's a fucking crock of shit."

"That isn't my opinion, Sir," Vince said softly. He fought to suppress a quaver in his voice. "I agreed with Lt. Anderson." He began to feel an uneasiness seep over him. He'd unwittingly put Captain Burke in a very bad light with his commanding officer.

"Yea, the kids got more on the fucking ball than I figured," Colonel O'Hara said lowering his voice. Then turning to the major seated at his left, he said: "You tell that fucking Burke to get that fucking bank book and tear the fucker up. Tell him that I don't give a shit how he gets it, but he better get the mothafucker and tear the living shit out of it."

The major took a notebook from his shirt pocket and began to write in it. The Province Senior Advisor paused and looked searchingly about at the faces of everyone in the room, as though he was expecting to find the captain seated there. "No! No, wait goddamnit," he said turning back to the major, "I want that goddamn book. I want to show it to some civilian types in Saigon who think the fucking Arvin officers are so goddamn pure."

Well, Grecco thought as he left the podium, the next time he visited Phong Tho, he'd have to find somewhere else to stay. That was for sure.

Vincent Grecco, II

Grecco lost trust in people. Friendship meant little to him anymore. Whenever he left a job, he no longer kept in contact with those he'd worked with. The moment he departed, they ceased to exist. If he ran across someone he'd once worked with, he felt nothing only perhaps an uneasiness.

It had not always been that way. Once Vince had placed great importance in friendship. There was nothing he would not do for a friend. Much of his time was spent helping others. No problem was too trivial. Never would he refuse an acquaintance money. Even if he were quite short, he felt it disgraceful to think of himself when a friend was in greater need.

The change was quite sudden. It occurred when the newspaper he had been working for went bankrupt. He suddenly found himself without a job in Eastern Washington's bleak desolate Columbia Basin during the coldest part of winter. Within less than a month, he hadn't a penny. His wife spent his salary as quickly as he earned it, so nothing was ever saved. But she couldn't be blamed. A small-town newspaper reporter didn't make much. Ninety bucks a week was all.

He went about to his friends and told them very frankly what had happened. He saw no reason not to. They had done the same when they were having difficulties. He had asked for nothing in return. At the time it seemed unnecessary. They were friends. He had helped them. Now they would help him. It was as simple as that.

At first, their refusals bewildered him. Then the puzzlement turned to alarm and finally settled into bitter hatred. Their response was always the same. They invariably told him that they were sorry, terribly sorry, and looked most distressed. They would then go into a long discourse concerning their problems. Some seemed

The Idiot's Frightful Laughter

quite trivial like keeping up payments on a new car. None was life-threatening. They all had jobs and steady incomes. Some could be considered affluent. None was suffering from a chronic ailment. They would whine about being short of money, having the usual doctor bills for the kids. There was the rise in taxes, a pending operation that they were saving up for, money owed the finance company. They were so aloof, so business-like with him. He had come at a bad time. He'd interrupted a favorite TV show, a bridge game, a ratchet ball match, a lodge meeting, the wife's birthday party, their tenth wedding anniversary.

But these were old friends, he would reassure himself. He had helped them in their hour of need. He would return in a couple of days. He assumed that by then their conscience would surely have begun to trouble them, and they'd be only too pleased to help. However, they grew even more estranged. Some made excuses that they had an urgent appointment, or that they were sorry, but the family was just leaving for the movie or a drive in the country. Some simply would not answer the door or had a member of the family inform him that they were not at home although he could see them quite clearly through the window. They acted as though he were a beggar asking for a handout. It became all too evident to Grecco why one might suddenly run amok in an office or workshop murdering his former boss and colleagues. As a newspaperman, Vince had spoken with mass murderers who had never before harmed a soul. They had been kind and loving fathers and devoted husbands. "He was a quiet man," those who knew the killer would say. "Always so thoughtful and considerate. I could never have imagined such a thing." Now Grecco knew. He knew all too well why they had snapped, for he harbored the same fearful impulse. How sweet revenge would be, he thought.

Vince had gone to the State Employment Office. He would dig ditches, collect garbage. He was quite willing to do anything. The Job Placement officer was indignant. "You're a college graduate," he retorted. "You have ten years' experience as a newspaper reporter. It's not fair taking work away from these people," he added pointing to those seated in the outer lobby. There were all types. Some wore clean work clothes and short barbered hair. Others were filthy with long matted dreadlocks and tobacco-stained beards. They wore tattered T-shirts and ragged pants. A few gazed back at Grecco with empty opaque eyes tranquilized as in an opium dream. "That's all these people are able to do," the bureaucrat added. He was impatient. Anxious to rid himself of what seemed to be some sort of muckraker. A reporter wanting to write about the seamy side of life. He was a busy man. He had no time for such trivialities. People needed his help.

How could this be? Grecco wondered. He was in competition with the dispossessed, the defeated, the retarded, the irredeemable, the drifters, the homeless, the junkies, the drunkards, the ex-cons. They had first priority to all the mean and ugly tasks. The grueling, backbreaking drudgery. Very likely some had once been just like him. They'd had a home, family, and job, but they were ill-equipped for life. They could not face its adversities. They were society's weak and hypersensitive, pampered or abused as children. They had dropped out, given up, lost hope. Life no longer held any meaning for them. They had turned to drugs and alcohol and crime as solace, seeking escape from the wrongs that friends and family had inflicted on them, wounded by an adulterous wife, a hostile sibling, a dishonest friend, a tyrannical boss. "Give me a break," Grecco pleaded. "Perhaps I can dig a better ditch. I have experience. I grew up on a farm. I was a forest service firefighter. I know all about manual labor." He was desperate. It was all too evident. It was in his voice, his eyes. But his insistence only made the bureaucrat more alien. He would not be pressured, not by the likes of this brusque newsman.

Vince fought to hold his rage in check. The compulsion to strike the office manager was so overpowering. He wanted to kill the smug sonofabitch, kick him to death. At that moment he wouldn't have cared what happened to him. Capital punishment was no deterrent.

Noting Grecco's crazed look, the Placement Manager moved hastily to an adjoining cubical. Peering back over the partition, he stood ready to sound the alarm, shout for the security guards.

The Idiot's Frightful Laughter

Vince had only one alternative left. Go on welfare. Either that or he and his family would be evicted. Thrown out onto the icy streets. He was already two months behind in payment. Where would they live? What would they eat? They would either freeze or starve. One or the other.

It had been humiliating. The Social Welfare Caseworker was suspicious. She scrutinized the stack of forms he'd filled out. "You're no kid. You're thirty-seven years old. Why haven't you saved for a rainy day? You owe it to your wife and kids," she said. The caseworker had small mean dark eyes set close together. Her lips were tightly pursed forming a circle of dry-prune wrinkles about the mouth. She looked as though she'd been sucking on a lime. It would take at least a month to process his claim, she said. In the meantime, she'd give him a voucher for the rent, and he could pick up some food at the agency's warehouse. Thanking her, Grecco explained that he would need some money for gas. His home was at a nearby town some twenty-five miles away. The social worker agreed to advance him the bare minimum; however, it would be deducted from his first month's allotment. "You been over to the employment office?" she asked. "I understand they're running a gas line to Soap Lake. They need men to dig the ditch. You ain't afraid to get your hands dirty, are you?" Vince tried to explain what had happened, but she only scoffed. "I've been working here for thirty years, and I thought I'd heard them all, but yours takes the cake."

A caseworker visited Grecco's home. She poked about in the kitchen and basement looking for hidden caches. She spoke with the neighbors. Was Grecco working? How about his wife? Did she have a part-time job? Did the kids work after school or on the weekends delivering papers or babysitting? After that, no one would associate with the Greccos. He was a leech, living off the hard-earned dollars of the taxpayers. It was as though the family had some horrible disease, were outcasts, lepers. "The poor woman," they would say of Vince's wife. "Putting up with that useless bum. I'd throw him out in the street.

It was bitterly cold, and there was no fuel for the furnace. The pipes were apt to freeze. Grecco gathered chunks of coal scattered about the ground at a fuel depot. He would tack a note with a five-dollar bill to the office door explaining what the money was for. Once he had filled the sack, loaded it in the trunk of his car and started the engine, he'd grab the note and money. It was stealing, but he could not allow his family to freeze.

Grecco's wife was outraged. The humiliation was unbearable. Maud would not speak to Vince. She left terse brief notes on the kitchen table. Do this. Don't do that. They had violent fights. Once when he tried to take the car keys from Maud, she struck him across the brow with a butcher knife. On another occasion, a neighbor called the cops. Grecco had pushed Maud up against the bathtub. As she fell backward into the tub her foot lodged against the toilet twisting her knee out of joint. The police gave Vince one last warning. Next time and it was a month in jail. No excuses.

It was 1962. Times were tough. The governor was under pressure to cut back on welfare benefits. The lazy beggars were bleeding the state dry. It was time to act. Put them to work. A bill was passed making it mandatory for able-bodied men to do menial tasks for government agencies. Grecco had the choice of cleaning up the school grounds or cutting brush along the bank of the Columbia River. He chose to clear off the river bank. He was assigned to a swampy area thick with second growth willow. It was bitterly cold. He didn't have suitable clothing for the subzero weather. He kept breaking through the ice soaking his loafers. The leather would freeze causing frostbite. He was alone all day. Others would come, but after an hour or so, they would leave. They'd get a doctor to say that they were too ill to work under such arduous conditions. Vince knew no such doctor.

Grecco explained his dilemma to the Director of Parks and Playgrounds. How could he look for a job and thus get off welfare if he were working forty hours a week cutting brush? It was a Catch 22. The Director had known Vince when he was a newsman. He'd been after him all the time to write articles about the deplorable conditions at the parks and playgrounds. The Director was all business. He loathed welfare recipients. They were parasites, sucking America's lifeblood. Hitler was right in some ways. Exterminate those who do not contribute to the welfare of society. Grecco would have to clear a certain amount of shoreline each day, or he'd have to report him to the welfare office. He was sorry, but that's the way things were. Couldn't play favorites, now could he? It was pleasing to see the hotshot reporter grovel at his feet.

It was finally agreed upon that Grecco could have Monday and Tuesday to look for a job if he agreed to cut brush on Saturday and Sunday. However, he warned Vince not to try any funny stuff. He'd be by on the weekends to check on him.

There was no work in the Columbia Basin for a journalist. Grecco must go to Seattle. However, he had only a few dollars in his pocket, not enough for gas a bus ticket. He tried thumbing a ride but was picked up by the highway patrol at Ellensburg. Hitchhiking on interstate highways was forbidden. They threatened him with either a fine or jail. Grecco had no alternative. He could not walk some two hundred miles over the Cascade Mountains in subzero weather. He went some distance from town and flagged a ride. The driver was nervous. He was not in the habit of picking up hitchhikers. One was always reading about how someone was either robbed or murdered. Then why had he stopped? Well, he wanted someone to help with the gas. When Vince told him that he was nearly broke, the driver dropped him off in the dark. He was angry. Grecco was an imposition.

The snow was six-foot-deep at the side of the highway. Grecco waited until sunrise dancing up and down to keep from freezing. He got a ride in the back of a truck to Seattle. The flatbed was covered with grease. All he had to sit on was a section of sewer pipe that slid about on the oily floorboards.

Grecco got a job at the Seattle World's Fair as a "Bubbleator" operator. It was surprising. For a week, he'd lived at a shelter for homeless people and ate at soup kitchens. He looked quite disreputable. His clothes were shabby, and his shoes needed mending. However, the personnel manager felt that he was just what was needed. They were looking for a work-weary astronaut who had spent a lifetime transporting space passengers throughout the universe. He fit the job description perfectly. He had to wear a spaceship costume, which appeared to have been copied from some caricature in a Flash Gordon comic strip. His spacecraft was a Plexiglas sphere-shaped elevator situated in the midst of the fair's main pavilion. All day he would stand on a platform behind an array of flashing colored lights meant to simulate a spaceship's instrument panel.

"Please step to the rear of the sphere, a century at a time," Grecco would chant peering out over the gaping faces of the multitudes that swarmed on and off the lift. "Occasionally he'd see the perplexed expression of an erstwhile friend. Vince would suppress the urge to flip his middle finger at him. "Kiss my ass. You miserable sonofabitch," he'd mutter beneath his breath.

Once everyone was aboard, Grecco would press a button, and the sphere would rise slowly seeming to sail through what looked like a sea of galaxies. "First floor, threats and thresholds, frustrations and fulfillments, challenges and opportunities," he would chant. Then a thumping sound could be heard coming from a speaker at the top of the sphere. "Kapakata, kapakata, kapakata."

"What's that pounding, pounding, pounding?" the transcribed voice of a child would ask.

"It's the heartbeat of man," Grecco would reply. Arriving at the second floor of the pavilion, he'd slide open a large glass door and say: "Please step off into the future." Then as though to himself he'd add: "We've all got to do that." The people, like flocks of sheep, would wander off down a dark passageway. Lights would flash on and off displaying photos of mankind's most remarkable achievements and grandiloquent voices would shout famous slogans from hidden amplifiers. Like a caged baboon, Grecco performed the gibberish over and over again every fifteen minutes, eight hours a day, forty hours a week. It was the apex of absurdity, Vince thought. He felt so ridiculous. What was he saying? What did it mean? He had no idea. But the masses loved it. They were elated. Flies in the marketplace. That's what they were, Grecco thought.

After a month of this, Grecco landed a job editing engineering documents at the Boeing Aircraft Company's vast industrial complex. His job was to cut away the gobbledygook making the engineering documents simple and easy for anyone at the plant to understand. This didn't sit well with the engineers. Vince and his colleagues were lowering their self-esteem. Made their reports so pedestrian.

A prestigious job with a great corporation did not ease Grecco's anger. His resentment continued to fester. He would fantasize over the most ingenious ways of liquidating all those who had betrayed his trust. He dreamt of waylaying them up some back alley and beating them senseless. However, Grecco also felt shame. He supposed that perhaps somehow they were right. That he had brought it all on himself. That he was weak and sentimental. Unsuited for the harsh realities of life. He was a hopeless idealist who had romanticized mankind. In reality, man was nothing more than an animal. The very worst sort of beast. He must train himself to be hard and ruthless. Humanity was a mass of worms to mash.

Grecco's self-loathing prompted him to go to Vietnam. There, there would be no masks. Man's true nature would lie open and exposed. Vince would become as hard and merciless as the worst of them. He would care for nothing. No matter how deplorable the circumstances might be, it would not faze him in the least. He would delight in other's misery. Laugh heinously at their whimpers. Men would grow to fear him. The fiercest warriors would tremble when he came near. They would not be able to meet his gaze nor control their voices. Never ever would he be weak and vulnerable again. He would be like the Samurai warrior of old. People would bow and quake when he passed by.

However, in Vietnam Grecco succeeded only in being incorrigible. Others regarded him as a grouch and kept their distance. His scorn meant nothing to them. They had seen too much mayhem to care. It took a fight at a bar to bring Vince to his senses. A Cracker from Swineboro, Georgia, raked Grecco's face with the shards of a broken bottle. "Had enough, son, or would you like some more?" he mewed pressing the jagged pieces of glass up against his face. Vince agreed that he'd had quite enough. Life was more complicated than he'd assumed. He'd gone much too far to the other extreme. If he was to survive in such a barbaric land, he'd have to assume a more tolerable behavior. There was no Zarathustra, Grecco thought. He was merely the ravings of a mad philosopher dying of syphilis.

A Hearts and Minds Sort of Guy

It was at least a month before Grecco saw the Aggrovilles again, and this time he went by boat; however not on board a sampan or junk, but on a U.S. Navy River Patrol Boat. Vince was anxious to see how those at Aggroville 12 were faring, but he figured it wise to avoid Captains Burke and Khiem.

The Navy had eight barges anchored in the middle of the Tien Giang River near the Sea of Reeds. From the outside, the barges looked like huge metal packing crates bound together with cable. However, the moment Grecco stepped inside, it was like passing through Alice's looking glass. The living quarters, the galley, and the recreation room were like those of any ordinary U.S. naval vessel. Adjoining the rec room was an officers cocktail lounge where cold beer and the best brands of Stateside whiskey were served. There was also a post exchange with a wide assortment of luxury items. One of the eight barges was a floating drydock. The river patrol boats termed PBR's were hoisted out of the water by two huge cranes and held suspended a foot or so above deck while repairs were made.

Grecco's FSR-4 rating entitled him to eat in the staff officers' mess; however, he was not prepared for such gracious living. The rosewood furnishings, linen tablecloths, napkins in ornate rings, polished silverware, crystal glassware, and china dishware wasn't at all what he'd expected. His shabby clothes and dirty boots made him feel quite out of place among the impeccably dressed naval officers. Here in the midst of all this desolation and dire poverty, officers wined and dined like royalty. Filipino waiters in starched white uniforms served platters of culinary delights. There were two kinds of wine and freshly brewed coffee. Steaks were broiled to one's taste, and there were fresh salads with one's choice of dressing and three kinds of soup and a choice of dessert. However, all through the meal, the officers complained of their sacrifice and the monotony of the post. They figured to the minute just how long before they'd be back in the world, back with friends and family, back to the comforts of suburbia. Two naval captains were comparing the merits of their wives' babysitters. Finding a competent teenager to watch the kids these days was a grave problem. Their poor suffering wives. Such trivia, Grecco though. It was disgusting.

After a second helping of sirloin steak and mashed potatoes drenched in thick brown gravy, Grecco boarded a River Patrol Boat moored alongside the barge. The mouth of the Dung Hoa Canal was some forty knots down the Tien Giang. It was another sixty knots up the canal to Phong Tho. From there it was twenty knots west to Aggroville 12.

Grecco was not at all optimistic. However, he didn't see himself as a cynic. No, that was not his nature. He regarded himself as a realist. In spite of all the crime and corruption that the allegorical Pandora encountered when she'd opened her parabolic box, there was still hope. However, that was long ago. A different people, a different time, Grecco thought. Since he'd arrived in Vietnam, what fragment of hope had he found? Day after day, it was always the same – death and destruct, greed and sadism. What hope was there? If being realistic and seeing things for what they were was pessimistic; then he was a pessimist. Under such circumstances, only a fool or a liar could claim to be optimistic.

He already knew what he'd find at Aggroville 12. The situation would be the same or worse. However, he could not help feeling concerned for those poor dispossessed peasants. It was his duty to see for himself. At the province warehouse, he'd found what was left of the relocation commodities promised them years ago. Only a very small portion of the cooking oil, bulgur wheat, rolled oats and cornmeal was left. With Colonel O'Hara's support, the food was loaded on a barge and sent to Aggroville 12. However, Grecco felt sure that it had never got there. It was very likely intercepted at Phong Tho.

Captain Kheim was at the pier when the PBR docked at Phong Tho. The district Chief looked sullenly at Vince for several moments and then sent a soldier aboard to get the skipper. Kheim was blunt and to the point. The American Chief Petty Officer could not go to Aggroville 12. It was off limits. That was that. He was under no obligation to explain why. "An order is an order," he said. "I am in command of this district." His troops looked ready for action.

"Bullshit," Grecco said when Chief Petty Officer Bud Malmquist told him of Captain Kheim's order. "Kheim has nothing to do with it. Just who in the hell does he think he is? This vessel belongs to the United States Navy."

The Chief was adamant. "First of all he's an officer and I'm an enlisted man. Second, this is his fucking district. It's his fucking country. We're fucking guests here. If he doesn't want us to go there, he must have a good fucking reason," he added.

"Yea, a very good fucking reason," Grecco said. 'He doesn't want anyone to know that he stole the fucking refugees' commodities and sold them on the black market. That's his reason."

"That's your opinion," Malmquist said smirking at him.

"It's not my fucking opinion," Grecco said. "It's a fucking fact. Ask Colonel O'Hara, The Province Senior Advisor and commander of the Special Forces throughout the area. I'm under orders to go there."

"Then go," the noncom said. "Who's stopping you? If the colonel's so keen on you going; then have him take you. He's got a whole fleet of choppers."

Grecco noticed that Captain Kheim was watching them. He and his troops had lined up along the pier and appeared to be anticipating something. The District Chief was probably anxious to get his hands on him, Vince thought.

"Okay, you win," Grecco said looking back at Malmquist. "Let's check out Aggroville 5."

Grecco stayed aboard when the crew went ashore to drop off some supplies for the MAT team. For one thing, he wasn't anxious to confront Captain Burke. Not after what he'd said about the Swiss

Bank Book at the briefing a month ago. No doubt the captain had caught a lot of hell for that.

Grecco sat on deck shielded from sight by a strip of armor plating that stuck up on either side to protect the grenade launcher. He picked up an M-16 Assault Rifle that was leaning against the bulkhead and chambered a round. Captain Kheim's men would have no trouble hanging a weight about his neck and dropping his overboard. He was ready; however, nothing happened. Kheim was biding his time. It was nearly an hour before the crew returned. Malmquist was holding a cold can of beer.

"Go get yourself a cool one," the navy chief said smiling. "Them dogface got their fucking fridge loaded with brew." He was his amiable self again.

"I'll pass," Grecco said forcing a smile." 'Beer makes me sleepy."

The noncom looked questioningly at him for a moment, then wheeled about and went in the cabin to fire up the engines.

It was cowardly hiding like this, Grecco thought, but then why invite trouble? Besides he didn't want Kheim and his gang tagging along. They had sure goofed things up for him at Aggroville 12. As for Aggroville 5, he preferred to visit it alone.

Two Vietnamese sailors came aboard. They were very young. Only eighteen or nineteen, Grecco assumed, but one never knew about Vietnamese. They had been assigned to the boat in order to be trained to take charge someday quite soon. It was the result of Nixon's Vietnamization Doctrine; an attempt to turn the fighting back over to the Saigon Government. They were wearing black berets perched jauntily at the side of their head and trim fitting fatigues. Their neatly tailored OD's contrasted sharply with the American crew's ragged denim shorts and bare chests. They sat on the gunwale at the fantail trying to be as inconspicuous as possible.

Grecco knew their story all too well. The seamen had been assigned to the PBR to learn how to operate it; however, instead they were being used as coolies, forced to clean the boat and help the engineer with the dirtier, more difficult repairs. When the vessel was eventually turned over to them, they'd know no more about its

The Idiot's Frightful Laughter

operation than they did the day they first came aboard. When they burned up an engine, as they were bound to do, the Americans would blame them. "Can't trust them dinks with nothing. Ruin everything they put their hands on," they'd say.

The small fiberglass assault boat skimmed the surface of the canal like a rocket. Water was sucked up through the hull and blasted out the stern just beneath the surface from two large fire-hose size jets that whipped the water into a great frothy whiteness.

Grecco looked about the PBR. It was bristling with armament. At the bow were two fifty-caliber machine guns protruding from a turret that swung in a two-hundred-and-seventy-degree arch. A Single fifty pointed out over the stern and mounted at mid-deck just to the rear of the skipper's cabin was an M-79 grenade launcher, which could also be fired point blank from the shoulder. On the starboard side, a thirty-caliber machine gun was fixed to a slender strip of armor plating. It could be switched to the port side in a matter of seconds.

On the river and large canal it wasn't hard to stay clear of the tiny sampans; however, on the smaller canals that linked to the main canal, it was a different matter. At normal cruising speed, the jets made from two to three-foot waves that slammed against the boats moored along the bank battering them up against the pilings and other obstacles. However, it was the ones caught afloat that were in greatest peril. A wave could easily capsize a sampan. The SOP was to move slowly while on a narrow canal, but this rule was rarely observed.

As the PBR started up the canal toward Aggroville 5, Grecco saw people frantically dragging their small craft up the sides of the bank, out of reach of the assault boat's wake. Vince also noticed a number of half sunken sampans strewn along the shore, their sides smashed against the pilings. Malmquist slowed down some after they left Phong Tho and entered a smaller tributary, but not nearly enough. When Grecco pointed to a sampan being slammed up against a large junk, the chief seemed not to hear. When he repeated the warning speaking more loudly, the noncom turned his head slowly and gave Vince a bland noncommittal look.

"So what?" he said. He spoke so softly that Grecco had to strain to hear above the whirr of the turbojets. Bud Malmquist looked to be in his late thirties. He had a broad square face burned a bright red by the tropic sun. His hair and eyebrows had been bleached such a pale blond that from a distance they looked white. When Grecco spoke with him at the boat basin, he had seemed quite amiable. He had smiled cheerfully, his eyes twinkling good-naturedly. However, that had changed along with the neatly pressed khaki uniform he'd slipped out of, carefully folded, and placed in a footlocker. He now wore a ragged pair of dungarees. The pants' legs had been cut off just below the crotch. He had a pea green bleach-stained T-shirt and a crumpled fatigue hat. On his face was an expression of sullen insolence. Malmquist was a rebel. He was in revolt against regimentation when it was safe to be so. Fuck the world. That was his motto.

Grecco felt an uneasiness creep over him. He lived too deeply within himself. What he saw was colored by a rather allusive imagination. It generally took time for reality to seep in. When the PBR left the barges, he felt as though he were embarking on a sight-seeing tour of the Sea of Reed with a bunch of fun-loving lads. However, the crew hadn't taken long to shatter that illusion. Yet there was nothing tough about any of them. Nothing that he couldn't handle provided they come at him one at a time. Most had removed their shirts. Even the youngest had thick rolls of fat that encircled their waists hanging down over their belts. Nor did they seem menacing. Three of them lay sprawled out on the deck, two asleep and a third reading a comic book. The cover had a picture of Spiderman swinging on a cord from a skyscraper. A fourth was sitting on the fantail strumming a guitar and singing in a low mournful voice. A reefer dangled from his lips.

The total lack of discipline troubled Grecco. There was absolutely nothing militant about these swabbies. What an example to set for the Arvin, Vince thought. The boat was so vulnerable. No one was manning the guns, on the lookout for a VC ambush. If this had occurred during World War II, they would have all been court-martialed.

The Idiot's Frightful Laughter

Grecco was reminded of an incident that occurred to him shortly after the close of the big war. An example of what happens when discipline and self-esteem erode. It was 1945 at Saipan in the Mariana Islands soon after the armistice was declared. He'd been transferred to the Fifth M.P. Battalion and ordered to stand hole watch aboard the Hamlin Garland, a cargo ship. The merchant seamen were the dreg of humanity. They were foul, sloven men with bloated dissipated features, bums rounded up from the waterfronts of cities along the West Coast.

Grecco was just eighteen when he stood six-hour watches at night three, four, five flights below the main deck. Often a figure would loom up noiselessly from behind piles of packing cases and float towards him, a grimy, ragged apparition. Its wide zombie eyes glazed from drugs. Vince would noisily slam a round into the chamber of his rifle and say in a tight-lip, harsh voice: Alright mate, up the ladder. Get a move on," trying his best to seem calm but tough. The figure would stand swaying before him, a bayonet pressed at his chest, not seeming to see Grecco, looking through him, through a millennium of darkness. "Up," Vince would order swinging the bayonet downward slicing his shirt and flesh. He'd jab slightly if the phantom didn't heed his warning. Then it would turn and go, seeming to slide slowly upward from rung to rung.

During the day, lying about the desk in the tropic heat, their clothing caked with grease and filth, they resembled decaying corpse rather than ghosts, In the bright searing sunlight, they held no fear for Grecco, only loathing and contempt. Yet there was the feeling that their breath or touch might contaminate him. It was this sort of eeriness that he now felt aboard the patrol boat.

Then it happened. It was a premonition. Grecco had known that something frightful would occur. It was as unnerving as a nightmare that one awoke from in panic. There on the canal before them, a little to the port side was a sampan, a tiny peapod pf a boat. A little girl sat transfixed watching with wide-eyed horror as the assault boat bore down on her. The sampan's other occupant, an old woman with her hair rolled into a bun at the nape of her neck, was facing the other way padding. She seemed not to hear the roar of the turbojet engine.

"Stop!" Grecco shouted. "Stop for christsakes!" he said waving one hand in the direction of the sampan and tapping Malmquist lightly on the shoulder with the other, for in spite of his alarm, he was hesitant of intimidating the chief.

As before, Malmquist turned slowly and stared blandly at Grecco. Still eyeing him, he pushed the throttle full speed ahead. The gunboat lurched forward. Four-foot waves rose above the gunwales. The fantail was a boiling torrent of foam. Grecco watched the tiny sampan shoot upward, ride the crest of a wave for an instant, then fall sideways disappearing into the turbulent wake. When the boat finally shot back to the surface, it was empty. The little girl and the old woman were gone.

Vince was startled by loud raucous laughter. The youth who had been playing the guitar was laughing loudly. He was standing at the fantail, his guitar still slung across his shoulder laughing. It was the kind of laughter that is heard at a roadhouse when a patron tells a foul joke. The frightful laughter of an idiot.

Grecco's mind flashed back once again this time to nineteen forty-six, twenty years ago. He was aboard a troop ship, the USS Mitchell, anchored in the Yangtze near Shanghai, China. A group of Marines were crowded along the railing. One was pointing at the water and saying something to the others. They were all laughing. It was the same coarse laughter like that of the guitar player. What they found so amusing was the body of a child, a girl Grecco guessed. She was floating face down bobbing up against the side of the ship, her long hair fanned out about her head, her arms stretched out at either side like a crucifixion.

> *How morbid a soul can man possess,*
> *To laugh at a sight of such great distress?*

That was all he could remember of the poem. He'd written it as an assignment for a freshman English class. The instructor had read it to the class, and later it was published in the college's literary magazine. The instructor had expounded on man's inhumanity to man. The poem was proof of how insensitive war made one to human suffering, but Grecco didn't believe that one needed war to make him behave barbarically.

"You don't see none of their people going out to save them, do you?" Malmquist asked pointing to where a group had gathered on the bank. "If them dinks don't care enough to help their own kind, I sure as shit ain't losing no sleep over them."

It was true. Grecco could see that no one had budged from the bank to search for the old woman and the small child, but what sort of rationale was that? That was no justification for murdering two innocent people. Malmquist was a cold-blooded killer. It was a war crime. The least he could do was to report it to the Navy's Criminal Investigation Division.

It was incredible, Grecco thought, glancing about at the crew. These punks had been exposed to the best that any civilization had ever been able to offer its youth, and yet look at them. Did they behave any differently than men fifty thousand years ago? Weren't they just as primitive, just as brutal and insensitive as the Neolithic cave dweller?

Here they were operating one of modern technology's most sophisticated pieces of machinery, a jet-propelled, fiberglass, armor-plated assault boats equipped with the most advanced sort of radar, starlight night scanner, and short-wave electronics, but where was their humanity? What effect had all the Christs, Buddhas, and Mahatma Gandhis had on them? Obviously nothing. Not the tiniest speck.

And how about himself? How about Vincent Grecco? What had he done to show his humanity? A woman and child drowned right before his eyes. Their boat capsized within an arm's reach of him. Had he made the slightest effort to rescue them? Couldn't he have dived after them or pulled the throttle back? Couldn't he have done something if he were really so concerned about humanity? Wasn't he just as much to blame as the Chief Petty Officer?

He knew how wrong it was drowning two helpless human beings. Didn't that make him just as guilty as the skipper? What remorse did Malmquist feel? How could he? Not after slamming the throttle full speed ahead and bearing down on the tiny sampan. He'd felt a perverse pride, a coward's sense of power. A self-righteousness that he found easy to rationalize. How was it that Vincent Grecco could be so masterful with an unruly assortment of skydivers?

He was so prompt to act, to see that everyone got a fair break. How was it that he could be so responsive to things that mattered so little, and quite helpless when faced with such grave consequence? He'd failed to stand up to Barban. Threats from the main office in Saigon had forced him to bribe his counterpart. He failed to report the slaughter of defenseless refugees by a drunken district chief.

However, it went back further than Vietnam. There was the doctor who'd purposely allowed his daughter to die of Meningitis. The divorce attorney who'd swindled him of everything – car, house, furnishing, the children. Then there were his employers, editors, and publishers, sour vehement men who incessantly harassed him. At night he would lie awake until the early hours of morn plotting the brutal revenge, but it all came to naught. When things mattered most, he'd grow passive. How he despised himself.

Grecco could no longer see the place where the sampan had capsized. They had left the scene of the crime far behind. No doubt the child and the old woman were dead, buried in the thick gummy mud at the bottom of the canal. In a few days, their bodies would fill with gas, rise to the surface, and float out to sea, bait for fish. How much better it would have been if he'd plunged over the side. He might possibly have saved one of them. He would never forget the child's startled look a moment before the sampan capsized. It would haunt him forever just as the memory of the child's body floating in the Yangtze River had and still did. But what difference would it make? Would he behave differently in the face of a future calamity? He was afraid that he would not. It seemed that there were but two kinds of people on earth – the savage and the drone,

The Idiot's Frightful Laughter

who was concerned but never able to act. He noticed that the sailors were watching him warily. He was not one of them. A miserable drone.

Aggroville 5 was ten clicks west of Phong Tho. There were no thatched huts perched on mounds of earth like those at Aggroville 12. The village was on a man-made plateau about the size of a football field that rose about four meters above the marshland. The huts were slightly larger, and most were made of bamboo and palm frond instead of reeds. There were no trees, shrubbery, or gardens about the homes. There was no sign of vegetation whatsoever. However, there was a neatness that he hadn't seen at the other resettlement camps. There was no litter scattered about, and the earth around the shacks looked as though it had been freshly swept. Beyond the village, Grecco saw what looked to be rice paddies. It was a lighter green than the reeds. If he'd been closer, he'd have seen the pale yellow of the kernels just commencing to mature.

Vince saw all this from the PBR that lay idling offshore. The crew were stopping sampans and junks that floated by on either side. They were checking the occupants' ID cards, searching for weapons, ammo, medicine, radio parts, anything that might be of use to the Viet Cong.

It was an ugly sight to watch. The fat, bare-chested seamen towering over the old men and women who resembled plucked sparrows in black pajamas. Grecco took a miniature camera from his pocket and focused the lens on Malmquist big belly. The navy chief was standing spread leg on the gunwale peering angrily down at a skeleton of a man who looked to be in his seventies. It was difficult to tell. The old man was kneeling in his sampan, his hands clasped together as though he were praying to Malmquist, the great fat demon god. The one of death and destruction, Vince thought, snapping the shutter just as the navy chief was jerking the ID card from the skeleton's clasped hands.

Grecco was afraid that he might not have the right f-stop and was preparing to take another shot when Malmquist saw him. "Hey none of that shit here," he said holding up his hand as though to block the lens.

"Just a personal memento," Vince said forcing a smile.

"Yea well let's have the film," the gob demanded stretching out his hand. "I ain't taking no chances. Don't want to turn up on the front page of no newspaper."

"Now wait just one fucking moment," Grecco said struggling to assume an expression of righteous indignation. "I'm a US AID official. I have an FSR rating of four. That's comparable to a brigadier general. We're part of the State Department. I'm not about to do anything that might jeopardize my career." However, Vince was thinking: I'll fix this sonofabitch. Just off hand, I know a half dozen city dailies that would fight over a shot like this. It's got punch, human interest, news value, everything a city editor craves. It's something the wire services would snap up and dispatch to newspapers worldwide. The world will know the real Chief Petty Officer Bud Malmquist. He'll be a symbol of all that is sick and ugly about this war, about the United States of America, the whole human race for that matter.

"Okay," the naval chief said dropping his hand. "The skipper said that you were okay, so that's good enough for me." However, there was nothing in his tone of voice or expression to indicate that he meant what he'd said. Malmquist had no use for civilians. They had no loyalty as far as he was concerned. They were mercenaries. In it for the buck. Ready to serve whoever paid the highest price. Look at that Daniel Ellsberg fucker. He was a big shot in the State Department. A lot higher up than this bird, and he threw it all away. Turned over all the Pentagon's top secrets to the press. He must have made a hell of a haul off that. On easy street for the rest of his life. Well, a photo of me checking some slope's ID card ain't going to put this character on no easy street. Maybe get him a hundred buck at the most. He ain't going to sacrifice his career for that kind of chicken feed, not unless he's a lot dumber than I figured he is, the chief thought.

The skeleton was still on his knees with his hands clasped before him when Malmquist finally got around to handing back his card. He had a long stringy goatee and mustache. His eyes were moist and red. In the corners were gobs of white matter. He was

The Idiot's Frightful Laughter

trembling, as he took the card and wrapped it with awkward care in a piece of plastic and tucked it away beneath his shirt. He was still shaking, as he unwound the rope from the gunboat's mooring and pushed out into the seemingly motionless current. As he dipped his paddle into the murky water, his trembling seemed suddenly to cease, and his face took on a grave expression. He looked strong and resolute, as he bent against the oar. The timidity evaporated, as he pushed his sampan with firm even strokes up the canal. He sat straight, his head held high and proud. Had it been a game he'd been playing? Grecco wondered. After all, these swabbies, especially Malmquist, with their thick hairy bodies and gruff strange-sounding voices might well pass for demons in a land where a stone or a tree is revered as a god.

It was noon when the patrol boat pulled in to shore. The keel sliced through the thick greasy black mud sinking into the sludge. Cases of C-rats were torn open and cans of food set out on the engine to heat. Children waded waist deep in the mud to beg for candy, gum, anything the gobs might wish to throw them. The men would toss the treats into the mud. It amused them to watch the kids wrestle about in the goo, pulling, tugging and thrashing about until they resembled tar babies.

Slipping away from the crew, Grecco made a standing broad jump from the bow. Missing the bank, he sank in the mud over his boots splattering his slacks and shirt with black splotches.

"Hey wait! You ain't going in there alone," Malmquist shouted. "The skipper said to keep a watch on you."

"No problem," Vince said turning and waving in an off-handed manner. "I always go alone. Easier that way." He flashed a horse-tooth smile supposing that it looked more mocking than reassuring.

"Not this time you ain't," the chief petty officer said. "Captain's orders. Said to take good care of you. Anything happens to you and it's my ass."

"Okay, okay," Grecco said waving his hand before his face as though he was driving away a swarm of flies. What a bore, he thought. Both a monster and a bore, but then he ought to be getting used to it by now. Wasn't that nearly all that he'd run into since he got to Vietnam? There was Haynes who was simply a bore and Barban who was both a bore and a prick, and Simoni and Bledsoe and Whitewash, and Eisenschiml. They were all bores. Yes, he'd had about all that he could stand.

Malmquist came to the bow with the guitar player, but now he had an M-16 Assault Rifle slung across his chest. "Lardner's your man," the chief said slapping the youth on the butt. "He's a good boy." The kid smiled indulgently.

"Does he have to bring a weapon?" Grecco asked. "It doesn't inspire the friendliest sort of feelings."

"How in the fuck you expect him to protect you?" Malmquist's face reddened even brighter than it usually was. He'd had about all he could take from this smartass civilian. If it weren't for the captain, he'd jump down there and rub the bastard's face in the mud.

"How about a forty-five?" Grecco's voice was thick with appeasement. Making the swabby angry was not a good idea. "It's less intimidating," he said.

Lardner widened his eyes and shook his head. "No way. I can't hit the fucking side of a barn with a forty-five."

"Okay," Vince said motioning for him to come along, as he turned and headed for the village. He stopped suddenly and wheeled about pointing at Lardner, as he was easing himself over the side. "Get a shirt and boots," he ordered. "It'll make a better impression on the village elders."

By the time Lardner had caught up with Grecco, he was in the outdoor market. It was nearly deserted. Like public markets everywhere in Southeast Asia, business was conducted in the mornings between five and eight. To the right was a soup kitchen where half a dozen men were seated about a long rickety table drinking tea. Vince assumed that they were the village elders. Two wore the traditional mandarin dress. They had black loose-fitting tunics that came to their knees, white cotton trousers and tightly bound pillbox shaped turbans. Their hair was tied in a bun at the nap of the neck, and they had wispy goatees. The other men had

The Idiot's Frightful Laughter

loose white collarless shirts and black baggy slacks. All of them wore thick wooden clogs. Confucian scholars, Grecco figured. Two hundred years of colonial oppression hadn't changed a thing. Only ethnic cleansing could do that.

Grecco and Lardner sat at a table adjacent to the elderly men. A thin mangy dog lay sprawled on the dirt beside Vince's chair. Large yellow fleas scampered about on the mongrel. For several minutes Grecco watched the insects with fascination. It puzzled him because they didn't seem to be burrowing beneath the cur's fur, but instead raced aimlessly over its surface. Vince nudged the beast in the rib gently with his boot careful not to touch the fleas. The emaciated creature rose slowly. Its sad cowed look told of the many kickings and beatings it had endured. Dogs don't have an easy time of it in Asia, he thought.

Lardner looked at the dog that gazed at him from beneath the nearby table where it had move. "It ain't right. That little girl drowning this morning," he said.

"Oh?" Grecco said raising an eyebrow. I thought you found it quite hilarious, he wanted to say.

"I don't care a thing for these adults," the gob continued. "They can look out for themselves. But little kids and dogs. They's different. They don't know the score."

"Yep," Grecco said nodding slowly. His lips pursed looking as though he was giving the sailor's commentary very serious consideration. And the old woman, he thought. I suppose she knew the score? Had plenty of time to save herself and the child if she'd had a mind to? Vince felt like screaming, an idiot's sort of scream. Mock sentimentality. Americans were boiling over with it. They were the sort of sadists that liked to laugh and cry at the same time. They were set on getting their money's worth.

"Beer," Grecco said motioning to a man with a cloth bound about his waist. "I want a beer," he said in halting Vietnamese.

"Two?" the waiter asked brushing bits of food from the table on to the ground.

"You want a beer?" Vince asked turning to Lardner.

"Gook beer?" Lardner asked. He was startled.

"Yea," Grecco said.

"Naw," he said. "I don't touch nothing gook with a ten-foot pole," His face was wreathed in the most repugnant sort of expression. He looked as though someone had just puked all over him. "Ain't you afraid you'll get the screaming shits? It can kill you, you know?"

"Look," Vince said staring intently at the swabby trying to appear very earnest. "Do me a favor, will you?" He waited a moment for the request to sink in. "Don't use that word around here, Okay?"

"What word?" Larson asked, his mouth dropping open in an expression of utter perplexity.

Grecco leaned across the table and said very softly, "Gook."

"Sure," Lardner said rearing back slightly. "Well, what do I call them then?"

"Them," Grecco said sarcastically.

"Them?"

"Yea," Vince said nodding. "Them people." God, where do they get these miscreants? He must have no more than an eighty I.Q.

At the adjacent table, the village elders had been quietly watching the two Americans since they entered the marketplace. They looked as though they wanted to talk. "How are you?" Grecco asked the men in very formal Vietnamese clasping his hands and bowing slightly in the classic Confucian manner.

Four of the men returned the greeting. The other two made no response. They looked angrily at him. Vince offered to buy them each a beer. It may not have been the proper thing to do, but then he hadn't met an American yet who knew how to behave around Vietnamese. Even Gutschinritter had doubts at times, and he spoke fluent Vietnamese and was sincere and sympathetic, which was not the case with most Americans. They were either nauseously obsequious and artificial or rude and overbearing. The four who had responded thanked him most graciously but said that they preferred rice wine. The other two remained silent, so Grecco ordered four glasses of the wine. It was homemade and very strong.

The Idiot's Frightful Laughter

One of the two angry men began to speak crossly to Lardner.

"What's he saying?" the gob asked Grecco. He was growing uneasy. He shifted his hand to the stock of his rifle.

Vince smiled reassuringly to Lardner. "He wants to know why you're always stopping his sampan and asking to see his identification papers. You stopped him three times yesterday and once this morning."

The gob eyed the man coldly. "Tell him all gooks look alike to me. I can't tell one from another."

Grecco stared at the oaf for several moments. Can't be more than nineteen, he thought. No more than a year out of high school if he ever went. I must be a good twenty-five years older than he is. As old or older than his father. What's the jerk's father like? Vince wondered. A bigot too, no doubt. May have been in the Navy during World War II or the Korean War. Bragged about all the gooks he'd killed. Where the hell was the generation gap that Vince was always hearing about? The kids that were so outraged with their narrow-minded parents. Intent on making America a more tolerant, more peaceful nation? Oh, sure, he knew of the counter-culture. There had always been student organizations that spoke out against the system. Those who aped some fashionable philosophy. Whatever became of those idealists in four or five years? What happened to all their anger and lofty ideals? How really sincere were they? They usually confessed later that they were disillusioned, but what they really meant was bored, and soon fell back into dad's outstretched arms. Then came all those hackneyed clichés: 'They'd thought that dad was the dumbest guy on earth; however, they had finally woken up and realized that what he'd been telling them made a lot of good horse sense.' A whole grab bag of prejudice handed down from father to son for the past one thousand years.

Lardner saw that the elder was pleased with what Grecco had told him. He nodded and smiled pleasantly at the sailor. "What did you tell that dink?" the gob said narrowing his eyes.

"I told him that you were sorry. However, you checked too many ID cards each day to remember them all," Grecco said.

"You're one of them WHAM birds," the sailor said curling his lips in disdain.

"What?"

"WHAM" Lardner repeated. "Win Hearts And Minds. W..H..A..M, WHAM."

"No," Grecco said looking piteously at the callow youth. "It's just that I don't see any point in needless antagonism. I find these men quite worthy of respect."

"Ball!" Lardner said shaking his head as though he'd never heard anything so absurd. "A Dink's a Dink. I don't care how he acts. They're all the same. They'll shake with one hand and stick a knife in your back with the other."

Interesting, Grecco thought. A Korean had once told him the same thing about the Japanese. Instead of "dink", he'd used the word "Jap". Well, perhaps there was some credence in what his Korean friend had said. The Japanese had made a sneak attack on Pearl Harbor while their ambassador was at the White House signing a peace treaty with President Roosevelt. Twenty-four thousand sailors and marines were killed in their sleep and a fourth of the fleet sunk. But the Vietnamese had never done anything treacherous to America. Not like that. In the beginning, Ho Chi Minh had been an amiable trusting ally.

Vince looked back at the elder whom he'd just spoken with. He no longer looked hostile. Have you been having any difficulties?" he asked.

"Yes, yes, we are worried about the rice crop," one of the mandarins broke in. The others nodded in agreement. "It's nearly ready to harvest. If it's harmed, we'll have nothing to eat."

"Who would harm it?" Grecco asked looking at the pale-yellow sheaves of grain growing nearby. It'd be ready for harvest in a week or so, he assumed.

"Those aircraft," the mandarin said pointing at several helicopters hovering high overhead. "We are afraid that they may ruin our crop. Whenever they skim near the ground, they knock the kernels from their stocks."

"What's he yapping about?" Lardner asked.

The Idiot's Frightful Laughter

"He says that the choppers are apt to ruin the rice crop," Grecco said.

"What the fuck," the oaf exclaimed. "If you'd keep the fucking VC out of here, there wouldn't be no need for no choppers."

"What did the boy say?" the mandarin asked.

"He thinks there may be Viet Cong in your village," Vince explained. "That's why the helicopters are here."

"No! Never!" the old man said making a downward motion with his open hand. "We are Hoa Haos. We hate the Viet Cong. They murdered our holy seer, the eleventh reincarnation of the Lord Buddha."

"Perhaps it was a mistake?" Grecco said.

The village elders were alarmed. "It is possible, but not likely. Nevertheless, we could never forgive them for such a horrible mistake," one of them said.

"No! No! I know for a fact that it was no mistake," one of the others said. "They sent a squad of killers to slay him."

"What did they say?" Lardner asked.

"They hate VC," Vince said.

"Haw!" the gob scoffed. "Yea, I'll just bet they do. I'll just bet. That's why I'm carrying this here weapon, eh?" he said slapping his M-16.

"Why does he slap his gun?" an elder asked.

"He hates the Viet Cong too," Grecco said.

"Ah! Good! Good!" they said nodding amiably to Lardner.

Grecco glanced about the market. The sun was directly overhead. Except for three children who were watching them some distance away, there was no one in sight. It was siesta time. Everyone was resting, he thought. The custom was the same all around the equator. However, it had not been this way when he visited Aggroville 12 last month. Things were a good deal more peaceful here. That was a good sign, he figured, or was it? They may have given up hope altogether. "Have you received any food for the past month or so?" he asked.

"Nothing," several said in unison. Then they smiled amiably. "We are used to their lies. We no longer pay any attention to them," a mandarin said.

"What about other villages?" Grecco asked. "Aggroville 12 especially."

"No, it is not so bad with us. Our soil is all right. It has been treated for alkali," an elder said looking gravely at Grecco. "But for Aggroville 12, it is very bad. Their land is sour. It has too much alkali. We have tried to help them, but we have so little to spare. And if the helicopters continue to skim above our rice paddies," he said waving his hands at the choppers that hung motionless several thousand feet overhead, "we will have too little for even ourselves."

Lardner stood up and slung his rifle over his shoulder. "I don't know about you," he said, but I'm getting back to the boat. I don't aim to stay here for the night and let Charlie slit my throat." He made a motion with the edge of his hand across his neck.

Grecco clasped his hands and bowed to the elders. "I know of where I can get a book that may be of interest to you," he said. "The author claims that Prime Minister Diem had your holy seer killed and blamed it on the Viet Cong."

The elders shook their heads in disbelief. "If this is true," one of them said, "we have been on the wrong side." The six elders stood watching Grecco and Lardner until they had slipped from sight.

Another seed sown for the revolution, Vince thought smiling to himself. Just trying to set the record straight is all. Blow away some of the smokescreen. Nothing wrong with that.

Back at Phong Tho, Grecco learned that he had no cause to hide. There was a new MAT team there. Captain Burke and the others had been replaced several weeks ago.

Cuong, the interpreter, was the only one he knew. The building, its interior, everything had changed. The only familiar landmark was the large plaster statue of the Madonna near the bank of the canal. The compound had been destroyed, and Sergeant Shaw was killed. Both Captain Burke and Lieutenant Anderson were critically injured and medivaced to a US military hospital in

Okinawa. The other two noncoms were at a hospital at the US's big naval base at Cam Ranh Bay.

"No, the Viet Cong hadn't done it," Cuong said. Charlie hadn't bothered them since Vince previous visit. It was Sergeant Shaw who'd destroyed the outpost. He'd unwittingly ignited a tank of butane with an acetylene torch. He was welding a stand for the fuel cans when he passed the flame over a leaky connection. The explosion drove him through one side of the shack and out the other. The hut burst into flame badly burning the other team members." Cuong said that, fortunately, he was sitting on the latrine perched over the shit fish pond and saw the whole thing. He thought that they were under attack and dropped down into the pool of shit with turds floating about his head.

The new bunkhouse was made of white pine packed in by chopper from Can Tho. It also had a concrete floor; however, the furnishings looked about the same. There was a new fridge with cases of beer and coke stacked at either side. Six double-deck bunks with pea green mosquito nets lined both sides of the room. Up against the third side was a shortwave transmitter. Above it hung a bulletin board. All sorts of memos were pinned helter-skelter about on it. Piled on a table in the middle of the room were a dozen burlesque magazines, a copy of the *Police Gazette,* and a number of GI Joe comic books.

"Here's to Sergeant Shaw," Cuong said handing Grecco a can of ice-cold beer. "Let's drink to the memory of Sergeant Shaw," he said tipping his head back and taking a long lusty swallow.

"Hey, go easy on the brew, Cuong," a short red-faced grunt said. He stood glowering down at the interpreter. Grecco noticed the staff sergeant stripes on his shoulder. Here it goes again, he thought, winking at Cuong. The interpreter looked noncommittally at the military advisor for several moments and then winked back at Vince. "Yep, here it goes again, Grecco thought, nodding to Cuong, one eyebrow cocked quizzically. Perhaps he'll meet the same fate as Sergeant Shaw? After all, the gas leak may not have been an accident.

Them People Lack Will

Grecco had never met a Vietnamese quite like Tex. His real name was Nguyen Van Hieng, but those at the MAT team at Kien Ngu District called him Tex because of his cowboy hat and a pistol slung low on the hip. It was an old six-shooter with the long barrel; the kind generally seen in cowboy movies. However, no one had ever seen him fire it.

Tex was the Deputy District Chief and spoke a very upbeat sort of American English. Three years before while attending college in Saigon, he was one of six students selected to make a PR tour of The States. The U.S. Information Service sent him on a speaking circuit of college campuses throughout America. He and his colleagues had been coached on just what to say about such things as the Communist menace and the people's struggle for freedom. Often, they were handed prepared speeches full of fictitious accounts of supposed hardships and abuses that they were alleged to have suffered. "It was all a crock of shit," Tex said. "Made me want to puke."

Nevertheless, Tex thoroughly enjoyed his six months in The States. It was the high point of his life, and he sought to relive the highlights of his sojourn with the GIs at the MAT team. Sergeant Wingarter, a quiet, soft-spoken man in his early forties, was the only member of the team willing to share those cherished memories with him. The other soldiers treated him with amused derision.

Often of an evening, the mild-mannered sergeant and Tex would go off to some soup kitchen, a thatched hut with several tables where noodles and rice soup were served. Sergeant Wingarter would sit quietly listening to Tex tell over and over again of those joyous days in America. Tex would make frequent innovations, embellishing events as time passed; however, the sergeant would pretend not to notice. He would smile and nod at

The Idiot's Frightful Laughter

appropriate times rarely ever making a comment. A sensitive chap, he understood how important these fantasies were to Tex.

The other U.S. Advisors would chide Wingarter for going off so often of an evening with Tex. They would kid him about the girls they were supposedly seeing. Insisting that he and Tex had a dozen on the hook and fucked a different one every night. The sergeant never bothered to deny the accusations. He knew that it was all said in good humor. "Aw you guys are just jealous," he'd say, "just because you don't have what it takes."

The team leader, Captain Dan Gross, a sour little man who had been passed over twice for major and no longer had any hope of ever rising above the rank of captain, was quite incapable of seeing the humor in anything, and Sergeant Wingarter's situation was no exception. As foolish as it may seem, he had convinced himself that Tex and the sergeant were slipping off of an evening in search of women, quite likely the wives of Arvin officers; those were assigned to other provinces. And so the day prior to Grecco's arrival at the Kien Ngu District, Captain Gross had given Sergeant Wingarter strict instructions not to go off with Tex anymore. In order that it didn't appear personal, the order included all those on the team. During their off-duty hours, they were to stay at the compound and have nothing to do with the Vietnamese. For an advisor to be told to have nothing to do with the very people that he was there to befriend and inspire was at cross-purposes. It will create enemies, not allies. That's how Sergeant Wingarter saw it, but he was a model soldier and so said nothing.

Grecco had only been at the advisory team's headquarters a short time when Tex showed up. He sensed the enmity the moment Tex stepped into the bunkhouse. No one spoke. The Deputy District Chief stood peering about from one to another with wide-eyed wonder.

"What can I do for you, Tex?" Captain Gross finally said without looking up from a computer printout that he'd been studying. Tex only smiled a mirthless grin and nodded his head. He was a tiny man with chopstick arms and legs. The large long-barreled pistol slung low on the hip made him look off balance.

Spotting Grecco, he walked across the room and taking his hand shook it vigorously. "You're here to check on the refugees?" he said.

"Only to see if I can be of any assistance," Vince said smiling amiably. That was the tack that Simoni expected his advisors to take. "It's their ball game," he had told Grecco as he was leaving for Lang Son. "You're just the coach. Let them carry the ball."

"Yea, you betcha," the Deputy Chief said pulling his had free of Grecco's grasp and nodding earnestly. "Glad to have you." Then he walked over to Sergeant Wingarter, who was staring intently into a half-empty coffee cup. "How about a cup of java, pal?" he said placing a hand on the sergeant's shoulder.

"Ya betcha, Tex," Wingarter said going over to a large stainless-steel percolator big enough to serve fifty men. "Cream, no sugar," he said looking at Tex for the first time. His large soulful eyes and drooping reddish mustache reminded Grecco of a Saint Bernard. How could such a gentle looking man be a staff sergeant in a combat unit? He wondered. He looked more like a small-town shopkeeper or craftsman.

Grecco was quite unprepared for all the hospitality Tex showered upon him. The Deputy had the hamlet chiefs at three different resettlement centers prepare a huge meal for his guest. Tex explained that he'd been treated like a king in The States. Now it was his turn to return the favor. He had not told Vince that he must eat three meals, or he would not have eaten so much in the first place. The dishes at each home were very similar – fried shrimp, baked crab, fish soup, fried rice, and small pieces of either pork or chicken. Each meal was followed with large glasses of beer with chunks of ice bobbing about in them. Each time, Vince was urged to drink a half dozen toasts of lasting bonds of friendship between the Vietnamese and Americans. With each toast, Tex would insist that they chugalug a full glass of beer. "Bottoms up," Tex would shout or other such platitudes as: "Down the hatch" or "Here's mud in your eye." After struggling bravely to complete the meal at the third camp, Grecco felt as though he would burst. However, the Deputy District Chief had still another treat. It was a special delight

The Idiot's Frightful Laughter

specially prepared for his honored guest, or at least that was how Tex explained it. This Vietnamese delicacy was raw congealed duck blood mixed with rice. Noting Vince's look of revulsion, Tex explained that the host would be most offended if he did not eat every morsel of the large platter of blood pudding with great gusto. Even if Grecco had been famished, the task would have been revolting. However, after consuming three large meals and countless glasses of beer, the thick gooey mess was immeasurably more nauseous.

Vince realized that he'd been had. Tex had placed him in a most precarious situation. For several moments, he sat gazing with stupefaction at the leering faces of Tex and the hamlet chief as they urged him on. It reminded him of the time in high school when he'd been initiated into the varsity football team's letterman club. They'd blindfolded him and had him eat spaghetti blindfolded informing him that the noodles were worms. However, this was no trick. It was the real thing. It resembled black raspberry Jell-O with tapioca. He felt himself grow ill. Bile rose in his throat. He fought back an urge to vomit. He must under no circumstances insult these gracious simple people. The blood must be eaten and done so with gusto. If not, he would cause Tex to lose face and bring shame not only to himself, but to all the other advisors in the district, or so he imaged. As he ate, he closed his eyes and tried to imagine that it really was raspberry pudding. However, it seemed puzzling that no one else was eating this so-called special Vietnamese delicacy. Perhaps it was their custom to reserve the treat for the special guest.

Seeing how ill Grecco looked, Tex insisted that he lie down on a pallet for half an hour. He told Vince that the village elders were very pleased with him. He had done them a great honor. No other American in the district had eaten raw duck blood, not even his very best friend, Sergeant Wingarter. When Grecco asked Tex why he hadn't partaken of this special Vietnamese treat, he shook his head and spread his lips in a look of utter disdain. "Eat that shit," he exclaimed. "Hell no." He preferred hamburgers and beefsteak and oh yes, pizza. That was his favorite.

Grecco stood transfixed on the path leading from the resettlement camp. He'd been had. Really had. The whole nine yards of it. The urge to kill the little sneaky cocksucker was overwhelming. So often Vietnamese had told him that Americans were like children. So this is what they meant. Americans trusted others at face value. They were not looking for hidden motives; not on guard against trickery. Like children, they were open-hearted. That was what the Vietnamese both appreciated and scoffed at. Tex had pulled a fast one on this very gullible American. Vince thought of all the nonsense his orientation officer at USAID had handed out to him. "Bend like the bamboo. Don't stand firm and unyielding like the mighty oak." This sort of crap had made Grecco an easy prey, for the Vietnamese's perverse sense of humor. He would be the laughing stock of the district if not the entire province. Everyone would know. He had lost beaucoup face.

A few days later, Tex took Grecco by outboard motorboat to his "Hawaii". It was a small emerald green island in the midst of the great Mekong River. They docked the boat at an Arvin outpost on the tip of the football-shaped isle. "This is my Diamond Head," he said.

Tex's Hawaii was no tropical paradise, but it was quite pleasant. At the end of the island was a grove of mango. The grass had been cut and benches placed beneath the trees. A hedge of bulrushes ran along the bank giving the site a trim orderly look. And in spite of the Arvin outpost nearby, it was quiet. A cool breeze blew across the point. In order to hold on to his most cherished memories of America, Tex had made life a little pleasanter for himself than he would have otherwise.

Beneath the mangos was a restaurant. It was nothing more than a small thatched roof supported by slender poles. "This is my Hawaii Hilton," Tex said. The proprietress, a plump little old woman, set a bottle of wine on the table. Tex referred to it as "Chinese medicine". The woman's mouth was stained a bright reddish-orange from chewing acacia nuts wrapped in betel leaves. "One glass of this," Tex said, "and you can make three babies tonight." Grecco saw pieces of bark, flowers, leaves, and roots

The Idiot's Frightful Laughter

floating about in the murky mixture. What kind of babies? He wondered. Downing the drink in one gulp, Tex said: "It makes the pecker hard like stone." Looking at Vince's quizzical expression, he added: "No shit, Jack. I kid you not."

Tex insisted that they down three glasses of the concoction. Grecco compared it to a mixture of rubbing alcohol and formaldehyde. It was worse than anything he'd ever drunk. He noted with some interest that Tex didn't like it any better. Taking it for medicinal reasons or perhaps as he intimated, an aphrodisiac, Grecco thought, No doubt about it. It did have an after effect, but not the sort that Tex has predicted. It was a bilious nausea that lasted for several days.

For lunch, they were served heaping platters of tiny fried shrimp. The proprietress's son took a sampan to a marsh nearby and cast a net for the small creatures. He tossed it in a wide arch like a cowboy throwing a lariat. The crisp crunchy seafood tasted only of shell. There was no discernable flavor of flesh.

Anxious to make a favorable impression on Grecco, the deputy district chief had carefully organized his tour of the resettlement camps. He had done such a thorough job of it, that Vince had no opportunity to visit with the ordinary people. Tex had scheduled meetings with the village and hamlet councils throughout the pacified third of the district. The meetings were held at schools and village headquarters far away from the camps. Tex spoke such eloquent Vietnamese that Grecco could not follow him, and from the officials' bored listless expressions, he sensed that they weren't grasping much of it either. As for his interpreter's translation, it was so brief and skimpy that Vince ceased to listen to him. However, it eventually dawned on him that Tex wasn't discussing any of the things pertaining to the welfare of the refugees. Instead, he was mimicking the sort of speeches he had given at college auditoriums in The States. Those full of hyperbole and glittering generalities. Those that had made him want to puke.

In the evenings when Tex was not talking with Grecco about his American dream, he was worried about the way things were deteriorating between him and the guys at the MAT team, especially Captain Gross. "Weren't they Americans and wasn't he a great admirer of America? Weren't they here to make Vietnam as magnificent as America? And what Vietnamese in the district, in the province, in all of Vietnam was more anxious for that than he? He'd had so many good friends during his short stay in America. They were all so eager to talk with him and invite him to their homes for dinner. They were so anxious to assure him of their sympathy and support. Of course, he had seen the war protestors, but that was unreal. They were far off shaking their fists and shouting: "We love Ho Chi Minh and Madam Binh." It was all so comical. He felt as detached from that as though he was watching a movie.

However, Captain Gross was not unreal. Not in the least. Tex had no feeling of detachment when it came to the team leader. Gross was very concrete. He and his team were Tex link to America. Some of them especially Sergeant Wingarter had kept the dream alive and vital. But Gross was a threat. He was rocking the foundation. He had turned the others against him. That piece of shit.

Grecco saw the gravity of Tex's dilemma and felt compelled to somehow reassure him; however, the duck blood episode had made him wary. Tex was a loose cannon. Just how far could such a guy be trusted? He might play Vince against the other Americans. Use him as a buffer. Tell the Province Chief what he'd said. Colonel O'Hare would be sure to find out. Grecco had best keep his own counsel.

There are all kinds of American, Vince had told Tex, just as there were all kinds of Vietnamese. Captain Gross was an exception. Tex should not identify Americans with him. Besides, he was due to rotate back to The States very soon. His replacement would be different. They'd get along just fine. That was more or less what Grecco told him.

The poor sonofabitch, Vince thought. They've sure blown a lot of smoke up his ass. He's wallowing in the American dream like a pig in shit. He's the kind that will feel bitterly betrayed someday. He'll end up hating Americans and set out to get even.

The Idiot's Frightful Laughter

"Look Tex, come to Lang Son. You can stay at the CORDS' compound. I'll find you a bunk and introduce you to some good guys," Grecco said. There were two IVS gals that he knew Tex would dig. The two country boys who helped Rufus Burns with his farm project were good eggs. He'd throw a party for Tex. Pass him off as a VIP. He'd like that. He was so great at fantasizing, a star performer.

However, Grecco felt a pang of guilt. What hypocrisy. Why was he perpetuating the myth? Gross was just as much America as Wingarter. In fact, if a survey were taken, Vince figured that the captain would be way out in front. There were twice as many Gross as Wingarters. It was best for Tex to wake up to what the real America was like. The sooner he got over the *Reader's Digest* fantasies, the less painful it would be for him.

The evening before Grecco was to return to the province capital, Tex invited him for dinner at the District Chief's home. It was a large old colonial mansion with very high ceilings and big bay windows. Tex had gone to a lot of trouble making the arrangements. The table was set in the most traditional American fashion. There were even napkin rings.

Emily Post would have found nothing to complain about. However, the big surprise was the food. Waiters wearing white tunics carrying heaping platters of hamburgers, cheeseburgers, French fries, and fried chicken paraded into the room. Such a feast must have taken days to prepare. Where had he found items like cheese and salami, and how had he ground the meat? If Captain Gross and his team only knew what they were missing out on. The sonofabitch had turned down the invitation for the entire MAT team. As a consequence, the District Chief and his entourage had not shown up. Tex took the refusal very hard. It was a slap in the face. That mean sonofabitch, Grecco thought. He would have to think of some way to settle the score.

They had just begun to eat when Tex set his hamburger down and sat very still; his eyes grew wide as though he were in deep concentration. Then he rose slowly and moved back to a corner of the room and sat down on the floor. He moved so stiffly and looked so lifeless that he might have been pantomiming a marionette.

"Mortars!" a waiter said gesturing with his hands and pointing to the ceiling. "Incoming! Boom! Boom!" he said as though it were a very routine thing that he was quite accustomed to announcing at meal time. Grecco had heard the popping sounds and assumed that the rounds were striking quite nearby. He recalled seeing chicken wire stretched a foot or so above the rooftop, so there was no danger of one dropping through the ceiling. The wire would detonate the explosive.

Vince was astonished by the Deputy Chief's reaction. It was so contradictory. It would seem more in character for the cowboy to lead a charge blasting away with his six-shooter, but then what did he know about Tex? He had simply accepted him at face value, and now suddenly he had a very different impression of him. Didn't Tex realize what a cowardly spectacle he was making of himself? How would he ever be able to look his staff in the face again?

Grecco went over and sat down on the floor beside Tex placing a hand of the terror-stricken deputy chief's shoulder. "Tex," he said, for christsakes get hold of yourself. Suddenly Tex sprung to his feet and bolted from the room. He dashed out the door and across the courtyard towards a bunker at the base of an old water tower covered from top to bottom with sandbags, so there was no danger of a shell dropping on top of the shelter. The District Chief and several of his aides were standing at the opening to the bunker. When Tex reached the entranceway, The Chief gave his deputy a shove back out into the yard. Tex stood crouched over like a cat poised to leap. The District Chief pointed at Tex, and he and his officers laughed as they might at a cowed dog. Finally, he motioned for Tex to come inside the bunker.

Grecco stood in the doorway of the mansion watching the miserable spectacle. Hearing someone moan, he glanced to his left. Two Arvin were carrying another soldier. Blood was coming from his mouth. They carried him into the room and laid him on the floor. The wounded soldier lay perfectly still. His eyes were all that moved. They had a glassy dazed appearance, a look of infinite terror. A sight that Grecco would remember for a long time.

In a few moments, Captain Gross, Sergeant Wingarter and the team medic arrived. Grecco passed around the platter of hamburgers and cheeseburgers. They were a great treat. The three Americans gulped them down hungrily; however, the two Arvin scarcely touched theirs. The medic made a hasty check of the wounded Arvin, and then sat down at the table and began picking the salami off a pizza.

Nothing serious," he said. "Just a tiny piece of shrapnel at the back of the mouth. However later that evening when they were told that the Arvin had died at the district hospital, none of the team including the medic was surprised.

"Them people lack will," Captain Gross said. "They just give up and die. It's funny. They don't seem to have the will to live," he added shaking his head with a sort of disconcerting look.

"What about the Viet Cong?" Grecco asked. "No one could accuse them of a lack of will."

"No," Sergeant Wingarter said. "They are fearless, and they sure as shit got plenty of will. I remember one little fucker, a platoon leader. A piece of shrapnel the size of your fist ripped open his stomach, and his guts fell out. Well, sir, the little bastard pushed them back in, and then tied his fucking pith helmet over his stomach to hold them in. He just kept right on fighting. It took a bullet between the eyes to stop him." Wingarter paused a moment for it to sink in. "There's a real man by anyone's standards," he said nodding his head very solemnly and looking intently at the wall as though he was watching the whole episode unfold before his eyes.

Yes, and then there was Tex, Grecco thought remembering how the muffled sound of mortar shells exploding had terrified him, causing him to panic and run blindly outside. The pistol-toting Walter Mitty who dreamt of being John Wayne. Why was it he who wanted so much to be an American and not the Viet Cong platoon leader? The Arvin and the Viet Cong might be the same race, often kin, but they were very different people. Captain Gross had put his finger on it. It was will. The will to be free of foreign domination.

Sheridan Peterson

The will for dignity. The will for honor. Hollow abstractions for some perhaps, but not for the Viet Cong. What sort of dignity had we given the Arvin? Grecco wondered. Nguyen Cao Ky, South Vietnam's Air Marshall and Prime Minister promenading about with his pearl-handled pistols, his black jumpsuit and fuchsia scarf, and a baseball cap covered with gold braid. How did he stack up alongside Ho Chi Minh for dignity?

Banana Cat

It was midday, and a bright equatorial sun blazed down on the tropic forest. However, on the floor of the jungle beneath three canopies of foliage, it was as dark as it is at sunset. The terrain was a profusion of bramble and vines. The air was still and sultry. Not a leaf stirred.

In order to move about in the undergrowth, a man needed a large machete to slash his way through the giant iridescent green colocasias that wound all about him. He had to be strong to do this for long, for the hemp was hard as mahogany and as limber as bamboo. And always he must be on the alert for green venomous snakes that may drop on him at any moment from overhanging vines. Yet there was an awesome beauty. The jungle was a luxuriant botanical garden, a perfusion of huge violet flowers and silver tinted leaves.

From beneath a mass of greenery, a spot of amber emerged. It was the head of a jungle feline, a banana cat. She was small and yellow with brown blotches, long spindly legs, and a monkey-like tail. The cat was setting out in search of food. Within her lair were three newly born kittens, their eyes not yet open. As she crept stealthily beneath the undergrowth, her pointed nose sniffed beneath the leaves and decayed logs in search of a rodent or toad. The cat had a perpetual look of alarm, for her ears were pointed and stuck straight up, and her large, bulging eyeballs looked as though they might pop from their sockets.

High overhead, she heard the sound of birds. In an instant, she began to scale a huge tree, her long sharp claws digging deep into the trunk's soft bark. Upward she scampered until she saw patches of blue sky and bright sunlight. High above nestled amid clusters of camphor leaves was a covey of blue and yellow parakeets.

Sheridan Peterson

The banana cat lay quite still against the trunk studying the terrain. Her scheme was to get above her quarry and drop down amidst them. Edging out along a branch just overhead, the feline crept ever so cautiously. Only her monkey-like tail was distinguishable swinging like a metronome just above her rump. The branch gave slightly beneath her weight as she moved out on to it. Gradually the bough bent down towards the flock of parakeets chirping loudly to one another; their bright colors reflecting the beams of sunlight.

Directly overhead, the jungle cat lay very still for several moments gauging the plunge. She singled out her prey, selecting the most succulent of the flock. All that moved was the tip of her tail swinging slowly with measured intent like a whip before the lash. Then rising slowly up on her haunches, she sprang dropping into the midst of startle birds. Nailing one with her front paws, the cat jammed the head into her mouth. She free fell down through the thick limber foliage finally grasping a limb. She wound her legs tightly about it holding on until the momentum ceased, then she slipped along the branch and down the trunk. With the head still firmly clenched in her jaws, the banana cat took her prey back to her lair where the three hungry kittens were waiting.

It was the banana cat's habit to prowl about after dark. Each night her nocturnal excursions took her further and further from her lair. Food had grown scarce, for the noises of war had frightened much of the wildlife away.

One night she came to a bare mound of earth. The jungle had been cleared away and coils of razor-sharp concertina barbwire had been strung about the clearing. Behind the wire were mounds of earth. Men were inside these caverns. The banana cat smelled the strong aroma of meat cooking. The odor was different from anything she had ever smelt before. The rich pungent odor made her very hungry. The cat lay in the undergrowth for a long time until she could no longer hear any sounds coming from the bare mounds of earth. Growing bold, she crept up to the edge of the outer coil of barbwire. She noted that there were two barricades with a bare space between them. She scratched a tunnel beneath the outer coil and through to the open space. As she slunk cautiously across the bare space, she touched a wire with her paw. As she pressed gently down upon it, there was a loud explosion. A fuselage of steel balls the size of large marbles smashed into the banana cat ripping her into tiny shreds.

"No sweat, man," a sentry said. "Just another fucking monkey set off a claymore. Blew it to smithereens."

That Perfect Place

On his first night back at Lang Son, Grecco had gone with Greg Kalick to the Green Beret's slop chute for a beer. They had asked Rufus Burns, a big black man from Sutton, West Virginia, to join them, but he had refused. He would not go there until they took that "George Wallace for President" poster off the back bar.

Grecco told the Deputy Senior Advisor of how Burns had argued with the mess sergeant at Tenth Transport where they'd had lunch that afternoon. The cook, a fat black man from Biloxi, Mississippi, had told Burns that he was for Wallace.

"You're an Uncle Tom," Burns had shouted jabbing his finger at the cook.

"Now you be careful what you say," The mess sergeant said. "I ain't no Uncle Tom. I'm as proud of my black skin as you or anyone else."

"Then how come you're voting for a racist like Wallace?" Burns said rising up on the balls of his feet.

"I don't believe that about him. That's all politics. He had to do what he did to get the white man's vote," the cook said shaking his head up and down. "Shucks, he's one of us. He's for the little fellow; the guy who's got to sweat for a living. Yep, that's who he for."

"I see you're forgetting mighty fast," Burns said placing his hands on his hips and thrusting out his jaw. "Already you forget about him standing in the doorway of the school building so no black children could enter. Yea! And you forgot what his police done to the King and all those civil rights people at Selma. Yea, and Wallace having the Grand Dragon of the Ku Klux Klan in his cabinet. Yea, and how he made a hero of any peckerwood that killed a black man."

The Idiot's Frightful Laughter

"Aw shit, man, you talk like one of them Rockefeller liberals," the mess sergeant said. "like I told you, and I'm telling you again. That's all politics."

Well, you're betraying your race," Burns said spinning about and walking off. "You're a traitor to the black race. That's what you is."

Grecco could see that Burns was trembling with rage. "I'm ashamed," the big black man said. "I'm downright ashamed of my people."

"Some," Vince said.

"Some?" Burns said wheeling about and staring bug-eyed at Grecco. "Man! You don't know what you're talking about. There's lots."

Grecco supposed that a good many Jews voted for Hitler's National Socialist Party in the 30's thinking that it was for the downtrodden. Once those bigots get in power, the tables turn. Politics! Yea, that was where it was all at.

The first thing that Grecco noticed when he and Kalick entered the slop chute was the large orange on black Day Glo poster of "Wallace for President" taped to the back bar. "Burns kicked up quite a fuss about that poster the other night," Kalick said. "But I see that he was just wasting his breath."

"Where's Colonel O'Hara?" Grecco asked looking about the room. He was always there at this time of evening talking in a loud booming voice.

"Haven't you heard?" The Deputy Senior Advisor said appearing somewhat surprised. "He got wounded the other day. Sergeant Caldiero triggered a mine. Killed him and wounded the colonel in the right leg. Nothing serious. Cut some muscle and tendon was all."

"Lucky," Vince said looking behind him at a Filipino rock band that were noisily tuning their instruments.

"Yea," Kalick said. "The men are afraid his luck's going to run out. This here's the third time he's been wounded in the past nine months. Major Gaspar is determined not to let him in the field anymore."

Grecco looked astonished. "Why? What are they saving him for? Retirement? For a desk job in the Pentagon? To advise Arvin whom he hates, especially his thieving, lying counterpart, Colonel Binh? Let O'Hara be out there with combat and death and destruction. Things he dearly cherishes. That's where he belongs. So what if he gets killed? Do you think he cares? He'd sooner have it that way than a slow, lingering death thirty or forty years from now in some veteran's hospital, a lonely old forgotten man."

Vince thought of when he had been a Marine some twenty-five years ago, he had known guys like O'Hara. Not a lot of them. Most guys lose an appetite for war once they come face to face with it. But there were guys like his fire team leader who thrived on combat. He could talk of nothing else. He would describe in graphic detail how a comrade in the platoon was killed without a flicker of remorse. Grecco could well remember the time he had dashed into their tent shouting: "The war's over! The war's over!" His fire team leader had looked at him as though he'd been badly betrayed. "I thought you liked combat, Vince?" He said. His voice was full of despair. He'd been cheated out of invading the Japanese mainland. What a nasty trick.

"O'Hara's a war lover. Gaspar's a fool not to see that," Grecco said downing a shot of bourbon and chasing it with a beer. Kalick looked thoughtfully at Vince for a moment and then nodded. He was in full agreement.

Not long ago, Grecco had bummed a ride aboard O'Hara's command ship. The Huey was on its way to Chau Duc on the Mekong River at the Cambodian border when the Colonel was notified of an Arvin attack on a nearby Viet Cong stronghold. He halted the helicopter directly above the VC entrenchment. The air strike began with two A-1 Skyraiders. They screeched down beneath the chopper lacing the hillside with CBU-19 Cluster Bombs containing tear gas to blur Charlie's anti-aircraft gunners' vision. Then a squadron of F-4 Phantom Jets with time-delayed bombs plunged out of the sun leveling off just above the bunkers. More Phantoms swept in with two hundred tons of ordinance. Finally, the A-1 Skyraiders made a frontal attack on the fortification

The Idiot's Frightful Laughter

bombarding it with a fuselage of 20mm cannon shells and cluster bombs. It was overkill, Grecco thought. Nothing could survive that.

Within a few minutes of the bombardment, a squadron of Hueys landed nearby and a company of Arvin disembarked. They were still climbing out of the helicopters when the Viet Cong came swarming out from beneath the smoldering rubble bristling for a scrap. The Arvin dropped their weapons and fled for the choppers that were already several feet off the ground. They scampered on to the skids frantically clawing their way back inside the aircraft. It was a turkey shoot. The VC picked them off like clay pigeons and then proceeded to shoot down the helicopters.

"Look at them little sonsabitches," O'Hara shouted above the roar of the rotor blades. "Tough little mothafuckers. Man, I wish we had them on our side." He was beside himself with ecstasy. He stomped up and down on the floor of the chopper and waved his beret about.

O'Hara's feeling for Charlie wasn't simply the admiration of one professional soldier for another. Grecco knew that it went far deeper. It was a love. O'Hara not only loved to kill. He loved those who were trying to kill him. Pitting one's wit and skill against those gutsy insurgents was great sport. He had been outfoxed by them a number of times, and this, no doubt, had only heightened his competitive spirit. Once when a sniper had shot him in the shoulder at close range, the colonel had waved a fist at the tiny combatant crouching in the fork of a tree. "Lots of guts, pal, but you can't shoot worth a shit."

Grecco downed a second shot of whiskey and chased it with a glass of beer. "What gives them the right to deprive O'Hara of running his life the way he wants to?"

"I see what you mean," Kalick said. "I'll speak to the major about it."

"Don't bother," Grecco said. "He wouldn't understand. I don't believe even O'Hara would. It's an impulse. It doesn't bear up well against simple logic." Christ but Kalick is naïve, Vince thought. Telling Major Gaspar to let Colonel O'Hara go ahead and get killed.

Sheridan Peterson

How has the Province Deputy Advisor managed to survive thus far? He's like Dostoyevsky's Prince Myshkin.

Rufus Burns was furious when Kalick told him the next morning at breakfast that the "Wallace for President" poster was still on the back bar. If it was still there that evening, Burns was going to see O'Hara about it. Either the Province Senior Advisor took it down, or he could find himself another ag man. That was the Agriculture Advisor's ultimatum.

Colonel Wild Bill O'Hara was no Southern peckerwood. The only prejudice he apparently had was for those cowardly bastards that wouldn't stand up and fight, Grecco figured and that wasn't necessarily a prejudice. Burns may stand a better chance this time. It all depended on how he handled it. The colonel didn't like to be challenged, not without a fight.

Burns was big and tough enough to have played tackle for a professional football team. He wore a wide-brimmed straw hat, tight-fitting Levis, a denim jacket and hobnail boots. He was born in a tiny mining town in West Virginia, the youngest of fourteen children and the only one of them to finish high school. His six older brothers all quit school at fourteen to work in the coal pits. During the summer vacations, Burns worked in the mines shoveling coal onto a conveyor belt. Graduating from high school, he was awarded a scholarship to attend Tufts University and was one of the first blacks to enroll at the University of North Carolina's graduate school where he earned a master's degree in agronomy. Leaving school, he spent eight years in Africa, first in Nigeria and then in Tanganyika testing soil and experimenting with hybrids. He told his African friends that it was a suitable occupation, for blacks in America were all hybrids to some degree. Burn's friends didn't know whether he was joking or not.

Africa left a deep impression on Burns. The black man had got rid of Whitey. He was finally free to determine his own destiny. The experience had made Burns understand the real worth of black power and the need for a separate black nation. As he saw it, there was no chance for blacks in a country dominated by whites. Burns saw himself as an exception, a showcase to ship abroad, show the

Africans what hard work and determination can do for the black American – for the chosen few.

Unlike most of the other advisors, Burns was seldom at his desk during the day. He was either in the field or at Can Tho or Saigon in search of things like baby chicks or rabbits or seed of some sort. Fishponds were a favorite of his. He was always after the peasants to dig more and more holes. Fish made *nuoc man*, a sauce high in protein. It was as popular with the Vietnamese as catsup with the American. The Agricultural Advisor was always ordering tanks of fingerlings, a special breed from The Philippines; a long slender fish with a black back and white belly that could thrive in the foulest sort of water.

Although Burns worked hard improving the Vietnamese's living standard, he did not like them. He felt their racial prejudice and bitterly resented it. They were worse than the white man. He considered their treatment of the Montagnard and Cambodians scandalous and told them so. However, there were those whom he made an exception of. There was one in particular. She was Co Thiet, a lovely woman in her early twenties who had followed Burns to Lang Son from Go Vap. He had gotten her a job as Kalick's private secretary. The Deputy Senior Advisor was delighted to get her, for apart from her beauty, she was also very proficient. Co Thiet was the daughter of the Province Chief of Go Vap, and had graduated from business college in Dalat.

Never had Grecco met anyone as devoted to another person, as Co Thiet was to Burns. It was the devotion of an adoring daughter for a gruff but dutiful father. It was the stuff that dramas were made of.

One morning soon after her arrival, she came to Grecco's office and stood demurely before him. "Where is father?" she asked.

He was busy drafting the end-of-month report and had not noticed her come in. "Where is who?" he asked looking up in surprise.

"Father," she repeated. "Where is he?" she bowed slightly, her hands clasped before her in a gesture of respect; an old fashion custom that Grecco had noticed only on rare occasions usually among the very old. He had not yet had a chance to take a good look at her and was for a moment entranced by her elegance. She had the classic beauty of those from the central coastline. Her face was oval rather than round like the Southerner. Her eyes were large, gentle and elongated. She had a small straight nose that turned up slightly at the tip. Her mouth was large for a Vietnamese with lovely red lips. However, it was her body that intrigued Vince the most. It was not the skinny shapeless form that one ordinarily associates with Vietnamese women. Rather she had curved hips that pressed out at either side of her pale yellow *ao dia*, a pair of firm resilient breasts that moved slightly as she breathed.

"Father?" Grecco asked. "The priest? Is that who?"

"Oh! No, no," she exclaimed laughing. It was melodious like the sound of small jungle birds chirping after sundown. "No priest." She walked to the door, turned, clasped her hands and bowed. "No priest," she said again and was gone.

Whenever Burns returned after being gone for a day or so, Co Thiet would rush up to him, and while they were talking, she would take his huge fist in her hands and squeeze it until he pulled it gently from her grasp. He only spoke with her long enough to find out if she had had any difficulties. However, she would never mention those who had propositioned her and been so gently but firmly rebuffed, nor did he ever visit with her in her room. If he wished to speak with her, he would send a maid to get her. They would meet in the rec room, the lights on and the door open.

Grecco was deeply touched by the relationship, the filial love of a pale beauty for a stern black giant. He supposed that others less idealistic, more cynical than he, saw the relationship as a clever ploy; a sinister plot to ensnare a young girl's heart. For one thing, Vince knew that Burns was too proud, too militant to give the bigots such satisfaction. Besides he was a loyal husband and devout father. It wasn't in him to betray his wife.

The Province Chief at Go Vap had the introspection to see this. He had the insight to know a decent man when he met one. His daughter was safe with Burns, as safe as she would be at home with him. He had asked Burns to be her guardian and had told Co Theit

The Idiot's Frightful Laughter

that she was to trust and respect the solemn black giant, as she would her father. In a sense, Co Theit was simply carrying out her father's orders. However, Grecco knew that it went beyond that, for by accepting Burns as her surrogate father, she had quite innocently transferred her filial love for her father to him. For Vince, it was a beauty he had not expected to find in this war ravished land. It was the yin-yang of Confucianism, he thought. In good one can always find a speck of evil, and in evil, a speck of good. This was the speck of good.

What Grecco liked most about Burns was that he accepted Vince at face value. Burns believed Grecco when he said that he favored black power and felt that the white man must pay dearly for what his ancestors had done to the blacks. He showed no trace of surprise or doubt nor did he seem the least bit pleased. Even when they disagreed as they had about uncle toms, Burns always spoke with him as though he was arguing with a younger brother who had not had the firsthand experience with racial bias that he'd had. He never held Grecco's white skin against him. As far as Burns was concerned, he was part of the brotherhood just as long as he never broke that trust. It was as though Burns was intent on giving anyone every possible chance to make a human being of himself. However, Burns had no use for those who played both sides. "Anytime a man says: 'I'm not prejudiced but…' I know that he's the worst kind of bigot but hasn't the gut to admit it. At least George Wallace admitted it. Not now, but in the beginning, he admitted that he hated blacks. Wallace said: 'Look at me, everybody. I'm a one hundred percent racist.' Well, you can't accuse him of being a hypocrite, now can you?"

Grecco didn't know why Colonel O'Hara had refused to remove the "Wallace for President" poster from the back bar. He wouldn't give Burns a satisfactory answer. Just the usual stock reply one expects from a military man, especially from the commander of a Special Forces Battalion. "I'm in charge here, and as long as I'm in charge that poster stays until I feel good and ready to have it removed. Is that clear?" That was Colonel O'Hara's reply. Three days later, Burns was packed and off to another province.

Sheridan Peterson

There was no room in his heart for racists. If he couldn't find racial tolerance where he was, he'd look for it elsewhere. A noble quest, Vince thought as he waved farewell to his good friend at the airstrip. He hoped that somewhere on this earth he'd find that perfect place, but he was not at all optimistic.

A Final Appeal

When Grecco visited the Special Forces' A Camp a stone's throw from the Cambodian border, he had not expected the Green Beret to be overjoyed at having a civilian in their midst. However, on the other hand, he had not anticipated such sullen disdain either. It was not that he was ill-treated. Quite to the contrary. He shared Lieutenant Longnecker's private quarters. The unit commander had an air conditioner, and Vince had use of his transistor radio and tape deck with Joan Baez latest hits. "I don't give a shit if she is a fucking hippy," Longnecker said. "She's the best fucking folk singer going." What's more the lieutenant assigned him a desk with a typewriter but made it clear that he wanted Grecco to write his report before he left. He wanted a copy. If anything unpleasant was to be said, the commander wanted to confront his accuser then and there.

Grecco assumed that the sullen reception was quite likely due to something that had occurred prior to his arrival. For one thing, the men weren't leaving camp. When he made a tour of a nearby refugee settlement, Captain Dung, Longnecker's counterpart, accompanied him. The lieutenant introduced them and then made some excuse about having to get out the monthly report and left.

Grecco found the refugees a good deal better off, then those at Premier Diem's Aggrovilles, but not nearly so free. The heavily fortified strategic hamlet was surrounded by two barbwire fences. Mines had been planted between the two barriers. At each corner of the compound was a lookout tower manned by a guard with a fifty-caliber machine gun. The refugees' identification cards were checked each time they entered the camp. Each thatch hut had a garden consisting chiefly of taro root and sweet potatoes. However, there was no sign of animals anywhere. There were no chickens running in and out of the huts, nor pigs rooting in the yards. The fish in the canal appeared to be the peasants' only form of protein. However, when Grecco asked a peasant what he did for meat, he promptly pulled a small wicker cage out from beneath a pallet that they were sitting on. In it was a rat, a small fierce-looking rodent no more than a foot and a half in length. It leaped at Vince pawing at the bars with its sharp claws, its fur bristling like the quills of a porcupine. Grecco sprung to his feet. The Vietnamese all laughed. They were surprised to see such a tiny animal frighten such a big man. It was so cowardly. Nevertheless, Vince was badly shaken. There was nothing he loathed or feared nearly as much as a rat. Captain Dung explained that the marshes were full of them and that they were easy to trap. "A small one like this is very tender," he said. "It tastes better than chicken." Grecco felt ill recalling that he had eaten some once thinking it was rabbit. As a matter of fact, he'd had several servings.

The refugees had a school. It was simply a thatch roof supported by large bamboo poles. A good strong wind could easily blow it over, Grecco figured. The pupils' desks were made from crates that once held artillery shells. The teacher was a young Nung corporal. Vince saw that he was writing English sentences on a chalkboard, and the pupils were busy copying them down in their notebooks. Later they would chant them over and over after the teacher until they'd memorized them. Why English? Grecco wondered. Of what possible use was English for these refugee children?

Directly across from the Special Forces Camp, two American medics and three Vietnamese nurses had set up a table and stacked some packing boxes beside it. A dozen or so peasants had lined up for treatment. Had all this been arranged for Grecco's benefit? Were the school and the clinic staged for the Refugee Advisor's benefit? It seemed so. It looked as though they had been thrown together in haste.

Most of the patients complained either of a headache or stomach discomfort and diarrhea. The diagnosis and treatment were always the same; aspirin for headaches, a pill to relieve acid indigestion or Kaopectate for diarrhea. What a hopeless waste of

The Idiot's Frightful Laughter

time, Vince thought. They need lab tests. Probably they had worms or amoebas or both and had had for a very long time. Quite likely vital organs like the liver were affected. They needed strong drugs and lots of them. These treatments were simply cosmetic, as useless as the witch doctor's treatments, and in a sense worse, for witchcraft involved the element of faith in an omnipotent power, and that sort of faith might give one the will to overcome his illness.

It soon became clear to Grecco that the Americans were prisoners of their own choosing. They had not only isolated themselves from the refugees whom they'd come to protect, but also from their comrade-in-arms, the Nung mercenaries. The Green Beret had barricaded themselves inside a triangular fortress surrounded by a double apron of razor-sharp concertina barbwire. Between these rolls of wire was a minefield separating them from their allies, the Nung tribesmen. The mines had been set out very recently, buried quietly in the dead of night; however, it was feared that someone, possibly a child might slip through the wire and be blown up. Grecco had overheard all this at the rec room. He had gathered the information in bits and pieces and fit them together. Who was this "Captain Quik"? Lieutenant Longnecker was either mad or terrified; a puzzling dilemma for a Special Forces Commander to be in. Why were these besieged men so afraid of their comrades, the Nungs? It was a comedy, a comedy that was due to be tragic.

The dilemma gradually dawned on Grecco. These dozen or so American counterinsurgents had all the luxuries of home and then some. They lived in private quarters with air conditioning and hot showers. Their clubroom had a bar stocked with cold beer and the very best Stateside whiskey. There was a tennis court and a golf putting course. Their meals were as good as those in any Stateside installation. Fresh vegetables were flown in nearly every day, and what's more, they had a Chinese cook from Can Tho.

The A-camp was a microcosm of America; the cornucopia of all that the destitute of the world craved. The problem occurred to Grecco while he was watching a movie. It was based on Pasternak's famous novel, *Doctor Zhivago*, a show that Nungs would enjoy even though most of them might not understand much of the English. Why hadn't they been invited? Even their new commander had not been offered an invitation. They could surely hear it and imagine what they were missing. What's more, they knew about the cases of ice-cold beer, the whiskey, the filet mignon, and the casseroles and rump roast and ice cream and freshly baked pies and cake. In bleak contrast, these fiercely proud tribesmen had only fish and rice and maybe a banana or a papaya for dessert. What was such discrimination all about? Vince thought. All this nonsense that the Americans were always telling the Vietnamese? This talk about democracy and equality? What utter bullshit.

But then Grecco saw some Vietnamese in the audience. They were the three pretty nurses whom he'd seen helping to treat the patients at the clinic the other day. They were sitting at the front, each with an American who had his arm about her waist. One soldier had a hand inside a nurse's blouse fondling her teats. So these guys even had prostitutes. What more could they want – surfing and water skiing?

The truth finally came to the surface. It was worse than he'd imagined. The revelation occurred on the afternoon of his last day in camp. He was scheduled to leave early the next morning and was in the admin office typing a second draft of his report on the state of affairs at the resettlement camp. Lt. Longnecker had insisted that he elaborate on a few minor points. The situation involving the Nungs would, of course, have to wait until he got back to Lang Son. Jake Klicker, a very youthful appearing second lieutenant, who may have wanted to settle a score with his commander, spit it all out. Then again perhaps it was something that he had to get out of his system; a premonition that doom was near at hand.

Lt. Klicker slipped quietly into the office while Grecco was busy typing. The young officer had never as much as said hello to him since his arrival a week ago. When he walked over to where Vince was seated, he could tell by the officer's expression that something out of the ordinary was on his mind. "You're lucky you weren't here two weeks ago," he said looking nervously about to make sure that there was no one else in the room.

The Idiot's Frightful Laughter

Here it comes, Grecco thought, trying to hide the faintest flicker of curiosity. Any anxiousness on his part might be enough to change the lieutenant's mind. What had happened was that the Nungs had not been paid for more than a week. Relations between the Americans and their mercenaries had been deteriorating for some time. This had been the final straw.

The conflict had crested when Sergeant Brad Smithers' naked body was found crammed in a haystack. It had been there for several weeks before a peasant pointed it out to them. It was badly decomposed, and the face was not recognizable, for the sergeant had been shot at the back of the head at close range with what looked like a full clip of ammo. He was stripped of everything, even his skivvies. A finger had been cut off, and his gold wedding ring removed. What's more, his stomach had been slashed open and his spleen and liver removed.

Sergeant Smithers had accompanied a squad of Nungs on a reconnaissance patrol. When the Nungs returned to camp the following morning, the sergeant was not with them. They said that they'd been ambushed by a company of Viet Cong and that Smithers was captured. However, none of the Nungs had been killed or wounded. They showed no signs of having been in a firefight; and what was even stranger was that even though they'd had a radio, they hadn't called in an air strike on the VC.

The tribesmen hadn't liked Sergeant Smithers. He was a loud, overbearing cracker from the tobacco fields of South Carolina. On several occasions, Lt. Longnecker had cautioned him not to curse the Nungs; that they understood more English than they admitted. However, according to Klicker, the advice had gone unheeded. Nothing was ever proven. No bullets were found lodged in his skull, so no ballistic test could be made. Thus the bitterness and distrust mounted. The Americans began to go out on patrol with the Nungs in pairs, and then in three and sometimes four paying more heed of their mercenaries than to a possible enemy ambush. The distrust could not be disguised, and so tensions mounted. As far as the Nungs were concerned, whatever happened to Sergeant

Smithers he brought on himself. At any rate that was how it seemed to the Americans.

Just one week after the day that they were to be paid, their former commander told Lt. Longnecker that if the money was not paid immediately, they would take it by force. Very likely they believed that it had been withheld because of Sergeant Smither's alleged murder. The A-camp commander told the Nung very emphatically that it had not yet arrived. When it did, they'd get it.

That night the Nungs, who outnumbered the Americans by twenty to one, slipped into the compound and surrounded the rec room. The Green Beret had assembled there for a special meeting. The tribesmen were armed with automatic rifles, M-79 grenade throwers, and M-60 machine guns. The Americans so to speak were sitting ducks. The Nung commander gave them five minutes to hand over the cash, or they would open fire and kill everyone in the clubhouse. Lt. Longnecker was not easily intimidated. Facing the heavily armed mercenaries, he told their commander that he had radioed the TAC at province headquarters and requested to have aircraft armed and on standby. If the Nungs did not return to their quarters immediately, he would order an air strike and cremate them with napalm and white phosphorus. The bluff worked. After firing a volley of shots in the air, the tribesmen withdrew to their quarters. The money arrived the next day. Colonel O'Hara warned Lt. Longnecker that they'd better improve relations with their counterparts and do it quickly. However, according to Lt. Klicker, so far nothing had been done to defuse the volatile situation.

It wasn't clear to Grecco why Klicker had chosen to take him into his confidence. Evidently, the end seemed close at hand. It was a condemned man's final appeal. He may have hoped that the Refugee Advisor had some clout back at headquarters and could somehow make things right. It was a long shot, but the kid was desperate. He couldn't go on pretending that nothing had happened. It was more than any ordinary person could stand. It was as though the world had turned upside down, and he was trying to restore it to its rightful order.

The Idiot's Frightful Laughter

Three days later, Colonel O'Hara told Grecco that he'd left the A-camp just in the nick of time. The night that he left, Viet Cong sappers overran the compound killing all the Americans.

"What happened to the Nungs?" Grecco asked.

'Those cowardly bastards," the colonel said. "They ran off. There's no trace of them anywhere."

"Perhaps it was the Nungs who killed them?" Vince said.

"I read your fucking report," O'Hara said. "If you know what's good for you, you'll keep your fucking trap shut."

The Hamlet of Thoi Binh

Tho awoke as the first sign of daylight crept through the open doorway. Outside a pig rooted at the side of the thatched hut shaking the palm frond roof. A fine film of termite dust settled over her. Tho brushed the powder from her face. She was only thirty-eight, but years working out under the blistering tropic sun had made her look much older. Mai, the oldest, lay curled up like a kitten; her long straight hair had fanned out covering all but firm little buttocks. Mai was fifteen but was well developed for her age. She could pass for seventeen or eighteen. Her two brothers, Tan and Cay, lay as straight as fence posts between her and Tho. Tan, a slender delicate boy, was ten. He had nearly died of amoebic dysentery when only a year old. Cay, who was stocky and as thick-necked as a carabao, was seven. He did not look Vietnamese, and the villagers would tease Tho of having a Cambodian lover.

Tho heard the plaintive wailing of a baby in the next hut. The cry was so familiar to her. It was the sound of hunger. The mother's breasts hadn't enough milk for the infant. Often when Tho's own children had been very small, they would cry like that sometimes for hours until finally having exhausted themselves would fall asleep only to awaken a short time later and begin again.

Tho felt a baby's foot kick at her womb. It was vigorous, more so than the others had been. The birth was less than two months away. She had written and told her husband of the approximate day that it would come. She hoped that he could be with her then. The army had not granted him leave for any of the other children. Maybe it would this time? After all, he was now a platoon sergeant. That should entitle him to some special privileges; something as important as the birth of his child.

Tho arose soundlessly. She went to the fire pit and uncovered the hot coals. Laying a handful of straw on them, a speck of smoke

The Idiot's Frightful Laughter

arose. She fanned it was a palm leaf until the straw burst into flame. Then she put some more straw and a few twigs on the fire and continued to fan it until there was a bright yellow blaze that lit up the hut. Tho liked this time of day. The temperature was just right. By noon the heat was so unbearable. One could die of sunstroke.

Filling a cast iron pot half full of water from a huge earthen jar just outside the doorway, Tho placed the pot on the fire. Once the water was boiling, she dropped a handful of rice and several tiny sun-fried paddy fish in it.

While the broth was simmering on the fire, Tho went outside. She saw a bank of clouds far to the east glow yellow and then bright orange. Climbing down the bank of a stream that wound through the hamlet, she picked a cluster of mint and other aromatic leaves that grew in thick abundance along the water's edge. She was careful not to step on the fish traps that were hidden among the weeds. When she was a teenager, she had stepped in one. Her mother had spent hours pulling out the tiny bamboo splinters deeply embedded in her foot. She was lucky that the punctures had not become infected, for a boy her same age had stepped in one several months later and died of tetanus. He was a brave child. She remembered how he'd lain smiling up at her, his face wreathed in agony. The palms of his hands and the soles of his feet were an ugly green, but he never uttered a sound. He died so nobly.

When Tho got back to the hut, the children were up, and Mai was stirring the soup. Tan brought four bowls and a can of bamboo chopsticks. Mai filled the bowls while her mother dropped some of the aromatic leaves she'd gathered in each of them. She then raised the lid of an earthen pot. The brown pasty substance was alive with large white maggots. She dipped some of it called *nouc mam*, fish water, from the container careful not to get any of the maggots and poured a little into each of the bowls. The smell filled the hut with the thick sour odor of decayed fish. Tan held his nose. He had never got used to the nauseous stench.

The sun burst from the Sea of Reeds into a fiery inferno. Rays streaked in through the cracks of the thatched shack. After scooping out every last morsel with their chopsticks, they tipped the bowls to their lips and drank the warm broth. This was the only breakfast that they had ever known except on rare occasions when there was a chunk of port or muskrat to drop in it.

Tho could hear people stirring about outside. It was harvest time, and they were preparing to go to their fields. She and the children had been cutting and threshing rice for the past three weeks. Seldom did they work less than fourteen hours a day not counting the two-hour siesta at noon.

Tho rolled some cooked rice in a banana leaf and filled a small bottle with the poignant *nuoc mam*. That would be their lunch. In the meantime, the children had gathered together the scythes, a whetstone, and some reed mats to place about the thrashing bar. It was while Tho was banking the fire, that she heard a noise sounding like an approaching thunderstorm. She didn't have to tell the children what the sound meant, for they were already scampering for a hole at one corner of the hut. It had been made in igloo fashion by plastering layer upon layer of mud on bamboo matting. At first glance, it looked as though it might be a Dutch oven. Tho and the children had to squeeze close together in order for all of them to fit inside.

The first couple of artillery rounds fell short plowing into a rice paddy across the stream from the hamlet; however, the next ones came raining down on the nepa huts jarring Tho and her children about in their bunker-like beads in a rattle. Tho clasped her hands tightly about her swollen belly. She was more afraid of what the concussion might cause the eight-month fetus; than being blown into tiny bits by a direct hit. Once the foreign devils had fired canisters of napalm and white phosphorous. This she dreaded more than anything. Many of the villagers had roasted alive in their bunkers. She considered it somewhat of a miracle that the fiery liquid had not poured down over her hut.

No sooner had the artillery barrage stopped, then Tho heard the clatter of helicopters circling overhead. Then came the chatter of machinegun fire spraying the huts with a rain of lead. She grew tense, as the staccato came nearer trying to squeeze herself up into as tiny a target as possible. She held her breath, as the bullets smashed through the thatched roof and battered the hard clay floor. In the past, the bullets had not penetrated the bunker, but that gave her little solace, for these might be larger and stronger than before.

Then the choppers left, and she could hear the squeal of wounded pigs and the roar of fear-crazes carabao. Sometimes a bombardment would drive a water buffalo so mad that it would race about butting down the shacks or whatever else was in its path. Tho did not hear any of the others moving about, so she felt it best not to leave the safety of her bunker, for the barrage might begin again at any moment.

Then she heard shouts and rifle fire. They were soldiers. No doubt foreign troops, for their voices were too harsh to be Vietnamese. She and the children must get out of the bunker quickly, for that was the first thing these foreign devils would destroy. They'd lob grenades into them killing whoever was inside.

By the time Tho had reached the doorway, the soldiers had already crossed the stream. Several were firing wildly about. A shot hit a crazed buffalo between the eyes. It reared up on its haunches shaking its great crescent-shaped horns about and then collapsed on its side letting out a loud eerie bellow.

Tho squatted in the doorway, motioning for the children to crouch behind her. One was less apt to get shot if she were in the open where these lunatics could see her and know that she was unarmed. They stopped at each hut and ordered those inside out into a nearby field. Tho had never seen so many foreign devils before. They were huge, like giants, twice the size of Vietnamese. Some had pink shiny faces with blue eyes. Others were various shades of black and brown. In the past, there had only been one or two accompanying the Vietnamese soldiers. Now there were only these horrid demons.

A red-faced baboon motioned with his rifle for Tho and the children to go into a field. The villagers were herded together and lead to the bank of a dry canal and told to wait. Tho saw her home burst into flame. Everything she owned was gone: the three sacks of rice, the jug of *nuoc mam*, a cast-iron pot, a few clay bowls, two earthen crocks, the family altar with photos of her parents. It didn't amount to much, she thought, but how would they live without it? Soon the entire hamlet was aflame. The devils ran about shooting the animal – the carabao, the pigs, even the chicken, and the ducks.

Tho looked up at the foreign apparition towering over them; his rifle resting in the crook of his arm. His eyes were a pale blue; the color of the sky on a hot clear day. If she looked at them for long, she felt as though she might disappear within like entering a brightly lit cave. They were a cold emptiness and hadn't the warmth that the Vietnamese brown eyes had. They were the eyes of a demon. And the skin was so red, as though it might burn her if she were to touch it. The nose was even redder and so large and ugly. Tho's husband had told her of Vietnamese women who had married these monsters. How could they? She wondered. They must have been conjured by the demons. Such grotesque looking creatures were capable of most anything. She noticed that he was smiling, but what did it mean? she wondered. It was, of course, false. He was trying to hide his cruel face, but it only made him look more hideous, she thought, nodding her head thoughtfully.

The soldier reached into a pocket of his tunic and brought out a handful of candy, large chunks of taffy wrapped in colored plastic. He tossed a piece to each of the children taking care not to omit anyone. They're a strange lot, Tho thought. They burn our homes, kill our animals; then give our children candy. She saw another soldier running towards them. He was no taller than an average Vietnamese, but fatter, twice that of the ordinary Vietnamese. If one did not look at his face, he might pass for a rich Saigon merchant or politician. When he grew closer, she saw that he was angry. His features were twisted into a cruel grimace.

"What the fuck's the holdup, Wimple?" The angry little man said.

"Why nothing, Sir," Wimple replied. "You said to watch them, and that's what I'm doing."

"Watch them, my ass. I said waste them. The old man's fit to bust a gut," he said pointing to the chopper hovering several thousand feet overhead.

The Idiot's Frightful Laughter

Wimple heard Colonel Hardcock's gruff whiskey-drinking voice. The radioman standing to one side of the little man had turned the amplifier up. "Lieutenant Nalley," he was shouting above the clatter of the helicopter rotor blades. "I want to speak to Lt. Nalley."

"Yes Sir," he said. "This is Lieutenant Nalley, Sir.

"Listen turd head," Colonel Hardcock said. "Get your fucking finger out of your ass and grease those mothafucking VC. I want every fucking one of those commie cocksuckers zapped. Is that clear, Lieutenant?"

"Yes Sir," Lt. Nalley said snapping to attention and saluting the handset. "Right away, Sir."

"Every fucking one!" Col. Hardcock said. "You miss one. Just one of them fuckers, and I'll bust your ass down to buck private. You got that, Nalley?"

"Yes, Sir. On the double Sir," the lieutenant said saluting the handset. Then turning to Wimple, he said: "You heard the old man. Get cracking." Wimple could feel Col. Hardcock's eyes boring down on him through his high-powered field glasses.

Tho saw the tall soldier place the rifle to his shoulder and point it at them. He's going to shoot us, she thought. That's what the fat man ordered him to do. He said to kill us. A cold tenseness crept over her. She felt the infant moving about in her womb. Her legs felt weak; she could hardly stand. Her breath came in quick, short gasps.

Private First Class Wimple's teeth clamped together, and his smile froze into a grimace. The eyelids peeled back, and in those pale empty skies, a storm was building up. Tho looked at her two sons. They had not noticed. They were concentrating on the chunks of taffy that the soldier had given them. They sat with their eyes half closed savoring every morsel. Never had they ever tasted anything so delicious.

"Hey, hold on there, Wimp," someone shouted from where the huts were aflame. Wimple lowered the muzzle of his weapon and turned about. A sergeant and four other soldiers were running towards him. "Hold it up a sec, Wimp. We need the broad," the sarge said pointing at Mai. One of the soldiers grabbed her by the wrist and pulled her from the pack. Another pressed the muzzle of a forty-five automatic pistol to her temple.

"Be nice, baby or I'll blow your fucking head off," he said. "They forced her along the stream to a clump of bamboo. She stumbled over the lumpy soil looking very stiff and jerky.

Before Tho had time to think of Mai, she saw the rifle swing about, point at those to her left and begin firing. The muzzle waved up and down over the women and children in a slow easy motion. PFC Wimple had to fire three clips of ammo before the last one, a small boy with a hunk of taffy between his lips, stopped moving.

Once the soldiers had Mai behind the clump of bamboo, they grabbed her by the arms and legs and threw her down hard pinning her to the ground. They ripped away the teenager's clothing. Two of them raised her legs and spread them wide apart. The sergeant was the first to rape her rupturing the hymen. Mai screaming hysterically. The five GI's shifted places taking turns with the adolescent. She finally gave up all resistance. Her cries grew so feeble that they could hardly be heard. The one with the pistol first shot Mai in the cunt, then through the naval and the nipple of each teat, and finally between the eyes. He was so proud of his marksmanship.

A full moon had just risen as Truc stepped into the clearing where his hamlet had been. All that was left were the heaps of smoldering rubble. He had heard that Yank soldiers were in the area and was afraid that they might raze the hamlet. Ever since the foreign dogs had arrived, some seven months ago, they'd been setting fires to villages throughout the province. Where might they have taken his family? He wondered. How would he ever find them?

Truc stopped at where his home had been. Protruding from the smoldering ashes were chunks of clay pottery and the remains of a reed mat. The devils had blown up the bunker before setting fire to the hut, he thought. Truc kicked about in the ashes with a sandal uncovering a bowl of sand with several jo still stuck in it. It had

The Idiot's Frightful Laughter

fallen from the ancestral altar without breaking. He picked it up and set it on a pile of rubble. Then he found a piece of bamboo that was smoldering at one end and blew on it until it ignited. He then touched the flame to the tip of each jo stick. The rich pungent smell of jasmine filled the warm still air.

Truc stood for some time staring at the smoking incense as though in a trance. All he was wearing were a pair of black trunks and sandals cut from truck tires and bound to the feet with strips of inner tube. A conical straw hat hung at his back. The bamboo handle of a homemade knife protruded from the waistband of his trunks. In one hand, he held an AK-47 Chinese Assault Rifle. Its freshly oiled stock and barrel glistened in the faint moonlight.

A Ghostly sort of murmur broke the silence. The deep inhuman yet plaintive moaning shook Truc from his revelry. The sound came from a field to the west of where the hamlet had been. Climbing a dike, he saw that the moaning was that of his family's carabao. It had been maimed early that morning. The foreign devils had shot all four of its legs shattering the bone at the knee. Why had they crippled it so cruelly? Why hadn't they simply killed it? What pleasure could they get torturing the gentle old water buffalo? What harm had it ever done anyone? When Truc was just a tiny child, he had ridden the great lumbering beast about the rice paddies. Never once had it ever tried so much as to jostle him off. Yes, there were times when it was self-willed and stubborn. That was to be expected, but it had always been a docile beast. The foreign demons with their round cold eyes and long pointed noses had no compassion. Life meant nothing to them. It was the Vietnamese faith in the Lord Buddha that made them so humane. Truc thought of their divine teacher. What a great heart he had. He would not harm even the smallest insect. Truc knelt beside the carabao. Its large chestnut eyes looked anxiously up at the youth. They were filled with pain and fear. Truc drew his knife from his waistband. unwrapping a cloth bound about the blade, he laid it over the animal's eyes. Then pressing firmly with both hands drew the blade swiftly across its throat. The great beast jerked convulsively for several seconds and then lay still. A vapor rose from the crimson fountain of warm blood that splattered onto the ground. When the flow had ceased, Truc removed the cloth from the buffalo's eyes and gently pressed the lids closed.

Everywhere there were dead animals – pigs, chicken, ducks, carabao – slaughtered and left to rot. Packs of wild dogs and jackal were tearing at the carcasses. Truc drove the predators off. How could he save all of this meat? he wondered. His comrades were in great need of protein. Another day in the hot sun, and it would spoil. The flies were already busy laying their eggs in the torn flesh. Soon the meat would be crawling with maggots. One thing that could be said about the Arvin was that they were not wasteful. They killed the peasants' animals for a reason. They needed the meat, Truc thought. However, for this Yankee scum killing was a lust. They didn't care what it was, just so it was something to kill. For them, it was a sport, a sick, bloody sport.

Truc thought of Tho and Mai and his two younger brothers. Were they alive? Had they been moved to a resettlement camp? There had been no mention of it on the enemy radio, not a word. Had the devils killed them too? He'd heard of it happening at other hamlets. They'd shot everyone, women, children. It didn't matter. It all depended on their commander. He looked about. If they'd been killed, where were the bodies? The stream, he thought. They may have floated down the stream. But then it was too small. There was too little water. There were the paddies, but they couldn't be there, for most of the rice had been harvested. The bodies could be seen easily in the bright moonlight. Then he noticed the dogs and jackals fighting over something at the drainage canal. Chasing the canine off, he walked towards it with slow faltering steps. He was afraid of what he might find. The canal, dry at this time of year, was a good three meters deep. It was too dark to see well, for the moon was too near the horizon to shed light directly into the canal. He moved cautiously, for he was afraid of snakes. Cobra often lived along the sides of rivers and canals. They dug slender dens in the steep banks just above the high-water mark.

About halfway down the side of the canal, Truc stepped on something that caused him to scamper back up the bank. It was round and slippery like a reptile; however, he had felt it crack when his foot pressed down on it as though a bone had broken. Truc returned to where the hamlet had been and poked about in the rubbish until he found a can with an ounce or so of cooking oil. He soaked a cloth with the oil and then bound it about a bamboo pole. Crawling down just beneath the edge of the canal, Truc lit the torch by blowing on a live ember.

The youth stared in horror at the jumbled pile of bodies strewn along the bottom of the ditch. They were people whom he'd known all his life – aunts, uncles, cousins, nephews, nieces, childhood playmates, a girlfriend. There were at least two hundred bodies all riddled with bullets. Striking his knife again and again into the hard clay embankment, Truc though dark bitter thought. If I only knew where these beasts lived; where their homes were; who their parents, wives, and children were, I'd revenge my family, he thought. I'd kill every last one of these blood-thirsty monsters. He fantasized of just how he'd do it. What awful retribution he would extract, but at the same time, another part of him said that it was impossible. It was a hopeless daydream. There could never be any retribution; no evening of the score. The white devils lived in another world on the other side of the earth. How hopeless the Vietnamese' life was. It always had been, he thought.

Truc moved the bodies about as gently as possible until he came upon Cay lying stretched out on the bed of the drainage ditch drenched in blood. Turning his brother onto his back, Truc saw a row of bullet holes spread across his stomach. Another row ran from the left shoulder down across his chest forming an X at the navel. The little boy still had a piece of taffy clamped between his teeth. Truc took the candy and examined it. "Those cocksuckers!" he screamed to the dark void surrounding him. It was not Vietnamese candy, he thought, shaking his head in disbelief. It came from those blood-thirsty lunatics. What sort of madman would give a child candy and then riddle him with bullets? It was too cold-blooded; too grotesque to possibly imagine.

Truc carried his brother's limp body up the side of the canal and laid it on the ground. He could remember ever feeling so tired.

The thought of going in search of the others especially his mother was so unbearable. He squatted on the ground staring glumly at the bullet-torn body of his tiny brother. He thought of the American; those whom they'd captured. A few had been brave; facing their fate courageously. However, most of them had not. He recalled the terror in their eyes; how some had cried, begged for mercy. He detested such miserable cowards. No soldier who behaved like that should be allowed to live. But the brave ones? Prior to this, he had felt that they should be spared. It seemed senselessly cruel to kill them. Many were drafted and didn't want to come to Vietnam. Now it was different. Brave or coward, he'd kill them as he would a snake and do it with relish. Kill slowly, mercilessly. Make the bold shriek with agony. He would revenge his mother, his brothers, his sister; all those who lay butchered in this ditch, he thought, making a sword-sweeping motion with his hand of the mutilated corpse. He would devise the most ingenious sorts of torture, and when they cried for mercy, he'd spit in their face. "Did you show my mother mercy or my sister?" he'd ask. He would have a pocket full of candy. Yes. Candy. He'd stuff their mouths with it. Make them choke on it.

Where was his sister? What had become of her? He visualized her, as he had seen her the last time he'd been home some six months ago. What had these shit-eating pigs done with her? He shuddered, feeling his blood grow icy, shaking his head to drive away the image that crowded his mind; the picture of a dozen or more red-skinned demons, their faces mad with lust, pouncing on her one after the other. He pulled his knife from beneath the cord that bound his trunks and thrust the blade into the hard dry earth again and again; plunging it into the hearts of the foreign dogs. He would cut off their cocks and shove them down their throats.

They are not human like us, Truc thought. They do not have a God who is loving and merciful. They are Christian heathens; cannibals who drink the blood and eat the flesh of their Savior. No wonder they are savages. They are rich and fly about in great powerful machines, but what is that to the Great Lord Buddha? Didn't he turn his back on wealth and power? Didn't he teach that

The Idiot's Frightful Laughter

those things breed evil – greed, lust, hate? Must not one be poor and humble before he can find love and peace? But these savage foreign pigs' God is one of violence and greed and power. They are not human. They are mad dogs that must be killed. None should be spared. Truc was trembling with rage. His breath came in short deep gasps. He no longer felt tired. He was restless. His mind filled with an insatiable lust to kill the red-faced, long-nosed devils.

Making another torch, Truc went back to the canal and dragged the bodies about until he found his mother and other brother, but where was his sister? Where was Mai? There was no sign of her. He continued to move the bodies about until he was drench in blood. He held the torch close to each face so that there could be no mistake. Three times he did this, but without success. Mai's body was not among them.

Truc found a slender piece of metal which was pointed at one end. It had been used as a plowshare. He squatted near the bodies of his mother and brothers and began to dig at the ground, and then scoop up the loose soil with a piece of earthenware. As he dug, he had the feeling that he was being watched. Looking about, he saw a man standing very still in the middle of the field. He looked as though he might be wearing an Arvin uniform. Although the man appeared to be unarmed, Truc instinctively reached for his rifle. He sat at the edge of the pit and laid the weapon across his lap. He looked to either side and behind. No one else was in view. The Arvin began to walk slowly toward him; his hand held wide at his side.

Truc was sure of the enemy uniform when the man was some twenty meters distant, but he did not realize that it was his father until the soldier was only a few feet from him. Neither man spoke. What could Truc say? Weren't the foreign pigs his father's comrades? How many times had it been pointed out to him that the Arvin were puppets, running dogs, lackeys of the invaders? Those who had murdered his mother and brothers and quite likely his sister; for that matter all his childhood friends and relatives; everyone who he had known and loved killed by his father's allies.

Sheridan Peterson

His father sat at the other side of the partly dug grave. Why was he wearing a uniform? Truc wondered. Wasn't he afraid of being executed as a traitor? His name, Wha, was printed in bold block letters across his lapel. Perhaps he was more fearful of his foreign comrades; afraid of being gunned down from a helicopter.

Wha took a cigarette and then passed the pack to Truc. The youth looked at it. "Salem" it read. "Foreign devils," he snarled throwing the pack into the grave and madly grinding it into the loosely dug earth with the heel of his sandal. "Foreign pigs," he growled.

Truc thought back to when he was a child. When his father would come to visit them, he usually had some gold jewelry – a ring or necklace or bracelet. He never told them where he'd got them, and his mother never asked, but she knew. They all knew that the loot had been taken from peasant women like herself. It was common knowledge that Arvin troops plundered the enemy villages. At one time it was the Vietnamese soldier's only means of livelihood. Nevertheless, his mother felt ashamed. The jewels were very likely the life's savings of some poor family like her own. It was insurance for the time when the crops would be destroyed by famine or flood. The gold could be pawned, and enough rice bought to last until the next year's crop was harvested. However, with no gold, no insurance of any kink, the family was sure to starve.

Tho had never kept the jewelry. As soon as Wha had left, she would go to the province capital and sell it at one of the town's three gold shops. She would loiter about the shops to see how much others got for their gold. The price was always either going up or down. She hadn't the vaguest idea what it was ever worth. The jewelers were solemn-faced Chinese. They would quote a price, and no amount of persuasion could get them to change it. She would eventually sell the gold to the one who made the highest offer or otherwise go downriver to Soc Trang where prices were often higher.

When they were first married, Wha would make excuses about the gold. He was then serving with the French and seldom got paid.

The Idiot's Frightful Laughter

The Vietnamese NCO's usually kept the money of those in their command. However, with the Americans, there were plenty of ways for a Vietnamese officer to supplement his income without cheating those under his command. For example, it was a common practice to keep men on the muster long after they'd been killed. Some had entire companies of bogus troops jokingly referred to as "ghost armies". The deceased's pay was split among those from the company commander all the way up to the brigadier general. As long as they all got a cut, nothing was ever said.

On the other hand, the National Liberation Front never looted a hamlet. Such practice was counterproductive. As Chairman Mao had aptly put it. "The people are the water, and the guerrillas, the fish. Without the peasants' support, the insurgents could not survive." All the Viet Cong ever took was rice, and then only enough for three or four days. If they could, they would repay the peasants, leaving whatever they had as collateral. Never did they take a family's jewelry. If one was to do such a thing, the party would punish him severely. It was a very serious crime.

When Truc was sixteen, he had joined the National Liberation Front. One morning Tho found a note by the hearth. It simply said that he had joined the Front. He left the day after a platoon of Arvin had looted the hamlet. They had stolen the family pigs and chickens and fired into some of the huts killing a village elder and wounding a small child who died later that night.

Occasionally during a truce, Wha and Truc returned to the hamlet. If it was planting or harvest time, the father and son would work side by side all day in the paddies. The first time that they met after Truc had joined the NLF, he tried to get his father to change sides, but it was of no use. Wha agreed with his son; the leaders of the South Vietnam Government were gangsters. Such bloodsuckers could not hope to win, for the people despised them; however, Wha could not change. He was a staff sergeant and earned ten times what he'd got with the French. How could he support the family? What sort of pay would the Front offer a renegade Arvin sergeant? Would they dare trust him? No, it was impossible.

Truc looked at his father, at his lined worried face and nervous shifty eyes. He hadn't realized until that moment what a weak man his father was. A lifetime of corruption, of looting villages and robbing poor peasants of their life savings had left its toll. He no longer had any pride, no self-respect. However, in spite of this, Truc loved his father. He was a victim, a pawn of colonialism. Such a man would be of no use to the Front.

Somewhere deep within his psyche, Truc sensed that someday he might have to kill his father. He'd known others who had had to kill a father or a son. It was a test of loyalty. Nothing must stand in the way of the cause; the glorious struggle for a free independent Vietnam. Whenever Truc thought of aiming his rifle at the base of his father's skull and squeezing the trigger, an icy chill ran down his spine. Nevertheless, it was karma. He saw no other alternative. He had gradually conditioned himself for that dreaded moment. The thought had become less and less difficult to accept. It would not be done with passion. How could he hate this poor pitiful man – his father? No, it would be an act of love. He would see to it that Wha died bravely, with dignity. He would restore his pride, his self-respect. Truc would be performing a sacred ritual to honor their revered ancestors. Wha would gain a position of veneration among his predecessors. He would have earned a place of dignity at the family altar, that is if Truc was to perpetuate the family progeny. The time would come when he would feel a compulsion to perform his duty, free his father from such a mean despicable existence. He knew already what he would say to him; how he would appeal to his manhood. His father must not disgrace himself and the memory of his family, for very soon he would be reunited with his wife and children, with a long lineage of ancestors going back to ancient times. He must above all else face death with calm resignation. Truc would assure him of an honorable burial. Here was Wha's chance, or his soul would be forever damned to wander the earth an outcast. Those were the thoughts that Truc was frequently pondered over. He would explain all that to his father when the time came.

The Idiot's Frightful Laughter

The youth looked intently at his father sitting quietly at the other side of the partly dug grave. He imagined seeing tears glistening in his eye; otherwise, he seemed quite at ease. The look of indifference was the result of twenty years in the puppet army. Twenty years of servitude to foreign pigs. Truc thought.

The youth laid his rifle aside and picked up the plowshare. Squatting in the hole, he began jabbing at the earth, prying out large chunks of black alluvial sod. Wha pulled a bayonet from a scabbard hooked to his web belt and dug alongside his son. When they had finished, they laid Tho and the two boys' bodies in the grave. Spreading a reed mat over the corpse, they kicked loose dirt onto it; then they dug up large squares of turf and placed them even with the surface to hide the plot. Truc scratched their names on a piece of slate and slipped it beneath the turf. Someday when the war had ended, and the foreign dogs had left, he might be able to find the grave and give them a decent burial, he thought.

Dawn began to break, as they were finishing the task. Truc went in search of some jo sticks to burn at the grave while Wha packed water from the stream in a clay bowl to moisten the grass covering the site. As an added precaution, debris was scattered over it.

Now that it was light, it would be easier to find Mai's body, but they would have to be careful. Aircraft were sure to check the site of the hamlet within the next hour or so. Wha took a red scarf from his pocket and bound it about his arm. It was intended to identify him as an Arvin; however, it might simply make him a better target. Truc bound a bundle of straw about his assault rifle and put on a green T-shirt that his father had given him.

Truc could not help wondering how his father, a miserably corrupt mercenary, felt about all the carnage lying about, especially the mutilated bodies of his wife and children. He had said nothing, but surely this had changed him. How could he possibly return to his platoon and fight for those foreign sons of bitches after this? He must ask his father. He had to know. Then he would be sure of what to do. But first, there was Mai. She must be found.

It was Wha who found her body. He had said nothing. However, when Truc came upon them, his father had finished dressing his daughter's defiled corpse and was slowly and with infinite care sewing the torn clothing. Truc stood looking in awe at his dead sister's beautiful face, and at his father humming a wild plaintive tune. His face was as blank as death, but Mai's was not. Hers had the look of dazed bewilderment. Truc knelt and closed the adolescent's eyes and mouth giving her a reposed peaceful appearance.

The father and son had just finished placing the last piece of turf on Mai's grave when they heard the clatter of helicopter rotor blades. Instinctively Truc dashed for a clump of bamboo and squeezed his slender frame in amidst the stock's thick bramble. Their long slender thorns jabbed at his skin. He could not move out of the way of one without being struck by another. As the chopper hovered above, he kept the muzzle of his weapon pointed at the door gunner facing him, taking up the slack on the trigger. With the slightest indication of being seen, Truc would fire without hesitation. He was so excited with the prospect of destroying an enemy aircraft and its foreign dogs that he'd completely forgotten about his father. Then he saw him standing only a few paces from Mai's grave waving to those in the chopper. The red scarf was spread out over his shoulders, so as not to be missed.

Truc shook his head in disbelief. Who was this person anyhow? His wife and children murdered only the day before by those blood-lusting savages, and today he's waving to them as though they were his most trusted friends. It was incredible, goddamn incredible.

The helicopter circled about Wha several times. Truc saw the door gunner speaking to the pilot over the intercom. Then the aircraft banked slightly, and the man swung the machine gun about pointing it at Wha. A stream of red tracers jerked Truc's father about and then dropped him in a tattered heap beside his daughter's grave.

The chopper landed near Wha's body, its great rotor blades blowing sand and dust into Truc's face temporarily blinding him.

The Idiot's Frightful Laughter

When he had cleared his eyes, he saw the two door gunners jump from the aircraft and walk over to where Wha was lying. They were so close that Truc felt sure that he was as visible to them, as they were to him. He wiggled back deeper into the thorny bamboo thicket.

One of the gunners, a short stocky man with a fat red face, kicked Wha over on his back. The other, a lean black man with a pearl-handled pistol slung beneath his left armpit, knelt down and started going through Wha's pockets.

"Yep, he's an Arvin alright," the black man said handing a card to the other man. "This here's his ID card. Platoon sergeant with GVN's Twenty-Fifth Division."

"Shit," the short red-faced man said flipping the card onto the ground. "Probably a fucking deserter or spy. Ain't got no business out here anyhow."

"How you reckon?" the black man said rising and looking down at the other.

'How you figure he got them platoon sergeant stripes? He ain't no draftee."

"How I reckon?" The short man was angry. "Look, boy, I reckon this here's a free-fire zone as of yesterday, and no one including this here sergeant ain't got no business out here. That's how I reckon."

What a setup, Truc thought. The two gunners unarmed except for that fancy looking pistol, and no one manning the machine guns. He had two alternatives. He could shoot the pilot and then the gunners, but that was risky. It was safer to give the two a quick blast, and then run to the aircraft and spray the cockpit. It would be even better to shoot the pilot once the chopper was airborne. The crash would destroy the helicopter. Truc was trembling with excitement as he aimed the weapon at the hated enemy.

The black man gaped in disbelief at the muzzle of the AK-47 assault rifle poking from the clump of bamboo. A burst of fire hit him square in the chest knocking him off his feet. He sat down hard on the ground slumping forward on his face. Truc was out of the thicket and running as fast as he could when he shot the other gunner. The short red-faced man dropped to his knees. Truc fired another burst blowing the top of his head off. The helicopter was about ten foot off the ground and moving horizontally away from the youth when he caught sight of the pilot's helmet through a thick cloud of dust. He was peering out of his side window. Truc fired from the hip. The helmet rocked sideways, and the chopper dived nose first into a rice paddy.

Truc quickly removed the two machine guns, three M-16 assault rifles, and a radio transmitter hiding them in some brush. Then jammed his green T-shirt into the gas tank, he set fire to it with a smoldering jo stick from his mother's grave. The aircraft erupted into a ball of flame parts flying in all directions.

Truc was a good hundred meters from the burning aircraft running in a low crouched position through the unharvested rice when he remembered the pearl-handled pistol. Without checking his stride, he spun about and retraced his steps.

As Truc was pulling the gun from its holster beneath the black man's armpit, he heard a clattering noise overhead. Out of ammo, he pitched his assault rifle to one side. Grasping the pistol with both hands, he aimed at the helicopter some fifteen hundred feet above diving straight at him. By the time he'd emptied it, the aircraft had leveled off at about five hundred feet. Truc could swear he saw the gunner make a circle with his thumb and finger as he swung the machine gun about and aimed at him. The bullets hit three meters in front of the youth and then moved towards him, first striking his feet and then moving up his legs leaving a row of fifty caliber holes across the stomach, chest, and face. Truc fell backward, his arms flung out above his head still clutching the pearl-handled pistol with both hands.

"Spunky little fart, wasn't he?" a full-bird colonel said nudging Truc in the ribs with the toe of a brightly polished boot. "Trying to zap us with a fucking pistol," he added picking up the weapon and examining it. "Just can't figure out what makes them so gung-ho."

Private First Class Jerome Wimple didn't sleep well the night after shooting the women and children and helping to toss their bodies into the canal. He was worried. It was not the killing that

The Idiot's Frightful Laughter

bothered him. He'd become quite used to that. Three months, or even one month before, he wouldn't have wanted to do it, but now it was all quite easy. What upset him was the indifference; that feeling of nothingness. He might just as well have been shooting at tin ducks at a shooting gallery. If only he could have felt the thrill of Flaherty and Polanski got. They were never so happy, as when they were slaying dinks. For weeks after a raid, they would go into lurid detail about all the killing, raping and looting they'd done. And then there were the pictures. Photos of young girls being gang banged, and later their cunts sliced open while they were still alive, or throats being slit and stomachs disemboweled. At first, the photographs had shocked Wimple and later disgusted him, but now they simply bored him.

Then there was the hate. Wimple wished that he could feel the wild snarling smoke-belching rage that Lieutenant Nalley had. During the massacre, the stocky little shithead ran about among the burning shacks an automatic rifle held at his hip, bandoleers slung about his neck, pockets bulging with grenades, red-eyed drunk with hate; a raging, bellowing, hysterical lunatic. Medic Andy Ziolkowski had warned Wimple to be careful. Nalley was a dangerous psychotic, and so was Colonel Hardcock. They made a perfect pair.

Then there was another sort of hate; that of Platoon Sergeant Palmer. A silent, icy fury that showed only in a throbbing artery at the temple and the pallor of his tightly pressed lips. He killed with a knife, a large hand-crafted bowie with a rawhide handle. He'd slip the blade slowly and deftly across the throat; then wipe the blade on the victim's clothing with the dispassion of a yogi. If only I could have such cold-blooded passion, Wimple thought.

Even fear, to kill from fear was better than nothing; if he could only have that. The spine-tingling, eye-bulging fright that Hector Finkbeiner had; to see the enemy lurking behind every bush; huge grotesque apparitions who could transform themselves into harmless-appearing peasant women, children, pregnant mothers or new-born infants at a moment's notice.

Sheridan Peterson

Wimple was nineteen when he arrived in Vietnam. He came determined to like the Vietnamese. He had never been so set on anything in his life. It was his drill sergeant at Fort Dix who was chiefly responsible for this impulse, Sergeant Slocum and his father. They were both big bloated men who spent their leisure time guzzling beer and boasting about all the gooks they'd killed.

Wimple had hated Sergeant Slocum the moment he saw him. During the nine weeks that he had been under his command, the loathing had mounted to an unbearable peak. It didn't matter what the drill might happen to be, the theme never varied. "Kill Gooks! Kill Slopes! Kill dinks! Kill! Kill! Kill!" Slocum would scream. Whether it was bayonet practice, grenade throwing, obstacle course running, calisthenics, or scrubbing floors, it was all done in tempo to the drill sergeant's sagacious chant.

Wimple's father, Corney, had been a Marine during the Second World War. He was a supply sergeant on Guadalcanal and then served out the rest of the war as a quartermaster at Parris Island, North Carolina. His proudest memories were serving under Gunny Sergeant Lou Diamond at the Marine Boot Camp. The sergeant was supposed to have dropped mortar shells down the smokestacks of several Japanese naval vessels. Corney never tired telling how many gooks Diamond had killed with just one mortar round. Wimple noted that the figure grew larger as time progressed.

As far back as Wimple could recall, his father had never once changed his daily routine. He was a purchasing agent for People's Electric. He'd arrive home at nearly the same time every evening, go directly to the fridge, get a case of Coors, take it to the living room, place it beside his lounge chair, turn on the TV, and there he'd sit until supper was ready. Within twenty minutes, he'd hog down a three-course meal and was back at the TV drinking beer. If there was nothing of interest on TV, he'd call for Wimple. It was time to have a man to man talk. There were just two topics. If he were not telling his son of the gooks that he and Gunny Sergeant Lou Diamond had killed, it concerned his son's future. He had it all laid out for him. Wimple would attend a vocational school, study electronics; then go to work at People's Electric. There was no limit

The Idiot's Frightful Laughter

to the opportunities he'd have just as long as he kept his nose clean. That's all he had to worry about. Be agreeable. Get along. Work as a team.

Wimple loathed his father. He despised the rolls of fat that hung over his belt. He disliked the way he'd grunt and groan when he rose from his chair, his face red and swollen. However, what he hated the most was his righteousness. It was forbidden to disagree with him even on the most trivial topics.

As soon as he arrived in Vietnam, Wimple set out to make friends with the Vietnamese. However, it was not possible for an American enlisted man to meet honest, hardworking, reliable Vietnamese. They were leery of foreigners, especially American soldiers. Those that hung about the U.S. Army installations were the dregs of society

Jerome Wimple was assigned to the Twenty-Fifth Division at Cu Chi. Bordering the camp were hundreds of shacks patched together with palm fronds, scraps of wood, and flattened beer and soft drink cans. These were the gyp joints where hustlers and whores hung out. Pimps, beggars, money changers and black marketers pursued the GI whenever he left camp. Packs of little street urchins dogged his heels pulling at his clothing. "You fuck my sister? Okay? She number one cherry girl. No sweat. Okay?" They would chant tugging at his arm. The worst were the "cowboys"; teenage gangsters on motorbikes who waylaid GI's beating and robbing them. The assaults were invariably blamed on the Viet Cong. It made the servicemen feel as though all Vietnamese were their enemy, that none could be trusted.

Late one evening, Wimple was jumped by a gang of cowboys, as he was walking back to camp. He was beaten unconscious and robbed of his wallet as well as his watch and camera. He had two cracked ribs and a broken nose. It was lucky that he had not drowned, for he'd been thrown into a sewer drainage ditch. Military police found him the next day.

After that, hating Vietnamese came easy for Wimple. The cowboys had achieved what Sergeant Slocum and his father had failed at. They had converted him into a coldblooded killer. For a time he'd craved revenge; however, he was not the vindictive type; so the killing became as routine as his father's job at People's Electric. "It's just a job." Corney would say. "Somebody's got to do it."

Corney was proud of his boy. "A real chip off the old block," he'd tell his pals at the American Legion Club.

Colonel Hardcock had the bodies at the hamlet of Thoi Binh drenched with crankcase oil and set on fire. "It ain't sanitary leaving them bodies lying about," he said.

A Real Can of Worms

Grecco had thought that Major Biff Ziegler was simply another one of those close-minded military types; until he'd overheard him expound on a scheme to rid the province of corruption. "Until we do that, we'll never get anywhere with the people," he told Captain Phouc, his counterpart, whose name is pronounced "fuck"; a matter that U.S. advisors learned not to joke about. The captain wasn't one to be trifled with.

Major Ziegler was so engrossed in explaining his theory to the fierce-eyed little ranger officer that he did not notice Vince sit down beside him in the mess hall. "Here's a list of the worst sonsabitches," he said shoving aside his tray and spreading a sheet of paper out on the table. Twenty-seven in all. Get them and the others will fall in line." The major had worked out a detailed plan for the assassination of each of those on the list. "It's a test case," he added tapping the list of names with his index finger. "When the other provinces see how well it works out, they'll follow suit." Major Ziegler knew each of the marked men's day to day routine, and how they spent their evenings.

"Who'll do it?" Captain Phouc asked. He spoke in a very matter-of-fact manner, as though the plan was a very routine task.

"We need a hit squad," Ziegler said. "The cool calculating types." He made a slow conspiratorial sort of wink, as though to say: "No one's better suited than you." If one had just come in on the conversation, he'd assume that the two were talking about nothing more out of the ordinary than a new accounting system. "However we'll have to plan our tactics carefully," he added. "Don't want to make any mistakes that could backfire on us."

Major Ziegler was an advisor for a Ranger Battalion stationed at the outskirts of Lang Son. Once he'd asked Grecco to visit the camp and see what he could do for the troops' dependents. They were eligible for war damages and injury benefits but had been cheated out of them when the unit was transferred there from Soc Trang.

The dependents' quarters were as squalid and shoddy, as any Vince had seen. The Rangers' families were jammed into a narrow windowless shed resembling a chicken house. Each family regardless of size was allotted a space five-foot square, just large enough for a pallet. Ponchos were used to partition off the cubicles. The corridor down the center of the shack was so narrow that Grecco had to edge sideways along it, as children scampered between his legs. Sewerage lay in green, stagnant pools about the structure. Those who could not stand the congestion and filth had abandoned the security of the compound to build huts of bamboo and palm fond outside the barbwire enclosure. They had no protection from enemy attacks and were generally caught in the crossfire. Twelve women and children were killed at the outpost's periphery two days prior to Vince's visit. "There was no VC attack," Major Ziegler said. "They were shot from within the compound. A pig had detonated a mine causing a sentry to panic and spray the perimeter with machine gun fire. The victim's husbands beat the sentry to death with their rifle butts."

Grecco did everything he possibly could to help the Ranger's dependents. He took the matter all the way up to his former boss, Gilbert Jones, Director of US AID's Refugee Division for the entire country. He also sent a letter to South Vietnam's Social Welfare Ministry insisting that the Rangers were entitled to the nation's highest tribute. They were the country's most courageous fighting force. None would help. They flatly refused. It was a matter for the military and was outside their jurisdiction, they contended. Jones found it amusing that a professed peacenik like Vince would be championing the nation's toughest combatants.

Sensing Grecco's despair and assuming that he had done all that he possibly could, Captain Phuoc was always ready and willing to befriend him; however, his help on occasions proved quite embarrassing. For example, once when Vince was in the market haggling with a vendor over the price of papayas, the

Captain stopped his jeep beside the stand and interceded for him. After that, the vendor always picked out the largest freshest papayas for Vince at the most reasonable price. Another time when the Ranger Commander heard from Major Ziegler that a repair shop had switched spark plugs on Grecco's motorcycle, he told the mechanic that if they were not returned within twenty-four hours, he'd have his shop burned down.

Although Phuoc's support had embarrassed Grecco more than it had pleased him, he saw no way of discouraging such well-meaning assistance without offending the austere captain, so he had thanked him, being more careful to conceal his problems in the future. As a Refugee Advisor, Vince did not wish for the Vietnamese to feel any apprehension. He needed their trust and confidence. On the other hand, upsetting the Social Welfare Chief a bit wouldn't be such a bad idea. Surely Nguyen Chinh must have heard of Grecco's new found friend. Sometimes a little name dropping didn't hurt, he thought.

Major Ziegler's plan to eradicate corruption intrigued Grecco. He was surprised at how much the circumstances of the past year had changed him. When he heard that a District Chief, well known for his corruption, had fallen from a helicopter, Vince felt with a certain sense of morbid satisfaction that Major Ziegler's plan was being put into action, for the only other passengers in the chopper was a squad of Vietnamese Rangers. The pilot had complained that several of them had blocked his view, thus he was unable to see what had happened to the District Chief. He couldn't imagine how he could possibly have fallen from the aircraft. "He must have been drunk," the pilot concluded.

Nearly every day some province official was reported killed and never in the same way. Va Xiong, The Province Finance Chief, had pulled the pin from a hand grenade when he opened his desk drawer. A Deputy Sub-Sector Chief was ambushed less than fifty meters from his home. A Deputy District Chief struck a landmine with his motorcycle. A Battalion Commander drank a coke laced with finely ground slivers of glass. And always the Viet Cong were credited with the deaths. It was enhancing Charlie's popularity among the people.

"It's great the way the VC are cleaning up the corruption in the province," Grecco told Major Ziegler the next time he saw him at the mess hall. "It's becoming the cleanest province in the country."

"It's wrong," the Major said. "Those assassinations have made Charlie so fucking popular with the people."

"Why's it wrong?" Vince asked with a knowing leer. "Give credit where credit's due."

"Yea. Sure," Ziegler said suddenly springing up from the table and hurrying away. Grecco noticed that he had hardly touched the food on his tray. The Major has opened up a real can of worms, he figured. No telling where it might end?

Alden Wordsworth-Adams, Esq.

It was two months before Grecco got a reply from his report on conditions at Aggroville 12. One morning as he was leaving the office to meet with Mr. Chinh, the radio operator handed him a cable. It was very brief. It simply stated that an inspector would be there the following day to check conditions at the resettlement camp. It was not from CORDS, US AID, or the Ministry of Social Welfare. None of the places to which he'd submitted the report. The cable bore the seal of the U.S. Embassy. An embassy inspector? Was there such a thing? It sounded as though it might be a CIA spook, Grecco thought. But wasn't this a bit out of their line? However, tomorrow was quite out of the question. He'd made arrangements to accompany the Social Welfare Chief to Gia Lai Village. It would be the first time for Chinh to venture outside the province capital, and Vince was sure he was in earnest this time, for he had come to Grecco's quarters late the previous evening and asked for a helicopter. He was nervous; seemed under duress. He explained that the Prime Minister had ordered the Province Chief to see that the 1966 flood victims at Gia Lai be given their damage allotment immediately.

The flood had occurred two and a half years before. Long ago the money had been divided up among the Province officials and safely stashed away in anonymous Swiss bank accounts. If it hadn't been for a village councilman in Gia Lai whose cousin had recently been appointed IV Corps Commander of the Mekong Delta, the issue would not have been brought to the attention of the Prime Minister. And thus the Province Chief wouldn't have had to send his Social Welfare Chief there to mend wounds.

The Province Chief had to do a lot of hasty juggling to come up with the needed sum. The Finance Chief's bookkeepers worked late into the night manipulating figures about. Chinh was ordered to go to Gia Lai and personally distribute the money to the flood victims. The IV Corps Commander would no doubt be keeping the Prime Minister informed of how things were progressing.

Grecco was delighted. An order from the Province Chief had accomplished more than all the months he'd spent coaxing and cajoling the Social Welfare Chief. If things went well at Gia Lai as Vince was intent on making sure they would, Chinh might no longer be afraid to visit the resettlement camps. However, the message from the U.S. Embassy had complicated things considerably. Hadn't Vince also been trying for months to get help for the refugees at Aggroville 12? Now he'd finally got a response. How could he ignore it? It would be folly to allow the embassy official to go there alone. Captain Kheim would surely disguise things. Either take him to a different resettlement camp or send an advance party to see that the refugees were well subdued when the inspector arrived.

By breakfast the next morning, Grecco knew what he would have to do. Kalick would meet the U.S. Embassy official's plane and take him directly to the Province Senior Advisor's morning briefing. Greg would then introduce him to the Province Chief and give him a rundown on refugee conditions in the province with a special emphasis on Aggroville 12. By then Vince would have the Social Welfare Chief aboard a chopper and on his way to Gia Lai.

Unfortunately, the plan did not go well at the chopper pad. For one thing, Chinh thought that Grecco was joking. No matter how earnest he tried to appear, Chinh would not believe him.

"Yes, yes. Ha, ha. I know you Americans," Chinh said. "Everything is always a joke. That's your culture. Am I not right? Some do not like this trait of yours. Think it's childish. But I for one do. By and large, life is quite absurd, and so it is fitting and proper to treat it as such."

So when the helicopter began to rise, and Chinh saw Grecco standing on the landing pad waving farewell, he grew quite pale and looked as though he might jump.

That was not the only thing that dampened Chinh's departure. Vince had had trouble getting him aboard the aircraft. "Look,

The Idiot's Frightful Laughter

mister, we ain't got room for no dinks today," the door gunner shouted at Grecco above the roar of the engines.

"This is Mr. Chinh, the Province Social Welfare Chief," Grecco shouted back putting all the outraged indignation into his voice that he could muster.

"Oh Yea?" the gunner said looking skeptically at Chinh. He leaned over the pilot's backrest cupping his hands at the edge of the warrant officer's flight helmet. Grecco saw the pilot pick up a clipboard and run his finger down a list of names. Then he nodded to the gunner.

He's checking the manifest, Vince thought. The gunner returned to the doorway and motioned with a jerk of his thumb for Chinh to come aboard. At that moment, Grecco realized the mistake he'd made. Alone Chinh had little chance of getting a chopper back to Lang Son that evening. The chief would probably have to spend the night in Gia Lai, and Vince doubted if he'd sleep much. Probably lie awake all night, for the village was in a Viet Cong controlled area. There was a Popular Forces outpost in Gia Lai, but that was of little consolation. PF outposts were manned by local youth who worked in the rice paddies during the day and slept in an earthen fortification at night. It was an unwritten rule that if they left Charlie alone, he would leave them alone. Up until a year or so ago, most of the Viet Cong's weapons came from Popular Forces.

The odds were not in the Welfare Chief's favor, Grecco figured. He was a prize captive. Some of the villagers were sure to inform the VC. It would be easy to capture him. No trouble at all. Who would object? Certainly not the peasants. They'd either be pleased or totally indifferent.

On the other hand, if he got back, Grecco's situation would worsen, for Chinh would want nothing whatsoever to do with him. By now he's probably had his fill of joking Americans. Their humor has ceased to be funny, Vince reckoned.

When Grecco got to the CORDS compound, the Embassy Official was speaking with Kalick in his office. The first thing Vince noticed was the brightly polished attaché case in one hand and a small canvass traveling bag in the other. He noted that the man was very young and evidently Ivy League, Harvard possibly, a Dr. Kissinger protégé. He wore a charcoal gabardine suit and a slender black tie. His hair was permed resembling the bouffant which was then the rage with the affluent yippy set. Grecco got a whiff of aftershave lotion; the strong piney smell that professed to give one that manly sensual aura.

"Ah yes. You're Mr. Grecco, I presume?" he said with an affected sort of Back Bay Boston accent. "The one who wrote the report," he added pulling a copy from his attaché case. "I'm Alden Wordsworth-Adams. You received my cable, I presume?" He made it evident that he had no intention of shaking hands with such riffraff by shoving them into his coat pockets.

Grecco instantly hated the fop. He hated the faint smirk at the corner of his mouth, the tilt of his left eyebrow, the chilling flatness of his eyes; however, it was the voice that he hated most. It was so condescending, so bored. Vince didn't just hate him. It was more complex than that. He feared him; as though the youth had stripped him naked, saw his wasted life; all forty-two bleak useless years laid out one before the other face up; a loser who'd run as far as he could go, just ten miles from the Cambodian border, a fucking wop. That's what Back Bay Boston's finest was thinking, Grecco surmised.

"Do you mind?" Alden Wordsworth-Adams said opening his handbag and taking out a pair of freshly polished jungle boots. "Will it matter if I change here?" he asked turning to Kalick. He wanted to be sure he wasn't breaking protocol. Nothing mattered so much as that. Greg looked askance at Vince as if to say: "Where'd you dig up this creep?"

When the youth had finished lacing his boots, he put his oxfords in the handbag; then he removed his necktie, folded it in a handkerchief and placed it with the shoes.

Wordsworth-Adams had, what you might call, a head start in life. He was a member of the Eastern Establishment, a direct descendant of that rabble-rouser, Samuel Adams, a signer of the Declaration of Independence, and William Wordsworth, the greatest of England's Eighteenth-Century Romantic Poets. His lineage traced back to John Alden, who landed with the Pilgrims at Plymouth Rock in 1620. He was a national treasure.

Wordsworth-Adams had attended Groton, America's most elite prep school. It was there that connections were made which would serve one well later on. Groton's motto was: "To Serve Is to Rule." Its overt aim was to serve God, family, and state; however, its real intent was more subtle and insidious. It taught that there was a thing called privilege and by all means use it. Wordsworth-Adams graduated from Groton summa cum laude.

Although Boston's upper crust usually went to Harvard after Groton, Wordsworth-Adams decided that Yale might be somewhat more broadening. There he joined the Skull and Bones, the university's most prestigious club, where only those from the very best families were invited.

From Yale, the young aristocrat went to Harvard as a Junior Fellow. It was designed to spare the supremely talented the drudgery of struggling for a Ph.D. After all, anyone could get a doctorate, but few could be a Junior Fellow, the Harvard dons reasoned.

He entered the Foreign Service directly from grad school with expectations of becoming an ambassador. To begin with, he was quite willing to take some small country like Switzerland or the Netherlands; however, the Secretary of State explained the difficulty of getting Congress to confirm such a young man for an ambassadorial post no matter how small the country might be. He advised Wordsworth-Adams to spend a couple years in the field. Such experience was inimitable. Vietnam was a new frontier, a place to test one's mettle; a chance to earn one's spurs, so to speak. His rivals encouraged him. They hoped he might get wasted.

The Province Chief had known about Wordsworth-Adams' itinerary several days in advance and radioed Captain Khiem to be on the lookout for a VIP, so when he and Grecco stepped from the helicopter at Phong Tho, the District Chief had his entire detachment there to meet Wordsworth-Adams.

This time Captain Kheim had a Special Forces whaleboat armed with a machine gun. Throughout the trip to Aggroville 12, the District Chief was on his best behavior pointing out picturesque sights for Wordsworth-Adams to photograph – a fisherman casting a net, a peasant knee deep in mud trudging behind a lumbering carabao, a pair of ibis poking about with their long slender curved bills in the marsh, a boa constrictor skimming across the canal, a man carrying a snapping turtle tied to the end of a pole, a war-ravished Buddhist pagoda, naked children jumping from a pier into the murky water.

Grecco figured that Kheim had smoothed things over at Aggroville 12. The thought struck him the moment they'd disembarked at Phong Tho, and the closer they got to the resettlement camp, the more troubled he grew. The thought that this Ivy League nerd telling those at the embassy that Grecco was an alarmist was distressing, to say the least. He could imagine the fop passing the report off as sheer fantasy. However, there was one thing for sure. There was no way that the District Chief could get the commodities to the refugees. They had been sold on the black market long ago.

Throughout the trip, Wordsworth-Adams kept twisting about in his deckchair snapping pictures. A fucking tourist out on a lark, Grecco thought. The plight of a few thousand starving refugees wasn't of the remotest concern to him.

Grecco concluded that all was lost before he'd stepped ashore at Aggroville 12. Standing on the bank was a welcoming committee. It consisted of a dozen short plump men waving South Vietnam's red and yellow striped flags. They were very likely Catholic bureau chiefs from Phong Tho. Obviously, it was the first time that any of them had ever been to the village. And where were the refugees? They must be hiding in the marsh, Grecco reckoned scanning the reeds for any possible sign of them.

As Wordsworth-Adams stepped ashore, the welcoming committee crowded about him clasping their hands and bowing; telling him in sing-songy unison how honored they were with his visit. "They say that they are so happy to meet such an important person from the American Embassy," his interpreter said trying very hard to seem earnest.

The Idiot's Frightful Laughter

However, that was only the beginning of the charade. Captain Kheim had brought in a company of the CIA's smartly dressed Rural Development Cadre. They were posted at regular intervals along the route. The men were Saigon college boys and looked quite impressive in their neatly tailored black uniforms, wide-brim bush hats, and colorful shoulder insignias.

Bogus refugees clustered in the doorways of the huts. Their expressions were a mixture of fear and bewilderment. As Wordsworth-Adams passed, they applauded mechanically. Captain Khein had overdone it, Grecco thought. It was all too staged. Surely the fop would see through it. He was no idiot. But Vince had miscalculated. Kheim knew the American elite quite well. The more outlandish the circus, the more fervently it was embraced. Yes, by all indications, Wordsworth-Adams was a vain, callow imbecile; one of America's future leaders, ideal qualifications for a presidential candidate.

Captain Kheim stood in Grecco's path; his legs spread wide apart, his hands on his hips. He smiled sardonically at the Refugee Advisor.

"Where are the refugees?" Grecco demanded.

The District Chief bared his teeth and shook his head. "Ha, ha," he laughed mirthlessly. "Ha, ha ha."

Coung, the MAT team's interpreter at Phong Tho, had cautioned Grecco to be wary of Captain Kheim. "He hates you too much," he said.

Although the District Chief had refused to surrender his Swiss Bankbook, he had bitterly resented Colonel O'Hara's accusations. No one could call him a crook and get away with it. He would get even with the colonel. Just who did he think he was? Had he forgotten that he was a guest in this country? He had no authority over him. He was way out of line. Captain Kheim intended to address the matter to the commander of MACV when it was to his advantage to do so.

As for Grecco, Kheim would deal with him directly. He could not allow such a useless piece of shit to prey into his affairs. If he did not act decisively, others would feel free to follow suit. He would make no effort to disguise the execution. It would be done in broad view of everyone. No VC would get credit for killing him. It would be done in the classic French fashion. A coup de grace, a bullet fired at the base of the skull. If he resisted, Captain Kheim would backhand him across the face until he'd beaten him into submission, order him to kneel, bow his head, then the Captain would slowly pull the trigger blowing his brains out. Ha, ha, he thought, sweet retribution. Everyone would know that he had fired the fatal shot. He would be vindicated.

I am a scholar of American history, Captain Kheim thought. Such decisiveness is an old American tradition. Look how Aaron Burr restored his honor by brazenly shooting Alexander Hamilton in a duel. Was he made accountable for the killing? Certainly not. Burr was duty-bound just as the captain was to defend his honor. Grecco was as good as dead. Only the time of execution was to be set. However, the District Chief did not know that the Refugee Advisor's tenure was running out.

Grecco had more than just a premonition that his life was in danger. On the boat trip back, Captain Kheim had pointed his fingers pistol fashion to the back of his head. "Pow," he said bearing his teeth. Just in case, Vince got a 45 caliber M-3 grease gun from Kalick and slung it beneath his bush jacket. One should always be prepared for the inevitable, he reckoned.

Grecco got a peek at Wordsworth-Adams' notes when he sat beside him at dinner. They were full of quotes from Nguyen Van Cao, who'd passed himself off as the village chief. Actually, he was Phong Tho's, Deputy District Chief. "Cao's not the chief of this camp," Vince said pressing his finger on the youth's notes. "He doesn't even live here. He's the Deputy District Chief."

"Please Vincent," Wordsworth-Adams whined snapping the notebook closed and moving it to the other side. "This is confidential if you didn't know," he said giving Grecco an indulgent look.

"I'm cleared," Grecco said motioning as though to grab the notebook.

The Idiot's Frightful Laughter

"What level?" the fop asked sounding as though his mouth was thick with syrup.

"Super secret, Alden," Grecco said giving the youth a menacing look. Then picking up his bowl and chopsticks, he moved to another table. As he rose, he muttered "callow ass". He said it just loud enough so that Wordsworth-Adams could hear.

Captain Khein had done well on such a short notice, Grecco thought. The food was out of the ordinary for such a remote place. There was fish baked in tomato sauce, fried rice with shrimp, egg and Vietnamese salami, egg rolls and pork and chunks of bell pepper and large bottles of La Rue beer floating about in a tank filled with chunks of ice. A man with Khein's capabilities could make four-star general. There was no doubt about it, Vince reckoned. A ruthless power-mad tyrant of a general.

Wordsworth-Adams' briefing was the self-indulgent ravings of an imbecile, as far as Grecco was concerned. One who saw just what he wanted to see, nothing else. He began by telling Lang Song Province's Advisory Team of his inspection tours of resettlement camps near the DMZ in I Corps' Quang Tri Province. He spoke in graphic detail of malnutrition, starvation, disease, assassinations and the killed and wounded. He was most adept at painting a picture of despair and made no effort to hide the pleasure these descriptions gave him. Then the blow came like the stroke of a surgeon's scalpel. Aggroville 12 was in every way a model village, he said. It should be used as a showcase. Captain Kheim had done a splendid job, and Wordsworth-Adams would see to it that he got ample recognition. Then the youth looked questioningly at Grecco. "One of the problems was that too often advisors were not adequately trained for their positions," he said. "They had only their own environment as a point of reference. They supposed that the refugees should have the same standards of living as the advisor had in The States." His voice had a gentle troubled tone. The kind used for an unruly child. Grecco glanced at Kalick and saw the earnest look in his eyes. He was nodding his head in agreement.

Grecco felt himself grow hot inside. Blood rushed to his head and stung him blind. He stood up and glared at the pompous buffoon. Forcing the thickness from his throat, he blurted out: "You saw nothing! Nothing! You understand?" His voice was quivering. He was shaking with fury. "Kheim put on a four-ring circus for your benefit with the CIA's RD cadre and his Catholic cohorts and the big feast." He was shaking quite beyond control, and he saw that Wordsworth-Adams was taking careful note of it. "You were duped, man, duped."

The Back Bay Bostonian looked concerned. He turned to Kalick and nodded. It was a slow knowing sort of nod; then he turned back to Grecco. "I spoke with IV Corps Regional Refugee Director in Can Tho. A Mr. Simoni, I believe his name is? You know him of course?" He paused for confirmation. "He said that you were having difficulties relating with your counterpart." He gave Vince one of those condescending indulgent smiles. "Your problem is so obvious. You are much too impetuous. An advisor must have the most infinite patience. Wouldn't you agree, Greg?" he said turning back to Kalick.

Grecco took a deep breath and paused until he had things under control. He must be calm, he thought. He must not lose control again. He must have that cool condescending air. "I should laugh. Yes, laugh," he said. "This day has been such a mockery. At this very moment, Captain Kheim is very likely telling his pals what a fool he made of that imbecile from the embassy.

Wordsworth-Adams' condescending indulgent smile turned to one of sullen contempt. "Yes, Alden, I must agree with you," Grecco said. "You are right. Most certainly the District Chief did a splendid job. He is to be complimented. What he did in such short notice was masterful. I too was impressed. However, I am troubled. What had he done with the real refugees? Where were they? I couldn't find a single one. And all those other people posing as refugees, who were they? Several I recognized as clerks from the District office. Then much to my amazement, there was Mr. Nguyen Van Cao, Phong Tho District's Deputy Chief posing as the village chief. Quite a demotion, wouldn't you say, your eminence?"

The Idiot's Frightful Laughter

Seeing that Worthington-Adams was about to speak, Grecco held up his hand. "I must say though, Alden, you really got the royal treatment with all that bowing and flag-waving and chanting praise to such an esteemed personage as you. And then the CIA lent their Gestapo as bodyguards, and the Special Forces provided a whaler with a fifty-caliber machine gun mounted on the bow. Yes, let me repeat that this day has been a fantastic mockery, and you, Alden were the dupe." Kalick winked at Grecco. He was pleased with the Refugee Advisor's performance. He'd put the prig in his place.

Not waiting for Wordsworth-Adams to reply, Grecco wheeled about and stomped from the room. "The people of Phong Tho will not forget the illustrious Mr. Alden Wordsworth-Adams for a long time. It was such a marvelous charade," he said slamming the door on leaving.

Grecco climbed astride his motorcycle and kicked down hard on the starter. The manifold gave off a couple of ear-shattering blasts, and the bike roared out of the parking lot spraying gravel at the guard asleep at his post. He sped several miles north of town; spun about at the ruins of a Shell service station that a VC sapper squad had blown up several months before and headed back. As he passed the Social Welfare office, he thought of Chinh. He'd better check and see if he was still in Gia Lai. It was late, and the helicopters would be heading back to their base at Sa Dec soon.

A clerk at the office told Grecco that they'd had a driver at the chopper pad for the past couple hours waiting for Mr. Chinh. If he didn't make it within the next thirty minutes, he'd have to sweat it out at Gia Lai for the night, Grecco reckoned.

Major Gaspar was at the TOC when Grecco arrived. "Good evening, Major," he said waving as he walked past. The major looked through him as though he were invisible.

"Would you dispatch a chopper to Gia Lai to pick up the Social Welfare Chief," he told the Filipino radio operator. "He's evidently been forgotten."

"Nobody forgot him," the major broke in. "We don't have no choppers to make a special run for no gook."

"Gook!" Grecco exclaimed wheeling about and staring at the Latino with openmouthed wonder. He's the Province's Social Welfare Chief," he said with all the indignation he could muster.

I don't give a rat's ass if he's the fucking emperor of China," the Major said. "We ain't sending no chopper out to pick him up." His face had turned a bright red, and his fists were clenched so tight the knuckles turned white. He wasn't accustomed to being challenged.

"But he'll be killed for christsakes," Grecco said. "Gia Lai's in the heart of VC territory."

"So what?" Gaspar said. "He ain't worth a shit anyhow."

It was useless arguing with the major. He had to find Colonel O'Hara as quickly as possible, for the last helicopters would be leaving for Sa Dec in twenty minutes. "How about a spic, Gaspar? Is a spic worth saving?" he asked as he stomped out the door.

"What did you say?" the major shouted after him. "Come back here, and I'll stomp the living shit out of you, you smart ass fucking wop.

When it comes right down to it, we're all gooks, Grecco reckoned. Each and every one of us is a gook of some sort or other.

Colonel O'Hara was in the clubroom. He was leaning back in a rattan lounge chair. His left leg encased in a cast was stretched out before him. "The Social Welfare Chief is still in Gia Lai," Grecco blurted out breaking in on a conversation the Colonel was having with a young lieutenant.

"What the fuck am I supposed to do about it?" he said. He was annoyed with Grecco's abrupt intrusion.

"It's VC controlled. Charlie will either kill him or take him captive," Vince pleaded, his eyes wide with expectation.

"Let him stay there," O'Hara said regaining his composure and smirking good-naturedly at Grecco. "It'll do the mothafucker good. It's time he spent a little time in the field."

"But he'll be killed, and I'm responsible for him. I got his chopper and . . ."

"He ain't going to get killed," O'Hara broke in. "If all you're worried about is saving your fucking ass, I'll take the fucking blame." The colonel was growing annoyed again, and the young lieutenant was giving Grecco a steely look. "They got a PF platoon there. He'll have them on their toes all night. Make them earn their pay for a change."

Grecco was suddenly aware that leaving Chinh at Chai Lai had been planned. It was their way of getting even with him for being such a wimp. "But don't you see? This'll destroy all the work I've done for the past three months," Vince pleaded.

"Balls!" O'Hara shouted. Everyone in the clubhouse stopped talking and turned to look at the colonel. "Balls," he repeated. Then turning to the lieutenant he said: "These fucking civilians think they know more about how to run this war than we do."

Grecco sensed that O'Hara was quite enjoying himself. He was testing this civilian's fighting spirit; and as for saving Chinh, that was quite out of the question.

Colonel O'Hara broke into a wide-mouthed sardonic grin. "Sit down for christsakes and take it easy." Grecco slumped into a lounge chair facing him. It was all so absurd, he thought. Here he was. The only American in the province who didn't believe in any part of this mess that corporate controlled politicians had started; and yet he was the only one who was making a serious effort to see the system work, and then being knocked down for it. It was madness, utter madness. Memories of a mental institution where he'd worked nights while attending college came back to him. He remembered the inane laughter of an idiot. The haunting, mirthless shrieking cries that went on and on; an idiot's frightful laughter. That's what it was. That's the feeling he had when he gazed at the Colonel; that smug egomaniac. Yes, of course, it was the same sort of feeling. The wide-mouth sardonic smile, the loud bellowing laughter, the arrogant belligerent threats. Yes, he was the inane laughter of the mindless idiot; the very personification of this senseless slaughter. Yes, yes, of course, Grecco thought. It was the idiot's frightful laughter. That was it.

"Bring this fucking civilian a drink," O'Hara shouted to the bartender. "What'll it be Vince?" he asked. He was smiling good-naturedly at the befuddled Refugee Advisor. I like this sonofabitch, the colonel thought. He's different. He's not afraid to get out in the field and take his chances with Charlie. He tries. Godamnit that's something. That's more than the other mothafucking civilians do.

"Vodka and orange," Grecco murmured. He felt burned out. What a day. What a hell of a day. He didn't even want to think about it. Not for now anyway.

"Bring him a screwdriver," O'Hara yelled snapping his fingers. "That's a fucking woman's drink," he said turning to Vince. The lieutenant laughed. He no longer looked belligerent, quite amiable as a matter of fact, Grecco noticed.

It was two days before a helicopter went to Gia Lai. Grecco felt an enormous relief when he saw Chinh step from the helicopter at the Lang Son chopper pad that evening. However, he didn't walk out to greet him. He knew that the Social Welfare Chief wouldn't be pleased to see him, not now, nor tomorrow, nor a month from now. But what did it matter? He'd be out of a job soon, and someone else would be the refugee advisor for Than Uyen Province, and the humbug would go on and on until every last American had left. Yet Grecco knew that it mattered. It mattered tremendously.

Things always seemed to end like this for him. Everything he'd ever done. Every job he'd ever had invariably ended the same. He had always put everything he had into whatever he did, and what had it got him? Enemies. Yes, enemies. If he had not been so eager, so ambitious. Had not pushed so hard, he'd have been more successful. It was funny, he thought. It was a fucking paradox because what he was striving for so earnestly was recognition. Even after he realized this, he knew that it wouldn't matter. Nothing would matter. Nothing would ever change. He could not change. He'd continue to be as he'd always been. It was not possible to change after all these years. The pattern was too deeply ingrained in his psyche. He would go on knocking himself out, for a recognition that he knew he had no chance of ever getting. Instead, he'd arouse negative impulses like jealousy and distrust. Maladjustment, that's what the social psychologist would call it, an inability to adjust, fit in, conform. Who had he to blame? Kheim?

Simoni? Barban? Bledsoe? Eisenschimi? Hadn't there always been such people? They were the consequence, not the problem. One had to be more circumspect. He must realize that generally speaking others were not so idealistic, especially those who chose to come to Vietnam and serve the military-industrial complex. He was quite out of his element. The idealist was back in The States protesting the war, burning draft cards, going to jail, not promoting it.

Why hadn't he been prepared for this sort of world? Why hadn't his parents, his teachers, society prepared him for it? Why had they always insisted that he reach for the unattainable? Why hadn't they told him to stay in step? Keep pace. Don't be a loser. However, on the other hand, don't win either. Tie. That was the thing to do. That took skill, timing, and calculation. It was safe. It meant success. If he'd been taught that, then he'd have it made. Have all the recognition, appreciation, respect he could handle. Now it was all too late for that. But wasn't there somewhere in this world where a sprinter was needed? Weren't the Viet Cong that sort of people? Nothing was holding them back.

The Late Night Massacre

The first time Grecco saw one of his strategic hamlets razed to the ground by artillery fire, he was devastated. It wasn't the first time that he had seen mass slaughter. As a teenage Marine on Iwo Jima, he'd seen plenty of carnage. During the mop-up, the Japs had staged a *bonsai* attack. Wave after wave of wild screaming zealots lead by sword welding officers had hurled themselves at him. Hundreds of bodies piled one on top of the other before his machine gun. However, they were soldiers intent on dying. It was their sacred duty to die in battle for their emperor whom they worshipped as a living god. This situation was different. These were innocent peasants – women and children and the elderly – blown to pieces for no plausible reason whatsoever. Bits of bodies lay scattered about. It was horrifying.

These people were not strangers to Grecco. They were good honest farmers whom he had spent countless hours trying his best to put their lives back together. Gradually they had come to trust him. He was a father figure. They would share their problems with him. There were so many. An Arvin had stolen one's carabao. Agent Orange, a deadly dioxin, had damaged their rice crop. A helicopter door gunner had shot a village elder for sport. A teenager had been mistaken for a Viet Cong and imprisoned and tortured. A young girl had been gang-raped by a squad of U.S. Marines. A tank had run over a Lambretta killing the driver and his passengers. These problems had bonded him to them, for sometimes he could get indemnities for them. Never had he felt so close to others. Never had he struggled so ardently to protect a people. They were so strong and yet so vulnerable. He was really all they had. They were at the mercy of everyone. Both the Viet Cong and the Americans demanded their unwavering support. There was no escape. They lost no matter what they did. Pulling back some palm font, Grecco found the head of an infant. The day before, he had held the child in his arms. Vince wept. He didn't care who saw the tears. He had loved these people as a father loves his children. Now they had vanished in an instant, blown into oblivion, and for what? What had they done to deserve such a horrid fate?

Late one night a barrage of artillery shells had struck the village without warning. That evening a howitzer had been airlifted to a nearby Special Forces A-camp. It had been reported that a division of NVA troops was moving through the area. Having no idea where the troops might be, the soldiers had fired at random into the countryside. As usual, no enemy soldiers had been killed. It would have been a miracle if they had. Only the local residents were killed, murdered in their sleep, blown to bits by 175mm missiles.

The resettlement camp had been Grecco's first assignment at Yen Chau Province. Earning their trust had not been easy. When he first met with them at the relocation camp, they were angry and rightly so. American troops and their Vietnamese puppets had destroyed their village burning their homes and killing their livestock. Bulldozers had transformed the ancient site into a barren lot. Nothing was left. Like jackal, the Arvin had come in the wake of the Americans taking whatever they had a use for. The peasants had been loaded onto trucks and driven to a campsite surrounded by a barbwire fence. Civil Defense guards with fifty caliber machine guns peered down at them from their towers.

They would rotate their gun about threateningly pointing them menacingly at their captives. The peasants were frightened. They regarded these lackeys as nothing more than ruthless cutthroats. The people's fear congealed into a bitter hate for foreign troops that occupied their country. What had they ever done to these pink-faced, long-nosed barbarians? Why were they treated as common criminals? In time Grecco got the Province Senior Advisor to have the barbwire fence and the guard towers removed. Although they must walk for miles each day, they were allowed to farm their rice paddies. All this Vince had done, and they appreciated it.

Concerning the massacre, Grecco had done the only thing he could do. He'd written a report detailing the atrocity and sent it to the Refugee Director, a faceless bureaucrat in Saigon. There was no reply. There never was. However, the report had been passed on to Colonel Wild Bill O'Hara, the Province Senior Advisor and commander of Special Forces camps scattered throughout the province. He was mad. Who'd that goddamn civilian think he was? He had a good mind to kill the mothafucker.

"Your ass is mud," the adjutant said. "The colonel's going to rip your ass wide open." Grecco couldn't bear to look at Major Gaspar's fat mottled mug. It reminded him of one of the pigs in George Orwell's *Animal Farm*. Which one was it? Yes, of course, Napoleon. Yes, that was the one. The fascist pig, Vince thought. What an excellent caricature.

In a minute or so Grecco would be standing ramrod straight before Colonel O'Hara. "Yes Sir. No Sir. Very well Sir" he'd be saying. One didn't mess with Wild Bill, not if he wanted to live. He'd take him on a little joyride on his private helicopter and take pleasure in personally booting him out the door over the vast Sea of Reeds. No one would ever find his body buried deep in the thick alluvial mud. Accidents do happen, don't they? The Colonel was one mean sonofabitch.

Reporting to The Province Senior Advisor wasn't protocol. It just wasn't done, Grecco thought. Greg Kalick, The Deputy Senior Advisor, was his boss. That's whom Vince was supposed to report to, not this Nazi fucker. However, the Colonel was king. He made the rules to suit himself. He'd dismissed his deputy as inconsequential. He didn't care if Kalick had been a World War II fighter pilot who'd been awarded the Silver Star for valor. He was still a fucked up civilian, and Wild Bill had no use for civilians no matter who they were. They were the reason, for all that had gone wrong with the war. Well, Grecco could see some truth in that. The corporate controlled politicians were the ones that started this mess, and there was no end in sight. Things were getting worse by the day. Nevertheless, he was glad that O'Hara and his ilk weren't running the show. The first thing they'd do was drop a nuclear

The Idiot's Frightful Laughter

explosive on Hanoi. But Kalick? Why Kalick? He and the colonel shared the same fascination for combat. They were like drug addicts. They were never happier than when they were in the thick of battle. However, that made no difference. As far as Colonel O'Hara was concerned, Greg was a birdbrain civilian, and civilians were an inferior species.

Colonel O'Hara was seated at a large metal desk. He was leaning back in a swivel chair, his boots propped at the corner of the desk. As always, he was wearing his Green Beret set jauntily at an angle just above the right eye. He had the grimace of a puma just before it struck. "At ease, Grecco. Who're you trying to fool?" he said dropping his boots to the floor with a thud and leaning forward on his desk. "You ain't no soldier."

"Yes Sir," Grecco said. He knew that the less he said the better.

"Cut the bullshit, Vince, or I'll stomp the living shit out of you." Wild Bill stared menacingly at him forcing Grecco to drop his gaze. "You think I can't?"

"No Sir," Grecco said struggling to keep his voice under control.

"You bet your fucking ass I can, he said standing and walking up to Grecco until they were just inches apart. "I'll twist your mothafucking head off and jam it up your ass." Then he backed off a couple feet and looked appraisingly at his adversary. "What are you sweating for? Ain't scared, are you?"

"No Sir," Grecco said. In a fair fight, he figured that he could easily whip the old bastard. O'Hara must be well past fifty; a good ten years older than he, but fairness wasn't part of Wild Bill's vocabulary. The slightest provocation and he'd whip out his forty-five and put a bullet between Vince's eyes. Anything goes in war. That's how Wild Bill saw it.

"No Sir," O'Hara said mockingly. "You sure as fuck better be," he added stepping back behind his desk. "What's the meaning of this bullshit?" he said waving a sheet of paper at him. "You tired of living, asshole?"

Grecco figured it was best to remain silent. The question was rhetorical. It didn't warrant an answer. Colonel O'Hara's eyes were red. It was obvious that he wanted blood. The situation was growing more perilous by the moment. Vince felt totally helpless. The least movement could trigger a disaster.

"Artillery shells struck the An Son Resettlement Camp Wednesday night killing 137 refugees. The shells were fired from a nearby Special Forces Camp. They were reported to have been fired at random into the countryside intent on hitting suspected enemy troops infiltrating the area," O'Hara read in a histrionic tone. "Fuck you, Vince," he said slamming his fist down hard on the metal desk. The bang caused Grecco to jump. "You cocksucker," the colonel shouted saliva spewing from his lips. Grecco's eyes were riveted on O'Hara's right hand that gripped the handle of a forty-five caliber pistol strapped to his hip. His thumb unsnapped the flap, and the weapon slid a couple inches from its holster. "You chickenshit sonofabitch. Do you have any idea what this would do to my career if it got into the wrong fucking hands?" he demanded. "I'd be fucked, royally fucked."

He picked the report back up and began to read some more; however, his hands were trembling so badly that he had to set it back on the desk. Leaning over, he read: "It is recommended that an investigation be conducted by a team of independent investigators, and that appropriate action be taken to correct this atrocity, and that those found responsible be court-martialed, as an example for others." O'Hare remained crouched over the report for several seconds until he had regained his composure. Pulling open a drawer to his left, he withdrew a K-bar, a military type hunting knife. Sliding the blade from its sheath, he made a slashing motion as though to slit his neck. "I ought to cut your mothafucking throat," he said. He was smiling, but there was no sign of mirth in his eyes. It was the grimace of a warrior preparing for the attack.

Then O'Hara sat back down and folded his hands behind his head. "Relax joker," he said. "I ought to nail your ass to the wall, but I'll let it pass this time." He smiled. It was the broad affable kind of grin that a boy shows after winning a fist fight. The shake-and-make-up sort of smile. "You're an ex-jarhead," he said. "You've seen some combat. You're not one of these chickenshit hearts-and-

The Idiot's Frightful Laughter

minds assholes, are you? He paused for a moment, as though waiting for some sort of acknowledgment. "What do you think we are doing here, playing ring-around-the-rosy?"

"You're not going to win the war by slaughtering innocent civilians, Sir," Grecco said. "You're only generating hate. The peasants are turning to the Viet Cong as the lesser of two evils."

"Har, har, har," O'Hara boomed. "Lesser of two evils. Win their hearts and minds. Love the mothafucking gooks. Is that it, Vince? Har, har, har." The colonel's fury had passed. He was in a jovial mood. "Grab them by the balls and their hearts and minds will follow. That's my philosophy. They're all fucking commies. Every last one of them."

"I beg to differ, Sir," Grecco said. Struggling to keep his anger under control, he added: "Have you ever been at the main gate of the Twenty-fifth Division's camp at eight in the morning, Sir? Hundreds of peasant women and some elderly men are lined up at the gate. The guards don't bother to search them. They trust them. Never once have they ever caused any trouble. They cook the GI's meal, clean his hooch, wash his clothes, and do whatever else he may want at the moment. Then in the night, these same dutiful peasants are slaughtered in their sleep." Grecco could see that Colonel O'Hara was no longer smiling. There was an expression of utter disdain on his face.

"Listen up, Gyrene," O'Hara said jumping to his feet and thrusting a finger at him. "Those fucking gooks know where their bread is buttered. They're not stupid. They know when they've got a good thing going. Who do you think gets that food that they carry home every evening? I'll tell you who get it. Charlie gets it. You don't think so, eh? Well, I know so. I saw it. VC had our grub in their packs. How do you think they got it, heh? From then fucking gooks that you are so crazy about. That's who."

He doesn't get it. He just doesn't get it. You simply can't reason with such a numbskull, Grecco thought. "Let's look at this from a strictly military point of view, Sir," he said. "Killing innocent civilians is counterproductive. Sure, some of them may be supporting Charlie. They're afraid not to. What alternative do they have? Destroying their ancestral homes and moving them into penal colonies is only compounding the problem. You're just driving them into the arms of the VC. Above all else, they want out of the stockades. They want to go home and start rebuilding their lives from scratch, reclaiming their ancestral graves, planting rice. That's their idea of freedom, and nothing matters more than that to them. That's what they want, and Charlie is offering them that choice. Sure, he may be lying, but he's their only hope, and after all, he is Vietnamese."

"Har, har, har," O'Hara boomed. "You're as full of shit as a Christmas goose, Vince, but goddamn it, I like you. You're the only goddamn civilian in the province that's worth a good goddamn," the colonel said. He was smiling from ear to ear. "I like your spunk. I've seen you a number of times out there in the rice paddies up to your ass in shit. I can't figure it out. How in fuck do you keep your ass from being blow off?"

"It's the peasants, or the gooks, as you call them, Sir," Grecco said. 'They protect me. They warn me of dangers. Where not to step. Where a sniper is. That sort of thing. They're wonderful people. They'd lay down their lives for me."

"I'll be frank with you, Vince. I admire the little bastards," O'Hara said. He looked genuinely sincere. "I admire their courage. They're the best. The best fucking fighters in the world, bar none. I'd give my right nut to lead a platoon of VC guerrillas; I would, Vince. I sure as fuck would. Look at all these tanks and planes and helicopters we've got. They don't mean shit, Vince. Charlie takes the powder from one of our five-hundred-pound duds and blows the living shit out of us." O'Hara pointed at the floor. "Right now, Charlie's down there digging a whole fucking city – hospitals, armories, radio rooms, printing presses. You name it, he's got it. He's going to kick our ass, Vince, and you know why? Because we don't have his guts. He'll die for what he believes in. Did you ever see those piss ant Arvin torture a VC? Well, I have. I considered myself privileged. Your fucking rights I did, and that VC knew it too. It was like we were comrades; that we shared a mutual contempt for the fucking shit for brains Arvin. The VC didn't so

The Idiot's Frightful Laughter

much as make a whimper, not one fucking whimper. He died like a fucking man, Vince. Not a sound. Goddamn it, Vince, I respect that kind of trooper. They put us to shame."

O'Hara walked around from behind his desk and put a hand on Grecco's shoulder. "I'm a soldier, Vince. Kill or be killed; that's my motto. That's where we differ, Vince. You're busting your ass to save lives, and I'm trying my goddamnest to kill every mothafucking sonofabitch that gets in my way." He walked back behind his desk and sat down. "That's what I'm paid for. I wouldn't shit you, Vince. I like my job. I wouldn't trade it for the world. Sure, innocent people get killed. I won't deny that. Passions run high in combat. My men are like soldiers anywhere in the world. They get a taste for blood. Like the predatory animal that they are, they love to kill. You know that, Vince. You were a Marine. Killing is what Marines do well. That's what's being a Marine is all about. It's the same with any combatant. Why do you think guys kill deer? For the meat? Fuck no. It's the thrill of hunting it down and killing it. It gives the hunter a burst of adrenaline. It's an animal instinct. It's in the genes, Vince. Goes back to prehistoric man."

True, Grecco thought. Killing was a primitive instinct. The survival of the fittest. He thought of his platoon sergeant. He was as cold-blooded as they came. Sergeant Palmer had told the men at the slop chute prior to the invasion, "I'm going to kill that useless sonofabitch." He was referring to Lieutenant Finklestein, their platoon leader. Everyone knew that it wasn't idle chatter. The sergeant meant what he said. It was just after sundown of D-day that he pressed his forty-five caliber pistol at the base of the platoon leader's skull and blew his head apart. No one objected. They felt that it was for the best. Lieutenant Finklestein was a fuck up. He'd have got them all killed. Grecco had thought of that many times. There was no getting around it. It was first-degree murder. It explained why so many second lieutenants got killed. The ratio was way out of proportion to that of others. But that's war, Grecco thought. What had that to do with innocent women and children who wanted nothing to do with the war?

"I know what you're thinking, Vince," O'Hara said. "Why in the fuck are we fucking with these poor fucking peasants? That's it, isn't it? He adjusted his beret so that it set just above the left eye. He looked ridiculous, Grecco thought. Like a meaner-than-shit boy scout leader, a bulldog with a beanie.

"Well, I ain't lifting a finger to stop them. Not one finger," he said shaking his index finger about. "And you know why? I'll tell you why. Because I don't want any of my troops to feel restrained. Combat troops should never feel restrained. They've got to act on impulse no matter what the consequences may be. It's a fight for survival out there in the jungle. He who hesitates is dead. You know that, Vince. You goddamn gyrene."

Walking back to his quarters, Grecco wanted to cry. In some cultures, men felt free to cry. It was an outlet for such things as rage and impotence. In Greece men cried for all sorts of things. It was great therapy. But in America, men did not have that luxury. They got drunk and had fist fights. Yes, some beat up their wives. That was their way of working off their frustrations, and as far as Grecco was concerned, it was not a satisfactory alternative. Not by a long shot.

Like a Child with a Toy

Grecco was surprised that Greg Kalick would get involved with Co Hi even in the most casual manner. She was Colonel O'Hara's girl. Everyone knew that. Wild Bill made no effort to conceal it. Officially she was an interpreter for the staff at the Special Forces compound, but she never did any interpreting. She did nothing whatsoever for anyone but O'Hara. She was twenty-three, had a slender, shapely figure and was very cute and provocative. Her baseball cap and camouflage fatigues didn't lessen her sex appeal in the least. The garb only made her more desirable.

The Colonel was insanely jealous of her and was quite frank about it. Any soldier who showed her the mildest sort of attention was dressed down for it. Grecco recalled the time Captain Burk aroused O'Hara's wrath. He like everyone else knew how possessive the Colonel was; however, he had not thought that buying Co Hi a beer would be interpreted as anything other than a gesture of politeness. Later O'Hara cornered the captain behind the bunkhouse. "Look, Captain," he said jabbing a finger at Burk's chest. "I want to make it clear here and now. Co Hi is my goddamn girl. If she wants a beer, I buy it. Is that clear?"

When Captain Burke told Grecco of the incident, he seemed more disillusioned than angry. Life was much more tolerable for an officer if he admired his commander. "The Colonel is like a child with a toy," Captain Burke said, "so infantile." The captain wouldn't have dared say that to any of the troops.

Kalick explained to Grecco one evening that Co Hi wanted to leave the military advisory corps and work for Cords, or more specifically for Kalick. Co Thiet would be leaving soon, and he'd need a secretary. Co Hi explained that O'Hara was too possessive. His jealousy was so unbearable. She wanted to work in a freer, more relaxed atmosphere. Kalick had taken the bait. The trap was set. Some people never learn, Grecco thought.

Greg agreed to hire her provided she got a release from the military, but more specifically from Colonel O'Hara. Obviously, it was only a trick to arouse Wild Bill's ire, Grecco reckoned. She might feel as though she was losing control of him. Why was it that Kalick couldn't see through her scheme? Greg was O'Hara's deputy. The Colonel would literally pulverize him if he suspected for an instant that his Deputy Senior Advisor was trying to lure Co Hi away, or simply carrying on a casual flirtation.

Kalick informed Vince that Co Hi would be over that night. O'Hara was attending a conference at MACV in Saigon. Greg wanted Grecco and Co Thiet to accompany them to a restaurant in town not frequented by Americans, especially military.

Co Thiet, rather reluctantly, consented to go once Grecco was able to convince her that it was strictly business. She was due to join Rufus Burns at his new location the following week and felt guilty at leaving Kalick on such short notice. Vince explained that Co Hi was considered as likely replacement. Co Thiet could explain to her just what the job involved.

Grecco suggested a restaurant that was nothing more than a roof made of bent and battered sheets of corrugated tin. The holes had been patched with flattened soft drink and beer cans. Its sides were covered with pieces of chicken wire to ward off grenades. It was located alongside a canal at the outskirts of town. The channel was nothing more than an open sewer, causing a pungent stench to hang in the moist tropic air. The place was frequented by a noisy crowd of drunken Arvin who littered the floor with scraps of food. Large fat rats scurried about beneath the tables competing with a couple of mangy dogs for the leftovers. The only time Americans ever went there was when they were invited by their Vietnamese counterparts.

As was usually the case, the joint was quite crowded. Avin sat at two long tables that protruded outside to the edge of the canal. They were loud and boisterous, and from the look on the manager's face, Grecco figured that a fight might break out at any moment. If

The Idiot's Frightful Laughter

someone tossed a grenade at them, Vince saw that there was nowhere to take shelter; so he sat facing the soldiers ready to toss the missiles out into the canal if one came his way. He knew that he would have to move quickly, for there were only six seconds from the time the pin was pulled to when it detonated.

Soon the Arvin became very quiet. They glared at them. There were angry murmurs, and Grecco caught a few derogatory remarks directed at the women. He grew tense feeling sure that they were in for trouble. Within a few minutes, the Arvin left the joint. Several stood about Kalick's jeep at the edge of the canal.

Vince ordered for them. He enjoyed showing off his Vietnamese; even though it was mediocre, to say the least, causing the two women to laugh. "Oh your Vietnamese is number one," Co Hi said mockingly. "Maybe you take my job?"

"All we have left is rabbit," the waiter said.

Grecco had thought it strange, for he had never seen any rabbit in the delta or anywhere else for that matter. True, quite recently Burns had introduced some from Taiwan, but they wouldn't be ready for the market for another six months. They were just babies. However, he saw that the bones were very small, and thought that they may be Burn's rabbits after all. The meat was very tender and tasty, so he had a second serving. He noticed that Kalick had not touched his. He looked about at the others. The women were nonplus; however, a faint smile flickered at the corners of Co Hi's lips. Why were they all watching him so intently, he wondered? "What is this?" he asked pointing to his plate.

"Rat," Kalick said. "Didn't you know?"

"Sure," he said trying to look blasé. He glanced at a fat sleek rat beneath an adjacent table. It had reared up on its haunches. Holding its front paws out before it, the rodent watched him anxiously; as though it was begging. Grecco looked back at his plate. This was different, he assured himself probing it with a chopstick. It's paddy rat, lives on rice and other seed and such. The Cajun in the Louisiana bayou would probably refer to it as muskrat, a delicacy in that part of America. It's clean, he told himself. "Of course I know what it is," he said. "Just wondering if you did,

Greg." However, he could see that they knew he was lying. The women were smiling at him. Yes, he thought, how could he be sure that it was paddy rat?

Co Thiet remained silent throughout the meal, appearing to be quite absorbed with her meal. Vince had never seen one eat so daintily. Her chopsticks moved rhythmically from bowl to mouth with slow deliberate motions lifting small morsels of food so tiny they could hardly be tasted. It was her way of telling everyone that she was a lady and not to believe what the soldiers had said. She was refined and cultured; the daughter of a Province Chief. That was Vince assumption. She reminded him of the geisha girls he'd seen at tea houses in Kyoto at the end of World War II.

On the other hand, Co Hi had grown quite oblivious to such insults. For the past several years, she had frequently endured their coarse remarks and had grown to despise Vietnamese men, seeing them as another species, quite different from herself. She shared the GI's contempt for the Arvin. She could do this, Grecco thought, for the Americans had accepted her, treating her as though she were Caucasian. By behaving so, she soon came to believe it. She was the Vietnamese version of William Faulkner's Joe Christmas.

There was nothing dainty about Co Hi. She tipped her bowl to her lips and scooped the food into her mouth with her chopsticks talking to Kalick as she ate. She was angry with the military, she said. Soldiers were so rude and coarse; always talking bad and making passes at her. She was tired of having them pinch her butt every time the Colonel's back was turned. She liked civilians. They talked nice and had good manners. They knew how to behave with a lady.

My god, Grecco thought, the bullshit's really getting deep. Just how much can Kalick take? It appeared as though he was swallowing the bait hook, line, and sinker; the poor sonofabitch. Vince thought of Grant Olson's mother. She was so contemptuous of men. "They're like little boys," she'd say. "You've got to watch them all the time, or another woman will come along and lead them away." Well, Kalick was a perfect example. Co Hi had him right in the palm of her hand. He was so pliable, so easy to seduce. She was leading him to the slaughter.

Such an obvious ploy, Vince thought. It was the old bid for power; getting the two most influential Americans in the province to fight over her. Why was Greg letting himself be drawn into such an obvious trap? She didn't want to leave O'Hara; and as for being pinched on the butt, that was a sign of status. It meant being attractive, desirable, something of worth. It was a kind of power. Whenever a GI made a pass at her, he put his career on the line; he took the chance of getting a poor performance evaluation or a demotion or possibly both. All she had to do was hint about it to Wild Bill, and the guy was finished, major or private, it made no difference. Now she was out for bigger game; the biggest trophy in the province; but then what if she made a play for a general, O'Hara's commanding officer? What would happen then? Then it would be the Colonel whose neck was on the block. It would be his career that was at stake. Given the chance, Co Hi would take it. Vince was sure of that. She was too addicted to power to pass up the Grand Prix.

When they left the restaurant, a half dozen Arvin moved some distance from Kalick's jeep. Grecco noted that the soldiers were watching them quite intently, so he dropped back a bit to see what they might be up to. "Shit," Kalick said looking accusingly at the Arvin. The seats were covered with black greasy mud from the canal. The smell was horrible.

Vince felt himself relax. Thank God it was only mud, he thought. This was a warning. Next time it might be much worse; a grenade with a trip wire fastened to the steering column.

Greg found a stick and a rusty tin can and scraped the mud from the seats. Then he rubbed them with handfuls of straw. The manager handed him a damp cloth. After scrubbing the upholstery for some time, he washed the cloth in a large clay jar at the rear of the kitchen and handed it back to the proprietor. In the meantime, the Arvin had ambled closer to see how the prank was being taken. They may want a showdown, Grecco thought and cautioned the others to be careful and not rile them. The Arvin were armed.

The incident seemed to have pleased Kalick. It had given him the opportunity to prove that he was a gentleman and knew how to look after a lady. Vince was amused. Greg had lost all sense of reason. Co Hi could ensnare him any time she chose to. The next day, Grecco gave Kalick a knowing wink. "Be careful," he warned. "You're playing with dynamite."

Colonel O'Hara didn't waste any time. The day he got back, he cornered Kalick at the club. "So you want Co Hi?" he said. Greg was caught quite off guard. Before he could explain, Wild Bill said: "Well, you ain't getting her," and walked off.

A few weeks later, Vince had a look at Greg's performance evaluation. O'Hara had rated him as totally incompetent in every area of endeavor. He hadn't a single redeeming trait. Grecco was impressed with how well Kalick seemed to take the rebuke, and what was even more surprising was that he held no resentment for Co Hi. "Power corrupts," Greg said.

"Yes, totally," Grecco replied. Did Kalick realize just how apropos his remark was? He doubted it.

That Déjà Vu Feeling

The increased pressure for Grecco to visit Aggroville 12 before his departure made it all too evident to him of just how determined Captain Kheim was to settle the score. On two separate occasions, the District Chief had come to Lang Son in search of him. Khein had explained to both O'Hara and Kalick that Grecco's presence was of the utmost importance.

"I wouldn't trust that mothafucker," Colonel O'Hara said. "He's got a hardon for you because of that Swiss Bank Book."

However, Kalick accused Grecco of hyperbole. "You're overreacting, Vince. Why would he want to harm you? Don't let yourself get carried away. Captain Kheim's a good guy. He's one of us. Loves America. Remember what that embassy guy said?" Grecco wasn't sure who was worse, a sinister, selfish Prima Donna like Barban or a numskull like Kalick. They were both dangerous.

There was one site that Grecco hadn't visited. The resettlement camp was along one of the Mekong River's major tributaries near the Cambodian border. It would give Vince the excuse he needed. Major Boyd Hargreaves, the MAT team's commander, had been after him to inspect the camp. He was proud of the accomplishments the team had achieved and was anxious for recognition. Grecco wanted to keep the trip a secret. It wasn't all that far from Phong Tho. Captain Kheim's boys could slip up on him through the Sea of Reeds whenever it suited them.

Colonel O'Hara wasn't happy with Major Hargreaves. He'd threatened the major with a poor performance rating if he didn't shape up. In spite of the colonel's pressure for him to kill more Viet Cong, Hargreaves's "body count" remained the lowest in the province. He simply was not a combatant. He'd always worked behind a desk. He'd transferred to an advisory position, because promotions came more quickly in the field, and he was afraid he wouldn't make colonel before he retired. However, he soon saw his mistake, for he was unsuited for anything remotely connected with combat. However, he did have a knack for civic action programs and had thrown all his effort into community welfare programs.

Grecco was impressed with how the major had integrated the refugees into the nearby community making them a viable part of the society. Hargreaves was especially proud of the schools. He had assigned each trooper to a school with a list of things he wanted developed. Vince was especially interested in the ingenuity of many of the training aids, and how modern and comfortable the classrooms looked.

The major beamed with pleasure when Grecco told him that his projects were by far the best in the province, but he knew that O'Hara wouldn't care in the least. Killing, that was all that mattered to Wild Bill. "Fuck the hearts and minds shit. Grab them by the balls. That's how to get their hearts and minds," he told Major Hargreaves.

However, what truly amazed Grecco was how gracious the team lived. Nothing in Vietnam could have prepared him for such refinement, especially at such a remote outpost.

The outpost was on the Tien Giang River, a major tributary of the mighty Mekong River. Surrounding their quarters was a carefully landscaped flower garden. They'd hired a peasant to keep it trimmed and weeded. At the center was a fountain. The water sprayed from a ceramic urn and splashed onto two stone swans painted to resemble flamingoes. The team had removed them from the yard of an abandoned French colonial mansion several kilometers upstream.

Grecco was surprised at how cool they'd made their quarters. The walls had been removed and replaced with screen. The eaves were extended to keep the rain from blowing in. In case of a storm, canvass curtains could be unrolled about the building within a matter of minutes. Vince thought of how alarmed Kalick would have been, for there was no barricade of any kind. They were sitting ducks, so to speak.

The Idiot's Frightful Laughter

Those who'd been there told Grecco that he'd like the food. It was as good as you'd find in New York's best restaurant. Well, he couldn't vouch for that, but it was the best he'd had in Vietnam. The team had the good fortune of having two very excellent cooks. One had once been a chef at a five-star hotel in San Francisco. The other's father owned a chain of restaurants in the Chicago suburbs. They took turns competing with one another working alternate days throughout the week, and then together for the big feast on Sunday.

When Grecco saw the table set for Sunday dinner, a lump formed in his throat, and his eyes misted over. How long had it been since he'd seen a linen tablecloth and napkins rolled up in ornate rings and porcelain plates and cups and saucers and long-stemmed wine glasses? It had been a long time. Well, of course, there'd been the officer's mess on the barge last month, but that was different. It was a matter of Navy protocol. However, this was a labor of love. A lot of care had gone into providing such refinement. He was transported back to his childhood surrounded by the beaming wine-flushed faces of his parents and brothers and sisters. There was a table with platters heaped high with steaming pasta and straw-covered flasks of Chianti. The warm vibrant tenor voice of Enrico Caruso boomed from a wind-up Victrola in the alcove. He fought back an overwhelming urge to weep. The recollection was so ecstatic.

Major Hargreaves had been watching Grecco's reaction and could see that he was deeply touched. He was a sensitive man and could empathize with him. He could tell that the décor had awakened memories. He patted Vince on the back. Here was a worthy guest, he thought; one capable of appreciating the truly important things of life. It was a moment such as this that made the effort worthwhile. Colonel O'Hara's reaction had been so cold and sarcastic. "You'd make someone a good wife, Boyd," he'd said.

When Grecco considered the primitive surroundings and the sort of food available at the district market, the feast seemed nothing short of a miracle. It showed just what the human spirit was capable of. They had gathered all sorts of herbs and spices at the market and got an Indian family to show them how to make various curry dishes. Dinner had three different kinds of casserole baked in earthenware pots, a roast and bowls of gravy and fresh salad. They raised the lettuce and tomatoes themselves to avoid the danger of amoebas and other intestinal disorders.

At Grecco's first meal, the chef had placed before him a platter heaped high with cream puffs and ladyfingers. There were also cakes and pies and puddings. And for Sunday dinner, the chef from San Francisco made a baked Alaska, the first that Vince had ever tasted. The ice cream had been churned in an old hand-cranked machine that had once belonged to a French family.

One evening just at sunset, a tall gaunt youth came to visit the MAT team. Grecco had watched him approach from a long way off paddling down the murky river in a small sampan. Vince had thought him Vietnamese until he stepped ashore, for he was wearing the traditional black pajamas and straw conical hat of the delta peasant.

"This is Joey Ravelston," Major Hargreaves said placing an arm fondly about the youth's shoulders. "He's an IVSer." So this was the International Voluntary Service guy that Grecco had heard so much about. He was so different from Candy and the others that had been at Lang Son.

"I shouldn't associate with this troublemaker," the major said shaking Ravelston good-naturedly. "He gets me in trouble with Major Vien. Thinks Joey's a Communist." He gave Vince a knowing wink.

Ravelston lived on a large island in the middle of the Tien Giang River. He'd been assigned there as an agriculture specialist more than a year ago. The volunteer had become very popular with the peasants, so popular that they had built him a house, the largest, sturdiest structure on the island. They spent four months building it and had not told Ravelston until it was finished. Early one morning, they'd come to his dwelling with an oxcart and moved him and his belonging to the new house. They were fond of him not simply because he was able to adapt so quickly to their culture or because he taught them ways to improve their rice and sugarcane

The Idiot's Frightful Laughter

yield, but chiefly because he'd shown them how to protect themselves against corrupt government officials in a safe non-violent manner.

When Major Vien, The District Chief, refused to give them the water pumps that CORDS had promised them, Ravelston rounded up every man, woman, and child on the island and lead them to the district capital. For three days and nights, they sat in front of Major Vien's home. There was a danger that they could be shot or beaten; however as long as Ravelston was among them, the possibility was remote. He was their protection like the household god they burned jo sticks to and worshipped each morning and evening asking that no harm comes to the family that day.

They had prepared to remain in the District Chief's front yard for at least one week, so on the evening of the third day when the soldiers pulled up before the house with a truckload of water pumps, and Major Vien handed them out personally, the peasants were convinced that Ravelston had superhuman powers. From that moment on, he was their most precious possession. They would fight to keep him.

Your boss isn't too fond of me either, Ravelston said smiling at Hargreaves. A long strand of blonde hair hung down over one eye.

"O'Hara!" the major exploded with a loud guffaw. "He ordered me to run you out of the district. Lucky you got the pumps by then." Hargreaves took a can of beer from the fridge and poured the brew into a large frosted glass. "This'll wash the *nouc mam* down," he said handing it to the youth.

"Well, it looks like he got his wish," the IVSer said. "I'm leaving at the end of the month. Orders from Washington."

"I didn't think Wild Bill would go that far?" the major said frowning angrily.

"Naw, it wasn't O'Hara. It had nothing to do with him," Ravelston said. "Forty-six of us IVSers are being kicked out. We sent a letter to LBJ protesting the bombing of North Vietnam in particular and the war in general. All those who signed the partition have been ordered out of the country. It was stupid of me. It was a dirty trick to play on those I'm here to help."

No one said anything for a long time. The three of them sat staring at the floor. Hargreaves reached in his pocket; and fumbled for his cigarettes. Pulling one from the pack, he lit it and flicked the match on the floor. Glancing nervously about to see if any of his troops were listening, he looked back at Ravelston until he caught his eye. Then he smiled an earnest man-to-man sort of smile. "Frankly Joey, I'm a professional soldier. I'm duty bound to support this war; any war my country gets involved in, but the truth of the matter is I don't believe we have any business here. I think it's criminal the way we go about killing these half-starved little peasants and blowing up their country. I don't know why we're here. I have my suspicions, but I have no proof. However, I don't believe any of the reasons I've been fed. They're all pure bullshit. Any simpleton could see that if he wished to."

"If he wished to," Ravelston said nodding his head and looking pensively at the major. "That's just it. Most people don't want to face the truth. It's too painful, too self-incriminating."

Late that night, Grecco was awakened by the man on radio watch. "Incoming!" the soldier shouted, as he ran past Grecco's bunk. "Incoming."

Instinctively Vince bounded out of bed and ran for the bunker in the pitch darkness. It was a reflex action from his Second World War days some twenty years ago.

But how was it that he knew right where to go, for he hadn't bothered to find out where the bunker was when he first arrived. He crawled the last ten meters to safety scrambling like a frightened turtle on hands and knees, for someone had knocked him down and then trampled over him, kicking him in the head. At the entrance of the bunker, hands had grabbed hold of his head and pulled him in just as an explosion rocked the building sending sheet metal and timber flying in all directions.

A satchel charge of plastic explosives hit the river bank about ten meters from the team's bunkhouse killing one Arvin and wounding two others. The blast knocked out the screen along one side of the building scattering the furnishings about. Grecco found his bunk turned upside down. The explosion would have given him a nasty jolt if he hadn't awakened, he thought.

The next morning Major Hargreaves showed Grecco where the satchel charge had been launched. It had been hurtled from the edge of a rice paddy over a thirty-foot clump of bamboo, above an ornate ancestral tomb, and a muddy creek and into the compound. Vince estimated the trajectory to have been from a hundred and fifty to two hundred meters.

The walls of the nearby homes were full of holes; shrapnel from mortar shells the Arvin had fired in retaliation. There was no one about. Grecco figured that most of the occupants had either been killed or wounded.

"Most ingenious," Major Hargreaves said kneeling down to better examine the two-foot-square groove in the moist earth where the explosive had been launched. "The little buggers dug a sloping trough," he explained. "They had to get the angle to within a fraction of a degree; then they sat one satchel charge on top of another one and lit the fuse of both charges. The bottom one exploded propelling the other towards the compound. The fuse on the second charge had to be carefully measured so that it ignited just prior to impact. It's a very touchy business. Takes very careful timing," he said shaking his head with a look of wonder.

Grecco had that déjà vu feeling. He felt that this had somehow happened to him before. Then it suddenly occurred to him. The day before he had seen two peasants digging at this very spot. The two men in black pajamas and straw conical hats were carefully shaping this launch pad. He had noticed them while he was riding with the major along a road about fifty meters at the other side of a rice paddy. "Look," he'd said nudging Hargreaves. "There's a couple of VC laying a mine."

"Don't joke, the major had said, "You're quite apt to be right."

Grecco remembered that Major Hargreaves had appeared nervous. Would he go that far to avoid an encounter with Charlie even when he and his troop's lives were at stake? Was it possible? Vince wondered. Yes, considering what he'd told Ravelston the evening before, it was quite possible.

Killer Cong

Luke Molloy was only thirteen when he was arrested for helping a man hold up a gas station. He was the lookout. Spotting a cop slip out from behind a hedge, he blew three short blasts on his whistle.

In his haste to escape, the man shot the attendant in the chest killing him. Luke was found hiding in a ditch nearby. Two days later, he pointed out his accomplishments in a police lineup. He was an unemployed farmhand who was wanted for armed robbery in two other states.

Luke's mother appealed to Father Flannigan for help. He'd founded Boy's Town, a boarding school in the Kansas countryside for delinquent adolescents from "good" Catholic families. It was self-supporting. The boys did all the farm work: raising and harvesting the crops, looking after the livestock, and running the cannery. In return, they got a tenth-grade Catholic education. Theoretically, it looked like a good deal. Everyone benefited.

However many of the staff were pedophiles. They themselves were the products of Catholic boarding schools and had been sexually abused as children. Soon after Luke arrived at Boys Town, he was assigned to shovel cow dung into a cart and wheel it to a pile at the rear of the dairy. One evening a huge burly man in charge of the livestock dragged Luke into the hayloft and raped him. This went on every night for six months until Father Buchanan, who taught Latin, took a fancy to Luke and had him transferred to cleaning the classrooms. The priest was more demanding than the ranch hand. In addition to buggering the child, he made Luke suck his cock. Sixty-nine was a favorite position of his. Whenever Luke balked, the sodomite beat him with a razor strap coving his body with deep welts.

The Idiot's Frightful Laughter

Luke once tried to kill the priest. He stole a butcher knife from the kitchen and hid it beneath the pervert's bunk. When he had Luke in a sixty-nine position, the youth tried to drive the blade into his kidneys, but missed, jabbing him in the buttocks. Father Buchanan tied Luke to a bedpost and beat him unconscious with his razor strap. This went on for several days. After that, the pedophile had nothing more to do with the child. He wouldn't even let him attend his Latin class, not that Luke wanted to. Father Buchanan told the monsignor that Luke was a thief.

Luke Molloy drew further and further within himself. He would sit alone at a corner of the walled-in playground sulking. He dreamt of the day that he would return with a rifle and kill the priest. First, he'd shoot him in the scrotum and then between the eyes. He would pin a note to the dead priest's robes. It would say: "This is for buggering little kids. May he burn in everlasting Hell." Once he tried to run away. A sheriff found him hiding in a cornfield. He had pleaded with the officer not to send him back to Boys Town. He was terrified of what Father Buchanan and the others might do. The sheriff would not believe him even after he'd showed him the welts that covered his body. He only laughed. "Serves you right," he said. "Them priests don't put up with no nonsense. They'll make a believer out of you."

The punishment hadn't been as severe as he'd expected. The playground prefect had slapped him about and made him stand in a corner at the end of a long row of toilets for a month. In the evenings, he knelt at his bed long after the other boys had gone to sleep. He was transferred to the cannery. Each afternoon after class, he cut corn from cobs into large half gallon cans with a paring knife.

At sixteen he left Boys Town and set out on his own. He headed west working as a ranch hand and cowboy; however living in a bunkhouse in close proximity to older men troubled him. It not only brought back bleak memories of Boys Town but more alarming he grew aware of his own homosexual impulses. He felt a need to be near older, more assertive men. He tended to behave strangely in their presence. The yearning to touch them mortified him. He was more frightened than ashamed. If the men suspected that he was a homophile, they'd kill him. The realization that he was like Father Buchanan, the despicable sodomite he'd vowed to kill, grew more and more unbearable. Intent on getting things back under control, he built a cabin in the mountains near Riggins, Idaho and cut off all ties with others. He was determined to rid himself of what he considered a dreadful sickness. Finding a woman and getting married seemed like the most sensible solution, but women were actually of no interest to him, and they intuitively knew it. He was spoiled fruit, so to speak.

Luke Molloy became a guide, tracking bear and cougar for trophy hunters from the East. He trained a couple hounds to run down bear and tree them. Once Luke had one trapped in a tree, he'd go to the Riggin's saloons that lined both sides of Highway 95 in search of clients. He frequently found them decked out in safari suits and Aussie bush hats slumped over a bar. They were often too drunk to walk through the brush to where the bear clung helplessly to the top of a fir. Nevertheless, they always insisted on carrying their rifles. It was dangerous, for they were apt to shoot themselves or one another.

The dogs would snarl and leap about at the base of the tree frightening the drunk neophytes. However, if Luke was to take the dogs away, the bear was quite apt to climb down and attack his client. They were often so intoxicated that they could not aim their weapons and sometimes shot the tree trunk a foot or so in front of them. Frequently Luke had to steady the gun for a dude and tell him when to pull the trigger. Usually, they would fire a dozen or more shots before hitting the bruin. Occasionally one of them was too afraid to shoot, so Luke had to kill the terror-stricken beast as it clung to the waving treetop.

Usually all the wealthy Easterners wanted was the head; however, some had them skinned. The carcass was left to rot, food for coyotes and carrion. They'd mount the head and hang it in their conference room. Tall tales were spun of how they'd wrestled the beast to the ground plunging a pocket knife into the heart.

Luke hated the phony bastards and didn't mind letting them know it. Occasionally he'd lose his temper and kick a drunken sot

The Idiot's Frightful Laughter

in the ass. His antics were soon known among the trophy-hunting set and business dwindled. It wasn't long before he was broke and had to sell his dogs.

Luke joined the rodeo circuit traveling about the country bulldogging steers. He started drinking heavily. Whenever he got drunk, he'd pick a fight with the biggest, roughest looking cowpoke at the bar. He didn't know when to stop and would nearly kill his opponent kicking at him as he lay unconscious on the floor. The word soon got about among the bartenders that Luke was a troublemaker, and they refused to serve him. "Your kind ain't welcome here," they'd tell him gripping a baseball bat beneath the bar.

"You better get moving, or I'll call the sheriff."

The Vietnam War was just what Luke had been waiting for; the chance to fight and kill and get paid for it. Violence, that's what he craved. It was the perfect catharsis. It released those pent-up tensions and made life more tolerable. It was a narcotic that he had to have. The more violent he was, the greater the esteem. That was war.

He chose the Marine Corps. That's where the fighting was. They were mean mothafuckers. They didn't take shit from no one. In boot camp, the old homophile longings returned. He reacted violently to these yearnings. A friendly gesture was enough to evoke a fight. He fought nearly everyone in the platoon. His ferocity was so intense that even his drill instructor became concerned. "Sir, I got me a real psycho," the DI told his commander. "He don't get along with no one. Fighting all the time."

"So what's the problem, Sergeant?" the captain said. "Isn't that what we're all about? Sounds like he'll make one hell of a fine Marine."

In Vietnam, Luke found all the fighting he could hope for. His cool ferocity under fire earned him kudos among the troops. He rose rapidly in rank, making platoon sergeant at twenty. Wanting to lessen the odds, he transferred to LRRP, Long-Range Reconnaissance Patrols, operated by the CIA. His patrols spent months behind enemy lines. They'd slip into the very midst of a

Viet Cong encampment, sometimes having to fight their way out against overwhelming odds.

Whenever Luke was back at camp, he was constantly training his troops. He became deeply attached to the death-defying Montagnard tribesmen, relishing their hate for the Vietnamese. He shared feelings very similar to theirs, a smoldering rage for revenge. His was the outrage against the indignities he'd suffered as a child. Theirs was the Vietnamese's racial bigotry. Luke spent as much time as possible at the Yard villages. For the first time in his life, he felt at ease among others. He relished the tribesmen's relaxed, uninhibited lifestyle. There were no sexual taboos. Anything was permissible. Homophile shame had no meaning to the Montagnard. The young warriors lived apart from their women in barracks called longhouses. These buildings, some fifty meters in length, were perched high on stilts and entered by climbing a notched log. Luke moved into one of them. He was a blood brother; their white chieftain and warlord.

Luke underwent their blood-letting ceremonies and drank coconut shells of warm raw blood drawn from a puncture in the neck of a live water buffalo. He thus had the unique distinction of becoming the blood brother of the Hre, Sedang, Rhade and Renago mountain tribesmen. Each had a distinct culture, history, and homeland. Luke wore their tribal bracelets as proof of brotherhood. He, who the Yards called "Killer Cong", gradually integrated the tribesmen into his patrols until they comprised more than half his troops. Their loyalty was never questioned. They were ready and willing to die fighting for their white brother, the Killer Cong. From the hundred that rallied to his call, he picked only the very best, the fiercest, most ferocious. In recompense, he let them do whatever they wished with their Vietnamese captives. Torturing a Vietnamese, any Vietnamese, was the highest reward they could hope for. Luke could empathize. How he yearned to torture Father Buchanan slowly to death in the most agonizing manner. How sweet the revenge would be. He fantasized on how he'd do it someday if he ever made it back to the world. He'd cut off the pedophile's cock and jam it up his ass; then make him swallow his balls. That was poetic justice.

Killer Cong selected his weapons with care. Firepower was the name of the game. His men were walking arsenals. Luke had a cut-down Chinese RPD machine gun. It was so compact and balanced that the killer could practically write his name with it. He also had a Soviet RPG anti-tank grenade launcher, and a .380 Walther PPK automatic pistol with a Sonics suppresser. His platoon had a 60mm machine gun that hung on a strap from the gunner's shoulder, several compact Uzi submachine guns, and a couple M79 bloopers. Each grunt carried a dozen or so golf ball-size Dutch V-40 grenades in his jacket pockets. The tiny explosives weighed just 3.5 ounces but spewed over four hundred fragments. The point man wore an NVA uniform complete with chest-type web gear and carried an AK-47.

Packing eighty pounds of equipment, they trudged through a terrain of deep gullies and steep ridges that dropped abruptly off into ravines stretching west into Cambodia and Laos. They operated along a three-hundred-kilometer strip of land that bordered the two nations. Their primary mission was to capture enemy soldiers and bring them in for interrogation. The higher the rank, the better. They would hide in the jungle until late at night and then sneak into a remote mountain village and pounce on an enemy officer while he slept. Sometimes they'd waylay a small band of North Vietnamese soldiers traveling along a trail. Once the Yards had had their fun, the captives were bound and gagged and marched back to their base camp where they were turned over to a sadistic gang of Arvin interrogators who worked for the CIA. It was better for an NVA to die fighting or kill himself, for if captured, he was sure to be tortured to death.

Frequently Killer Cong's patrol traveled for days through jungle sprayed with Agent Orange, an herbicide laced with the deadly dioxin, TCDD. The once luxuriant forests were transformed into a barren wasteland. It was a landscape of rotting snags and withered undergrowth. The ground was littered with the decaying corpse of tropical birds and other wildlife. Clusters of dead fish shimmered on the surface of murky ponds. The defoliants accelerated the trees and other vegetation's growth literally causing them to grow to death.

Assured that the herbicide was harmless, the grunts drank from the streams and ponds of polluted water in bomb craters. It was ironic that they took care to put Halazone tablets in their drinking water to ensure that harmful germs were killed. Frequently huge C-123 cargo planes swept low overhead spraying them with the deadly dioxin, soaking their clothing and skin. They wore the same fatigues for weeks, and at night slept in defoliant's saturated undergrowth, they're bodies soon covered with a rash. They felt dizzy and nauseous and suffered from migraine headaches, stomach cramps, and deep depressions. Those who made it back to The States invariably died of liver, prostate or testicular cancer. Others succumbed to heart attacks, kidney failure or lymphoma. Their children were often deformed; some with parts of the brain missing or their bladder on the outside of their body. Still others had heart defects, sprung pelvises, double hernias, cleft lips, missing nose or eyes, clubfoot, water on the brain, webbed toes, cancer, gastritis or no forearms. The government did nothing. It turned a blind eye to the miseries, insisting that Agent Orange was harmless. In spite of the overwhelming evidence, the Veterans Administration stood firm refusing to acknowledge the existence of dioxin poisoning. It wasn't until decades later when it was too late that the VA finally acknowledged the existence of the deadly chemical.

One day Killer Cong's patrol stumbled onto a prisoner-of-war camp some ten kilometers inside Laos. A half dozen bamboo pens were hidden from sight by a thick tropical canopy. Each held four or five prisoners. Three guard shacks were arranged in a triangle facing the cages. Two NVA soldiers manned each post. They sat on stools with AK-47 assault rifles across their knees smoking and laughing loudly to one another. They didn't appear to have a worry in the world. They were obviously quite oblivious to the danger that lurked nearby.

The Idiot's Frightful Laughter

Carefully scanning the treeline surrounding the compound, Killer Cong detected a movement. A guard immerged from a well-camouflaged hut hidden from view by the dense jungle foliage. The shack faced a bare yard. It occurred to Luke that others might be confined in pits in the field. There was that eerie déjà vu feeling. He had a premonition that this had all happened before. His thoughts flashed back to Boys Town. He remembered the chicken wire pen at one corner of the playground where recalcitrant boys were confined. It was no wonder that the sight of bamboo cages caused him to feel such wrath.

A guard went to the middle of the field, lifted a heavy lid and dragged a prisoner from the pit by the collar of his flight suit. The American airman was covered with mud. He struggled trying to stand but kept collapsing on the ground. Killer Cong supposed that he'd been forced into a cramped position for such a long time that there was no life left in his legs. The guard kicked and jabbed the man brutally in the ribs with the muzzle of his rifle shouting curses at him. "You son of a whore, this is for your napalm," he shouted kicking him in the ribs. "This is for burning my people alive, you American pig." The airman could only crawl. Each time he tried to stand, his right leg would collapse, and he'd fall back on the ground. The guard continued to kick and jab at the prisoner, as he tried again and again to rise. The ruthless beating went on until the airman was too weak to move. Finally, another guard appeared with a bamboo pole. They lashed the man to the pole with thin strips of hemp and carried him screaming into the main hut at the center of the compound. Luke figured that the guy's right leg was broken, perhaps shattered. The troops watched the North Vietnamese soldiers carry him like a hog to slaughter into what they supposed was the command shack. It was all Killer Cong could do to keep his men from attacking the outpost. The Yanks found it hard to restrain themselves. Watching the Vietnamese beat a fellow countryman was intolerable.

North Vietnamese soldiers moved in and out of the operations hut. Killer Cong counted twenty-five in all. Just as it was growing dark, an officer stepped out on the porch. He had red patches on his epaulets. Metal insignias were affixed to the patches. Luke assumed that this was the commander of the jungle prison. Sometime Later, the American airman, who'd been carried into the shack, was brought back out. He was hanging unconscious from the pole. Evidently, he'd been tortured until he passed out. A guard opened one of the cages and ordered two of its occupants to carry the airman inside. Luke could see the two were also Caucasians, most likely Americans. Their clothes were in rags.

At sundown using a hand signal, Killer Cong ordered his men to withdraw a quarter of a kilometer from the compound and regroup. They needed to formulate a pattern of attack. Most wanted to strike immediately; however Luke cautioned them to wait. The prisoners needed to be evacuated quickly before reinforcements could arrive. They would need a half dozen choppers. They would also have to have help, for the prisoners were obviously too weak to walk. It would take at least another squad to pack them to the landing site. The jungle was too dense to hoist them out among the trees. They'd get hung up in the branches. Killer Cong needed another day to reconnoiter the camp and see if more NVA troops were camped nearby. He radioed operations and gave the officer on duty his coordinates. He requested aircraft and reinforcements for the following day.

Prior to sunrise the next morning, Killer Cong and his men moved back to their observation points. Because the prison was so well hidden inside Laos, the NVA did not expect Yank or Arvin troops, and so had not placed any booby traps or punji stakes about its perimeter. What's more, there were no heavy weapons in place. At 0600 hour, a soldier stepped out on the porch of the operations hooch and blew three short blasts on a whistle. Ten more men came from the shack. They were joined by fourteen others from the guard shacks and elsewhere. All twenty-four of them lined four abreast facing the command shack, Then the commander with the red patches stepped out onto the porch facing the formation. He spoke to them in a nasal high-pitched voice. This went on for about ten minutes. Luke assumed that they were getting their daily dose of

The Idiot's Frightful Laughter

Communist propaganda. He then saluted them. They returned the salute holding it until he'd stepped back inside the shed.

Killer Cong was elated. Back at their bivouac area, he told his men: "It's like shooting fish in a barrel." He drew a diagram of the enemy troop formation before the operations hut; then he separated the diagram into squares, each representing an enemy soldier and gave the squares numbers. Each member of the recon team was assigned a number. On command, they were to shoot the one in the square that corresponded to their respective number.

The next morning, Killer Cong's team moved into position and waited for the drama to unfold. As expected, at 0600 hour sharp, an NVA soldier stepped out onto the porch and blew the whistle. As before, the soldiers quickly formed rank and stood at attention facing the prison commander. As he began his nasal high-pitched oration, Luke brought the flat of his hand down. Instantly a burst of automatic rifle fire erupted from the treeline tearing the formation to shreds. Killer Cong blew the commander to pieces with a burst from his grenade launcher. Within seconds, twenty-four enemy soldiers and their commander lay dead. Luke was delirious with joy.

The point man ran ahead lobbing grenades into the command hut. As the troopers broke open the bamboo cages and shot the locks from the tiger pits, Killer Cong called in an air strike. Within minutes Skyraiders dropped out of the sky leveling off at around three hundred feet. Canisters of napalm tumbled into the jungle. Three sides of the camp's perimeter burst into billowing waves of orange flame and clouds of black smoke. After each assault, the A-1's rolled over and struck again with napalm and white phosphorous until the jungle about the outpost was ablaze with giant plumes of flame and smoke. Cinders sailed about burning holes in the troops' fatigues. The heat scorched their lungs and stung their eyes.

As the dive bombers departed, the clatter of helicopters could be heard. Six Huey slicks emerged from the smoke. Four Cobra gunships followed circling above the prison just inside the circle of flame. The slicks landed in an opening some distance from the camp, and a dozen Yards jumped to the ground and helped carry the prisoners to the aircraft.

Killer Cong was pleased. His recon team had freed thirteen Americans and one Australian POW, and not a single man had been injured, let alone killed. The captives had thanked their liberators profusely. As the choppers lifted off, Luke looked at the emaciated captives. He hadn't felt such compassion for anyone before. The skeleton-like creatures looked so pathetic. Tears streamed from their dark sunken eyes. As the Hueys set off for the hospital Cam Ranh Bay, Luke gave them a thumbs-up salute. He felt a dark gloom lift from his heart. It was the closest he'd ever come to feeling love; a love for the abused, downtrodden of the earth. He felt of himself as a crusader. He was performing a worthy mission. However, there were those like Grecco who wouldn't have seen it quite that way.

Killer Cong never got the chance to even the score with Father Buchanan. A month later, he was reported missing in action. His recon patrol had vanished from sight. No one heard of him or any of his comrades again.

The Colonel's Hasty Exit

The party for the Province Chief had nothing to do with the fact that Grecco was leaving the province the following morning. Kalick had been planning it for some time. For one thing, it was a feeble attempt to mend the split between the civilians and the military advisors, but more specifically between O'Hara and himself, for the colonel had had nothing to do with Greg since he'd taken Co Hi out to dinner. Wild Bill was leaving the next day, and Greg was anxious to get him to provide a more amiable performance rating. What's more, relations between the Americans and their Vietnamese counterparts had deteriorated badly. O'Hara hadn't met with Colonel Tu for several weeks. The snub had angered the Province Chief, and he had ordered his staff to have as little as possible to do with the Americans. "They are no longer welcome in my province," he'd said.

Kalick was not surprised when Colonel O'Hara did not show up; however, he was noticeably distressed that none of the other military advisors had come. No doubt the colonel had ordered them not to.

Colonel Tu and most of his staff came; however, they gathered at one corner of the rec room and were stiff and very solemn, ignoring the Americans. Whenever an advisor spoke to one of them, he would look through him; his eyes opaque, seeming not to hear. The Province Chief had accepted the invitation only after hearing that Colonel O'Hara was being replaced. The new Province Senior Advisor would have a lot of apologizing to do, and Colonel Tu would take full advantage of the insult, demanding all sorts of compensations.

Grecco watched Kalick and Nakamura scurrying about with drinks and snacks for the Vietnamese. It was ironic, he thought. Was this how one adjusted to the culture? Neither the Province

Chief nor any of his subordinates would serve the Americans, no matter how eminent they might be. That was a task for servants. If Kalick thought that he was setting an example by giving them a taste of democracy, he was wasting his time. It wasn't that the Vietnamese were ignorant of such propriety. Humility was not foreign to the Asian. Buddhist and Hindu ascetics had been preaching such virtues for thousands of years, but when had religion ever intruded on the pace setter's lifestyle? They took whatever suited them and ignored what didn't. That was true everywhere, Vince reckoned, from the Potala Palace in Lhasa to St. Peter's Basilica in Rome.

The unexpected arrival of Bo Thi Vinh saved the party, at least that's how it seemed to Grecco at the moment. The Deputy Chief of Administration had transferred from Yen Bay that day. Since Vince's departure, Bo Thi Vinh had fallen out of favor with The Province Chief and was now the Deputy at Than Uyen.

Grecco had been at the party less than a half hour when Vinh arrived. The Vietnamese guest's arrogant behavior had distressed Vince, so it was comforting to have Vinh walk over to him the moment he entered the room and grasp his hand in both of his in a gesture of manly affection. His actions were all quite spontaneous. He had broken protocol by greeting Grecco before giving Colonel Tu so much as a nod. Stunned by the slight, everyone stopped whatever they were doing and stared wide-eyed at the deputy and Grecco, the lowly Refugee Advisor on his way out. Kalick was so surprised that he nearly dropped a tray of drinks. Suddenly realizing his mistake, Vinh abruptly broke free of Grecco and went over to the Province Chief. Colonel Tu made no effort to hide his displeasure. He stared icily at his subordinate, as he apologized for being so dimwitted as not to have followed proper protocol.

Vinh and Grecco had much in common to discuss. Both had transferred to Than Uyen Province because of incurring disfavor at Yen Bay. Both hated Hank Barban, and their assessment of the other American advisors was much the same. They also enjoyed reliving the most sportive moments in the province.

The Idiot's Frightful Laughter

By the time dinner was served, Vinh and Grecco were moderately drunk, enough at least not to care how disruptive they might be. Vinh told those at the table the riotous antics the two had engaged in embellished them somewhat. Then prompted by Vince, he performed some of his parlor tricks. He began by balancing two forks on the tip of a toothpick at the edge of a glass of water and concluded by lifting a full glass of beer with his teeth and drinking it with one gulp. When Grecco tried it, he bit off a large piece of glass dumping the beer in his lap. At this point, Colonel Tu, who'd been glaring angrily at his deputy, rose and left abruptly without bidding farewell.

Kalick put on a brave face and laughed about the incident, but Grecco knew that his boss was anything but happy, for it had only served to widen the breach even further between himself and the Province Chief. Nevertheless, Kalick had cause to celebrate, for he had just learned that Wild Bill's replacement was due to arrive on the same plane that Grecco would depart on. He was taking Colonel O'Hara's place as Province Senior Advisor. The Special Forces commander was being transferred to a combat unit at Ca Mau in An Xuyen Province at the southernmost tip of Vietnam. His outpost was an enclave in the middle of the U Minh Forest, a trackless mangrove swamp. It was the hideout of the most notorious Viet Cong guerrilla forces in the country. There were no roads, only footpaths and a network of canals teeming with poisonous snakes and swarms of malarial mosquitoes.

Grecco's feeling had tempered somewhat towards the colonel, for he'd been the only one to show any appreciation for what Vince had been trying to do for the refugees, and so O'Hara was angry when Grecco announced at a briefing several weeks before that he was leaving.

"Who says you're leaving?" O'Hara bellowed.

"My eighteen-month appointment ends in two weeks," Vince said. "I haven't been offered a new contract, Sir."

"You been sacked?" he said.

"Yes, Sir," Grecco replied.

"Who sacked you? Some civilian type? Give me his name. I'll put the sonofabitch straight," O'Hara demanded, taking out a notebook and pen. "I like your spunk, Vince. You're the first goddamn civilian that's tried to do anything, and I think you're on the right track. I'd like to see you keep at it."

Grecco felt his eyes moisten and a lump form in his throat. "I appreciate it, Sir. I'm sorry I didn't discuss this with you earlier. I… I've already accepted another job."

"Look, Vince," O'Hara said screwing up his eyes and thrusting a finger at him. "You're a big boy now. Make up your fucking mind. Do you want the job or don't you?"

"I'll need some time to think," Grecco said. "Can I let you know tomorrow?"

"Fourteen hundred," Wild Bill said closing his notebook and thrusting it back in his pocket. "Fourteen hundred sharp."

Grecco had stayed up past midnight drafting and redrafting a reply to O'Hara. The next morning at zero eight hundred he left the letter with the colonel's secretary. It was easier that way. The coward's way out. Saying "no" to Colonel O'Hara was quite beyond Vince's capability.

Grecco watched O'Hara's replacement leave the plane. He had short cropped gray hair and a pencil thin mustache. His gabardine uniform was tailor-made and neatly pressed. In one hand he carried an attaché case and in the other a swagger stick. He had stepped straight from behind a desk, Vince reckoned. From now on things would be a great deal different in Than Uyen Province.

They're Out to Win

Grecco hadn't been in Saigon a week when he received his performance rating. Kalick had written:

```
VIET-NAM PERFORMANCE EVALUATION REPORT
      Foreign Service Reserve Officers
           Department of State
     Agency for International Development
```

    Mr. Vincent Grecco is a most highly motivated Refugee Officer, exhibiting the utmost concern for these be leagued people. However, his patience with his counterpart is severely tried by what Mr. Grecco terms his counterpart's apathy towards his job and thus little rapport exists. However, Mr. Grecco has excellent rapport with the Deputy for Administration in the Province and the Districts where he spent a good deal of his time endeavoring to make these individuals responsive to the needs of the people and displaced persons.

    Mr. Grecco has worked tirelessly interviewing refugee families in every district and written more reports and maintained better files of his endeavors than any other US staff member. He affiliates himself with the Vietnamese and has a very close camaraderie with some of them. He has studied all refugee guidelines on policy and has distributed simplified versions to each district in an attempt to keep the districts abreast of policy.

    Mr. Grecco's extreme sympathy for the refugees and the underprivileged people has on occasions caused him to lose perspective and understanding of the job's objectives. He has wanted to take over his counterpart's job in order to accomplish what needs to be done. He is unable to anticipate the delays that occur in his program, and as a result, does not start a program soon enough to accomplish his mission on time which in Vietnam is not an uncommon failing.

Sheridan Peterson

> At social functions of mixed races, Mr. Grecco tends to spend the majority of his time with the Vietnamese engaging in parlor tricks that delight his audience, but sometimes alienate his American colleagues and the Province Chief in particular.
>
> Gregory Kalick,
> FSR-3 Dep. Province Senior Advisor

Well, it could be worse, Grecco reckoned. He could well imagine what Hank Barban would have said. But then what did such things matter? Kalick was being kind. In spite of everything, he had failed. There was no denying that. The refugees were no better off than the day he'd arrived. In some cases, they were likely worse off. It was the Captain Kheims who triumphed. All the power and influence were in their hands. The refugees, the underprivileged, the peasants, they could not be helped; until this gangster government was eliminated. As much as Grecco abhorred violence, he knew that Major Biff Ziegler had been right. However, he too had failed because he lacked the power and influence to carry his scheme beyond Than Uyen Province. Besides the Ranger Advisor had overlooked some of the most ruthless men in the province, like Captain Kheim. That sonofabitch was too sly to get killed. Ziegler's project had been haphazard and limited. It was obvious that the assassinations had failed to frighten Kheim. He and others like him had simply grown more cunning and cautious.

"What's going on here?" Grecco said the instant he stepped into Grant Olson's tiny apartment. Backpacks, sleeping bags, canteens, hiking boots, ponchos lay scattered about the room. A tent was spread out on the bed, and a rubber raft stood propped against the wall. "Planning to assault the south slope of Mount Everest?"

Olson arose from behind a huge carton that he was sealing with thick strips of masking tape. "Hey Vince! Some mess, eh?" he said making a sweeping gesture of the room with his hand. "Your joke is nearer the truth than you might think."

"Ah ha, then it must be Annapurna," he said nodding his head solemnly.

"Right on target, Vince," Grant said. Turning to Victoria who was standing in the midst of a pile of sportswear, he added: "Vince's mental telepathy is tuned into the right frequency, wouldn't you say, Vicky?"

Victoria laughed shaking her head to show that she didn't understand. "We're leaving for Nepal next week, Vince," Olson said.

"Nepal?" Grecco was surprised. "What in hell for?"

"Write a novel. Tell it like it is," Olson said. "Last desperate attempt to shake the intelligentsia out of their stupor."

"Oh sure, Grecco said. His look was a blend of pity and despair. "I figured as much, but why Nepal?"

"A hidden valley in the Himalayas," Olson said. He gazed out the window as though he could see the tranquil paradise. "What could be more conducive for thinking and writing?"

"About Vietnam?" Vince asked giving Olson a look of incredulous wonder.

"Sure. It's objectivity that I'm after," Grant said. 'I can't be very rational if I'm in a constant state of rage, can I?"

Grecco went to the window and gazed down at the trash littered yard five floors below. It had once been a lawn bordered by a hedge when the French officers and their Asian mistresses occupied the building. A few of the shrubs had somehow survived, and here and there patches of grass pushed up among the heaps of litter. "But specifically," Grecco said watching a rat the size of an ordinary dog scurry across the yard. "What's the novel going to be about specifically?"

"About everyone," Olson said walking over to where Grecco was standing.

"Those I've known or know of. They'll tell the story, the whole rotten mess. Tell it like it is."

"Well, leave me out," Grecco said walking about the room examining the camping equipment. I don't want anyone telling my story for me."

"But you and I'll be the protagonists, Vince," Olson said grasping his old friend by the shoulders and swinging him about so that they were facing one another. "The others will revolve about us."

"Just you, not me," Grecco said pulling himself free of Olson's grasp.

"But you're my alter ego, Vince. You're my aspiration, my idol," Olson said. His voice was high pitched and pleading. "We've been through so much together, Vince. The Marines, Smokejumpers, Skydiving."

Grecco sat down in a wicker chair and clasped his hands together as though he was preparing to pray. "Do you really think the novel will make any difference, Grant?" There was a smile on his lips, but his eyes were solemn. "Look how many books have been written about this fucking war. Have they made any difference? Do you know of anyone in The States who gives a damn what happens to the Vietnamese? I mean really grievously gives a shit? Not for a moment," he added slapping his hand down hard on the arm of the chair. "Sure, they care if a son or husband get drafted and has to put his life on the line. Then they become so idealistic, but not for the neighbor's kid and certainly not for the Vietnamese kid. He's expendable. And who will read your novel anyway?" he asked looking questioningly up at Olson. "The warmongers? The ones most responsible for this genocide? Of course not! They won't read beyond the first page. It's only those select few who, for some reason or other, object to the war. They're the ones who'll read it, and they're not the ones who need convincing. They already know it's wrong."

Olson felt his temper rising. He stood staring at the floor until his anger had cooled somewhat. "Okay, Vince, you've made your point," he said softly enunciating each word slowly and distinctly. "Now perhaps you'll tell me what your solution is?"

'If you're sincere, Grant," Grecco said snapping closed the lid of a first aid kit he'd been examining. "If this book isn't just a way to ease your conscience or win a laurel or two from the literary

The Idiot's Frightful Laughter

circles, then commit yourself. Join the Viet Cong. Put your life on the line."

'You're talking violence, Vince," Olson said holding up a finger as though he had caught his friend in grievous error. "A violent solution solves nothing. It only creates greater violence. You and I have had our share of bloodshed. I have I know. I thought you had too?"

Victoria came in from the kitchen carrying two tall glasses of lemonade. She thrust one glass at Grecco causing him to rear back in alarm. "Oh! Ah! Yes! Ha, ha. Yes, calamansi juice. Thanks, Vicky." He took a sip and smacked his lips. "Magnificent! Nothing like it to quench the thirst." He took a long drink, and then set the glass on the floor. "Damnit Grant, nonviolence is fine. I'm all for it, but what have the pacifists accomplished in Vietnam? Nothing and they aren't going to. They can protest and demonstrate all they want. It's not going to matter one bit to this gang of butchers. They know that all they have to do is ignore the peaceniks and they're powerless. People grow discouraged quickly. They feel quite helpless and soon give up. But rest assured Grant," Grecco exclaimed posing a finger in the air, "the Viet Cong will never give up, not after the price they've paid. They're out to win. You can be damn sure of that."

He's the Worst

Grecco took five twenty-dollar bills from his wallet and held them out to the Vietnamese pilot. "One hundred U.S. dollars," He could not see the man's expression, for he had on a pair of wrap-around dark glasses. He wore a black baseball cap and black coveralls with two gold lotus blossom insignias on each shoulder indicating that he was a captain. He had a lavender scarf tied casually about the neck. A pearl handle pistol hung at his hip. Aping his idol, Air Marshal Nguyen Cao Ky, Grecco mused, South Vietnam's Clint Eastwood.

"Why do you want to do this?" the pilot asked. His voice was flat, quite void of any feeling.

"That's not part of the bargain," Grecco said. "The bargain is that you fly me fifty kilometers north of Tay Ninh."

"One way?" the pilot asked taking the money and examining each bill carefully.

"Yes, one way," Vince said.

The pilot placed the bills in a chest pocket and closed the zipper. "Okay," he said turning and walking towards his helicopter. "It's a deal." Grecco picked up his parachutes and followed.

Once the chopper left the city, it dropped down to within a few feet of the ground. The downward thrust of the rotor blades pressed the young blades of rice flat against the earth. The aircraft hopped over rows of trees that bordered the streams and canals, as though it were playing leapfrog, or would zigzag in among them when there was ample space.

"Mad fool," Grecco muttered as he hooked on his parachute harness. 'Seen too many Hollywood movies." But then he may be trying to avoid detection by flying beneath the radar's field of vision, he reckoned.

The Idiot's Frightful Laughter

Soon the rice paddies were gone, and the chopper was skimming at treetop level over dense jungle broken now and again by plantations of evenly spaced rubber trees. It wasn't long before the aircraft began to climb until the jungle had faded into a blur of dark green, and everywhere there were craters left by bombs and artillery shells, pools of muddy water encircled by rims of red earth. This is Viet Cong country, Grecco reckoned. He glanced at his altimeter. Eight thousand feet. The pilot had climbed out of range of their heavy machine gun and missile fire. Vince saw what he supposed was Tay Ninh a good fifty kilometers to the south. At twelve thousand feet, the chopper leveled off. The pilot glanced back at Grecco and motioned for him to jump. Vince made a quick inspection of his harness straps and reserve. He had not thought to find out what the elevation was here. Surely no more than one, possibly two thousand feet. The terrain was, of course, higher than the delta; however, it still looked flat except for a couple pyramid shaped mountains about forty kilometers to the Southeast. He checks his altimeter. It had been set at sea level. If he pulled at three thousand feet, he should still have a good thousand feet before he hit the ground. However, he may still try to go lower, for he was afraid of being shot while floating down beneath an open canopy. It would have been better at night. He put on a pair of goggles and a white fiberglass helmet and knelt in the doorway scanning the landscape. Picking up a radio headset that hung from the fuselage, he pressed the switch and spoke into the mouthpiece. "Pull right until you're over that cluster of bomb craters at three o'clock," he said. Let's hope there's no wind. Landing in jungle is not my idea of fun, he thought. I'd be hanging from my shroud lines two hundred feet in the air.

Grecco picked up a small canvass bag from the seat behind him and snapped it to the harness between his legs. It contained a change of clothes, rations for one week, water, and a first aid kit. He'd thought about bringing a weapon and some ammo, but he wasn't sure how that might be interpreted, so he had left them in a box beneath his bunk. Now he was sorry. Of what good would he be to a guerrilla unit without a rifle? He felt naked and vulnerable.

As soon as the helicopter was above the craters, Grecco sprang from the door. He felt about in the air with his hands and feet until he had control of himself. He lay flat to the earth watching the needle of his altimeter tick off, 12,000, 10,000, 8,000 feet. There was a red line at 2,500 feet. That was where skydivers were supposed to reach for their ripcord. It was the safety margin. It gave the jumper ample time to open his reserve if his main malfunctioned. However, not knowing what the terrain was like, Vince decided to open at 4,000 feet. That seemed like a safe bet; however at 4,000 the bomb craters still seemed far away. He waited. There was a ground rush at 3,000 feet. The craters seemed to suddenly expand which meant that he was actually at less than a thousand feet. He pulled the ripcord. There was a moment's delay as the canopy slipped free of its sleeve. What a foolhardy way to estimate one's elevation, he thought as the parachute billowed out above him. Just in the nick of time, he thought. He was only a few hundred feet above the cluster of craters.

Grecco tugged at his steering toggles that were fixed to his front risers. He turned back and forth pulling first the left and then the right toggle until he'd maneuvered himself directly above a triangle formed by three craters. At an estimated thirty feet from the ground, Vince pulled down hard on both toggles to stop the forward motion. The canopy shot upward slightly giving him a soft landing. He was right on target. The guys at the club should have seen this, he thought a bullseye.

As soon as he landed, Grecco reached up and pressed the capewell at either shoulder releasing the shroud lines and canopy from the harness. The olive drab parachute came free and sank into one of the craters blending with the stagnant water. Unsnapping his pack from between his legs, Vince sprinted along the rim of the crater until he reached the edge of the jungle. He then unbuckled his harness and removed his crash helmet and jumpsuit. Rolling the harness, reserve, and helmet up in the coveralls, tossed the bundle beneath some vines. Then he got his wallet and took out a safe conduct pass written in Vietnamese indicating that he was a civilian who favored the Vietnamese battle for independence from foreign

The Idiot's Frightful Laughter

domination and had chosen to join their ranks. He unfolded it and placed it in his shirt pocket. After examining the contents of his pack to see if there was any damage, he slung it over his back and started west through the dense undergrowth towards the Cambodian border.

After clawing his way through a thick mesh of vines and bramble for about twenty minutes, Grecco came to a narrow but well-worn trail. Unconsciously he touched his shirt pocket feeling for the safe conduct pass. He crumbled it slightly to reassure himself that it existed.

The trail ran north and south. South was to Tay Ninh. He would go north. The thought of trip wires, mines, punji stakes, and barbed pits began to haunt him. He crept slowly along the path carefully examining the earth. His passport inside his sock began to hurt. He had hidden it there for fear that it might be confiscated by ordinary soldiers who had no idea what it was. There was also the possibility of an ambush. He might be mistaken for the point man of a reconnaissance patrol. For a while, he walked along holding his hands raised before him as a sign of surrender, but his arms soon grew tired.

At a turn in the trail, a North Vietnamese soldier stepped from behind a clump of bamboo. He was pointing an automatic rifle at Grecco, his finger pressed firmly against the trigger. The slightest twitch would send a burst of hot lead through Vince's chest. He stood very rigid; his hands stretched high above his head. He looked as though he might be grasping for something just beyond his reach.

The soldier wore a pith helmet and the grey uniform. An NVA, Grecco reckoned. That was luck. They were better disciplined and less apt to harm him; for they had not endured the personal abuse from the Americans for as long as the Viet Cong had. The soldier stepped to the side of the trail and motioned for Vince to pass. Clasping his hands and placing them on his head, he bent forward to avoid the overhanging vines.

"*Dung lai,*" "Stop," the soldier said pulling aside some brush to reveal a small tunnel through the jungle's undergrowth just large enough for a Vietnamese to squeeze through. Grecco unstrapped his pack and hung it from his chest; then he dropped to his knees and began to crawl. The twigs jabbed at his head and shoulders. The guerilla was patient and did not prod him whenever he stopped for a breath. It seemed like hours before they finally reached a clearing hidden from the sky by a grove of great octopus-like banyans. Tiny thatched huts were scattered about beneath the trees' huge twisted roots.

Huu Bien came out of one of the huts and examined Grecco's safe conduct pass. He had been sitting at a desk studying Vince for some time and had concluded that he was both educated and a civilian.

"Do you know Grant Olson?" Huu Bien asked.
"Yes, I know him," Grecco said. "I know him quite well."
"He is an American too," Huu Bien said. "He's a good man. The only one I met. The rest were bastards."

"Don't be fooled," Vince said. "He's the worst."